PENGUIN CANADA

GOOD TO GO

KIM ZARZOUR is a journalist whose articles have been published in *Today's Parent* and *Maclean's*. She is a former features writer for the Life section of the *Toronto Star* as well as a former columnist with *Home and School* magazine. She is the author of several books on schoolyard bullying, a contributing author of *Growing with Your Child: Pre-Birth to Age 5*, and a contributing writer for *Cup of Comfort for Inspiration*, and *Me to We: Turning Self-Help on its Head*.

SHARON E. MCKAY has been an author for more than twenty years and in the process has written more than fourteen non-fiction books. She has won or been nominated for the Sydney Taylor Book Award, the UNESCO International Youth Library, Europe's White Raven Award, and Canada's Governor General's Award.

GOOD
TO GO

GOOD
TO GO

A Practical Guide to

Adulthood

Kim Zarzour &
Sharon E. McKay

PENGUIN
CANADA

PENGUIN CANADA

Published by the Penguin Group
Penguin Group (Canada), 90 Eglinton Avenue East, Suite 700, Toronto, Ontario, Canada M4P 2Y3
(a division of Pearson Canada Inc.)

Penguin Group (USA) Inc., 375 Hudson Street, New York, New York 10014, U.S.A.
Penguin Books Ltd, 80 Strand, London WC2R 0RL, England
Penguin Ireland, 25 St Stephen's Green, Dublin 2, Ireland
(a division of Penguin Books Ltd)
Penguin Group (Australia), 250 Camberwell Road, Camberwell, Victoria 3124, Australia
(a division of Pearson Australia Group Pty Ltd)
Penguin Books India Pvt Ltd, 11 Community Centre, Panchsheel Park,
New Delhi – 110 017, India
Penguin Group (NZ), 67 Apollo Drive, Rosedale, North Shore 0632, Auckland, New Zealand
(a division of Pearson New Zealand Ltd)
Penguin Books (South Africa) (Pty) Ltd, 24 Sturdee Avenue, Rosebank, Johannesburg 2196, South Africa

Penguin Books Ltd, Registered Offices: 80 Strand, London WC2R 0RL, England

First published 2008

1 2 3 4 5 6 7 8 9 10 (WEB)

This publication contains the opinions and ideas of its author and is designed to provide useful advice
in regard to the subject matter covered. The author and publisher are not engaged in rendering health
or other professional services in this publication. This publication is not intended to provide a basis for action
in particular circumstances without consideration by a competent professional. The author and publisher
expressly disclaim any responsibility for any liability, loss or risk, personal or otherwise, that is incurred
as a consequence, directly or indirectly, of the use and application of any of the contents of this book.

Manufactured in Canada.

Library and Archives Canada Cataloguing in Publication data available upon request to the publisher.

ISBN: 978-0-14-305569-3

Visit the Penguin Group (Canada) website at **www.penguin.ca**

Special and corporate bulk purchase rates available; please see
www.penguin.ca/corporatesales or call 1-800-810-3104, ext. 477 or 474

TO THE TWO SAMS, FIRST OUT THE DOOR

Contents

SECTION TWO

Body Basics

SECTION THREE

The Big Picture

Honey,

This is it—you are finally moving out! But before you go, there are just a few things I think you should know. Did I tell you not to flush kitty litter down the drain? It'll gunk up the pipes. Oh, and ironing your shirt directly on the rug—bad idea. There's glue under there. And did I mention that cheap feather pillows can explode if you throw them in the washing machine? And not to defrost the freezer with a knife? And oh, there is so much I haven't told you yet!

But yes, I know, you gotta go.

It won't be easy out there—especially these days. That's partly my fault. I wanted you to have it all, from that pram that cost more than our first car, to the violin, karate, fencing, acting, Cantonese, hockey, voice, guitar, and drum lessons. Maybe I should have given you laundry lessons instead. Taught you how to do a budget, rather than a pirouette. But the fact is, I did the laundry for you. And the bill paying. And the paperwork. And now it's time for you to do it yourself.

That's why I've written this book. I have tried to think of all the things that I might have missed, all those things you'll need to know. Doubtless there are a few I left out—I couldn't possibly cover it all—but I have faith in your ability to figure it out. Surely you can work out how to make ice cubes, despite the fact that you have never, not once, done it yourself. I know that you will one day learn how to replace the toilet paper roll when it runs out. And, with luck, you will discover that you don't have to return a jacket just because a button fell off.

So here it is—your last lessons before you fly from the nest. Please take this book in the spirit with which it was written—with love.

Mom

The Homefront

Finding a Roof for Your Head

Where thou art, that, is Home.

—EMILY DICKINSON

You're on your way! There's the door, the world is waiting! But first you'll need a roof for your head, a place to hang your hat, and some way to heat up your can of Alphagetti. Chances are your new place won't be as nice as home, but on the other hand being homeless, squatting, or living in a car isn't nearly as romantic as it might appear.

Oh, and find something *before* you leave—it's cold out there.

Ask yourself:

- How much can I afford?
- Do I want to live alone or share my space?
- How long will I likely live there?
- Where do I want to live?
- What kind of housing do I want?

Let's break it down.

How Much Can I Afford?

Of all the things that will cost you money when you move away from home (and believe me, there are many), housing is number one. So how much should you spend? Try to keep the total cost of rent plus utilities below one-third of your net income. Another way to figure it out: take your monthly salary and divide it by three—that should be your rent. If you're moving to an expensive big city, it might be tough to find anything decent at that price, and you'll have to scrimp in other areas in order to afford a little bit more. Ideally, you'll want your housing, transportation, and food costs to come in at less than 65 percent of your take-home pay.

One way to find out if this is doable: before you move out, keep track of everything you spend for one month. Try grocery shopping for yourself for a week or two and estimate how much you might need for food for a month. Add on what you spend in a month for public transit or gas and car payments. Then scan the apartment rentals section in the local paper to get a feel for what you will have to pay. If you have friends who rent, find out how much they pay for heat and electricity. Add it all up. Show your list to your friends and whoever does the budget in your own home to see if you've forgotten anything. If the grand total comes in at less than 65 percent of your spendable income, go for it! (For more help making a budget, see page 336.)

TIP: Get a taste for living on your own by paying rent to your family and buying and cooking your own food. Might as well do your own laundry, while you're at it. This is called taking care of yourself, and if you do it for a while you'll have a pretty good idea of what life will be like on your own.

More than You Really Wanted to Know

It appears a growing number of young people, stymied by the high cost of rent, are swapping their services for shelter. Call it Extreme Renting. Are you good with pets? You could be your landlord's pet-sitter. Handy with repairs? Offer to fix stuff. Got a car? Maybe you could find a senior with a basement apartment and a need for transportation. If you can whip up omelets or casseroles, or don't mind scrubbing bathtubs, you might find a landlord or roommate willing to give you a break on rent in exchange.

But be very cautious. Bartering for rent can leave you exposed to financial scams, or worse. You might not be protected under local tenant-protection laws. Whatever bartering deal you come up with may be subject to tax. And your personal safety could be at risk. Don't get into this kind of thing without doing a thorough background check. Get your deal in writing—what you're expected to do, and what you get in return. Better yet, save your money, look for a rental in a cheaper neighbourhood, or find a roommate.

Don't forget these hidden costs of apartment rentals, and make sure you factor them in.

- Extra utilities like cable TV, phone, and Internet.
- Laundry—if you don't have appliances, you'll need to use a laundromat.
- Parking, if it's not included in the rent.
- Appliances—do you need to purchase or rent?
- If there is no rent control in your area, you'll need to determine the chance of a rent increase in the near future.
- Usually you are required to pay a security deposit, about the same price as the rent. (Ask if the landlord will let you pay this in installments.)
- Renters' insurance. (See page 29.)

Do I Want to Live Alone or Share My Space?

Roommates can make your first home less lonely. Not only will you have someone to share your misery with, but you'll have someone there to share laughs, secrets, midnight popcorn, and rent, too. On the other hand, roommates can make you nutty if they're not a good fit, or if you simply must have privacy at the end of the day. Be honest with yourself. What do you need?

If you have decided to open your home to someone else, think hard about what type of person you could live with.

How do your activities match up?

Look for someone whose working hours resemble yours. You don't want to be crunching pretzels in front of the TV and annoying the hell out of your roomie when he's trying to hit the books; nor do you want to try catching up on sleep while your roommate entertains.

How compatible are you in the kitchen?

Is your belly a bottomless pit? Is she on a perpetual grapefruit diet? Are you a goat cheese and sushi fan, or pizza and beer? If your tastes don't match, how will you handle groceries?

I'd come home at midnight and there she'd be, waiting up for me again. She'd say, "I was worried." I don't need another mother. And I don't want a new best friend. She wanted girls' nights and chats. I wanted a roommate who has her own life, her own interests, and pays half the rent. When I finally said something about it she burst into tears and ran into her room. When she packed her bags and left I was totally relieved.

—ELEANOR, 25

TIP: Beware rooming with an old high school buddy. If you've been out of touch during the post-secondary years, chances are you've gone separate ways and have little in common.

What are you both looking for?

Are you seeking a soulmate, a lifelong friend, or simply someone to help pay the bills and leave you lots of space? Beware of sharing with a buddy. Just because she's your best friend doesn't mean she'd make a perfect roommate. Sure, she makes you laugh with her klutziness or her crazy outfits, but can you live with that every day? Do you love her enough to put up with drinking from the milk carton? Hair in the sink? The perpetually misplaced can-opener? (A reasonable compromise might be to rent an apartment in the same building as your friend. That way you're close—but not too close.)

Finding a Roommate—Where to Look

It can be hard finding the right roommate, so start your search early. Word-of-mouth should be your first resource—e-mail your friends, co-workers, and classmates to find out who's looking. With any luck, you've started before you've even left home, talking about your plans with other graduating students in your last year at school with the hopes that someone is heading to the same town. You'll probably have to cast a larger net, though. Here are some options:

- Check to see if the city has an apartment-sharing service online.
- Online roommate-finding services can help. You can be more specific about your potential roomie, but there might be a fee. And definitely don't put your phone number or home address in the ad. Use e-mail. (See Resources at the end of the chapter for website suggestions.)

If I could do it all over again, in my last semester of university I would have posted a big ad asking if there was anyone else looking for a place in Toronto. I found out months later that there were at least a dozen ex-UBC students moving to TO and all were in the same boat I was in—desperately seeking a home in a new city.

—ADAM, 24

- Place—or check—ads in the local newspaper, alternative weeklies, and specific publications related to your hobby or passion.
- Check the bulletin boards wherever you hang out—favourite stores, libraries, coffee shops, laundromats, church, or workplace. Get permission before you post your ad.
- Visit university or college website housing boards.

How to Word Your Ad

Don't be too picky in your ad, or you'll get few responses. Besides, do you really want a Mini-Me? Make the ad casual and friendly-sounding. Don't forget to mention some details about you. If you are looking to move in with someone who already has a place, be clear about what kind of accommodation you're looking—or not looking—for (for example, no to basements, yes to private bathroom, willing to share kitchen, no pets). If you already have the place and just need a roommate, share some details about your apartment—the cost of rent, whether utilities are included, amenities, etc. Make the ad stand out with colourful markers or pictures of your place.

It never occurred to me to ask my roommate, "So, are you a nudist?" I really wish I'd known that little tidbit in advance.

—JOSH, 23

What you can't specify or ask about: Religion or race.

What you can: Gender. Whether you'll be sharing a bathroom. Smoking or non-smoking.

When writing your ad, it's important to remember that it will be viewed by the public. You don't want to leave yourself too exposed. Take reasonable precautions against identifying yourself (skip last names, for example), and make your first meetings in a public place, not your home.

Interviewing Potential Roommates

Now's the time to do some serious weeding. Be picky and take the time to do it right.

The face-to-face meeting: this is the fun/scary part. How do you tell the keepers from the *Single White Female* types? First off, treat the interview seriously. Be friendly and polite, dress nicely, be on time. You want the person to like you! Second, be honest about your own quirks and hang-ups, but don't be afraid to be picky. Know ahead of time what you absolutely won't put up with. (Toothpaste gunk in the sink? Smoking? Air freshener? Orgies?) Be prepared with answers to questions about yourself and, if you've already found your place, the apartment. You might want to bring your cellphone and the landlord's number in case the interviewee has questions that you can't answer.

Here are some key areas to keep in mind during the face-to-face interview.

- *Tidiness.* If you're a neat-freak—or the opposite—say so. Have a good look at the potential roomie. You can often tell how tidy a person is by his/her personal grooming.
- *Socializing.* Talk about how often you like to entertain friends, favourite at-home activities, your position on parties, and what you consider out-of-bounds behaviour.
- *Sleep habits.* Find out if you're early birds or night owls, sound sleepers or not.

Been there
Done THAT

So I asked him, "Do you smoke?" He says no. Great. Turns out that the guy doesn't think smoking dope is *smoking*. I'm not talking about the occasional joint here, I'm talking Reefers 'R Us. Then he decides to grow a few plants on the windowsill. I swear, he turned our apartment into a grow-op. Did I mention the electricity bills? The "guests" who started hanging out in the living room? Yeah, I split.

—JACK, 24

- *Your gut feel.* You can usually tell, early on, if you're a good fit. If you're getting creeped out, if the vibes just aren't good, then don't try to convince yourself you'll grow to like the person. Better to keep looking than get stuck with someone who makes you feel uncomfortable.

What to ask

- Are you a smoker? Of what?
- Do you have pets? Any allergies? If there's a pet in the picture, does it have any nasty habits I should know about?
- Do you have a boyfriend/girlfriend who sleeps over? How often?
- What's your normal method of dealing with bills?
- Are you an early bird or night owl? Introvert or extrovert?
- Do you usually cook your own meals or eat out? How do you envision sharing a kitchen?
- Do you play a musical instrument? Is it the drums?
- Have you shared an apartment before? Can I speak to your old roommate?

> *Been* there
> *Done* THAT
>
> There's nothing quite like watching a movie with a new guy in the living room while your roommate is having loud sex in the bedroom.
>
> —MEG, 21

During the interview, throw out some possible scenarios. What if you want to entertain your water polo team after a big game? What if she's having a dinner party and you've got an exam?

Ask some open-ended questions about hobbies, friends, pets. (You might want to know about his interest in reptiles.) What are his favourite TV shows? Talk about things you are passionate about, things that really annoy. And this won't be easy, but at some point you need to know if your religious practices mesh. Don't get me wrong, this isn't about being judgmental, but you need to know if your poker night conflicts with Roomie's Bible-study class. There could be some basic lifestyle differences that you will have to talk about honestly, openly, and without a hint of prejudice.

Of course, there's really no easy way to ask "Are you a racist?" or "So what do think about the Holocaust?" But here's the thing: *you are going to want to know this stuff.* Throughout the interview, do your best to read between the lines and look for "attitude" or secretiveness. Talk about the events of the day, for example. Frankly, one meeting won't do it. The easiest way to get to know someone fast is to meet his or her

Been there
Done THAT

I was interviewing this one woman and thought she was great. I then asked her about her last two roommates. She told me about how much money they made, how one had a STD and the other had an abortion, and she told me their names and where they worked. If I'd moved in with her, one day I was going to be her last roommate. Thanks, but I don't want personal stuff like that spread all over town.

—LAUREN, 23

friends. Potential Roomie might clean up his act for a nanosecond for you, but chances are he won't be able to get his best friend to do the same. Try to meet the girl/boyfriend. You'll likely be seeing a lot of that person (in the hallway, at 3 a.m.).

At the end of the interview process, if you're feeling hopeful, say so. Ask the interviewee for references from a previous landlord and a recent credit report, and promise to contact him as soon as they're checked out. If you're not so keen, let him know that you've got more interviews and will be in touch.

If you are the one being interviewed and you think you've found a good match, offer a copy of a recent credit report (for more on this subject, see the Finances chapter) and a deposit cheque, on the spot.

Making It Work

So you've found someone! You like him and he likes you—congratulations! Sit down, right now, and work out a game plan so that there's a chance you'll go on liking each other until the lease runs out.

"Dos" and "Don'ts"

- **Do** go together to choose the apartment, if you haven't got one already. Be sure you're each happy with who gets which bedroom.
- **Do** decide ahead of time who will pay what. It's the small things that will cause trouble: the cost of the newspaper delivery or laundry soap, for example.
- **Do** arrange a bill-paying routine, and stick to it. Decide who will write the landlord the cheque, when, and when roommates should make their contributions. Work out how you'll pay for late fees and damages.

- **Do** discuss, very specifically, expectations about housework and cleanliness in general. Who does what, and when? There can be a huge difference between "cleaning the bathroom when it's dirty" and "keeping the bathroom clean."
- **Do** discuss renters' insurance, and how much each should contribute. (See page 29.)
- **Do** communicate to nip troubles in the bud—both casually ("Can you *pulleeze* stop leaving the half-empty bag of chips on the counter?") and formally (with a biweekly talk).
- **Do** be considerate. No matter how hungry you are, unless you've agreed in advance, her Doritos are not your Doritos. Having said that, have a little compassion for Roomie caught in the clutches of the midnight munchies. As long as the Rocky Road is replaced, and this isn't an ongoing thing, suck it up.
- **Don't** sign the lease until everyone's read it thoroughly and you've had someone (parents? lawyer?) check it out too.
- **Don't** let familiarity breed contempt. Throw in some random acts of kindness once in a while to keep life pleasant. Make a surprise dinner for both of you, do one of her chores, pick up a favourite doughnut on the way home. Share your Doritos.
- **Don't** put utilities in your name only. If you do, it will be your legal obligation to pay, and late payments will wreck your credit rating. If that's not possible, try putting different utilities in different roommates' names.

TIP: When you're sharing a small space it's extra important that you respect each other's privacy. Pick up after yourself, keep the music down if your roomie's reading or headachy, let others know when you're having friends over. And always be friendly with the folks who run the building—you never know when you're going to have to ask the building superintendent for help with a plugged toilet or lost key.

Rules for Roomies

Write them out:

- *Locks:* Bathroom, bedroom, apartment—what gets locked, when, and who gets the keys.
- *Food:* Sharing—what's fair game, what's off limits. You might want to set up a container for food money to which each person contributes a set amount, with

TIP: Phone bills can cause havoc if roommates don't have the same long-distance "habits." If you can't agree on which phone service is best, or who made what long-distance call, try relying on cellphones, or setting up separate phone lines.

a grocery list that can be added to or checked off. Whoever uses the money to refill the pantry should leave a note, along with receipts.

- *Housekeeping:* From dishes to toilets to taking out the garbage. Sort it out now. Try a rotating chore list. Be as specific as you need to be (e.g., dishes must be washed within 24 hours).
- *Décor:* Talk about your "style" and what you absolutely cannot stand.
- Socializing: From dinner guests to overnighters— decide how often guests are welcome, and when a "sleepover pal" needs to start contributing to rent or expenses.
- *Grocery shopping:* Who buys what, when, and with what money? If your tastes aren't similar enough to make you want to share groceries, you might want to share just the staples—sugar, salt, bread—and keep separate cupboards.
- *Bedtime:* It's tough to turn a night owl into a lark, and vice versa, so set the ground rules now. (Earplugs, anyone?)
- *Room temperature:* Sure, it sounds like a minor issue now, but wait till the dead of winter and you're freezing in five sweaters because your roomie likes it "cool," or you're sweating in your undies because your roomie's "hot-blooded."
- *Noise:* When should the TV or stereo be turned down?
- *Drugs, booze, and smoking:* Deal with this now, and get it in writing.

And then there's the biggie:

- *Rent:* How much should each person pay? You can split it evenly, but that might not make sense if one of you gets a bigger or better bedroom or requires additional space. And if you're the one whose name is on the lease (or the utility or telephone bills), and you are responsible, you might deserve a break on the rent.

The Roommate Contract

Not sure how to get this all down in writing? Try this sample fill-in-the-blanks contract. But remember this word to the wise if you run into disagreements: "Blessed are the flexible, for they shall not get bent out of shape."

Fill-in-the-blanks Roommate Contract

Money

Deposits will be paid and returned to _____.

The rent is due _____ (when).

It will be paid _____(how).

Renter's insurance? Responsibility of _____

and paid by _____.

We will share the costs of _____.
(Consider telephone, cable, Internet, heat and electricity, laundry, kitchen and bathroom soap, toilet paper, paper towels, condiments for the kitchen, other grocery items.)

Appliances (if owned by one roomie)

We will share the repair costs of _____.
(Think stove, fridge, washer and dryer not small appliances which are often cheaper to replace, sadly.)

Personal Property

We will share _____. (newspaper?)

We will not share _____. (soap?)

Guests

It's okay to have guests over on _____.

It's *not* okay to have guests over on _____.

We will tell each other about stay-over guests _____ days in advance.

I will repair anything my guest breaks. _____

Signatures

_____   _____

Cleaning

The bathroom and kitchen will be cleaned _____ (how often, by whom).

The entire apartment will be cleaned _____ (how often, by whom).

Garbage day is on _____.

_____is responsible for taking out the garbage.

Smoking and Drinking

Smoking is allowed _____ (not at all, on the fire escape, etc.).

Drinking is allowed _____ (when, where).

Smoke detectors checked _____ (date? Mark it on the calendar).

Personal Space

Bedroom doors will be left open or locked _____.

The living room is off limits on _____.
(e.g. if someone is sleeping on a pull-out)

Painting will be done by _____.
(Think about bringing the place back to code before moving out.)

Arguments will be settled by _____.
(This one is hard. Get it right and your lives will be way easier.)

If someone has to move out suddenly they will be responsible for

_____.

(Finding a new roomie? Paying an extra month's rent? Decide.)

Roomie #1 It's a big deal to me that _____.

Roomie #2 It's a big deal to me that _____.

Roomie #3 It's a big deal to me that _____.

Health concerns _____ (who? what? Serious allergies?)

Signatures

_____   _____

Getting Along

Even if you do everything right, plan ahead, discuss the rules, and really like your roommate, at some point or another you are going to butt heads. Something he, she, or you do is going to drive someone right up the wall, and you're going to have to deal with it. And, since you're all grown-ups now, you're going to handle it without hissy fits or locking people out … right?

It's all about communication. If something's bugging you, speak up—but do so diplomatically, and don't nitpick. Some suggested approaches:

- Role-play what you want to say first. Your message should be calm and clear about what you want changed. Find a friend to act as your roommate and practise.
- Before you meet, think carefully about your roommate's viewpoint. Is there something you're doing that could be contributing to the problem? Can you offer a compromise?
- Decide ahead of time how far you're prepared to go. If the conversation ends at a stalemate, is there an impartial acquaintance you can call on as mediator? Are you ready (and able) to move out? Can you tolerate the problem until the lease expires?
- Don't ambush her at the door with your beef. Find a time when you're both relaxed, and alone.
- Use the "I" word a lot, rather than "you"—e.g., "I feel uncomfortable when …" as opposed to "You always …"
- If he's violating the terms of your lease, assume he has forgotten the specifics. Show him a copy and tactfully point out the terms. Have a remedy ready: if the terms are violated, what are the options?
- Remember what you liked about your roommate, once upon a time. Treat him as if he were still that person (which he is) and not a freak (oh come on, he's *not*).

TIP: Before you go postal over a dish in the sink, talk it out. Yell or scream and the battle is lost. Do not rattle off a list of offences starting with the day Roomie moved in. Focus on one problem only. And choose your time judiciously. Mentioning the used condoms in the bathroom should probably not be brought up when the parents are visiting.

We'd been sharing an apartment for two weeks, *two weeks*, when I apparently committed the treasonous act of inviting a co-worker over for a beer. Apparently I forgot that it was Roomie's night to study. Anyway, she called her mother, and her *mother* called me at work the next day to "talk about the problem." I mean …

—SARAH, 26

Troubleshooting

You know you're in trouble when …

- Roomie can't tell you what's bugging her, or communicates by slamming doors and giving you the silent treatment. You might be up against a lifelong personality problem.
- Roomie doesn't know the difference between privacy and secrecy and leaves you out of the loop on things that affect you, like the fact that she lost her job a month ago and now can't pay the rent.
- Roomie is always right; there is never room for compromise. Worse, he feels obligated by some higher power to always play the devil's advocate. Conversation always turns into argument. The operative word here is *always*.
- Little Miss Passive Aggressive understands the problem, then she ignores it, and you. Worse, she tells everyone but you about the problem. Or, a personal fave, Roomie says, "Everything is fine," when clearly everything is not fine. Good luck with that.
- The Space Invader has no sense of personal space, hence the junk all over the bathroom.
- The Borrower assumes that you won't mind if he wears that newly dry-cleaned shirt.
- Roomie is a pig. We're not talking about towels on the bathroom floor. This person leaves entire meals under the bed.
- Roomie has a serious body odour problem. There are a whole lotta people out there who: a) shower and put on dirty clothes, b) don't shower but think that layering clothes will cover any lingering stink, c) use cologne in places and ways that Calvin Klein could not even imagine, d) honestly think that their smell is—wait for it—pleasant!
- Roomie is great—too bad about her friends from hell. Her boyfriend gets drunk and breaks things—maybe on purpose, maybe because he's a complete idiot. Or Roomie keeps having parties, leaving hurricane-like damage in their wake.
- Roomie wants to save the world and brings homeless people to share dinner and the couch. (You might want to suggest that Roomie volunteer at the local shelter.)

I remember my first home on my own. I'd left a pampered life in the country to live in downtown Toronto. I had no idea that the neighbourhood I'd chosen was prime hooker territory. I used to sit at my window into the wee hours of the morning watching all the seedy stuff. The things I saw! I would never have told my parents —they'd have whisked me right back to the country! Every night, as I walked home from the university, I'd get approached by johns looking for a trick. I took to walking fast with my keys poking out through my clenched fist. (Like *that* was going to save my life!) I think I grew up more that year on my own than I did in the entire first nineteen years of my life. Sometimes, I wonder how I even survived.

—KRISTEN, 32

What Sort of Neighbourhood Do I Want?

Location is one of the key factors in your search for shelter. You won't be able to find something that meets *all* of your needs. Expect to compromise somewhere—but not on safety. Make a list of what's important to you in a neighbourhood, from most to least, and keep that in mind when you begin your search. Here are some things to consider.

Proximity to school or work

Do you like the idea of rolling out of bed with only minutes to spare and still getting in on time? Or will it drive you crazy knowing that work/school is always only a few blocks away? Are willing to put up with a long commute to really escape? How do you feel about getting up early to make the long trek in?

Safety

Find out what areas have the lowest crime rates. Call the local police station and public transit system for more information. If you have specific neighbourhoods in mind, hang around a bit, day and night, to see if you like the vibes. Can you see vandalism? Bars on windows? Talk to the residents. Can you walk alone at night? If you're female, talk with other women. Do they feel safe?

Atmosphere and amenities

Would you prefer an area with a family feel, or a trendy area with people your own age? Imagine what you will do with your time. Will you want to be near a park, library, cafés, shops, the gym? If you want to be near the local nightspots, will you still want to be near them when you're ready to sleep and the rest of the street is out partying? Is there an ATM connected with your bank nearby, or will you be forking over service fees every time you use your card?

Local transportation

How will you be getting around? Do you need easy access to public transit, or is good parking a must? How close is the nearest bus or subway stop? Walk it yourself to be sure. If you need to take major roads to school or work, find out how difficult it is to get to them.

What Kind of Housing Do I Want?

Some of your options:

Renting a Room in a Rooming House or Home

Pros

- You probably won't have to provide furniture or linen.
- It can be a less expensive choice.
- If you're boarding, meals might be included.
- It's good if all you need is a place to crash at night.
- The owner is generally interested in upkeep, so repairs will usually be done quickly.
- Parking is often included.

Cons

- You will almost certainly have to share a bathroom, and possibly both kitchen and laundry facilities.
- There might be stricter rules about sleepover guests and noise. The landlord might feel entitled to enter your space at any time.
- There might not be locks on your doors. (In that case—run!)

The ad said *"Two bedrooms, en suites, top floor of Victorian house, shared kitchen with landlord. Original fixtures and moulding."* What that really meant was decrepit, old, mouldy house with really bad wiring and toilets stashed in free-standing cupboards. Did I mention that the landlord kept his teeth in a cup by the kitchen sink?

—TONI, 19

Basement Apartment

Pros

- It's private.
- If it's in a home, it might be in a quieter, residential area.

Cons

- You might be required to share utilities and amenities (kitchen, laundry, heat) with the rest of the home.
- Noise might be an issue if walls/ceilings/floors are thin.
- It might be dark, damp, mouldy. Be sure there is a safety escape route.
- The landlord might feel entitled to enter when you are out, or might not observe respectful boundaries.

Co-Ops

Pros

- Plenty of social opportunities.
- Less expensive.

Cons

- Less private.
- Often "party central."

TIPS:

If you have a thing about noise, look for low-rises or townhouse rentals, which are often quieter. You may hear more of a noisy neighbour if you're on the lower unit; look for an upper unit, instead. Neighbourhoods with lots of seniors are also easier on the ears.

Shared House

Pros

- Can be less expensive.
- More social.

Cons

- Little privacy.

Walk-Up or Low-Rise Apartment

Pros

- Usually less expensive than a high-rise.
- Sometimes offers laundry rooms and storage lockers in the building.

Cons

- Rarely has extra amenities offered in high-rises.
- No elevator.
- Buildings usually older.

High-Rise Apartment

Pros

- Because they are more than five storeys, buildings usually have elevators.
- They often provide better security.
- Many offer extra amenities, like party rooms, pools, and gyms.

Cons

- More expensive.
- Can be less friendly.
- Located in more congested neighbourhoods.

Adding Up the Extras

To help you narrow your choice, decide on the following. Remember that each "extra" you absolutely must have adds to the cost of rent.

- Number of bedrooms, bathrooms, extra rooms.
- Storage space—what about your bike?
- Size of kitchen—counter space, appliances?
- Extra space for piano, exercise equipment, larger furniture.
- Modern building or one with hardwood floors and lots of character.
- Elevator.
- Large windows.
- Good view.
- Security system.
- Parking—indoor or out?
- Pets allowed.
- Pool, fitness centre—what are the hours?
- Air conditioning.
- On-site laundry facilities.
- Balcony, yard.
- Think about your hobbies—are there enough sunny windows to satisfy your green thumb? Is the oven large enough for your baking sheet or your world-famous roast turkey? Is there room for your mountain bike?

Where and How to Apartment-Hunt

Once you've got a list of what you want—ranked from most important to least—you're ready to start your search. So go. Go *now!* Finding an apartment is surprisingly hard work. You'll need to give yourself about two months. If you procrastinate, you will end up with something nasty and regret every night as you crawl into your cockroachy bed listening to the neighbours blast ABBA.

Best way to find awesome digs? Word-of-mouth. Spread the news. Be shameless. Tell everyone. E-mail

TIP: Classifieds are written in a unique lingo that will take some figuring out. For example, "1½ BA" means a one-and-a-half-bathroom apartment.
"W/fpl" = with fireplace;
A/C = air conditioning;
w/d = washer/dryer. And note: "cozy" means small.

everyone. You never know who might have a room to let or may have heard about a great place that's about to become available.

Some more places to check out:

Local newspapers (both the paper and online versions)

Check the paper as soon as it hits the newsstands. Don't forget smaller ethnic, community, and weekly papers, and publications like *Renters News* (in Ontario) available free at the local corner store. By scouring the classifieds, you'll learn a lot about the area, like neighbourhood features and going rates.

Websites that post available accommodations

Local newspapers often publish their classified ads on the Internet. Other websites to check out: www.craigslist.com, www.homes4students.ca, www.rent.com, www.rentnet. com, www.apartments.com, www.roommates.ca, www.rent.net, www.homestore.com, www.apartmentsearch.com. *Note:* While these sites are handy because they're updated regularly, they won't include all listings, and you probably won't find the really good deals there.

University/college housing lists

You don't need to be a student to take advantage of post-secondary school housing directories. Use the school's online housing list and visit the campus in person to see what's posted on the bulletin boards.

Local bulletin boards

Wander around your desired neighbourhood and look for bulletin boards in libraries, coffee shops, community centres, grocery stores, bookstores, laundromats, places of worship, even on telephone poles.

Neighbourhood scouting expeditions

Once or twice a week, in the morning if possible, scout out the neighbourhood for vacancy signs. Walk or bike so you don't have to waste time looking for parking. Dress nicely. If you find a "For Rent" sign in a building you're interested in, you can buzz the superintendent or property manager and check it out. Bring a notepad to help you keep track of what you find.

Also worth checking out

- Local real estate agencies—check the Yellow Pages.
- Real estate magazines.
- The Human Resources department where you work.
- Guides to available housing—available in some larger cities' municipal offices.

What to Do If You're Moving to a New Town

It gets a little more complicated if you're conducting your search from afar. Photos and online "virtual tours" just can't give you a clear enough picture—you really should see the place in person. Can you manage to get in a few exploratory visits to your new town? If you can, bring a friend or relative for company, safety, and a second opinion. Ask local folks about the going rental rates and best places to live. If you can't arrange to view apartments in person, try to find someone who lives in the area to view them for you.

TIP: If you're moving to a university town to start school in September, finding a place to stay can be difficult. One possible solution: move at the beginning of the summer when there are more vacancies. It will cost you a few extra months in rent, but if you can afford it (maybe by working in your university town for the summer, instead of back home?) then you won't have to compete with the swarms of returning students in the fall.

If you're moving to a new job in a new city, your employer might be able to help. You might find someone with rooms to rent through your college or university alumni group (also nice to find someone with whom you have something in common, and who can possibly act as a mentor/ambassador). Another option: sublet until you find your own spot. Many university residences are available in the summer. Contact the school's housing office. You can even borrow a buddy's couch for a while, if you just need shelter while you carry out your search. Just make sure you pay your host, help out with chores while you're there, and leave a gift when you go. A cellphone or voice mailbox will allow you to receive calls from potential landlords until you get your own phone line.

Viewing the Place / Meeting the Landlord

When you find an ad that looks good, get your butt out there quickly and check it out. Especially in tight rental markets, you'll need to move fast. Good deals get scooped. If you like what you see, be ready to submit your application the same day. Make sure that you've saved enough money for a deposit, first month's rent, and utilities.

TIP: Make sure you have a bank account from which you can obtain a certified cheque. Most landlords require you to pay first month's rent and a security deposit with a certified cheque or money order.

Meeting with a landlord is a little like a job interview. Remember that the landlord is looking for someone who will pay rent on time and be a responsible adult. Show him that you are. Dress neatly. Be cheerful, polite, and on time. Switch off your cellphone during the interview. Save your questions for the end of the interview, after the landlord has given you some information. Consider bringing a parent or older sibling with you—landlords might feel reassured to know there are "older and wiser" folks backing you up.

Apartment-Hunting Kit

Here's a list of everything you'll need to have with you when you meet the landlord. Keep the papers in a neat portfolio or briefcase.

- Road map, address, contact number.
- Cellphone in case you get lost or are running late.
- Notepad and pencil to keep track of what you did or didn't like.
- Camera (for pictures of rooms, building facilities, and the neighbourhood—not the sweet sunbathing neighbour or anything else that should remain private).
- List of questions to ask the superintendent, fellow tenants, or landlord.
- List of references (employers, teachers, friends, and former landlords). Better yet, gather some letters of reference beforehand.
- Chequebook to leave a deposit. (Make sure there's enough money in your bank account to cover the deposit and first month's rent.)
- Guarantor information (if applicable—see page 28).
- A letter from your current employer stating your salary and length of employment, or a recent pay stub or tax return to prove you have income, plus contact numbers so the landlord can reach your employer.

- Driver's licence.
- Job resumé.

Apartment-Viewing Checklist

If you can, bring "someone who knows something" (father/mother? neighbour? buddy in construction?) to inspect apartments with you. It's easy to be swayed by superficial touches and miss the major flaws.

- *Faucets in kitchen and bath, showers.* Is the water pressure strong, hot water hot? Do the plugs plug?
- *Toilet.* Make sure it flushes properly.
- *Leaks.* Look for evidence, like water stains on ceilings or floors.
- *Lighting.* Look for adequate ceiling lights (or you'll be forking out for lots of lamps). Switch them on to be sure they work.

> **TIP:** If you've found a place you like, visit at different times of the day. Find out whether it's a zoo at rush hour, or if it feels creepy at night.

- *Electrical outlets.* Two functioning plugs in every room? Are they three-pronged?
- *Appliances.* What's included? Does it all work? (If it's a gas stove, find out where the pilot light is. Does it light right away?)
- *Heat.* Electrical, radiator, or central heating? Can you adjust it yourself?
- *Windows.* Open, close, and lock, with screens? Well sealed?
- *Noise.* Stand quietly: can you hear traffic, neighbours? The rental isn't over top of a pub, is it?
- *Closet space.* Is there enough?
- *Security.* Are all doors well locked? (Look for deadbolts.)
- *Phone service.* Are there enough jacks for your phones and your computer? Can you get cellphone reception? High-speed Internet connection?
- *Water.* Can you drink from the tap?
- *Upkeep.* Inspect cabinets, closets, carpets, around woodwork, and under appliances for cleanliness, evidence of bugs. (Look for droppings, dead bugs, or traps. Is there a line of brown goo along the back of the cupboards or sink? Roach repellent, most likely.) Do the carpets need cleaning?
- *Laundry facilities.* Is there a hookup available in the unit? Laundry machines in the building? Is the laundry room clean? If there are no facilities in the building, how far is the nearest laundromat?

- *Fire safety.* Are there working smoke and carbon monoxide detectors and fire extinguishers? Is the fire exit easily accessible? If it's a large building, what is the warning system? What about a fire escape? If there are security bars on windows, is there a quick-opening device to allow you to escape? If you are thinking of renting in an older building, be sure to ask the landlord about fire safety features.

TIP: To impress the landlord, remember your manners when inspecting apartments and remove your shoes before you enter. Try not to have holes in your socks.

- *Intercom.* Does it work?
- *Air conditioning.* Are you kidding me? You should be so lucky! (If you are, be sure it works, then thank your lucky stars.) Remember that the higher you go in a building, the hotter it will be.
- *Outside.* Are the lawns cared for or neglected? Are there cigarette butts or empties floating around? Are the hallways clean and well-lit? Is there peeling paint? Is the elevator working?
- *Parking.* Is there a spot available? Is it reserved, covered, safe?
- *Neighbours.* Do they smoke? (It can be impossible to keep the smell out.) Do they look like grumpy old people who won't like your taste in music, or partiers who'll be up all night?

Questions to Ask Current Tenants

If you see other residents in the hallway, ask if they'd mind talking with you about their experiences in the building. Ask their opinion of the super or the landlord. Are they happy with how well maintained and clean the building is? Can they hear people talking through the walls? Do they know why the current tenants are leaving? Is the area safe? Is the commute safe? What is local traffic like? What about noise levels outside the building at different times of the day? If you don't see other residents, come back another time or ask the landlord if he can put you in touch with some.

Questions for the Landlord

- Who is responsible for general maintenance, grass cutting, clogged toilets, snow removal?
- What redecorating are you allowed to do? Does the landlord paint the apartment before a new tenant comes in?

- Is there room for guest parking? Are there special rules about overnight guests?
- Is there storage available? Where can you keep your bike?
- Are pets allowed—what kind?
- How are repairs handled?
- How much is rent? What does that include? (Any additional charges for heat, electricity, water, cable, or parking?)
- Are the appliances included? Who is responsible for appliance repair?
- If utilities are extra, what are the average monthly costs?
- Can you control heat in the unit?
- How much is required for a security deposit?
- Is there a lease? How long is it for? Is there an option to renew? (You don't want to have to repeat this search next year.)
- Why are the current tenants leaving?
- When were the locks last changed? What security is available for the unit? Is there a 24-hour security guard? Who can access common areas of the building?

Questions the Landlord Might Ask You

It's a two-way street. The landlord wants to know about you. (Think of it this way: if he's checking you out, he's also checking out the guy with the tattoos, mullet, and Harley.) The landlord is within her rights to contact previous landlords, call references, and run a credit check. Compile this information (and make sure the references are good ones) ahead of time. You might also be asked to fill out an application. The landlord will want to know:

- Your income.
- Where you work.
- How many people will share the rental with you.
- Whose name will be on the utility bill.
- If you have pets.
- If you smoke.
- Previous landlord's contact information.

TIP: If you're on a really tight budget, look for an apartment in a complex that shows lots of vacancies. The landlord might want tenants badly enough to negotiate on deposits, leases, even rent.

The landlord *cannot* ask personal questions about your ethnic background, religion, sexual preference, plans for marriage or children. He cannot require you to give him your social insurance number.

Signing a Lease

You're approved! The landlord likes you! He really likes you! But before you drag your futon inside, take a good close look at the lease, because this is serious stuff.

TIPS:
Will the landlord give you a break on rent if you pay early each month? Can't hurt to ask.
If you can commit to staying in a place for a longer period of time, offer to sign a longer lease. Landlords often prefer that and will reward you with lower rent.

A lease is a contract—a written document giving you the right to live somewhere in exchange for rent for a certain period of time—and it's legally binding. That means it's got the law on its side. That means you'd better know what you're signing before you sign it, because once you do, you're stuck. Put down the pen, pick up the lease, and read it through, very carefully, no matter how eye-glazing-over you find it to be. If you don't understand something, ask. If you've got roommates, have them do the same. Then show it to a trusted friend or parent, someone older and wiser.

If it's your first lease you'll probably need a co-signer (someone who signs too, guaranteeing that if you don't pay, they will accept full financial responsibility). Usually, it's your parents. Get permission. Get them to read the lease. If you have a lawyer friend floating around somewhere, get him to read it too. Heck, have the dog read it.

What to Look For

A lease spells out your obligations, and the landlord's. Here's what you should look for:

- Your name, your roommates', and the landlord's, properly spelled.
- Correct address of the rental property.
- Description of the rental unit and which appliances are included.
- What to do if something should break or needs repairs—and the timeline for repairs.
- Any damage you and the landlord found on your pre-rental inspection.
- Start and end date of the rental agreement.
- Rental fees, with or without utilities.
- Parking fees, if not included.
- To whom you make your payment, when, how, and what happens when your payment is late.

- How much security deposit is required and under what conditions you can get it all back, when you will get it back, and with what interest.
- When the landlord is allowed to enter the rental unit, and with how much notice.
- Rules for subletting.
- Notice required for terminating the rental.
- What happens if you break the lease.
- What happens at the end of the lease—whether it's renewed or becomes month-to-month, and at what rate.
- Allowable rent increases.
- Rules about tenant conduct, decorating, pets, smoking, waterbeds, roommates, and boarders.
- Emergency contact information for tenant and landlord (include phone, fax, and e-mail).

> **TIP:** Take photos or videos of the rental before you move in so you have proof that that hole in the wall really wasn't your fault.

Once you (and your roommates) have signed the lease, you should all get a copy. Keep yours somewhere safe.

Renters' Insurance

Don't doze off. I know this isn't riveting stuff but you still need to know it.

Picture this. Your sweet-but-ditzy roommate has decided to put together a five-course surprise dinner for your birthday, but the biggest surprise of all are the flames flying out of the pot of hot oil that she left on the stove while she ran down to hang balloons in the lobby. The landlord's snow-white cupboards are soot-black, and he wants them fixed, *now*.

Or … the toilet mysteriously flushes all weekend long while you're back home visiting family over Christmas break. You return to find your stereo system waterlogged and funny-smelling mouldy stuff growing along the baseboard.

Well, guess what? Even if it's not your fault, if your belongings are damaged because of a problem with the rental unit, you could still be financially responsible. That's why they invented insurance. Get some. Your landlord probably has some kind of insurance to cover the building but it won't include your belongings.

First, check out your parents' homeowners policy, and see if you can piggyback on it somehow. It's possible, if you are sleeping on your old bed, sitting on the old basement couch, and eating off the old kitchen table, that these "borrowed" items are covered. Alternatively, check to see if your auto insurer can write both policies; you might get a discount. Make sure you're covered for both accidental and theft, and be sure your computer is covered, since at this stage in your life it is probably the most valuable thing you own.

If it's a struggle for you to pay for insurance right now, at least try to find a policy with a higher deductible—that's the amount that you have to pay before the insurance payment kicks in. It should be less expensive. If the annual premium is out of reach, you can try monthly payments. And if you really can't afford full insurance, at least get "personal liability." That will ensure you're covered if you leave the stove on or bathtub faucet running.

To find the best deal, compare packages with different insurance companies via the Internet, consult a broker, and talk with friends who have policies.

TIP: Start looking weeks in advance for free boxes. Try liquor and grocery stores. Get as many as you can, in a variety of sizes. If all else fails, boxes can be bought, or even rented, from moving companies—check the Yellow Pages.

This Is It—the Big Move-Out

There might be nothing more liberating than packing up all your belongings and hitting the road. But don't just go racing out the door—there are a few things you've got to do before you leave.

Moving can be a great adventure—or a stress-filled disaster, depending on how well you've planned. And chances are you'll be doing this moving thing a few more times over the coming years. Follow these steps for smooth moves.

Packing and Planning

1. Make a list of what you want to bring—which furniture, accessories, and personal items to pack. (Um, honey? That Metallica poster? Don't bring it. I have a special place in mind for that one.)

2. Pile up the stuff you don't want and give it to your younger sibling, or to a charity, or hold a garage sale.

3. Find out from the landlord what utilities you're responsible for turning on and whom to call. Call the utility companies at least one week before you move in and arrange to have everything hooked up the day you arrive. Don't forget phone,

Internet, and cable TV. Most places pay for water; it should be on when you move in. Some landlords include heat in the rent. If yours doesn't, and you have gas, call the gas company in the area. If it's winter, it's probably already on—you just need to transfer the account to your name.

4. Plead, beg, and bribe your friends to help you move. Offer pizza, pop, beer (when the move is done), and promises of reciprocation (don't flake out when they call you on it!).

5. Find out if the apartment building allows moves at only certain times of the day. (You should also try to avoid moving during rush hour.) Reserve your moving truck—and "moving buddies"—for that time.

6. Book moving day off work.

7. Fill out a change of address form at the post office or online (http://www.canada-post.ca/tools/pg/manual/PGcoa-e.asp) for your new address.

8. Pack. Give yourself a couple of weeks. Start with things you don't use often (prints, photographs, old yearbooks—trust me, you'll want those—out-of-season clothes). Try not to make the boxes too heavy. You want to hang on to your friends—and your back. Put heavy things like books in small boxes. Mark the boxes "HEAVY," or "FRAGILE," or "THIS END UP," along with the rooms they should be moved to. Old newspapers are good for wrapping breakables. Seal the boxes with proper packing tape, available at office supply stores.

Moving Day

1. Pick up the moving truck as early in the day as possible.

2. Pack up your last-minute items—toiletries, linens, snacks, toilet paper, soap, alarm clock, a few disposable plates, cups, and utensils, and cleaning supplies—in a box marked "OPEN FIRST."

3. Hop into the truck and head off into the sunset. Wait. Turn around. Say a last teary goodbye. Now, go. *Go!*

4. Inspect the rental before you move in so that you are not held liable for damage that already exists. The landlord should accompany you. Bring a friend, too, if possible. Take notes, and

TIP: Leave a set of keys with a friend in case you get locked out.

More than You Really Wanted to Know

Most landlords require you to pay first and last month's rent plus a deposit to cover the costs if you damage anything. In Canada, the landlord can ask for a deposit in all provinces and territories except Quebec. When you give the landlord your cheque, be sure to get a receipt. That way, when you leave, you'll get the money back (or it will go towards the last month's rent), as long as you haven't:

- Damaged the property.
- Skipped out on the rent.
- Broken the lease.
- Left without giving proper written notice.
- Left without cleaning the rental to the same level as it was when you first took possession. (Remember those pictures you took? Now you know why.)

photographs, of any problems, including things like wall dents, scuff marks, peeling wallpaper, carpet stains, etc. Find out exactly how clean the landlord expects the apartment to be when you move out. Have the landlord sign the inspection notes, and keep the record with your important papers. When it's time to move out, you'll have something to compare, and the proof you'll need to get your security deposit back.

5. If time allows, scour the place before you put your stuff in it. Before you crash into your bed (or blankets on the floor), check that the smoke detectors work and windows and doors lock.

Setting Up House: What to Buy First

Face it. Your place is going to look like the "Before" pictures on *The Decorating Challenge* for a long, long time. Think of it as a rite of passage. You can't be a real grown-up until you've done some time on an uncomfortable mattress, watched a fuzzy TV on the floor, and eaten barely edible things from upside-down Frisbees and tinfoil pans.

After a while, the novelty of "roughing it" wears thin. But be patient. Don't rush out to buy the biggies like a sofa or bed right away. Sure, you'll eventually need somewhere to sit and sleep, but there's no sense in blowing your money now. Who knows if it will even fit in your next place, or whether you'll still like it by then?

If you're really itching to buy something to symbolize your independence, here are a few items that you might or might not consider essential. (Remember, most of these things are available at second-hand stores and garage sales.)

- Kitchen stuff—pots, pan, dishes, etc. (For a complete list, see Your Kitchen Tools, page 91.)
- Microwave, if there isn't one included.
- Curtains—old sheets or newspaper might work as a quick fix, but curtains or blinds should be one of the first things you purchase (after carefully measuring, of course).
- Linens, blankets, pillows.
- Sleeping bag (for friends).
- Bed frame and mattress set—remember, if you get a queen-size bed, queen-size bedsheets are more expensive.
- Alarm clock—because Mom won't be waking you up any more.
- Flashlight.
- Shower curtain—you'll need to wash or replace this every few months (they get gross).
- Toilet brush and plunger. (For what to do with them, see the Housekeeping chapter, page 74.)
- Folding card table, folding chairs—the real dining-room set can wait.
- Desk—if you're a student, it's a necessity.
- Lamp—at least one, for reading and backup in case the ceiling light burns out. Lava lamps don't count.
- Garbage cans—one for the kitchen, one for the bathroom, one for the bedroom (if you have one).
- Soap dispenser for bathroom and kitchen.
- Something for storing clothes—a used dresser, plastic drawers from a discount store, under-the-bed bins, or hanging shelves for the closet.
- Smoke and carbon monoxide detectors.
- Cleaning supplies. (See page 75.)
- Iron and ironing board. (For what to do with them, see Taking Care of Your Stuff, page 173.)
- Light bulbs, laundry detergent, dish soap.
- Basic tool kit. (See page 51.)
- Oh yeah—don't forget toilet paper. That's *your* job now.

TIP: If you've got roommates, rather than splitting the cost of furnishing the apartment, try dividing up who buys what. One person might supply the vacuum cleaner, the other purchases the microwave, for example. That way, you won't be arguing about who takes what when you go your separate ways.

Later, you can add:

- Comfy chairs/couch/futon.
- Bookcases—you can make your own with plastic milk crates or long boards perched on bricks.

Beyond the Milk Crate: Décor for Dummies (and the Broke)

Yippee! It's yours—a whole new place to fix up the way you like! All those years of watching HGTV will finally be put to good use. Before you start shopping for furniture and slathering on paint, however, there are a few things you should keep in mind. This is just a temporary home, remember; there will be many others. You are broke—or nearly. Your new place is tiny and your tastes are going to change a hundred times over. If it's a rental, you probably can't put nail holes in the wall and you might be stuck with nasty tiles or ugly cabinets. All this means you can't just go whole hog. You'll need to plan, and budget. And before you do anything else, you'll need to get yourself off that Pottery Barn catalogue mailing list, because honey, that's just cruel.

TIP: If you have a roommate with a sleep schedule different from yours, look for a vibrating alarm clock to tuck under your pillow.

Here's the deal: you've got to be patient. There's no need to outfit the place immediately. Wait for seasonal discounts and garage sales, and do just one room at a time. Start with the basics: a place to sleep, a place to sit, a desk for your computer, and a table for food (sometimes they're one and the same). Rule of thumb: don't sink a lot of money into something that won't go with you.

If you're really pressed for space—if you're in a dorm room or a bachelorette and your bed takes centre stage—focus on finding a comforter that really turns your crank.

Then pick up a few colours from the comforter as accent colours for your accessories. And if your new comforter is machine washable (or at least has a machine-washable cover, like a duvet), you can even skip the top sheet and the whole bed-making chore altogether. Leap (or crawl) out of bed, smoothe, and go.

Flowers and photographs are a quick way to make your new digs feel like home. If you're stuck with ugliness (and what cheap rental doesn't have some?) then your best bet is to cover it up. Inexpensive throw rugs are good for floors. Accessories like blankets and pillows that have just a bit of the ugly colour can distract from yucky tile or countertops. And there's nothing like a dimmer switch when you're really desperate. Check your hardware store for DIY instructions.

Where should you put your decorating dollars? Sleep's mighty important as you forge your way in the world. Get the best mattress you can find and some curtains to keep out the lights at night. If you're in a dorm and the mattress is already supplied, buy a zippered vinyl mattress cover and a cheap egg-crate foam mattress pad for on top. Linens can be purchased relatively inexpensively at outlet stores and sales. (See the Finances chapter, page 336, for best sale times.) If you have some basic sewing skills, buy extra flat sheets and make pillows and curtains.

TIP: A chandelier should hang about 70 centimetres (28 inches) above the tabletop.

When it comes to big-ticket items, like couches, rugs, or draperies, stick with neutrals. The more space they take up in the room, the quicker you will tire of something trendy. If you're lusting after the latest lime or lipstick-pink, try it on accessories like cushions and picture frames, which you can change when the trend is passé. Couches are really kind of stupid, anyway. I mean, who sits in the middle? Usually, people cling to the couch arm and don't squeeze into the centre unless they have to—which is why a loveseat makes much more sense.

Been there
Done THAT

I inherited two ugly old wingback chairs and, believe it or not, I spray-painted them! Okay, so it was dumb. I thought yellow would look funky, but it was just flaky—literally. Anyone who sat there ended up speckled yellow. So no, I wouldn't advise painting upholstered furniture.

—KATE, 28

TIP: Bring a tape measure when you buy larger furniture so you're sure it will fit through your door.

And you could skip the dining table, too. Try a coffee table, which can be found cheap at garage sales and thrift shops. Sit on cushions on the floor. Pretend you're in Japan. Another option: TV tables. Pretend you're living in *Leave It to Beaver*–land.

Windows

Covering the windows will probably be one of your first orders of business—unless you want an audience outside the building every night. For a quick fix, tape newspaper to the window. You can also drape a sheet or tablecloth across a tension or shower curtain rod. If it's a small window, you can use string to hang the fabric. If it's too long, sew or duct-tape a hem. If you've already got mini-blinds on the windows, you can soften the industrial feel by draping fabric over the top. On small windows, if you don't want to put holes in the wall for curtain rods, try tension rods.

Filling Your Empty Walls

Just because the landlord won't let you put holes in your walls doesn't mean they have to go bare. You can cover them with something interesting using Velcro, peel-and-stick, and other products designed to hold wall hangings temporarily. Check your local hardware store. What should you hang? Well, if you opt not to hang your original Matisse, there are other options (and we're not even going to mention the Ashlee Simpson posters, because those are long gone, right?).

- Old record album covers.
- Vintage clothing.
- Quilts.
- Pretty plates.
- Your niece's or nephew's artwork.
- Calendar pictures in cheap frames.
- Family photos in similar frames.
- Leftover fabric. (Cut cardboard to fit a frame, cut fabric slightly larger, glue ends to back of cardboard and stick inside frame.)

Remember not to just plunk your artwork in the middle of the wall. Small pieces will look silly if they're out of proportion to the wall size. Try to cover more than half the wall with artwork. Usually, that means grouping several similar pieces together. So that you're not hacking up the walls with nail holes, cut squares from newspaper the size of your pictures and arrange with Blu Tack or other sticky stuff to find the best layout. The art should be hung at eye level—when you're standing if it's in a hall (for example), or when you're sitting if it's in the living room.

Bathroom Basics

If you're sharing a bathroom, you'll want to keep your toiletries—and germs—to yourself. Invest in some flip-flops for the shower. Keep your jewellery in your bedroom, medicine in a kitchen cupboard, edit your makeup and shampoo to bare essentials, and keep toiletries in a small plastic basket from the dollar store. That'll cut the clutter. A rubber shelf liner (also from the dollar store) can act as a portable personal bath math.

The easiest way to spiff up your bathroom is with matching towels, shower curtains, and bath mat. If you're dying to liven up your new home with a sassy colour, the bathroom is the safest place. You can sometimes find cool colours in the hardware store's section of paint "mistakes." Just check with the landlord first.

TIP: For a cheap way to express yourself in a rental unit, look for funky switch plates, drawer pulls, and knobs. You'll find them in hardware stores. Bring the old pulls with you so you're sure you've got the right size, and hang on to them so you can put them back when you leave.

Small Space Solutions

- Wherever possible, add reflective surfaces like mirrors and glass. Instead of a bulletin board, post your reminders on a mirror with a dry-erase marker.
- Choose furniture that has legs rather than skirts.
- Buy the tallest bookshelves you can find.
- Try screens to hide storage bins or anything ugly.
- Use a drop-leaf table as a desk or dining table, or both. Shove it up against the wall when you're not entertaining.
- Keep colours and patterns simple and monochromatic.
- If you have space over your cabinets, store stuff in baskets tucked on top.
- Try a plastic garbage bin with a round piece of wood on top for an end table. Store stuff below, cover it with fabric.
- Trunks are great as both storage and coffee table.
- If you can't tuck things under your bed because there's no space, see if you can prop the bed onto cement blocks to make room.

Painting

Some landlords let you paint, others don't. And some say it's okay to paint as long as you don't paint the walls black, navy blue, or dark purple, because dark colours are such a pain to paint over. If you get the go-ahead, then go ahead—slowly. Try just one wall at a time. With any luck, and with a good choice in paint, just one wall is all you'll need to spiff up a drab room. You can even use this technique to camouflage a long room, painting one or both ends in a stronger colour to make it look less narrow.

TIP: A cheap plastic tablecloth (the kind with cotton backing) makes a great non-slip drop sheet. Find them at garage sales or dollar stores.

Which colour do you choose? Take a handful of paint chips home with you and tape them to the wall. Look at them at all angles, at all times of the day. Colours look different depending on the light. Once you've narrowed it down, buy a sample can of each and paint a bit of one wall. See which one grows on you. There are several types of paint surface: flat, eggshell, satin, semi-gloss, and high-gloss. If you're painting a living room or bedroom, opt for flat or eggshell. Glossier is better for kitchen or bath because it's easier to wash. Semi-gloss is often used on trim. Choose latex paint because it's easier to work with and easier to repaint. Ask the guy at the store if you'll need a primer coat (probably) and which colour you should use. Generally, white primer goes with light-coloured paint, tinted primer with dark-coloured.

Of course you're dying to get that paint on your walls, but before you do, there are some preparatory steps you must not forget.

First of all, move all your furniture, either out of the room or into the centre of the room, and cover it with sheets. Remove the switch plates and keep them in a place where you won't forget them.

Take a close look at the walls. Are there holes that need repairing, old "party dents" that you want to hide? Get yourself back to the hardware store and pick up some Spackle (putty) and a putty knife. (While you're at it, might as well pick up some painter's tape, a rolling pan and roller, and a few paint brushes. Ask the hardware store guy which he'd recommend. You'll need a couple of sizes.) Place a tiny bit of Spackle on the spot to be repaired, smooth it with the knife, and leave it for about an hour to dry. After you've sanded it smooth, wash the walls with a damp sponge, then apply painter's tape (masking tape is too sticky) to the edge of the wall and around windowpanes. Tape newspaper to the floor and tape a plastic grocery bag to enclose the rolling pan (for easier cleanup).

TIP: If you're adventurous or crafty (or have lots of time on your hands), most paint departments carry how-to brochures for painting faux finishes. Craft shops and DIY magazines and www.diy.com offer more ideas.

Now, finally, you're good to go. Use a screwdriver or claw end of a hammer to open the can. Take a hammer and nail and put about four holes in the rim of the paint can so that paint won't well up in the rim when it's poured. Stir the paint with the wooden stick the paint guy stuck in your bag. Check that the windows are open for ventilation. Start with the small brush and work on the edges first, then fill in the walls with your roller. If you're painting the ceiling, cut a slit in the centre of a coffee can lid and stick the paint brush handle through so the paint doesn't splash down onto your face. Read the can to find out how long to wait between coats. Pour any leftover paint into clean jars and label for touch-ups, later. Don't store paint in the garage; latex paint should not be allowed to freeze.

There! Not exactly easy, but I'm sure you feel proud, and doesn't it look much better? Invite your friends over—especially those who helped you—for an admire-my-paint-job party. Go easy on the booze. You don't need any more dents in the wall.

Plants

Another great way to add personality and life to a place is with plants. Plants can fill empty corners, hide ugly wall stains, and make the place look lived in—as long as they are actually living. That part can be tricky. You can't just plunk down any nice-looking bit of greenery and assume it'll be happy with a little water now and then. There are two keys to happy plants:

Location: Before you buy a plant, read the tag to see what kind of light it needs. Diffused light usually comes from a north-facing window. A plant that requires full sun should be in a south-facing window. Don't think you can persuade it otherwise. Plants can be stubborn that way.

Water: Stick your finger in the soil. If it feels moist, don't water it. Too much water can kill a plant just as easily as too little. The pots you put your plants in don't need to be fancy—just big enough to let them grow, with drainage at the bottom so the roots

Cost Cutters

Sources for setting up house on the cheap:

- Raid the family attic, basement, and garage. Get permission first.
- Wander over to the nearest university residences in December and May. Check out the bulletin boards and sidewalks for cast-offs.
- Second-hand stores, junk shops, antique fairs, classifieds, garage sales, auctions, flea markets.
- Hand-me-downs: spread the word that you're moving out and looking for cast-offs.
- Make cast-off furniture (but not upholstery!) funky with a can of bright spray paint.
- Check out scratch-and-dent sales, and IKEA's "As Is" room.
- Post notes on bulletin boards in large apartment complexes saying you're looking for cheap or free furniture.
- For free design advice: many furniture stores offer interior design assistance with a purchase; home centres have experts who can advise you; paint, hardware, flooring, and lighting stores can also help.
- Buy some folding lawn chairs at end-of-summer sales—great for impromptu get-togethers.

don't get waterlogged. To keep the soil from pouring out the drainage hole when you water, put a plastic dish underneath, or place a coffee filter in the bottom before you put your plant in. You can find cheap pots at discount stores and spruce them up with nail polish. Every time you water your plants, turn them so each side has equal time in the sun. Wipe the leaves a couple of times a year to remove dust. Deadhead (cut off) flowers after they've bloomed.

Feeling at Home

You've got your own cozy spot to relax, you've stocked the fridge, the phone's hooked up, and your favourite pictures are on the wall. You are master of your own domain! You can do what you want—sing badly in the shower or watch TV in your underwear—and nobody's going to stop you.

But.

Kinda quiet, no? Something's missing. *People*, maybe? If you're used to university dorm life, or a bustling home with lots of siblings, life on your own can seem kinda … *blah*.

Have you met the neighbours? Explored the neighbourhood? Well, why not? Take a deep breath, get up off that couch, and get yourself out there! Grab a map and start wandering. Find the nearest park. Scout out some cool cafés, or public tennis courts, or the closest library. If you have a dog, take your little "ambassador" with you and let him help you find where the other dog-walkers are. Make a point of getting out there every day, if you can. If you're in a university residence, make sure you hit the common room regularly, even if what's on TV is not your cup of tea. Fake it.

Making connections in a new community can be scary, but you need to stretch yourself to grow. Here are some more ideas to help you settle in:

- Smile at people and say hi. It shows you're open to making friends.
- Offer your help. If someone's sick, bring over muffins or a casserole. If a neighbour's going on vacation, offer to pick up their newspapers.
- Having a party? Invite the neighbours. It may head off any noise complaints. But remember to be thoughtful about the music volume, no matter how hilarious Kurtis's karaoke routine is.
- Volunteer. Call the local municipal offices to find out about community service opportunities, or contact the library, church, or school.
- Did you have a hobby or favourite activity back at home? Ask around to find out if there's a group or club in your new neighbourhood.
- Try something new. If you've always wanted to learn woodworking or salsa dancing, go for it!

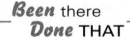

Been there
Done THAT

When I first moved out on my own, I confess, I got a little lazy. Didn't really feel like cooking for myself so I relied on canned sardines and microwave popcorn. Veggies went bad so I didn't bother buying them. I really didn't like scouring the tub, so I kinda just left it. Same with the inside of the fridge. Then my new boyfriend dropped by. I could have died! My advice? Don't let things slip, just because you're on your own.

—JENNIFER, 20

- Do a little networking with your friends back home to find someone who knows someone in your new town. Then meet that person for coffee and pick their brains about the area. Chances are you'll make a new friend.

Neighbour Troubles

Not that we want to put you off or anything, but neighbour troubles come with the territory. Remember, adulthood, like old age, is not for the faint of heart. I know you can cope with the noise, smells, creepy crawlies, and otherwise annoying things. It's all about living up close and personal. Here's a taste of what you might encounter, and a few solutions.

Noise

- You can start with earplugs, of course. You'll find them at drugstores. Look for the ones made from foam. They should fit snugly.
- Try running a fan or humidifier. They make white noise, which can cover up annoying sounds. You can even buy a noise machine at drugstores or department stores.
- Throw down some area rugs, hang heavy curtains—add more fabric, in general, to absorb noise.
- Ask your landlord if you can add some weather stripping around your doors and windows.

If all these Band-Aid solutions fail to block out whatever's bugging you, it's time deal with the problem head on. Yes, that means speaking with the noisemakers. No, it's not fun, but it's got to be done. And there's always the chance that they don't realize their sound is travelling.

But wait. Before you go banging on their door all in a huff, you'll want to lay the groundwork first. Whenever you see the neighbour, smile, act friendly, make small talk. If he thinks you're a nice person, you'll have better luck when you mention one day, casually, that you can sometimes hear (fill in the blank) and that it keeps you awake, or makes it hard to study, or makes it difficult to go to bed early so you can get up for your job in the morning—or whatever.

If you're lucky, this is all you'll need to do. Give it a week. If it's still a problem, raise the subject again, more specifically: ask him politely to turn it down or keep it down.

Try to keep it friendly and use humour, if possible. If it's music that's bothering you, explain that it might just be that the bass is set too high. If other tenants are bothered by the noise, encourage them to speak with the neighbour too.

Barking dog? If it's non-stop during the day, politely let the neighbour know. Assume the pet owner isn't aware of what happens when he's at work during the day. Brainstorm ideas. Offer to look up pet advice on the Internet. There are some nifty boredom-busting toys available for pets. But if your neighbour clearly doesn't care, call the local Humane Society to see what they suggest.

> ### *Been* there
> ### *Done* THAT
>
> The guy's bathroom in the next apartment was right next to my bedroom, specifically, against the wall that my bed was pushed against. You think hearing the neighbours having sex is bad? Try this one.
>
> —MAX, 24

If, after all that, you're still stuck listening to their Celine Dion CDs or the banging of the bed's headboard, get a tape recorder and record the noise. Let your noisy neighbours hear it—and the landlord, too. Maybe the landlord can arrange carpeting for the neighbour, or find a vacant unit for you in another part of the building. If all else fails, you'll have to decide whether you want to dig in your heels—get legal advice or call police—or just throw in the towel and find another place to hang your hat.

Smells

If you live in an older building that doesn't have good ventilation, smells can be a real problem. One night someone stir-fries, another night it's curry, someone in the building really likes his deep fryer, and that guy down the hall keeps burning the bacon. Sorry, honey, but there's not a whole lot you can do. You can ask the landlord if the ventilation system is working, but you can't ask him to forbid cooking.

If it's a smoker who's smelling up the place, and you have allergies, you can try getting a note from the doctor to bolster your case with the landlord, but other than that, open the windows. Welcome to city life!

Heat—or Not

Sometimes you don't have a whole lot of control over the temperature in your unit. If it's too warm in the winter months, let your landlord know. He'll probably be pleased to turn down the thermostat and save on his energy bills. If it's too cold, and the landlord can't help, here are some ways to warm your tootsies.

- Throw on a sweater and slippers.
- Wear socks to bed (warm toes warm the whole body).
- Learn to love flannel—especially for blankets and pyjamas.
- Simmer a pot of soup on the stove to warm you inside and out.
- Invest in better bedding—an electric blanket, heated mattress pad, or down comforter.

TIP: Rent is due on the day stipulated in your lease. In most places, it is considered late on the day after it is due. If you don't pay on time, the landlord can take you to court to seek compensation and have you evicted. Not paying will also hurt your credit rating. If you're having serious money troubles, you might appeal to a caring landlord, and he might have some sympathy, but consider it a red flag: you'd better read Chapter 13 (Finances) and get your act together now!

Eviction

Yes, the landlord can kick you out if your parties are too loud, your cheques keep bouncing, you're not doing what the lease said you should do, or you are doing what it said you shouldn't.

If you receive a notice of eviction you can try to fight it—with a written apology and promise to pay for repairs, if any. But generally, eviction notices are legal documents. If you get one, you need to take it very seriously.

If, on the other hand, you are the one who wants out, and your lease hasn't yet run out, you can try to appeal to the landlord. Sob stories sometimes work. If not, offer to sublet (and if you've got a great tenant in the wings, all the better), or simply suck it up and pay up.

Subletting

What happens if you absolutely must leave your rental before the lease is up? If you've got no choice but to vacate (maybe you found the perfect job in another town, for example), you are still on the hook for paying the rent, but you might be able to sublet. Subletting means renting your apartment to a temporary tenant. You are still responsible for the unit, but they now pay you money that you use to pay your rent.

Check your lease to see what the rules are for subletting, and let the landlord know what you're planning. You cannot charge more than you pay for rent, and the landlord cannot charge you a fee for subletting. Usually it is your responsibility to find someone suitable, and it is your responsibility if the sublessee causes damage to the unit or fails to pay the rent. Draw up a contract with the sublessee laying out the rules for rent payment and tenant responsibilities.

For more information on subletting, check the laws in your province on the Canada Mortgage and Housing Corporation website: www.cmhc.ca/en/co/reho/yogureho/fash/index.cfm

Leaving Your Apartment

When it's time to move on, it's important that you do it right. In all the excitement of moving out, don't forget:

- Give the landlord proper notice—in writing—that you do not intend to renew your lease. Check your lease to find out how far in advance of moving out you need to give notice. If you don't, you could end up paying extra.
- Provide your landlord with a forwarding address.
- Go through the apartment with a fine-toothed comb. It should be clean top to bottom and look just as good, if not better, than it did when you first moved in. If you're new to the cleaning thing, check the Housekeeping chapter for some tips. Otherwise, hire professional cleaners.
- Photograph—or better yet, videotape—the clean apartment, with the date. (Videotape the day's newspaper date for proof.)
- Inspect the apartment, with the landlord, and document the condition of the unit. Sign two copies of an inspection report—one for you, one for him—and put your copy with your other important papers.
- If the apartment passes the inspection, the landlord should send you your damage deposit.
- Return the keys to the landlord, blow your first home a kiss goodbye, and head off on your next adventure.

Moving Back Home

It can happen.

Say you need to regroup—you've had some time away and you're really not sure where you're headed. Or maybe you've decided it's pretty near impossible to find something decent to rent in the big city. Or you've taken a pay cut in order to get career experience. Or you just want to save your money rather than give it away to a landlord. For whatever reason, you've decided that you need to make a U-turn on the way to adulthood and move back home to the family nest. Is that so wrong?

Back in my day, any red-blooded North American who chose to move back home with his parents got branded with that big old loser "L" on the forehead. "He's *how* old, and still living at home??" Well, lucky you: today's young adults don't find that *wrong* at all. In fact, returning to the family nest has become so popular it's got a name, "boomeranging," and its own box-office hit movie, *Failure to Launch*. And if it's just a temporary measure and all sides are on board, boomeranging is sometimes the right thing to do. (Even if, as your parents, we shudder at the thought of returning to the days of clothes piled on the bedroom floor and the phone tied up for hours on end.)

But there are ways to make it work.

If you're undecided about whether to stick it out on your own or return to the nest, sit down and write out a list of pros and cons. Here's a start:

Pros

- As you forge your way in the competitive real world—be it the workplace or post-secondary education—you'll have a cozy warm place to return to, with people who love you, warts and all.
- It's a chance to bond with your family in a way you might not have had when you were in the throes of teenaged rebellion. You might be surprised to find that parents are people too!
- You can save money for a car, home, or graduate school.
- You might be able to drop out of the rat race for a while to figure things out, decide what you want to do next.

- No rent, or lower rent, means you can pay off your student loan sooner.
- Without the burden of rent, you can wait for the right job, take one that offers promise but a lower salary, or even an unpaid internship.

Cons

- Remember chores? Those this-is-your-family-and-everyone-pitches-in-here chores? Guess what? They're *baaaack!*
- Your social and romantic life won't be the same. Imagine having friends over for dinner or to watch a video—with Mom and Dad sharing the couch (because, of course, it's still your parents' couch).
- You will no longer have roomies handy for late-night chats, or friends living down the hall. (But maybe, just maybe, little sister or brother will do?)
- Kiss your privacy goodbye. You'll probably have to tell someone whether you'll be home for dinner, where you're going, and when you'll be home, because we parents, well, we *worry*.
- Your life will feel unsettled, your future on hold.

If You've Flown Back to the Nest

Whether this is your first choice, or last, you might as well make the best of it. Try viewing the family home as your launch pad—as opposed to lounge pad. Think *temporary*. You are aiming for independence, remember?

To stay focused and motivated, identify *why* you've returned home (to pay off debt, save for a house, find a job?). Write down that goal, your targeted timeline, and post it somewhere you'll see it every day.

Watch out for inertia (a.k.a. the TV and computer). They'll suck you right back into your old teenaged torpor. If you've got more time on your hands now that you're back home (thanks to Mom and Dad's washer/dryer and full fridge), then take advantage of it in a positive way. Set some goals: learn to cook, perfect your resumé, search for a better apartment, work on

Been there Done THAT

My boyfriend lives two hours away in another town. I fell asleep at his place, and, even though it was cozy and everything, I got up and went home at 3 a.m. just because I knew my dad would flip out if I stayed the night. He flipped anyway. He was waiting up for me. Now I have a curfew! I can't believe they think they can tell me when to come home at night! I'm not a kid any more.

—PATRICIA, 23

your relationships at home. (Maybe you can finally carry on a normal conversation with your siblings? Please?)

As for relationships with parents, well, that's a whole other matter. You are not the same child you used to be—but we, your parents, have changed too. And it's going to take some getting used to. It might be an idea to sit down and find out exactly how much things have changed. Specifically, find out how Mom and Dad's lives are different now that you've left home. And make a deal: you won't act like a child who needs caring for; your parents won't act as though you need surveillance or advice. Talk about your short- and long-term goals and how long you expect to be living there. Talk talk talk. It's the best way to find out what everyone's expectations are.

Surviving the Homefront

- The best place to start: a "bug" list. Make a list of what bugged you most when you lived at home. Mom and Dad should do the same. Now that you've got your lists, you've got some fodder for discussion. Show how mature you are. Stay calm and focused as you come up with ways to compromise.
- Sort out your responsibilities. To establish a new adult-to-adult relationship, make sure you're carrying your fair share. Offer to cook dinner. Run errands. Paint the porch. If you don't know how to do something, ask for a *lesson*, not help. It's an adult thing.
- Pay rent? Sure, great idea. Pay your rent on time and treat your parents with the same kind of respect you would a landlord. We'll be polite if you'll be polite.
- If you're not paying rent, then do something "mature" with your money, like pay off your student loan or save for your own place. If you can't afford to pay rent, maybe there's something else you can do around the house instead.
- Remember those good old days in high school when you slept late and lounged on the couch? Don't even *think* about it. Get up, all by yourself. If you don't have anywhere special to go just now, at least hit the gym or scan the classifieds. Meet people for lunch, distribute your resumé, get a part-time job—do *something*, until you figure out your next career move.
- So you want your privacy. Okay, that's fair. If you promise to keep your room bug-free and mould-free, then we promise to stay out. And if you don't want anyone touching your laundry, say so.
- Here's the thing: you are an adult sharing another adult's home. You respect us; we'll respect you. If you can't show up for dinner, at least let us know ahead of time,

okay? That way we know not to set a place for you. (And fair's fair—we'll do the same for you.) If you mention that you'll be home around 1 a.m. and find out you're going to be late, call. Because, you know, *we worry*. And if we're trying to sleep, please, keep it down. And one more thing: clean up after yourself. There. That's all the nagging we'll do—because it's all we'll *have* to do, right?

- What about the family car? Who gets it when and who pays for gas? That needs to be decided *before* it turns into trouble. Another source of trouble: the family bathroom. What if everyone's trying to get out to work at the same time? Who showers when?

- Some more things that will have to be discussed: long-distance bills, dating, friends, and loud music. Oh, and overnights. You might have to pass on the romantic sleepovers at home for a while. Come on, you can do it. This is *temporary*, remember?

Resources

Roommate-search services

www.roommateaccess.com
www.roommates.com
www.roommateclick.com
www.craigslist.org

Information on apartment renting

http://www.cmhc.ca/en/co/
You'll find a ton of useful info on Canada Mortgage and Housing Corporation's website.

Rental agreements

These are governed by landlord and tenant law specific to the province or territory where a tenant is renting an accommodation. While many similarities exist from jurisdiction to jurisdiction, each province and territory has its own legislation. Visit http://www.cmhc.ca/en/co/reho/yogureho/fash/index.cfm for fact sheets related to each province's landlord-tenant legislation.

Resources for apartment-hunters

www.craigslist.com
www.homes4students.ca
www.rent.com
www.rentnet.com
www.apartments.com
www.roommates.ca
www.rent.net
www.homestore.com
www.apartmentsearch.com

For home decorating and DIY help

www.freecycle.org
www.doityourself.com
www.bejanecom
www.diy.com

Change of address

Tell the post office about your change of address online at:
http://www.canadapost.ca/tools/pg/manual/PGcoa-e.asp

Moving back home?

www.movebackin.com
www.boomerangnation.com

2

Home Maintenance

One only needs two tools in life: WD-40 to make things go,
and duct tape to make things stop.

—G.M. WEILACHER

Home maintenance? How hard can it be? After all, you've lived in a home for years!

Okay, here's a pop quiz for you. If you know the answers, then you're good to go—see you in the next chapter. If not, read on.

1. Water is gushing out of a pipe in the garage. What do you do?
2. The lights have gone out. Where is the fuse box or circuit-breaker box? (What is a fuse box or circuit-breaker box?) What do you do when you find it?
3. It's time to change the filter in the furnace. What? Where? Why? How?
4. Where is the hot-water heater? Why should I care?
5. How do you get a bird out of the attic without a shotgun?

So, you're not Bob Vila after all. But if you're going to rule the roost in your house, you are going to need to be prepared.

The Tool Kit

Let's start with your basic tool kit. Yes, you get to go shopping! But don't get carried away here. This expedition could cost big bucks. Go easy the first time out.

First Shopping Trip

- *A toolbox.* Not too heavy, because once you add your tools, it will weigh a ton. And since you will need to carry it from location to location, do not get one that's too big.

- *Measuring tape.* A battery-powered tape that extends and retracts at the push of a button is great if you're trying to measure a room by yourself.
- *Power drill.* Cordless is handiest for short jobs. Buy a lightweight model with a high and low speed, forward and reverse (to undo your mistakes), and a keyless chuck (which means you can change drill bits without a key). Drill bits should be made of steel or titanium.
- *Hammer.* 12-ounce (.34-kilogram) hammers are good for hanging pictures, but if you are building a deck, opt for a 14- to 20-ounce (.40- to .56-kilogram) one. A steel shaft with a rubber handle is best. Graphite hammers are lighter but more expensive.
- *Set of screwdrivers.* One set gets you a Phillips, Robertson, and a flat-head screwdriver. (A Phillips screw has a cross-shaped slot on the head. A Robertson screw, which is arguably the better screw and a Canadian invention, by the way, has a square slot in the head. Now you know.) Plastic handles are best for sweaty fingers.
- *Adjustable wrench or vice-grips.* The jaws should expand to at least 3.8 centimetres (1.5 inches).
- *Some nails, screws, nuts, picture-hanger hooks, and bolts in varying sizes.* Robertson-head screws (they've got square holes) don't strip as easily.
- *Needle-nose pliers.*
- *Duct tape.* Just get it. It's a guy thing.
- *A utility knife.* Look for a sturdy metal handle with a safety lock that prevents the blade from coming out as you slice.
- *Plunger.* It doesn't belong in the tool kit, but you'll need one, so put it on your shopping list.

Second Shopping Trip

- A level.
- Small hacksaw and wood saw.
- Nail-punch set.
- Allan key set.
- Staple gun with staples.
- Wood glue, Crazy Glue, and small hot-glue gun.
- 16-ounce (.45-kilogram) claw hammer.
- Small handsaw with a 30-centimetre (12-inch) blade.
- Masking tape and carpenter's glue.
- Duct tape. Yes, get more.
- Long level. For hanging pictures and shelves or drawing lines for painting.

- Transparent plastic containers. For nails and screws.
- Spackling compound. To plug up the picture holes left by the last guy.
- Hangers and hooks. Enough for pictures, clothes, towels, and brooms.
- Stud finder. Locates wall studs, and some versions can locate live wires, too. Good to know!
- Scissors. A good pair.
- Safety goggles. Use them.

Buying a ladder

House-dwellers should have access to an extension ladder for outdoor work. If you borrow one from a neighbour, return it promptly and with effusive thanks. Chances are you'll need to borrow it more than once. If you decide to buy one yourself, be prepared. Ladders are not cheap—typically between $200 and $400.

If you are doing mainly indoor work, a basic 2-metre (6^1/$_2$-foot) aluminum stepladder is best. Make sure it's sturdy, with flat-topped, slip-resistant rungs and pivoting feet. (Do you want to spend the afternoon cleaning walls or lying in a crowded emergency room?)

Buying a snow shovel

A decent winter shovel will likely run you around twenty bucks. Buy two, in case a friend pops by to lend a hand. (Fat chance.) Buy an extra, smaller shovel to keep in the trunk of your car.

Find and Note

Renting a house? Think you might one day lend the place to a friend for the weekend? Here's what you must locate. Write it down in a little notebook. Not only will you discover the secrets of your new home, but when you win an all-inclusive trip to Cuba you can toss the book off to the dog-sitter, grab your bathing suit, and go.

Locate

- Main shut-off valves for water and fuel.
- Main electrical switch.
- Circuit-breaker box.
- Emergency switch for the furnace or burner.
- Hot-water heater thermostat.

More than You Really Wanted to Know

Finding the Circuit-Breaker Box or the Fuse Box. This nifty box is where all the household electricity is disseminated and regulated. Locate it while you've got light, because odds are the next time you need to find it, you will be in the dark. **Where is it?** Stand outside and look up. If your electrical service is above ground, (i.e., you see hydro wires), follow the wires from the pole on the street to the metal or plastic box attached to the outside wall—they may lead to the garage. **Not there?** Check out the basement, near the washer/dryer or furnace. **No luck?** If you are in a house that looks like your neighbours', ask where theirs is. Bets are yours is in the same place.

Now take a look inside the box. Newer homes have circuit breakers—small slide-switches labeled "on" and "off". Older houses have fuses instead of breakers. Fuses look like bottle caps and usually have an amp rating written on the side. Beside each fuse or breaker there should be notes that say "living room," or "office." Make sure the corresponding references are correct or you may turn off your computer instead of the power to your bedroom.

So you found it: Who cares? You will, if you plug something in and suddenly find yourself in the dark. Circuit breakers and fuses guard against fires and electrocution by tripping (breakers) or blowing (fuses) to cut off the power supply if wires are in danger of overheating. The most common reason why the breaker flips or a fuse blows is because you are running too many appliances at once. If that happens:

- Unplug the toaster, space heater, coffee maker—whatever made the lights go out.
- Find your way to the circuit breaker. If you've got the old-fashioned fuses, look inside the glass top and you'll see a little metal strip. The fuse is blown when that strip is broken in two. Replace it with a new fuse that has exactly the same amp rating (buy a handful of these now and keep them near the box). If you've got circuit breakers, find the switch that's flipped to "off" and flip it back on.
- Do not fool around here. Death by electrocution has little to recommend it. Know when to call in an electrician.

Air-Conditioner Maintenance

Lucky enough to have central air conditioning in your rental accommodation? Unlucky enough to have it break down during the annual summer heat wave? Here's

TIPS:

Want to Go Green?

- Use energy-saving compact fluorescent bulbs in as many outlets as possible.
- Lower your thermostat two degrees—you won't feel the difference between 22 and 21 degrees C (72 and 70 degrees F), but you will save a bundle.
- If you can, program the thermostat to lower the heat between 11 p.m. and 7 a.m., or lower the temperature before you go to bed to save as much as $100 a year.
- Your water heater should not be set any higher than 49 degrees C (120 degrees F).
- Unplug your electronics when not in use.

a thought: don't try to fix it yourself! This is one of those times when you really ought to call the landlord or building superintendent and have him take care of the problem.

Window unit

Unplug the unit before you do anything to it. Vacuum the front grilles, air registers, and air vents. When it's going full blast during the summer, replace or clean the filter once a month. Really. Use a brush to get rid of the lint on the washable filter, then dunk it in soapy water. Let it dry before reinstalling. Every unit is different, so if you are buying a new one, ask the salesperson to show you how to get the filter out. If you have inherited a unit and the handbook is nowhere to be found, Google the name of the unit; the manual might be online.

Store the unit in the basement during the winter. Unless the manual tells you otherwise, it's not really designed for sub-zero weather.

Beating the heat without AC

No air conditioner?!? How will you manage?

First, remember that residential air conditioning wasn't invented until 1928. People have been known to survive without it.

Duh |
moment !

How to Change a Light Bulb

This is no light-bulb joke. There is electricity running through the veins of your house, and that stuff can do you serious damage. If the light burns out, unplug it. (How easy is that?) If it's the middle of the night, leave it until morning so that you can clearly see what you are doing. Once you've unplugged it, gently unscrew and remove the bulb. Give it a gentle shake. If it rattles, the bulb is burned out.

If the light bulb breaks off in the socket, don't start poking around with a knife. (Don't ever do that. Stay away from toasters with that knife, too.) If it is not a free-standing lamp (i.e., can't be unplugged), *turn off the power* at the circuit-breaker box. Then cut an apple or potato in half and jam it, hard, up against the socket. Twist gently and ease the broken bulb out of the socket. (Did I mention turning the power off? Whatever you do, don't skip this step.)

Second, take steps to keep the heat outside. Block the sunlight by closing the drapes and blinds during the day. Incandescent lights can produce as much heat as sunlight, so turn them off, too. And don't use the oven if you can avoid it on a hot day. Eat salad or barbecue.

Ceiling fans are the most efficient and quickest way to cool a room without air conditioning. Cheap fans placed so that they cross-ventilate a room can cool the place off quickly. If it's too hot to sleep, fill a bowl with ice and place it in front of a fan. It will keep you cool until you drop off to Dreamland.

How to Unplug a Toilet

Ooooh, this is going to be such fun! First, lower the back of your pants so a fraction of your butt peeks out. Now you're ready. Begin.

1. Have a look in there. Is the toilet bowl half-filled with water? If not, either bail till it is, or add more water with a bucket.

2. Grab your plunger—which should always be kept handy, by the way. Stick the rubber funnel-cup thing at the end into the toilet's outflow passage. Plunge up and down ten times, as quickly and vigorously as you can. Really put your back into it!

3. Flush.

4. Repeat, several times, if need be.

5. Still plugged? Beg, steal, or borrow a toilet angler (also called a "toilet snake").
6. Insert the toilet angler's curvy end into the outflow passage. Crank the handle until the tip snags whatever is blocking the toilet. Pull back gently.
7. Know when to call a plumber (which is *before* your best friend's little brother, who once took a plumbing course in high school, gets in on the act).

And a brief word about plungers. Don't waste your money on the cute, decorative plungers that come with piggy or doggy heads. It's a toilet plunger, for heaven's sake, not a knick-knack! Buy the heavy-duty kind with a funnel-cup that looks like it means business.

Is the toilet wet where it shouldn't be?

Water on the outside of your tank doesn't necessarily mean something's wrong. A tank sweats when cold water in the tank causes the warm air outside of the tank to condense on the surface. There's not much you can do about that in the summer except rub it down with a cloth. If it's causing big problems, like leaving a pool of water on the floor, then talk to a plumber or an experienced salesperson in a hardware store. You might need a liner for the tank. To make sure the tank is not leaking, first wipe it clean, then add food colouring to the water in the tank. Wait an hour or more. Blot the underside of the tank (the bolt area) with white toilet paper. If the tissue is coloured then you have a leak. Time to call the plumber.

TIP: If you want to reduce the amount of water you use when flushing, gently place a brick, or a 2-litre (64-ounce) plastic pop bottle filled with water, in the bottom of the toilet tank. (Place it in there gently; if you drop the brick you might crack the tank.)

When the sink or bathtub is clogged

Commercial drain-unclogging products are caustic. Try 50 ml ($1/4$ cup) baking soda followed by 125 ml ($1/2$ cup) vinegar. After the fizzing stops, pour boiling water down the drain several times. Note that most drain-unclogging products are not suitable for unplugging a toilet. The chemical reactions they create to unclog a drain can actually crack and damage a porcelain or ceramic toilet bowl. If in doubt, ask the guy in the hardware store.

Appliances: Troubleshooting

Refrigerator

Problem: The fridge has stopped working.
Solution: Is the fridge plugged in? Is the thermostat (inside the fridge at the back) set at the right temperature? Vacuum under and at the back of the fridge and make sure that dust has not clogged up the vents. If it still won't switch on, call in the pros. Meanwhile, keep the fridge door closed. Most food will keep for twenty-four hours. If in doubt, throw it out.

TIP: Unplug any appliance before tinkering with it. Yeah, you know that already. I'm just saying ...

Problem: The ice-maker isn't working.
Solution: Check to see if the trip lever is stuck in the off position.

Problem: The fridge door won't shut.
Solution: Quit slamming it harder! Those plastic drawers and shelves aren't made for that. Open the door. Look at everything in the door's path, including the hinges. Clear the way. Close gently. If the fridge door will not stay closed, it's likely a levelling problem and has more to do with the floor than the fridge. Get a friend to help you prop the front up with a sliver of wood.

Stove

Problem: The electric stove burners are not working.
Solution: While the stove is off and the burners are cool, check to see if the coils are plugged firmly into the base.

Dryer

Problem: It's taking forever for the clothes to dry.
Solution: Remember to clean the lint-trap every time you use the dryer. Not only will a dirty lint-trap slow down drying time, but it creates a fire hazard. Before you call in the repair guys, read the owner's manual. Same goes for your washing machine. And your dishwasher. Heck—all your appliances. Those guys are expensive!

Calling in the Pros

Are you clear about what your responsibility as a tenant is when an appliance breaks down? If not, go back and check your lease. Your landlord will not be happy if he considers himself a handyman, and you went ahead and called in a professional rather than giving him a chance to fix something himself. On the other hand, when your toilet breaks down on Friday night and your landlord is on a camping trip and can't be reached till Tuesday, something has to be done! Just be as sure as you can, first, that you are not overstepping your role as tenant.

Reliable repairmen are worth their weight in gold. The best way to find one is through references. Ask a friend or neighbour.

Most repair companies charge double after regular business hours. Independent Mr., Ms., or Mrs. Fix-Its, however, might charge less on the weekends. You might be tempted to pay cash in return for a cheaper rate. Remember, though, that if you pay cash you have no guarantees and no records. If the toilet explodes (yuck) you might even have challenges with the insurance company.

Describe the condition of the appliance over the phone, and don't worry too much about technical terms. Ask questions. If the repair person uses language you don't understand, simply ask that he explain in layman's terms. Don't try to fake it. No one expects you to be an appliance expert.

Ask about costs. If he says that he can't give you a price until he sees the job, ask if there will be a cost for the inspection visit, and tell him that you expect a written estimate in advance of any work done.

When your appliance can't be saved

If your best efforts fail and it's time to call it quits, you'll have to get rid of the appliance to make way (hopefully) for a new one. If the appliance is one that you own, you'll have to deal with it yourself. If the landlord owns the appliance, don't dispose of it without checking with him first to see what he would like done.

In any case, don't just drag the thing to the end of the driveway. Appliances with doors (fridge, washer, dryer, etc.) can be deadly. Children have been known to crawl inside old appliances and suffocate. You are legally required to remove the door before taking it to the curb, or secure the door with rope and duct tape. A hefty fine will come your way if you do not comply.

Look up *garbage collection* in your phone book or go to your municipality's website to find out how to have the old appliance picked up.

Fireplaces

They look nice, but they require work. First, the fireplace has to be cleaned at least every two years; once a year is best. If you have just moved into a place and the previous tenant assures you that the fireplace was just cleaned, you might want to have it checked anyway. A good chimney sweep (yes, there really are chimney sweeps) will check the chimney from the top down and look for chunks of clay, chalky deposits, moisture stains, cracks, or loose bricks. If your chimney is plugged, you could be breathing the exhaust from your furnace, fireplace, or woodstove. If the chimney is deteriorating, you or your landlord should call a qualified chimney contractor. A neglected chimney can burn your house down, and a malfunctioning fireplace or woodstove can release carbon monoxide gas—which will kill you.

Keep the fireplace clean. If it is filled with ashes it will not vent properly.

And this is critically important: *Make sure you've got several smoke detectors and a carbon monoxide detector on every floor.*

Carbon Monoxide Poisoning

Carbon monoxide is an odourless gas. It's the product of fuel that has not burned properly. In most cases we are talking about a broken furnace. If your home's ventilation is inadequate and carbon monoxide gas is inhaled, it will deplete the amount of oxygen in your red blood cells. In other words, it can be deadly.

Symptoms

The symptoms of carbon monoxide poisoning are like those of the common flu. Light or mild exposure will give you a slight headache and affect your concentration. If you're exposed to a higher concentration, you'll experience a severe headache, weakness, dizziness, mental confusion, drowsiness, nausea, vomiting, vision and hearing impairment, and loss of muscle control. With extreme exposure comes loss of consciousness, brain damage, and eventually death.

If anyone in your home experiences these symptoms, and these signs lessen or disappear when they leave home, suspect carbon monoxide.

Signs of carbon monoxide leaking

Stuffy or stinky air (like the smell of something overheating or burning). There might be water condensation on the windows. (This could also mean your humidifier is set too high.) Occasionally there are smells of unusual gases. Carbon monoxide is usually odourless, but it is sometimes accompanied by exhaust gases.

If you notice these signs, turn off the equipment and contact a licensed heating contractor. If you suspect carbon monoxide poisoning in your home, get out and get help. If the carbon monoxide detector alarm has gone off and there are no medical symptoms, open all doors and windows, then call a heating contractor for an inspection.

How to Light a Fire 101

TIP: Running a ceiling fan on low will help circulate air—and heat—while the fire's burning.

Open the damper before you light the fire, and keep it open until you're certain the fire has gone out. There are different designs for the damper—practise with yours to avoid getting it wrong and filling your home with smoke, setting off the smoke alarms, and summoning the fire department. Crack a window in the room but close upstairs windows to avoid a back draft that could bring smoke back in.

The store-bought three-hour logs are safe and convenient, but if it's romance you're looking for, there's nothing like the old-fashioned crackling log fire. Start with tinder (something like scrunched-up newspaper, not coloured newsprint). Next add pieces of kindling (finger-sized sticks and branches) in a criss-cross pattern. Light the paper. When the kindling catches, add a couple of small split logs on the flames. Burn hardwoods like oak, hickory, and ash that have been split and dried at least six months earlier. Softwoods like fir, pine, and cedar create more smoke and creosote. Do not burn garbage or painted or pressure-treated woods; they can release toxins. Leave space between the logs to allow air to circulate. A fire is too big when you cannot see the top of the flames (i.e., the flames reach up into the chimney).

Fire Extinguisher

Buy one. Just do it. This is not negotiable. Sure it's butt-ugly mounted up on the kitchen wall—too bad.

There are two common types. The one you want has the letters "ABC" on the label. This one extinguishes wood, paper, and cloth, plus flammable liquids and electrical fires. ("BC" types are for flammable liquids and electrical fires only.)

Hang your fire extinguisher near an exit and in plain sight—not in a closet. In a panic, you might not remember where you put it.

TIP: Record your address above the telephone. Not only might you want to tell the firefighters where the fire actually is (and in a panic, your brain can turn to mud), but friends and family will need it when ordering pizzas or taxis.

Point the extinguisher hose at the base of the fire and work up slowly. Always keep your back to the exit. Know when to quit and just get out!

Planning for emergencies: Figure out how you'd get out fast in case of an emergency. If you have roomies, designate a meeting place—across the street, perhaps—should you need to evacuate the building. Firefighters have been known to search for someone in a burning house only to discover that that same person is watching the fire from afar.

Household Chores

Seasonal Jobs

If you're renting a house, or if a yard is part of your rental property, you might or might not be expected to handle some of the outdoor work that comes with the changing seasons. Make sure that you and your landlord are on the same page about this. Hopefully responsibilities are specified in your lease.

And if you do have to tackle some of these chores, here's what you should remember.

Winter

- Drain and shut off all exterior water taps. If they freeze, they could burst and spew water into the basement.
- Turn birdbath bowls upside down so they won't freeze and crack. (In fact, if you own them yourself you should just get rid of them, or use them as a base for potted plants. They can create breeding places for mosquitoes. If you must have them, change the water frequently.)
- Check the weatherstripping on doors and windows. If your windows are old and not airtight (you can find out by holding a candle next to them), then cover them with plastic sheeting. You'll save a small fortune on the heating bills. Sheeting is sold on a roll at large hardware stores.

Spring

- Pull out the refrigerator and vacuum the coils behind.
- Clean flower beds and fertilize lawns.
- Clean outdoor gutters.
- Reattach outdoor hoses.

Summer

- Check air conditioners and install and/or clean as needed.
- Deal with your dirty windows:
  —Dust off the window and windowsill with a clean paintbrush.
  —Wash the windows on a cloudy day. Direct sunlight causes streaks because the cleaning solution dries before you can wipe it off.
  —25 to 45 millilitres (two to three tablespoons) of vinegar to 4 litres (1 gallon) of water will work just as effectively on windows as the expensive commercial cleaners.
  —Wipe horizontally on the inside and vertically on the outside (or vice versa). That way you'll know which side the streaks are on.
  —Pour white vinegar in crevices and between bricks in the walkway to kill weeds.

Fall

- Check the undersides of outdoor furniture for insect larvae before storing it. If you have a pressurized glass tabletop, don't set it in the basement and load it up with stuff. When the temperature changes it might shatter.
- Clean the leaves out of the eavestroughs or there will be a snow buildup under the shingles or plywood. When the snow melts because of the indoor heat, it thaws and leaks through, causing major damage.
- Trim trees and bushes.

TIP: Buy a professional squeegee from a janitorial supply store—it's worth the extra cost. And wipe the squeegee blade dry with a cleaning cloth after each stroke.

TIP: Once the cold weather sets in, everyone will be calling to have their furnace checked. Do it before the rush. Ask for a discount if you call in the summer.

- Clean outdoor drains and/or gutters.
- Get the chimney cleaned. Have the furnace serviced.
- Plant bulbs.
- Clean leaves and debris from the central air conditioning unit.
- Make sure the garden hoses are empty of water.

Burglary Prevention Tips

- If you do buy that snappy new computer or plasma-screen television, don't advertise the fact by leaving the box at the base of the driveway. All a wannabe thief has to do is cruise the neighbourhood on recycling day to see who bought what. Rip up boxes and turn them inside out.
- Walk around the house every so often. Look at it from a burglar's viewpoint—the basement windows, the condition of the doors, and access to the roof.
- 40 percent of home invasions occur because a door or window was left unlocked. Lock the door behind you when you go in, or out. Install a peephole.
- Replace all locks immediately after moving into a new home.
- Record the serial numbers on all your cool stuff and put the list in a safe place.
- A simple wooden pole can secure sliding glass doors. Lay it along the base track.
- If you feel vulnerable, or live in a suspect neighbourhood, consider getting an alarm system. Until then, paste some fake security stickers on the windows.
- Check out the local Neighbourhood Watch. Go to a meeting. Really. It's a great way to meet your neighbours. They are your best defence against theft. They are the ones who will report a big white van outside your house—the one your new plasma TV is being loaded into. And if you are broken into, tell your neighbours—they might be next.

Been there
Done THAT

I told my neighbours that I was going away on vacation. Their fifteen-year-old son advertised it, and the house was gutted. Now I only tell my brother. He just drinks my wine.

—ANDY, 25

- When you go away on vacation, be sure to put several lights and the television on different timers to give the appearance that someone is home.
- The old advice was to stop mail and newspaper delivery when you go on vacation. Do it if there is no reliable person around who can pick up your mail. If there is, keep it going. No need to tell all the delivery people that your house will be empty.
- When you leave for vacation, offer your driveway to a neighbour. A car in the driveway is a good deterrent.
- Burglars do not like small yappy dogs. (They know that big goofy Labs will roll over for a hunk of meat.) And contrary to popular belief, burglars do not enjoy a challenge. If they hear a dog (or see evidence of one), they'll move on to someone else's place. A note here: a dog is a person too. (You know what I mean!) Don't buy a dog just to keep your house safe. Buy a dog because you want a dog and can care for it. (And no, I don't want it when you decide to tour Australia for a year.)

What to Do If You Are Broken Into

1. File a police report. Hand over that list of serial numbers you have stashed in a safe place.
2. Call the insurance company. Give them the serial numbers of all your cool stuff. (Now you get to hear about all the loopholes in your home owners' insurance policy—like you are only insured on Tuesdays if it's raining.)
3. Thieves, unlike lightning, are pretty likely to strike the same place twice. Now that they have taken all your old stuff, they know that you are going to buy new stuff! Be careful discarding boxes. Change the locks. Do what you can to take your house or apartment off the thieves' must-nab list. Home insurance companies have a real problem with people who make multiple claims.

Pests—Up Close and Personal

We saved the best for last: how to deal with mice, rats, bats, birds, bees, and other nasty things that can invade your home. It's guaranteed you and your new home will encounter a few. Again, be clear with your landlord whose responsibility it is to deal with this kind of problem. There might be some pretty hefty costs racked up before you're done.

TIP: If you are renting a house or apartment, talk over possible treatments with the landlord. Obviously you'll want the least toxic product available. He or she is not living with the fumes. You are!

Listed below are mostly alternative ways to deal with critters without using expensive and possibly unhealthy commercial products. If you do choose to use chemicals, read the instructions on the products carefully and wear disposable vinyl or rubber gloves. If you have leftover chemicals, check the instructions for proper disposal methods.

The Bugs

Cockroaches

Cockroaches are nocturnal and prefer dark, warm places with access to water. Under the sink in the kitchen is a hot spot. You need to get rid of them. They contaminate food, plates, and utensils, destroy fabric and paper products, leave gross stains, and they stink. Cockroaches that come into contact with human poop in sewers or animal or bird droppings might transmit bacteria that cause food poisoning. There is more, but I think you get the point.

If you are having the place fumigated, make sure that all your dishes and food are well covered. Clean away any residue left from the spray before you put the dishes back in the cupboard.

If cockroaches have access to food, sprays alone will not get rid of them, not over the long haul, anyway. You'll need an integrated strategy.

Here's where the work begins. It will take a full day but it will be worth it. Buy a caulking gun and literally plug up every crack in the kitchen, especially under the sink. This is not 100 percent foolproof, particularly if you have rented a place above a restaurant, but it's a good start.

Traps can be effective. They can be bought or made. To make a trap, take an old soup can and coat the inside with petroleum jelly to prevent the roaches from escaping. Use a slice of white bread as bait. Place the trap along the edge of the wall or behind the stove and the refrigerator. You will know if you still have a problem within the first 24 hours of placing a trap.

Once the roaches are gone, take steps to make sure they stay away. Most important is to keep the place clean! Remember that cockroaches need food and water. Even crumbs or mildew can be a food source.

- Store food in glass jars or sealed plastic containers.
- Keep garbage in containers with lids.
- Get rid of piled-up newspapers and magazines that can become "roach motels."
- Check under the sink for plumbing leaks. Plug them up.
- Vacuum cracks to remove food and debris. Get rid of the vacuum bag.
- Clean up food surfaces where food or drinks have been spilled.

Earwigs

Earwigs are completely creepy-looking. They are long, flat, and have pincers or forceps. Just nasty. But despite what your babysitter told you, they do not crawl into your ear as you sleep and bore into your brain.

TIP: Blech! Bugs in the bag of flour or cereal! Freeze the bag, then throw it out.

Earwigs rarely fly and do not crawl long distances. They *do* crawl into laundry baskets, luggage, newspapers, wooden furniture, fruit and vegetable bags, and so on. They like the damp, garbage, flower gardens, compost piles, and wood piles. They also like the light.

You can trap them outdoors in cardboard boxes baited with bread. Punch pencil-sized holes near the bottom of the box. Smear a little petroleum jelly on the inside walls of the trap. They go in … but they do not come out. Indoors, vacuum them up and get rid of the bag.

There are lots of insecticides labelled for earwig control. Use them according to directions.

Silverfish

Silverfish are small insects without wings. Nocturnal and zippy little things, they hang out in bathtubs or drains. Outside, they live under rocks, bark, and leaves, and eat vegetable matter. Indoors, they will feed on almost anything, including book glue, wallpaper paste, gum, cotton, linen, rayon, silk, sugar, mould, and breakfast cereals.

Make a trap by sticking masking tape around the *outside* of a small glass bottle—this helps them climb up. Lay a piece of bread *inside* for bait. The silverfish will climb in, but will be unable to get out because they cannot climb on smooth surfaces. Once captured, drop the silverfish in a bucket of soapy water.

Infested items such as clothing and books can also be placed in a green garbage bag, which is then sealed and placed in the freezer. Freezing will kill all life stages.

Termites

Termites look like flying ants. They nest in the ground and gain access to the house through basements or lower levels when there is moisture and wood-to-soil contact, or through cracks and crevices in the foundation. Prevention is key. If you're in an area known for termite troubles, repair leaks, improve drainage, and remove any old tree stumps or dead trees that might harbour the pests. Place wooden structures (like sheds) on patio stones and think twice about using railway ties, wooden posts, or other wooden materials in the garden. Also, don't stack firewood or lumber against the foundation. The wood can provide a hidden path into the house. Vines, ivy, and other plants that touch or cling to the house should also be avoided.

When in doubt, call in the pros. Most companies will provide a free inspection.

Bedbugs

Bedbugs are insects. If you want to get technical, *Cimex lectularius* is the species most commonly found in homes. They are oval-shaped with no wings, paper-flat, and about 6 millimetres ($^1/_4$ inch) long. After feeding they become bloated and turn dark red. Eggs are whitish and the size of a pinhead. Clusters of ten to fifty eggs can be found in the cracks and crevices of your mattress.

Mmmm. Lovely. There's more. Bedbugs have a one-year life span, and a female can lay 200 to 400 eggs. They can survive up to six months without feeding.

The good news is that there are no known cases of disease associated with bedbug bites. Most people are not aware that they have been bitten. People who are more sensitive to the bite can have a localized allergic reaction, but that's about it.

The bad news is that they feed on human blood, bite at night, and munch all over a human body. They arrive via furniture and clothing and can be found in folds of mattresses and box springs, cracks in the bed frame and headboard, under chairs, in couches, beds, dust covers, rugs—well, just about anywhere. And they can travel from apartment to apartment along pipes, electrical wiring, and other openings. Now aren't you going to sleep well tonight!

If you have them, don't panic, just deal with it. You might want to call the city health department for advice. Vacuum all crevices on your mattress, bed frame, baseboards, and any objects close to the bed. (Use a nozzle attachment.) Empty the vacuum bag immediately and discard it. Set out glue boards or sticky tape to catch the bedbugs. Wash all the sheets in hot water and pop them into a hot dryer for at least thirty minutes. You might also want to cover your mattress with a plastic cover and buy a new pillow.

Examine any items that you are bringing into your home. Furniture put out by someone else for garbage pickup could be infested with bedbugs. Use caution.

Fruit flies

They're the annoying little things that appear out of nowhere and keep getting in your face whenever you're in the kitchen.

Keep your compost and recycling bins outside. If you can't, make sure that you rinse the cans before you toss them in the bin. Get rid of moisture around the sink. Forget the pretty fruit bowl. Keep your produce in the fridge. That will help prevent the problem.

Now, to kill the little suckers that are already here—your options:

- Pour a little wine in a saucer. The flies will be drawn to it, get drunk, and die happy.
- Take a large, plastic soft drink bottle and cut it across about a third of the way down from the top. Put very ripe fruit (tomato, orange, banana peel) in the bottom of the bottle with a bit of water. Take the top third of the bottle, without the lid, and put it into the bottle upside down, making a funnel. The flies can fly in but not out, and that's that.
- Mix 50 millilitres (1/4 cup) of white vinegar with a squirt of liquid dishwashing soap. Add water until it bubbles. Leave it out. The fruit flies are attracted to it and get trapped in the bubbles.
- Leave a bit of beer in the bottom of the bottle. Flies go in and don't come out.

If none of those fun activities work, check your houseplants. It's possible that these aren't fruit flies, but rather gnats that are hatching in your plant soil. (Run double-sided sticky tape around the outside of the pot to catch them.) Still got problems? Stop watering your plants for a bit and let the soil dry up.

TIP: Get rid of ants by filling an old spray bottle with equal parts white vinegar and water. Spray around door jambs and windowsills.

Fleas

Fleas get into the house, and rugs, via the dog. Call the vet for treatment (although Granny swears by mashing a garlic bud into the dog's food once a week). You might also want to buy a flea spray for the carpet and furniture.

Vacuum everything, twice, and toss the vacuum bag immediately. Spray the house. Then do it all over again tomorrow.

Precious teddy bears and blankets should be steam-cleaned. Alternatively, if you have a large freezer, pop pillows and blankets into a garbage bag and leave them in the freezer for a month.

The most important area to clean is the dog's sleeping area. If pooch sleeps on a pillow, toss it.

Wasps, hornets, and yellowjackets

Before attempting to deal with a wasp nest, be sure that you have an antihistamine, such as Benedryl, on hand.

If you're going to take on a wasp, hornet, or yellowjacket nest, do it in the late evening when all the little critters are tucked in for the night. Do not shine a flashlight directly into the nest. (No need to announce your presence.) Use a commercial product, *read the directions*, spray away. (Do wear long sleeves and pants while doing this.) Wait a day and check for activity. You might want to give the nest a second dose, just because. When you're sure there's no more activity in there, remove the nest and burn it. Easy.

Hornets are a whole other matter. They're downright mean. If that's what you're dealing with, then really, *really* take care. And if the nest is hard to reach, or if you've had any previous allergic reactions, for heaven's sake, call in the pros.

Mice and Rats

If you are renting your home, it is the landlord's responsibility to deal with rodents. Your concern should be prevention. But a little knowledge can't hurt.

Rats are active at night and generally avoid contact with people. Snap traps are preferable to poisonous bait, as they are non-toxic. Baited traps (peanut butter is the preferred bait) are put in areas with rat activity. Pre-bait a trap. (That means set out the bait once without the trap.)

Glue traps are sometimes used to catch mice. A tray or sheet is smeared with strong adhesive. When mice trot over the glue trap, they get stuck. But this doesn't immediately kill the mouse. It could take days for the thing to die, which seems a little mean.

Humane live traps are an alternative. They look like little plastic tunnels. The peanut butter bait goes at one end of the tunnel. The mouse goes into the tunnel, has lunch, and waits for you to pick up the trap and release it outside. Take it far, far away from the house or it will be back tomorrow.

These traps contain no pesticides and, unlike a snap trap, which breaks a rat's or mouse's neck, they do not present the risk of seriously hurting Fido's paws—or your own.

There are plenty of poisons that will kill rodents eventually. However, it's common for a mouse or rat to nibble on the poison and then stagger back between the walls to die. The only way to then remove the smelly dead mouse or rat is to break a hole in your wall. There goes your security deposit.

Poisons are also dangerous to any visiting children or pets who might accidentally ingest the pesticide.

Also dangerous—rodent droppings. Once the mice or rats are dead or gone, open the doors and windows to let fresh air in. Put on a pair of vinyl or rubber gloves. Do not sweep or vacuum up droppings, urine, or nesting materials. Use a paper towel to pick up anything gross and dispose of it in the garbage. Spray the area with bleach and water: 375 millilitres ($1^1/_2$ cups) of household bleach per 4 litres (1 gallon) of water, or 1 part bleach to 9 parts water. Let the solution soak for five minutes before mopping it up. Use the bleach solution to clean all countertops. If you even think that bedding or clothing has been exposed to rodent urine or droppings, wash everything with laundry detergent in hot water. Wash your hands with soap and warm water after removing the gloves. Oh, what the heck, take a shower.

Phew! Never want to do that again, right? To make sure there are no repeat visits, check your house for gaps or holes that a pencil can fit into. Look for holes everywhere—around vents, plumbing, water and gas lines. Seal them up. (Try lath screen or lath metal, cement, hardware cloth, steel wool, or metal sheeting. All are available at the hardware store.)

Yes, it's hard work, and yes, it's gross, but so are mice mating in the back of your stove.

More rodent prevention tips

- Put Fido's food away, and do not leave pet food or water bowls out overnight.
- Rodents will eat fruit that's fallen from fruit trees. Pick it up.
- If you haul garbage to the curb, use thick plastic or metal containers with tight lids.

Raccoons

You can try all the gizmos and home remedies you want (ultrasonics, mothballs, mashed jalapeño peppers slathered on the garbage bins) but really, you have to stop providing them with food. Start with the easy-access birdfeeder. Get rid of it, hang it from a wire or a thin metal pole, or stick it on a non-climb window. Remove anything that might be seen as a tasty treat by your new best friend, Mr. or Ms. Omnivore. What's left? Making a physical barrier or calling pest control. Careful trapping the little critters. There are laws about this sort of thing.

Birds

How do you get Tweetie out of the house? The bird is more terrified than you are, and it has more on the line, so stop panicking. Put on a pair of peck-proof gloves. Lightly dampen a large, old beach towel. (They are usually lighter than regular towels. Remember, we are trying to keep the bird alive.) Fling the damp towel over the bird. Wait until the bird has settled, then gently pick it up, towel and all, and take it outside. Lift off the towel. Are you standing back?

Bats

I know that bats are great for the environment, but really, they belong in a belfry, not your attic.

   If a bat is flapping around in the daytime, it might have rabies. This is not to say that most bats have rabies. They do not. However, according to the National Center for Infectious Diseases (NCID) in the United States, most of the recent human rabies cases in the United States have been caused by the rabies virus from bats. (Any wild mammal—like a skunk, raccoon, fox, coyote, or bat—can have rabies and transmit it to people.) Without fast and appropriate medical intervention, rabies is fatal.

True, bats have got a bad rap. Most species are not blood-sucking, and even those that are will only very rarely feed on human blood. They are not blind. They are neither birds nor rodents. They are nocturnal (kind of like you). Bats do play an important role in our ecosystem. They eat insects. Acknowledged. Just don't touch one, okay?

Bats have tiny teeth—so small that you may not be able to tell if you've been bitten. If you wake up and a bat is in your room, get yourself tested.

Only a lab can confirm rabies in a bat, but if you find a bat that is active during daylight hours in a room in your home or out on the lawn flapping around, or unable to fly, be suspicious. If you are bitten by a bat or get any bat saliva into your eyes, nose, mouth, or a wound—wash and get medical advice immediately.

To keep bats outside where they belong, caulk around any openings larger than 5 or 6 millimetres ($^1/_4$ inch). Use window screens and chimney caps. Fill electrical and plumbing holes with stainless steel wool or caulking, and keep your exterior doors closed.

If a bat does get in, call Animal Control or Public Health. If that's not possible, put on leather work gloves, grab a small box or coffee can and a piece of cardboard. Have tape ready.

The bat will land, eventually. Approach it slowly and place the box or coffee can over it. Slide the cardboard under the container. Tape the cardboard to the container securely, and make air holes. Call animal control and get advice as to where you can have the bat tested for rabies.

If you are sure no one has been touched or bitten, restrict the bat to one room and leave a window open. The bat should leave on its own.

Resources

Lower your heating bill

Read *Keeping the Heat In*, published by Natural Resources Canada. Call 1-800-387-2000 in Canada or 819- 995-2943 outside Canada for a copy.

For more information about bats and the risks they pose

www.cdc.gov/ncidod/dvrd/rabies/Bats_&_Rabies/bats&.htm

3

Housekeeping 101

My idea of superwoman is a person who scrubs her own floors.

—BETTE MIDLER

Picture this. It's the day after a party, or perhaps it's just a Saturday morning and the Cleaning Fairies have called in sick. The place is a dump. There are twenty or so half-filled glasses dotting every flat surface, pizza and Chinese take-out boxes everywhere, empty buckets filled with chicken bones, and crumpled bags of something called "Gourmet Take-Away" sitting on the couch. The cushions are off the chairs, a pair of boxer shorts dangles from the rafters, and every dish you own is either in the sink, in the fridge, stacked in a corner, or stashed in the oven. The floors are sticky, the rug has a suspicious stain on it, and the bathroom looks as if it should be attached to a gas station somewhere in Montana. I am not even discussing your bedroom—it's a wonder you haven't *caught* something in there.

Where do you start?

Absolute Cleaning Basics

1. Put on a CD or grab your MP3 player.
2. Open the windows.
3. Grab a large garbage bag, and make sure the recycling bins are handy.
4. *Go!* Start filling. Begin with the boxes, bags, and garbage. Once you get that junk cleared away, the job will seem much easier to tackle.

5. Collect all the clothes before more stuff gets spilled on them. Put the dirty clothes in the washer, add detergent, and push *start*. (If you need to know more, see page 174.)

6. Put the pillows and furniture back where they belong.

7. Collect all the dishes and take them into the kitchen. Fill up the sink with hot water and a squirt of soap, and leave the really evil dishes to soak. If you have a dishwasher, start the first load now. (See page 76.)

8. Arm yourself with a cloth or paper towels and a spray bottle of 1 part water to 3 parts white vinegar. Wipe down all surfaces, including the bathroom. If you are slowing down, find some new tunes and crank up the volume.

9. Clean from the top down. In other words, leave the floors until last.

10. Sweep and vacuum. Here's a weird little tip from the carpet-obsessed: *rake* your carpet before vacuuming to loosen the dirt and raise the pile—it will make vacuuming more effective. (Bet you won't do *that!*) And another idea, particularly if you have a dog: sprinkle the rug with baking soda. Let it sit overnight if you have the time, or for a few minutes if you don't, then vacuum.

Your Clean-Up Kit

Collect in one place:
- 1 pair of rubber gloves.
- 1 bucket.
- Mop.
- Broom and dustpan (like Grandma has).
- A decent vacuum cleaner and extra bags.
- A box of rags (old washcloths and tea towels, or buy some at a hardware store).
- Paper towels.
- Stiff-bristled brush.
- Pot-scrubbers—for the hard gunk.
- Any old socks that have lost their mates. (Use them as mitts to dust door and picture frames and baseboards.)

TIP: Where to keep the garbage bag twist ties? At the bottom of the garbage can. When the bag is full, lift it out and there are the ties. They never get lost.

TIP: If you do use commercial cleaning products, be aware of what you're breathing in. Many products contain ethylene-based glycol ether—not something you want to fill your lungs with. Be sure to keep windows open while you clean, and afterwards to air the place out. Toss used paper towels in the garbage outside and head outdoors yourself for a few hours until the fumes have dispersed.

Tackling the Kitchen

Sorry kid, but it's gotta be done. Start by removing the dirty dishes from the oven or fridge or wherever else you've stashed them and put them in the sink to soak in hot water.

Clean the microwave by placing a small bowl of water inside and boiling it on high for five minutes. The steam will loosen the splatters. Wipe clean.

Clean chrome taps in the kitchen—or bathroom, for that matter—with a sprinkling of flour. Rinse, then buff with a soft cloth. Club soda and seltzer water work well on chrome, too. Rub a stainless-steel sink with baking powder and buff with balled-up newspaper.

Loading the Dishwasher

Position the dishes so that they are facing toward the centre of the dishwasher, to get the full blast of water. Mix small plates with large ones. Load pots, pans, and large cookware on the sides. Place glasses and mugs in rows between the prongs on the top rack. Mix the flatware (forks, spoons, and knives) so that the items don't nest together. Knife blades should go down into the basket to prevent nasty cuts when emptying the load. Place bowls down the centre of the top shelf. Make sure no items touch or they might get chipped.

Loading the Dishwasher

Rinse off all food before loading

Top rack

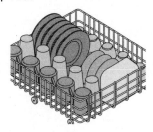

Bottom rack

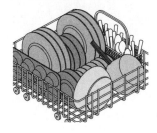

Cutlery rack

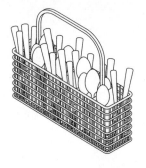

Been there
Done THAT

At my first apartment I was blessed with a dishwasher. I forgot to buy dishwasher detergent, though, so I poured in some Tide. Do you know how much lather that stuff produces? My floor got really, really clean. Good to know: dish and laundry detergent are not interchangeable.

—BRETT, 30

TIP: If the dishwasher has a bad smell, it's likely caused by food trapped at the bottom, or dirty plates that have been sitting for too long. If you must leave dishes for a day or two, run the load through a "rinse and hold" cycle. To get rid of the smell, run the dishwasher on empty with two cups of white vinegar instead of detergent.

TIP: Wash a wineglass by holding the base, then plunging and swishing the glass in very hot, sudsy water. Quickly rinse in hot, clear water. (Cooler water might shatter the glass.) Dry upside down on a paper towel or clean tea towel. For streak-free glasses, add a little vinegar to the rinse water. Lipstick stains on the stemware? Rub salt on the rims.

Dishwasher "no gos"

Cast iron, wooden bowls and cutting boards, anodized cookware, and Grandma's gold-rimmed china and plates should not be put in a dishwasher. Careful with that delicate stemware, too. There's a good chance the stems will snap off. Note that knives will become dull; pewter, brass, and bronze will tarnish; iron and tin pots might rust. Sadly, you should wash all these by hand. If you have Grandma's sterling silverware and you flatly refuse to hand-wash it, either give it back or wash it separately from the stainless steel.

That pan with the baked-on food that you just pulled from a smoky oven won't come clean in a dishwasher either. (What? You believed the ads?) Elbow grease is required here. Try sprinkling a pan

---

Duh moment!

How to Hand-Wash the Dishes
(Last seen on *The Andy Griffith Show*. Aunt Bee was the one washing.)

Fill up a clean sink with hot, hot water. If the sink is made of porcelain and hard on wineglasses, sink a tea towel and press it flat against the bottom of the sink. Wash glasses first, cups next, utensils and dishes after that. Rinse in clear water. Save the dirtiest stuff for last—that's usually the pots and pans. Let everything drip dry—unless your tea towels are clean and you've got nothing else to do.

TIP: Broken glass? Don't, just don't, stick it in a plastic bag. Someone, somewhere, is going to get cut. Wrap it first in thick newspaper before discarding it. Use tape if you must to prevent glass shards from slicing through the bag. If you're throwing out large quantities, mark it "Broken Glass" for the garbage collectors—their job is hazardous enough without nasty surprises like that.

with baking soda, adding some water, and letting it sit for a while. Maybe someone else will come along and clean it … or not. You might also try mixing kosher or coarse salt with water to make a paste. Salt is an abrasive, but it's not too abrasive. Don't use salt on a non-stick skillet, though, because it will ruin the surface.

A word about kitchen dish towels: If you have just bought them, wash them before you use them. They have been handled by all sorts of people, plus they have natural oils that can reduce absorption. After use, wring them out and hang them to dry. If you stick them back in the drawer wet they will grow bacteria and mould. Toss them in the wash at least once a week.

The cutting board that cuts both ways: Wash your plastic board in the dishwasher, or scrub with soapy water and a brush, then sterilize it with a solution of 1 part white vinegar to 4 parts water. Leave the solution on the board for two to five minutes, rinse, and dry with paper towels. You can also use a bleach solution for really mucky boards (e.g., post chicken-cutting). Make sure cutting boards have a chance to air-dry in between uses.

Dealing with the Fridge

Finally—a fridge of your own! If it came with the apartment, you're in luck … or not. If you get an unpleasant whiff of something every time you open the fridge or freezer door, chances are the plastics have absorbed odours from the food choices of previous tenants. (Example: some mad tipsters have suggested that paintbrushes be frozen until you are ready to clean them. Bad idea. The fridge might never recover from that paint smell. Which would you rather buy… a new paintbrush or a new fridge?)

So what do you do? A good cleaning with a baking soda and water paste might remove most of the odour, but if all else fails, mask the odour with, say, coffee. Keep an open coffee container in the fridge. In the end you might just have to live with the smell.

Cleaning Cupboards

When dust obscures the names of the soups on the cans, it's past time to clean out the cupboards. Empty the entire cupboard out onto the kitchen table. Toss out the old mustard packets from MacDonald's, plastic cups from Burger King, and the plum sauce packets from Chung Choo Chow. Wipe the shelves down with a damp cloth and a squirt of vinegar and water. Only put back what you will actually eat. If you come across a can that will not sit flat on the counter (i.e., one that is bulging or dented) *toss it!* Botulism poisoning is about as yummy as it sounds. (For everything you ever wanted to know about botulism, go to: www.bt.cdc.gov/agent/botulism/hcpfacts.asp.)

Cleaning the Oven

Alas, there *is* such a thing as an oven that is *not* self-cleaning, meaning you have to clean it the old-fashioned way. Does your oven smoke every time you turn it on? Do you know for a fact that the cheese from the pizza dripped through the oven rack?

TIP: So that you won't have to do this oven-cleaning thing too often, spread aluminum foil on the bottom of the oven to catch drips. Do the same with cookie sheets for fast cleanup.

Okay, here's what you do. Buy an oven-cleaning product and read the directions. Don't do anything unless the oven is turned off and completely cool. Make very sure the room is well ventilated and that you are wearing gloves. Spray. Try not to breathe the fumes. Wait until the stuff turns into dust and then wipe clean with a damp cloth. If there are little particles left try vacuuming them up. If the cookie sheets are in an awful state, clean them with the same product.

A word about self-cleaning ovens—there is work involved. The oven will have to be *locked* before you turn it to the cleaning setting. Read the manual carefully and follow the instructions exactly. *Do not* leave the house while the oven is "cleaning itself," and *do* block off the entrance to the kitchen in case your dim roommate decides to bake cookies.

How to Mop a Floor

The kitchen floor might be the one you need to mop most often (although the bathroom is another strong contender for this title). The job requires some equipment: a mop and a pail. Said equipment can be as simple or as complicated as your finances allow.

No matter what the floor type, sweep it first. Use a pencil eraser to remove black heel marks from the floor.

- *Hardwood floor.* Use a wood cleaner mixed with water. Rinse the mop out several times. Dry the mop. Buff the floor with a dry cloth stuck to the end of the mop.
- *Linoleum or vinyl floor.* Use a mild detergent and rinse with warm water.
- *Ceramic floor.* Mop with hot, soapy water. Dry and buff with a cloth.

Beautifying the Bedroom

Assuming this room hasn't seen *too* much action, cleaning it shouldn't be a horrid job.

Make the bed first, and see what a difference it makes. If you haven't got a laundry hamper yet, run out and buy one. Use it, and again see how much better everything looks. If you will not hang up your clothes, at least fling them on hooks. (Check out the chapter Taking Care of Your Stuff. That cashmere sweater you dropped last month's rent on will not fare well dangling from a peg.)

If you are too lazy to dust (aren't we all?), then at least run a lint roller over flat lampshades every once in a while. If the shades have folds in them, you can turn your blow-dryer on the low setting and blow the dust off. Same thing with curtains. Of course, the stuff has to land somewhere. Good luck with your allergies. At some point, you *are* going to have to dust.

For a Lovely Living Room

Start at the top of the room and work down. Spiderwebs near the ceiling? Tie a rag to a broom and sweep them away. While you're at it, clean the wallpaper by dusting it down, top to bottom.

Cover your hand with an old sock and dust the mini-blinds and shutters. A dollar store paintbrush works well too, especially on keyboards, telephones, and in other odd places. Wipe mini-blinds, shutters, and TV screens with a damp fabric softener sheet to get rid of static.

Stains

*   *Water marks on wooden surfaces.* Make sure the area is dry, then rub half a Brazil nut onto the mark. What? No Brazil nuts lying around? Try mixing equal parts baking soda and non-gel (white) toothpaste, then rub that into the mark with a damp cloth. Follow with furniture polish. Other options: rub with cooking oil, mayonnaise, or Vaseline. Test in an inconspicuous area first. And if the furniture is an heirloom from Grandma, better call an expert.
*   *Grubby fingerprints on walls.* Rub with stale, moist white bread. Or try rubbing spots on the wall with lukewarm white vinegar.

Carpet Diem!

> *I'm not going to vacuum until Sears makes one you can ride on.*
> —ROSEANNE BARR

There are some firsts you'll never forget: your first breakup, the first dent in your car, and the first stain on the first rug *you ever paid for yourself.* Can't help you much on the first two, but here are some suggestions for the carpet.

*   Act before the spill or stain spreads too far, or penetrates too deep into the fibres.
*   Scrape up as much as possible of whatever spilled with a spoon or blunt-edged knife.

Been there
Done THAT

It was my first full-time job. I was out on a home visit with a client. Just as I was leaving, I spilled grape juice all over their carpet. I was mortified, apologized, and then left! I didn't realize until much later that it would have been a difficult stain to remove, and that the rug was probably very expensive. To this day I regret not offering to pay for the cleanup.

—KARLA, 42

If it's red wine, dab soda water on it.

- Blot up liquids with a clean cloth, towel, or paper towels, using plain warm water to dampen the spill without rubbing.
- Always work toward the centre of the spill to prevent spreading.

Things that you should not do

- **Do not** lift the carpet or roll it up.
- **Do not** rub the stain. Always blot it up.
- **Do not** try to dry it with a blow-dryer.
- **Do not** use solvents, detergents, turpentine, or other solutions.

TIP: Red wine on a rug is a killer. Quickly, pour on white sugar. It will absorb the wine. Leave it until the sugar turns red, then brush it up or suck it up with a vacuum. Now pour on some water and blot the remaining stain. The trick is to blot, not rub the stain into the rug.

There are some spills and stains that are impossible to deal with, like wood glue, hair dye, furniture stains, shoe polish, permanent marker pens (what was your first clue?), and paint. When they happen, you are left with no choice but to call in professionals. Keep the stain moist by covering it with a damp cloth.

Renting a rug cleaner from the supermarket is an option, although those machines can leave a good deal of cleaning solution on your carpet. The carpet becomes sticky and not nice to romp on. Add up the cost of the rental, the cost of the suds, and, if you are hoofing it, the cost of the taxi to lug it home. You might discover that calling a rug cleaning service is only marginally more expensive.

If you call in the pros

- Ask for references. Really! If they dither and say, "We don't give out the names of our clients to protect their privacy," say that you understand and hang up.
- Ask about their cleaning methods. There are three: hot extraction, bonnet cleaning, and shampooing. This is a tad technical, but if you have inherited Grandma's Persian carpet, you'd better listen up.
  — Truck-mounted extractors, used by most of the pros, recover about 80 percent of the cleaning solution chemicals. Drying times takes between 6 and 12 hours. This is big-boy stuff.

— Bonnet cleaning is topical and involves injecting a dry detergent into a cloth buffer and running it over the rug. There is no drying time.

— Steam cleaning is the most popular because it gives a good, generally deep clean. In general, go for the steam clean. You might also want to ask about the use of more environmentally friendly cleaners (they can use a club-soda–like cleaning solution).

- Ask about drying time.
- And, of course, the million-dollar question: How much? Does the cost include moving the furniture and spot removal?
- When you make the appointment on the phone, tell them that you will require a written guarantee *that lists all services* before work can commence. You might as well learn to play hardball now. It will save you a bundle as the years go by.

More than You Really Wanted to Know

You already know about baking soda, of course. (An open box in the fridge absorbs odours.) But did you know that you can replace the bad smell with a good smell? Dip a cotton ball into vanilla extract (found in a tiny dark bottle in the baking section of the grocery store) and place the cotton in your fridge. You can also dab a bit on a warm light bulb to make your home smell yummy. (Don't go overboard!) And after cleaning in the kitchen or bathroom, add a squirt of lemon to what you're washing to leave a fresh scent.

Bold Bathroom Cleaning

It's the combination of steam, mould, dampness, and dirt that makes the bathroom a virtual hothouse of gross. That, and the fact that your roommate keeps forgetting to flush. If you keep on top of it, though, your bathroom won't ever get too hellish.

What you'll need

- A roll of paper towels.
- A sponge.
- A squirt bottle of water and vinegar mixture.

- Disinfectant (for the bigger and grosser jobs).
- Old toothbrushes.
- A squeegee.

Store your kit under the sink (assuming that small children never visit.)

When you are in the shower and everything's still wet, sponge down the damp walls with your water-and-vinegar solution. Keep a squeegee hanging on a hook to swipe down the glass shower door (if you've got one). If you've got a buildup of stains and lime scale on the shower doors, try cleaning with white wine. To clean the grout, add a little bleach to the water-and-vinegar solution and scrub with an old toothbrush.

TIP: Loofahs and sponges can harbour germs big time. Let them soak overnight in lemon juice and water. If they are still suspect, boil them in lemon juice and water.

Wipe the mirror with a cloth and the vinegar solution.

Once the soap holder is shiny clean, dab it with a tiny amount of baby oil. That will make it really easy to clean off any soap residue later.

Either buy really cheap curtain liners (under $5) and toss them out every second month, or buy a good shower curtain that can be washed. To wash a shower curtain, soak it in warm water, baking soda, and lemon (or add a bit of bleach). Leave it for an hour or so and then wash it in the washing machine on a "delicate" setting. This should handle any mildew. If the curtain is plastic or vinyl, do not put it in the dryer. (But if you did toss it in the dryer by mistake, you can now use it as a baseball.)

Blitz bath stains with 1 part vinegar to 5 parts water. Unclog a showerhead by first dismantling it and then soaking it in the vinegar and water solution for twenty minutes.

There are two main things that make the bathroom really stinky: mould and mildew, and bodily functions. Cleaning will take care of the mould and mildew, while a lit candle will take care of the bodily function smells. Just be sure the candle is contained and totally safe and nowhere near your curtains. Think small tea-light candles.

Removing Stains from the Toilet Bowl

I know, you think the toilet cleans itself every time you flush.

It does not.

Remember that box of baking soda that you put, opened, in the back of the fridge? After about three months it loses its odour-absorbing powers, so take it out of the

TIP: Always wear rubber gloves when cleaning up vomit, blood, or poop. When you remove the gloves, wash your hands.

fridge and toss it in the toilet. (The contents—not the box.) Let it sit for a bit before flushing.

Every once in a while, though, nothing else will do—your toilet bowl needs a hands-on approach. When that happens, empty the bowl with a bucket and sponge. (This is where the rubber gloves come in handy.) Now, sprinkle the inside of the bowl liberally with cleanser and give it a general cleaning using a bowl brush. (Forget the day you reached legal drinking age. *This* is the moment when you finally realize that you are a grown-up.)

If you've got hard-water marks in there that won't go away, try this: pour a can of cola in the toilet bowl. Let it sit for about one hour, then flush. If the stains are still there, take a wet pumice stick (found in any drugstore) and work directly on the deposits. (It's soft on porcelain but hard on deposits, so it won't scratch the bowl.)

TIP: If someone in the house has the flu, clean the surfaces in the bathroom and kitchen frequently with soap and water or a cleanser. Then spray on disinfectant. Throw away the paper towels or cleaning cloth. Spray doorknobs, telephones, and light switches with disinfectant. Alternatively (and more easily) keep a container of disinfecting wipes handy. Use often.

Duh moment!

How to Use the Potty

If you are sharing a place with roommates, bring this up at your first—possibly only—*Let's Set a Few Ground Rules* meeting. (Chances are no one shows up for meeting number two.)

To the males in your midst: Be Down-Sitters. To put it bluntly, *sit* on the potty/can/throne. To make the idea more appealing, put a magazine rack beside the toilet. Fine, it might not work.

To everyone else: Flush with the toilet lid down, to prevent the spraying of germs and other undesirable airborne contaminants.

Getting Rid of Stuff

You already know what to do about garbage, right? We're talking about where it goes, when, how much you're allowed to toss, and what should go in the recycling bins instead. If you don't, call your local municipality and ask. But remember, not all garbage is garbage.

What's Hazardous Waste?

Basically, hazardous waste is garbage that's bad for the environment. That can include:

- antifreeze
- batteries
- brake fluid
- chemical strippers
- chlorine bleach
- contact cement
- drain cleaners
- fire extinguishers
- flea collars and sprays
- herbicides
- insect repellent
- insecticides
- kerosene
- lawn chemicals
- lighter fluid
- lye
- mothballs
- nail polish remover
- old propane tanks
- oven cleaners
- paints
- pesticides
- pool chemicals
- prescription drugs
- solvents
- spot removers
- stains and finishes
- toilet cleaners
- used motor oil

It should go without saying, this is stuff you don't simply throw away. What do you do with it? First, find out if your community has a hazardous waste depot or collection days. Your local public works department should know.

Here are some more suggestions:

- Computers: www.rebootcanada.ca
- Sports equipment: www.kidsport.on.ca
- Art and craft supplies: www.sketch.ca uses art to help street youth, homeless, and at-risk young people.

Been there
Done THAT

A 25-year-old Ontario woman died after hosting a New Year's party in 2007. She and three others who were hospitalized had apparently been poisoned after drinking a home-made punch that had been stored in a container that once held windshield-wiper fluid.

TIP: Always store hazardous products tightly closed, in a well-ventilated area, in their original containers. Never use the empty containers to store other materials.

- Cellphones and rechargeable batteries: www.call2recycle.org. (Be sure to erase names and numbers in the phone's memory.) Local electronics retailers might recycle them, or try www.charitablerecycling.ca, or www.think-food.com
- Inkjet and laser printer cartridges: www.think-food.com, www.diabetes.ca (click on "support us").
- Hazardous wastes, including paint, oil, batteries, and tires: http://www.canadiangeographic.ca/magazine/mj06/feature5_side.asp

Hiring Help

Hiring regular cleaning help will cost you big bucks, but if you're lucky, you could make it work. Say there are four of you sharing a house, all gainfully employed and able to contribute $30 to $40 a week. It might make sense to let someone else do the busy work while you focus on your careers.

There are two ways to go.

1. Independent cleaners are self-employed. To find one, ask neighbours and people you work with. Check references.
   Pros: Independents are usually more flexible and may be cheaper.
   Cons: They can bail on a whim.
2. Cleaning services. There are several from which to choose. Consult the web or Yellow Pages.
   Pros: Cancellation is not likely, although it can happen.
   Cons: Services are not as flexible. Some will not change beds, for example.

Note: Cleaners will quickly learn more about you and your life than your best friend ever did. Your garbage alone is a treasure trove of private information. With that in mind, you might want to treat your cleaners with respect. When the cleaner comes to the door, take her coat, hang it up, and ask if she needs anything. (Yes, most cleaners are women, although more guys are getting into the act.) Introduce her to everyone in the house. She needs to know who is there, for her own comfort and safety. You may point out the radio and CD player. Music is a great motivator.

A cleaner is there to do a job, not to serve you. Do not ask her to make you a cup of tea, but if you are making some for yourself, pour a cup for the cleaner, too. Don't worry that a tea break will cost a few precious minutes of cleaning your house. If she has just finished cleaning someone else's place, a cup might be just what she needs. And we all do better work when we feel considered and respected.

Decide what you want cleaned. Emptying the dishwasher might not be the best way to use the cleaner's time. Before work begins, sit down with the cleaner and talk about what you want done. You might want to leave a list.

Most cleaners would rather not have you lolling about. Either leave the house, or take yourself off to another room.

Some cleaners bring their own products; others will provide you with a list of supplies to pick up.

Always have the money ready, and if the cleaner has done something special, add a tip. Speaking of tips, no matter what your religion, or the religion of the cleaner, it is customary to tip at Christmas. Typically a full day's pay is the norm if this person has worked for you for six months or more, depending on your relationship. In some cases a bottle of wine or a gift certificate will do.

Resources

For information on botulism

www.bt.cdc.gov/agent/botulism/hcpfacts.asp

For disposal of unwanted clutter and hazardous waste

www.rebootcanada.ca
www.kidsport.on.ca
www.sketch.ca

www.call2recycle.org
www.charitablerecycling.ca
www.think-food.com
www.diabetes.ca (click on "support us")
http://www.canadiangeographic.ca/magazine/mj06/feature5_side.asp

4

Getting to Know
Your Kitchen

The woman just ahead of you at the supermarket checkout has all the delectable groceries you didn't even know they carried.

—MIGNON MCLAUGHLIN, *THE SECOND NEUROTIC'S NOTEBOOK*, 1966

Hungry? What's to eat? Now that you're on your own, *you* are the only one who can answer that question. Nothing says "grown-up" like taking care of your own empty belly.

Here are the options: You can take lessons from Mom's School of Cooking-by-Phone. You can eat ice cream for breakfast and put Pizza Pizza on speed-dial. *Or* … and here's a concept: you can learn to cook.

First off, meet Your Kitchen. You might have to step over the empty pizza cartons, but I know you can find it. After all, the beer fridge is in there somewhere. Believe it or not, your kitchen is good for much more than just storing beverages and peanut butter. Use it wisely and treat it right—your body and soul will thank you.

First, you need to know what equipment to put in the kitchen. And food—where to get it and how to store it right. Then you need to know what to do with all that stuff so that the food continues to be edible—tasty, even—and doesn't make you sick. Study this chapter, and with any luck, you'll be holding sophisticated dinner parties in no time.

Your Kitchen Tools

Hopefully you've already got a fridge, stove, and sink in there. Now, what else will you need?

Pots and Pans

Pots (otherwise known as saucepans) and pans (also called skillets) are the hardest-working pieces of equipment in your kitchen (aside from you, of course), so you want to buy the best you can afford. If they're too thin or wobbly, you'll end up with a lot of burned messes and pizza delivery again. Here's what to look for.

Pots

Used for cooking pasta and soup, pots are deep, with lids. You'll get the most use out of a pot with a 3- to 4-litre (roughly 3- to 4-quart) capacity. A stockpot—which is much bigger, with about a 6-litre (roughly 6-quart) capacity—is handy for boiling corn-on-the-cob, pasta, and big batches of soup, but probably bigger than you need at this point in your life. Stainless steel is probably your best bet, although it can be expensive. If you can't afford stainless steel, aluminum is fine, but you'll have to keep an eye on your cooking because it burns more easily.

Pans

Used for just about everything else you do on a stove, a frying pan, or skillet, is shallow, usually without a lid. Your pan should be about 30 centimetres (12 inches) in diameter, and can be of the same material as your pots. Pans can also be "non-stick"—specially coated (possibly with Teflon) so that you don't have to add a lot of fat, and food won't stick. You don't want to scratch a non-stick pan, so use only plastic or wooden utensils when cooking, and wash them with a dishcloth (not a pot-scrubber). Replace a non-stick pan every few years, or when you start to see the coating flake off. There is some controversy over the health effects of the non-stick coating. If you prefer, you could just stick with stainless steel. Stainless-steel pans are heavier, last longer, and are not as delicate. If you have burned something in a stainless-steel pan, try cooking it off by adding an inch of water to the pan, placing it on the stove to boil, and scraping the burned food with a spatula.

TIP: Keep an eye out for estate and contents sales in the classified ads. You can sometimes pick up good pots and pans, cheap. Second-hand stores like Goodwill are also good sources.

Knives

Forget the "steak knife set" you picked up at the dollar store. If you haven't already sliced your fingers with those, you will, because those cheapies rarely keep their edge for more than a few uses—and dull knives are the most dangerous. You don't need to buy top-of-the-line blades, but you should invest some money in good, heavy knives at a reputable store so that they—and your fingers—last a long time. If the store clerk looks as though she's knowledgeable, ask her what she recommends—explaining that you're poor, on your own, and just starting out.

You'll need two special kinds of knives to start.

TIP: If a good knife set or pots and pans just aren't in the budget, there's always Christmas and your birthday. Forget the gift cards from the mall boutiques and ask Santa for kitchen essentials instead. You will impress everyone with how grown-up you've become.

Chef's knife: This one is heavy, with a 15- to 25-centimetre (6- to 10-inch), slightly curved blade. Hold it in your hands to see if it feels like a good fit before you buy it. It's good for cutting up fruit and vegetables. One hand grasps the handle, the other pushes gently on the top (dull edge) of the blade. Rock back and forth, pushing down.

Bread knife: This has a 20-centimetre (8-inch) serrated (zigzag) blade. It's good for slicing baked goods, bread, and tomatoes. Slide it back and forth gently, like a saw.

TIP: To keep blades sharp, don't toss them in the cutlery drawer. Store them in a wooden knife block or on a magnetic holder.

Cutting Board

Look for either plastic or wood. There is still some controversy over which is less likely to harbour dangerous bacteria—wooden boards can be sanded down, and have also been found to have natural bacteria-killing properties, while some plastic boards are made with antibacterial materials.

A big board is most versatile, but make sure it's small enough to fit in the sink for cleaning, with a groove running around the edge to direct juices away. A rubber underside is helpful to keep it from skidding around. If you can't find one with a rubber bottom, buy a non-slip underpad or rubber shelf liner from the dollar store—or, in a pinch, you can fold a tea towel under the board to keep it steady.

I confess, I stole four wooden cutting boards from a restaurant I worked in when I was seventeen. I still have them—thirty years later. We just sand them down and rinse them every few years.

—TERRY, 50

Here are a few more tips:

- Buy boards of different colours for different uses—a red board can be for cutting raw meats and poultry, green for cutting fruits and veggies—so there's less chance of cross-contamination.
- Avoid tiny boards—unless you like a separate board for garlic, because that's about all they're good for.
- Avoid glass boards—they'll dull your knife.
- When you start to see grooves in your board and it's hard to clean, it's time to replace it.

TIP: Don't pour your ingredients into a measuring spoon over the pot or bowl you're mixing in. One misstep and you've dumped way too much right into your masterpiece. Measure over the sink, instead. Anything that overflows can go down the drain.

Measuring Cups and Spoons

Plastic cups are for measuring dry goods, like sugar and flour. Scoop out the ingredient from the bag or container and level the top with the flat edge of a knife. Glass cups are used for liquid, and are marked on the outside. Place the glass cup on the counter and bend down so that the cup is at eye level, so you can read the marking and be sure you've measured accurately. Don't use your regular cutlery for measuring spoons; they're not the same. If possible, buy narrow measuring spoons; they'll fit better into spice jars.

Duh!
moment!

Tsp is short for teaspoon, tbsp is short for tablespoon.

Imperial versus metric measures

Most Canadian cookbooks use metric measures, while American recipes tend to use imperial.

Utensils

Here are some absolute essentials:

Imperial Measures	Metric Measures
1 cup	250 ml
1/2 cup	125 ml
1/3 cup	75 ml
1/4 cup	50 ml
1 tbsp	15 ml
1 tsp	5 ml
1/2 tsp	2 ml
1/4 tsp	1 ml

- *Can-opener*—look for one that twists smoothly and has easy-to-grip handles.
- *Wooden spoon*—so you don't burn your hands when stirring something hot, and you don't scratch your spiffy new non-stick pan.
- *Spatulas and "flippers"*—you might want a heavy, slotted, stainless-steel one for flipping heavy food, or a similar plastic one if you have a non-stick pan. A rubber, flexible spatula is good for scraping batter out of mixing bowls.

TIP: When measuring brown sugar, make sure you pack it into the measuring cup firmly, unless otherwise directed.

- *Spring-action tongs*—handy for lifting hot corn-on-the-cob or buns, flipping chicken on the barbecue, and serving salad or chicken wings. They're available, cheap, at the dollar store.
- *Ladle*—this is a large, deep-bowled spoon for scooping out soups or sauces. Make sure it's strong. If it's too light it will droop under the weight.
- *Veggie brush*—for scrubbing fruit and vegetables. You can find one at the dollar store.
- *Vegetable peeler* (swivel type)—for peeling fruits and veggies, along with shaving the rind from oranges and creating chocolate curls for fancy desserts.
- *Bottle opener*—get one that also punctures can lids.
- *Corkscrew*—the ones with arms that you press down to lift the cork are probably the most user-friendly for a novice.
- *Cheese grater.*

TIPS:

When opening a can with a can-opener, don't cut completely around the top. If you leave a fraction of the lid still attached, you can carefully lift it open with a spoon, dump out the contents, then push the lid back in. If you don't, the lid (which will not be perfectly clean) will fall into the food—and you'll risk cutting your fingers trying to fish it out.

Cut your pizza with scissors. Clean them first. Use an oven mitt to hold the hot pizza.

Other Necessities

- *Oven mitts*—if you buy the fabric kind, remember to toss them in the laundry once in a while. The waterproof mitts made of silicone are pricier but better, because they'll protect you if you spill water or oil while carrying a hot pot.
- *Meat thermometer*—it's not always easy to tell when food is fully cooked, so keep it simple: stick a thermometer into the thickest part of the meat, compare it with the chart that comes with the thermometer (or see page 164), and you'll know when dinner's done.
- *Casserole dish*—you may not think you need this, but you will. Use it for Rice Krispie squares now, and save the casserole-making for when you're feeling more ambitious.
- *A set of plastic containers for leftovers*—make sure the lids fit well and the sides are translucent (so you can see what's in there). Don't use them in the microwave unless they say "microwave safe" on the label.
- *Large mixing bowl.*
- *Ice-cube tray.*
- *Salt and pepper shakers.*
- *Dishcloths, dish towels*—five should be enough.
- *Paper-towel holder.*
- *A large colander or strainer*—good for draining pasta, cooked veggies, washed berries, etc. Metal lets you rinse both hot and cold food. Look for drainage holes (as opposed to slits, which allow some food to escape).
- *Fire extinguisher*—read the instructions before you need it. Don't store it above the stove.

- *Cookie tray*—good for cookies, of course, but also for catching spills in the oven (placed under whatever you're cooking or baking) .
- *Kettle*—a plug-in kettle with an automatic shut-off is a very good idea, or a stovetop version with a very loud whistle.
- *Pitcher*—for making juice.
- *Drying rack*—for dishes.

TIP: Don't have a biscuit or cookie cutter? Use a cup or soup can. Don't have a rolling pin? A pop or wine bottle works very well.

And don't forget, when you make your first foray into a grocery store, you'll need:

- Aluminum foil.
- Plastic wrap.
- Garbage bags.
- Plastic freezer bags.
- Paper towels.
- Pot scrubbers.

Also Nice to Have on Hand

- *Muffin tins.* Plan ahead, bake up some healthy muffins, and throw them in a freezer bag in the freezer. Then you've got a cheap, easy, microwavable breakfast to go. Muffin tins are also handy for mini-meatloafs, potatoes, and stuffed peppers.
- *Immersion blender.* Once you discover this handy little tool, you'll wonder how you existed without it. Plug it in, stick it in a bowl or pot, and you can whip up smoothies, soups, and sauces in no time—and it takes up less space than one of those freestanding blenders.
- *Hand-held electric mixer.* Most baking recipes call for beating or whipping of ingredients, and only early Canadian pioneers (also fond of butter churning) dared attempt this by hand.
- *Microwave.* If we're realistic, you're going to use this appliance more than the vacuum cleaner. We all know about your microwave popcorn habit, of course. But it can't be beat for days when you're rushing out the door, or dead tired at night and just want to heat something frozen and flop on the couch. Remember, though, there are drawbacks—leftovers taste better reheated on the stove, veggies may lose more nutrients in the microwave, and thawing food often partially cooks it, too, so you need to be careful about how you use it.

- *Contact grill.* If you've got the money for it, this appliance is great for fast and healthy cooking. If you've prepared ground beef or chicken patties and stored them in the freezer, you can quickly whip up barbecued burgers on a cold winter night. Also worth trying: grilled veggies, fancy grilled cheese sandwiches, and quesadillas. Look for one with removable plates (easier to clean) and an on-off switch. (Other kinds require you to unplug to turn off—you'd hate to burn your first place to the ground.) Remember to use your grill on a counter that doesn't have overhead cupboards.

How to Shop at the Grocery Store

Remember that self-filling fridge at home? Sorry to be the one to break it to you, but there is no Tooth Fairy, and there is no Fridge Fairy, either. If you don't fill that thing, it's going to stay empty.

You knew it had to happen sooner or later. The grocery shopping is your job now. And you'll have to do more than just make a beeline for the snack aisle. You're going to have to push a cart up and down all those monstrously loaded aisles. The days of begging me for fruity-sugar-cocoa cereal are gone, kid. You're on your own. Walk on in, grab a cart, and get shopping.

What should you buy? What—you don't have a list? For shame! Well you can't just stock up on ramen noodles, pop, and cold cereal, you know. That really won't do. If you seriously don't have a clue, you could sign up for a store tour. Many of the larger local supermarkets offer free tours with nutritional advice, and even cooking classes, for newbies. But if you can't see yourself traipsing behind a "tour guide" with notebook in hand, then here are a few pointers to help you understand what the supermarket is all about.

The most important thing to remember when it comes to grocery shopping is that there is nothing "accidental" about supermarket design and layout. These are sophisticated, complicated, tricky places, all designed with one thing in mind: to separate you from your money. It's a bit like a game. One team (the grocer) wants your money and doesn't care so much about your health. The other team (that would be you) wants to hang on to money and live to be 110. You think it's coincidence that you can never find a clock in a grocery store? Or that the things you buy most regularly—bread, butter, milk, and eggs—are placed far apart and at the back of the store? That the chocolate bars are always conveniently nestled up next to the cashier? Ever wonder why the cinnamon bakery smells seem to whomp you in the face the minute you enter the store? Believe it—every square inch of your "shopping experience" has been carefully planned.

Be prepared with knowledge. Know what you want and how much you're willing to pay. Know how the grocer is trying to trap you, and how you're going to fight back. If you shop with a full belly (no weakness there) and a sharp mind, you won't set out for milk and veggies and come home with Pringles and Fudgie-Os.

Your Secret Weapon: The List

Keep a list on the fridge door, and a pen nearby. Any time you run out of something, make a note. Then—and here's the important part—bring the note with you when you go to the grocery store. Sure, it destroys the joyful spontaneity of the shopping experience, but if you don't want to spend half your life going back to the store to get things you forgot, and if you don't want to spend the equivalent of a case of beer buying forgotten items at the local convenience store, then by golly you will take a list!

You will also need to start paying attention to grocery store sales flyers and coupons. Flyers are usually delivered around the same time each week in your local newspaper. If you don't get newspaper delivery then you may find the flyers displayed near the store entrance. Most items that you need go on sale at some point, and if they're not perishable—soups, toilet paper, canned goods, etc.— and if you have the room, you can stock up. If the store runs out, ask for a raincheck. That's a little piece of paper that guarantees that you get the sale price when they restock.

> **More than You Really Wanted to Know**
>
> About one-third of the stuff on grocery store shelves could be classified as high-fat, high-sugar "junk food."

How to Shop with Your Brain

Some things you need to know:

- The healthier, less-processed, fare—fruits, vegetables, meats, and dairy—tends to be shoved along the perimeter of the store. Often, you've got to walk past the just-baked smells of the bakery. Back away from the cinnamon buns!

- Less-healthy items—like super-sugared, feebly fibred cereals—are usually placed at eye level. Retailers pay grocers to have their products placed on the centre shelf. If you want something less expensive and better for you, look way up, or way down.
- Beware the belly of the beast—the middle of the store. That's where they've got your number—pre-packaged foods, high in salt, sugar, and fat. It's a nutritional minefield. If you must venture down those aisles, do so with purpose. Grab what you need and go. If you're feeling snackish, opt for nuts and popcorn, or buy the single-serving sizes.
- Skip the samples. They're usually just overpriced, less-than-healthy fare that isn't moving off the shelves. Remember what I told you about how to deal with the stoners in high school? Just say "No."
- Sales and coupons don't mean you must buy. A discounted item might look like a great deal, but if you weren't planning to buy it, and you don't really need it, then it's not a "deal" for you.

TIP: Fill the main part of your grocery cart with healthy stuff—whole grains, veggies, dairy, and fruit. Save the little section at the top of the cart for treats.

- Read labels carefully. Look at the list of ingredients—does it read like *War and Peace*? Can you pronounce all the ingredients, or does it look like a science project? Usually, the fewer ingredients, the healthier the food. (See "How to Read a Label" below.)
- Watch out for claims like "made with real fruit." There might be only a tiny fraction of "real fruit" in there. "Low fat" doesn't really help if the food is loaded up with sugar. And don't be fooled by the words organic or diet. Pigging out on anything pre-packaged is still pigging out.
- Find the unit price—it's usually on a card that gives the pricing information next to products at the grocery store. The unit price lets you compare brands, or find out how good a deal that sale is, or if the price of the store brand really is better than the name-brand price.
- Forget buying food in bulk. You might get a better price with that great big jar of pasta sauce, but if you're not going to eat it, you're not saving money.
- Don't be fooled by "special products" in bins in the middle of the aisle. They're usually things you didn't set out for and wouldn't normally find in a grocery store— like toasters or frying pans. Chances are, you'll find these things cheaper elsewhere.

How to Read a Label

On most packaged foods, you'll find an ingredient list and also "Nutrition Facts." Ingredients have to be listed in order of predominance, with the ingredients used in the largest amount first. Avoid foods with first ingredients sugar, glucose-fructose, or corn syrup, or hydrogenated fats or shortening.

The Nutrition Facts help you compare products according to their nutritional value. The "% Daily Value" helps you figure out if you're getting a little or a lot of a particular nutrient.

Here's an example, from a box of microwave popcorn:

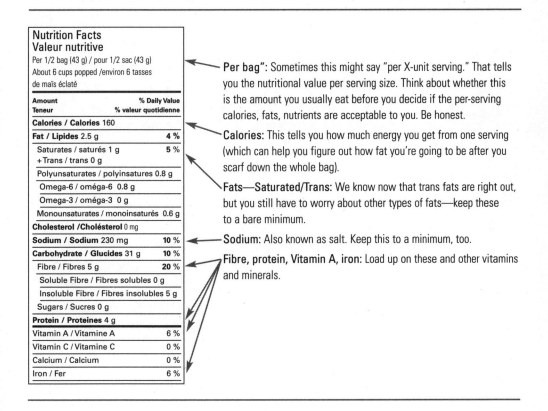

Nutrition Facts / Valeur nutritive

Per 1/2 bag (43 g) / pour 1/2 sac (43 g)
About 6 cups popped /environ 6 tasses de maïs éclaté

Amount / Teneur	% Daily Value / % valeur quotidienne
Calories / Calories 160	
Fat / Lipides 2.5 g	**4 %**
Saturates / saturés 1 g +Trans / trans 0 g	**5 %**
Polyunsaturates / polyinsatures 0.8 g	
Omega-6 / oméga-6 0.8 g	
Omega-3 / oméga-3 0 g	
Monounsaturates / monoinsaturés 0.6 g	
Cholesterol /Cholésterol 0 mg	
Sodium / Sodium 230 mg	**10 %**
Carbohydrate / Glucides 31 g	**10 %**
Fibre / Fibres 5 g	**20 %**
Soluble Fibre / Fibres solubles 0 g	
Insoluble Fibre / Fibres insolubles 5 g	
Sugars / Sucres 0 g	
Protein / Proteines 4 g	
Vitamin A / Vitamine A	**6 %**
Vitamin C / Vitamine C	**0 %**
Calcium / Calcium	**0 %**
Iron / Fer	**6 %**

Per bag": Sometimes this might say "per X-unit serving." That tells you the nutritional value per serving size. Think about whether this is the amount you usually eat before you decide if the per-serving calories, fats, nutrients are acceptable to you. Be honest.

Calories: This tells you how much energy you get from one serving (which can help you figure out how fat you're going to be after you scarf down the whole bag).

Fats—Saturated/Trans: We know now that trans fats are right out, but you still have to worry about other types of fats—keep these to a bare minimum.

Sodium: Also known as salt. Keep this to a minimum, too.

Fibre, protein, Vitamin A, iron: Load up on these and other vitamins and minerals.

Now, let's take a closer look at the supermarket, section by section.

The Produce Section

Bright, shiny, colourful, showered all day long with a soothing mist—how could anyone resist? It's good to buy here—your body will thank you. But you want to be smart about what you toss in the cart, or it will all turn to mush at the bottom of your fridge. Some suggestions:

- Don't buy those enormous bags of fruit and vegetables. Sure, they're cheaper, but really—will you eat that many kumquats? Pick out as many as you think you will eat and put them in one of the clear plastic bags grocers place around this section.
- When picking fruits, look for plumpness, tenderness, and bright colour. The paler the fare, the less healthy it is. Go for variety.

TIP: As soon as you get home from the grocery store, wash, chop, and put your veggies in see-through plastic containers. You'll be more inclined to reach for them when looking for a snack. Try not to cut more than you'll eat in two days, though, since they start losing nutrients like vitamin C as soon as they're cut.

- Don't be tempted by the high-fat, high-calorie dips and spreads that are snuggled up next to the fruits and vegetables. You'll ruin the healthiness by adding all that gunk.
- Pre-cut, pre-packaged produce is usually more expensive, but if you find you're throwing veggies out because you never get around to preparing them, go ahead and buy the bagged stuff. Salad greens or mini carrots are especially convenient, and if all you've got to do is rinse, then you'll be more likely to eat them. Even if it says pre-washed, wash it anyway.
- Pick up the fruit before you buy it. Does it feel heavy? That's good. See any mould, soft spots, bruises? That's bad. Put it back.
- Some produce just isn't worth buying in the winter. Tomatoes, for example, can be tasteless in the cold months. When buying produce, pick it up and smell it. If your tomatoes smell like earth and tomatoes, great. If not, they've probably been chemically ripened. Take a pass.
- When fruit is in season, load up. Things like strawberries freeze well, and are delicious in smoothies and oatmeal in the dead of winter. Cut the fruit up into chunks and freeze them on a baking sheet. Once they're frozen, toss them into small freezer bags to enjoy in small servings. (*Note:* watermelon, citrus fruit sections, raw

green onions, lettuce, cabbage, cucumbers, radishes, tomatoes, and other high-water–content fruit and vegetables do not freeze well. The texture and colour of raw potatoes can also change when frozen.)

- Sometimes fruit is shipped to stores before it's ripe. To ripen, place the fruit in a small, clean paper bag. Loosely close the bag and leave it at room temperature for a day or two. To speed things up, you can add a ripe apple. Check it occasionally, removing what's ripened to eat or put in the fridge.
- Avoid buying pre-cut, pre-packaged produce. It's usually more expensive and probably not as fresh—or nutritious.
- Find out when the store gets its produce delivered. Many have shipments in time for the weekend rush, so your best bet for fresh fare might be late Friday or early Saturday.

Corn

So you set out to buy some fresh ears of corn and you see them all dumped in a bin in various states of undress. Do you just pick the top half-dozen, or do you root around like everyone else? What are these people doing, anyway, ripping off the leaves and peering inside like specially trained corn doctors? Maybe this is too complicated and you should just go grab a couple of potatoes instead …

Wait! Don't give up yet! You don't need to take a course in corn inspection. Simply pick up a cob. Does it feel light and scrawny? Toss it back. If it feels thick and round, it's probably good to go. You can also pull back just the top of the husk and check the kernels. They should be all about the same size, undented, and without gaps. A few brown kernels at the end won't kill you. The silk (yellow fibres) should be moist, not brown and dried out. Eat your fresh corn as soon as you can; it will taste better. Just peel off the husks (use a damp paper towel to remove the silky stuff) and dump your corn in boiling water (you'll probably need your biggest pot) for 5 to 7 minutes. There! That wasn't hard, was it?

Been there
Done THAT

I love getting up early on Saturday morning to buy all my veggies at the farmers' market. It's way cheaper there. And it's fun. I find all kinds of weird things and I'm experimenting a bit now. I could never do that in my small town back home.

—CORINNE, 23

The Meat Department

Keep raw meat (beef, lamb, poultry, and pork) separate from other foods in your cart. Most meat comes in huge, family-sized portions—way more than you'll need. You can divide it up yourself in zippered freezer bags at home, or you can ask the butcher to package just the amount you need. Also, look for the section in the freezer aisle where the grocer has piled all the meat items that he's reduced for quick sale. This meat is still perfectly good—it's just reduced because the sell-by date is near and the store wants to clear it out.

Cuts of beef

First off, beef comes from a cow. (You knew that, didn't you?) Not all beef tastes the same, though. When butchers chop the beef into servings for the supermarket, they label it according to where it's from, as follows:

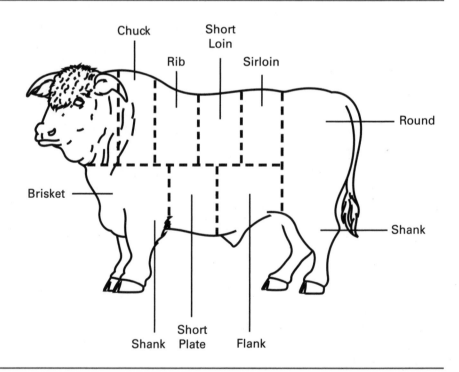

The type of cut tells you which of the cow's muscles you've got, how it should be cooked, and how long you'll need to cook it. Hard-working muscles (neck, shoulder, butt, and leg) are tougher and require long, slow, moist cooking methods, like braising, boiling, and stewing. These cuts are called *chuck, brisket, shank*, and *round*. Less-used muscles are more tender and need dry-heat methods, like sautéing, grilling, roasting, and broiling. These are the *rib, short loin*, and *sirloin* cuts. Short loin is the tastiest of all; it produces high-class restaurant steaks like Porterhouse, T-bone, and filet mignon. These will be the most expensive cuts. Save them for that heavy date.

Hamburger is made from ground beef—but not all ground beef is the same. Your burger can be made from *ground chuck* (the juiciest, because it has a high fat content), *ground round* (healthier, because it has less fat), or *ground sirloin* (also lean, but more flavourful, and more expensive, than ground round).

Still confused? Ask your butcher. (You'll find him in a white coat behind the meat counter. Ignore the blood stains; he's usually quite friendly.)

What's a "poultry"?

Poultry: that would be chicken, turkey, duck, goose, capons, and pigeon. (Yes, *pigeon.*) You'll find it in the refrigerated section near the meat counter. You're probably most familiar with the white meat (which comes primarily from breasts and wings) and dark (which comes from thighs and drumsticks). Each has a slightly different flavour; be sure to check which cut your recipe calls for. When choosing, look for poultry that is creamy-white to yellow in a package that is unbroken and cold to the touch (to reduce chances of bacterial contamination).

White meat is leaner (i.e., better for you), and skinless is leaner still. For ease of preparation, boneless, skinless chicken breasts can't be beat. You can also buy ground chicken or turkey and use it in place of beef, although it is not necessarily lower in fat than beef. If fat is something you're concerned about, then look for low-fat ground chicken or turkey.

You will likely buy chicken in larger packages than you will eat at one time. When you bring it home from the store, separate the chicken in portions you're most likely to use—one or two breasts, for example—and freeze them in freezer bags. Chop one or two breasts before freezing so you've got quick additions for a stir-fry or soup.

Poultry Parts

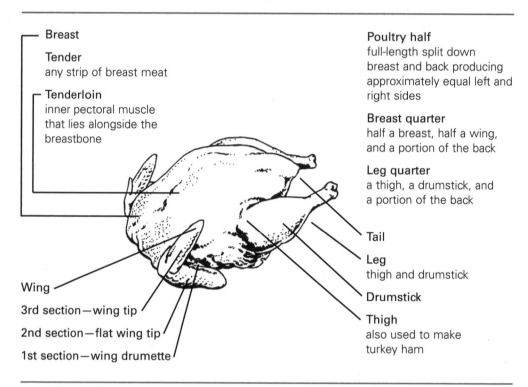

Breast

Tender
any strip of breast meat

Tenderloin
inner pectoral muscle
that lies alongside the
breastbone

Wing

3rd section—wing tip

2nd section—flat wing tip

1st section—wing drumette

Poultry half
full-length split down
breast and back producing
approximately equal left and
right sides

Breast quarter
half a breast, half a wing,
and a portion of the back

Leg quarter
a thigh, a drumstick, and
a portion of the back

Tail

Leg
thigh and drumstick

Drumstick

Thigh
also used to make
turkey ham

How to buy pork

If you haven't yet figured it out, pork is pig. You'll find pork in the meat department, divided according to the part of the pig from which it comes: the loin, the leg, the shoulder, and the belly.

The loin is the most tender and lean section. It produces pork roasts, cutlets, chops, cubes and strips, back ribs, and country-style ribs. Pork chops can be prepared quickly and are a great option when you're cooking for one. Tenderloin can be cut into cubes for kabobs or strips for stir-fry.

The leg can be cut into roasts, steaks, schnitzel, cutlets, scallopini, cubes and strips. These cuts are usually less expensive than the loin and can be made more tender by marinating or cooking in liquid.

The pig's shoulder produces the least expensive meat: the pork butt and shoulder. It's best when cooked in liquid. And the belly is where those yummy processed (but often less healthy) products come from, including side ribs (spareribs) and bacon.

You'll also find ground pork (look for lean or low fat), pork sausage (usually ground from trim or picnic shoulder), back bacon, and ham—which is usually sold fully cooked and requires only reheating.

Cuts of Pork

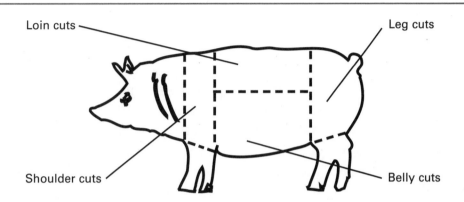

Loin cuts

Leg cuts

Shoulder cuts

Belly cuts

More than You Really Wanted to Know

Ever wonder what exactly is that mystery meat inside your humble hot dog? While each hot dog company has its own secret recipe, essentially, hot dogs are cooked sausages—or, as *Consumer Reports* likes to call them: "tidy little bundles of sodium, additives, and fat." Yum. Here's what you'll usually find inside:

- Meat (usually beef, pork, chicken, and turkey).
- Meat fat.
- "Variety meats," "meat by-products," or "mechanically separated meats (MSM)." This is where you could find the dicey stuff. A special machine forces bones, which still have edible meat attached, through a high-pressure sieve or similar device to strip away the edible remnants. What you get is a kind of pinkish "meat paste."
- Cereal filler.
- Egg white.
- Spices (onion, sugar, garlic, salt, pepper, mustard, nutmeg, etc.).
- Preservatives, colouring, MSG, and sodium nitrate.

(continued)

If you're still salivating for a frankfurter, chew on this: eating lots of processed meats like hot dogs has been linked to an increased risk of cancer and heart disease. Look for nitrate-free organic varieties, or at the very least, brands labelled "all beef" or "all pork." And don't worry—an occasional treat at the ballpark is okay. Just don't make a habit of it.

The Fish Counter

You've probably heard it before: fish is good for you. But some types of fish are better than others. To avoid ingesting too many contaminants, limit consumption of tuna steak, swordfish, shark, and marlin (they all contain mercury). If you like salmon, opt for wild salmon (which includes most of the canned product) to reduce your exposure to PCBs. Eat as much bass, clams, haddock, halibut, cooked oysters, Pacific salmon, pollock, shrimp, snapper, sole, tilapia, and trout as you want. If you don't particularly like fish, try tilapia—it's mild and doesn't taste "fishy."

When buying fish, explain to the seller how many people you want to feed and he or she will advise you about which one to buy. If the sign says "Fresh Fish," don't assume it's just been hauled off the boat. That just means it's not frozen. The freshest fish should be packed in ice, or in trays on top of ice; it should have firm, smooth, shiny flesh that bounces back when touched (if you can't touch it yourself, ask the fishmonger to poke it for you); and it should not smell fishy. Find out when the store gets its delivery, then try to shop that day.

The Bakery

Ever heard of "willpower"? You're going to need it here. Plug your nose and walk quickly. Go directly to the high-fibre fare and look for bread that offers at least 3 grams (.1 ounce) of fibre per slice. Whole wheat flour should be the first ingredient. If you find it hard to get past the treats, chew gum so the smells don't get to you. Don't forget to pick up some whole wheat tortillas—great for wraps.

TIP: Keep those grubby fingers out of the bakery bin! See the tongs hanging nearby? Use them. Pawing the pastry is rude and unsanitary.

Look for the bin that's full of day-old and reduced-price items. You can score some deals here. Inspect for mould. The shelf life of these items is limited, so what you buy here should go into the freezer for up to three months, to be withdrawn and defrosted as needed. Never store bread in the fridge. At room temperature it will stay fresh for about four days.

The Dairy Aisle

Look for "low fat" or "fat free" on the label. Watch out for yogurts that are loaded up with sugary stuff. You'll also find eggs here. Open the carton and check to see if any are cracked or dirty. (Jiggle the egg a bit. If it's cracked, it will stick to the container.) Return these containers to the shelf slightly open so the grocer knows.

At the Deli Counter

Avoid the "white" prepared salads, like macaroni and potato. They're usually high in fat. Look for salads in a vinegar dressing, like bean, coleslaw, and carrot. When buying cold meats, ask the grocer which are fresh (as opposed to processed). These will have less salt, sugar, and preservatives.

Frozen Foods

If ice cream is on your list of essentials, you might want to choose boxes of individual ice cream bars. Otherwise, you'll end up with the tub in your lap some night, the spoon mysteriously returning and returning …

This is the best place to buy juice. Frozen concentrate is usually much less expensive than ready-made. While you're here, pick up some frozen spinach. It's great to toss into just about anything, and you'll feel so nutritionally virtuous!

There will, admittedly, be some days when all you can manage is TV dinner on the couch. If you haven't planned ahead and frozen your leftovers from previous nights, then you'll be grateful to at least have something, so don't feel too guilty about buying a few ready-made dinners, or frozen entrees in one-person sizes. Plus, they're a great way to control your portions when there's no one there to say "What, you're having *more*?" Look for low-fat versions to go on sale and buy a few. But don't rely on them too often or your grocery budget will tank in no time.

Don't forget to pick up some frozen vegetables. They can be healthier than fresh when local fresh is out of season. Broccoli and cauliflower are good bets, but pick whatever you think you'll eat. One really handy item is a bag of frozen chopped onion. Try chopping an onion when you're in a hurry and you'll find out why. (For more on onion chopping, see the chapter Making It Edible.)

At the Checkout

Do your best to avoid eye contact with the chocolate bars staring you in the face as you wait in line. Take the opportunity, instead, to leaf through the magazine rack for quick decorating or workout tips, or read the tacky tabloid covers full of shock, insult, and exclamation marks and be thankful you are who you are. Check to see that each item is scanned correctly, and speak up if you notice a mistake—it happens more often than you might think. Some stores now even have checkout aisles that use price scanners instead of checkout staff—which is handy if you need to distract yourself from the chocolate bars.

Cost Cutters

- Don't shop when you are thirsty or hungry. You'll end up spending way more than you planned and you'll arrive home with food you will never eat.
- Processed foods, frozen dinners, and gourmet fare will bump up your weekly grocery bill.
- Plan a weekly menu before shopping. Don't panic-shop after work for that evening's dinner.
- If you're shopping for just a few things, take a basket, not a cart. That way you will be less tempted to throw in extras.
- Stick to groceries at grocery stores. Prices are usually higher on non-grocery items like shampoo and vitamins.
- Buying in bulk can save you money—or not. Potatoes in the 10-kilogram (or 20-pound) sack might be cheaper, but not if they go bad before you can eat them. If you love the idea of buying in bulk, get together with friends and split the goods. Make sure you have some place to store what you buy (see advice on storing below).
- Buy generic brands. Once the package is open and the glitzy advertising is gone, only your wallet will know the difference.
- Good buys: bananas and eggs—nutritious and cheap. Buy chicken thighs instead of breasts—much cheaper. Also good choices: beans, brown rice, carrots, popcorn, canned light tuna, carrots, and flank steak.
- Clip and save only those coupons that are for products you regularly use. Buying something you won't use because you have a coupon is just silly.
- Use cash to pay for food. This will force you to stay on budget and help you to avoid impulse purchases.
- Fill up on fruits and veggies. They're healthier and cheaper than packaged food. For the best deals, find a local farmers' market. Don't buy too much or it will just rot.

- Buy produce that is fresh and in season. Buying peaches in December is not smart.
- Sift through the reduced-price bin in the produce department. Stores often sell perfectly good produce dirt-cheap if a new shipment has just arrived.
- Buy day-old bread and freeze it. It will taste just as good as fresh. Only thaw what you need.
- Snobbish about tap water? Don't waste your money on bottled stuff—invest in a filtered pitcher.
- Don't be fooled by "3 for $2" specials. You don't have to buy three. If it doesn't specify otherwise (e.g., "Only Available in Quantities of 3"), then you should still be able to get one at the sale price.
- Be realistic. Are you really going to eat all that celery? If not, you might as well put your money in the garbage, because that's where the celery will go.
- Avoid the glitzy grocers and shop at no-frills stores. You might have to bag your own groceries, but the prices are often much lower.
- Eat less meat. Need protein? Learn to love beans.

TIP: If you hate crowds, shop on Monday or Tuesday. The next least-crowded time is Saturday evening. For the freshest food, shop on Friday afternoon or Saturday morning, when shelves are filled for the weekend rush. If you're shopping for fish, don't go on Sunday. Fish isn't usually delivered on weekends. Your best day, overall, is usually Wednesday.

What to Put in Your Grocery Cart

Here's a list of ingredients that you might want to keep in your kitchen. Most of these things will keep a good long time. (See specific expiry dates on page 116.)

Your Pantry

Stock your pantry with:

- *Peanut butter, jam.*
- *Rice*—brown rice is best for nutrients and fibre.

- *Olive oil*—it doesn't have to be the pricey, extra-virgin kind. You might also want canola or vegetable oil.
- *Tomato sauce*—watch for sales and stock up.
- *Dried fruits*—keep a bag in your desk or glove compartment for when the munchies hit. Some of these—like dried strawberries—actually taste better than candy. Dried cranberries are great tossed into salads or oatmeal.
- *Vinegar*—regular white is the most versatile, but cider and balsamic are nice to have, too. Just mix with a bit of olive oil for a quick, inexpensive salad dressing.
- *Canned fish*—flaked tuna or salmon is good because the breaking up work is done for you.
- *Pretzels*—these make a healthier snack than chips.
- *Chocolate syrup*—good if you don't like to drink plain milk, and it also fancies up desserts or ice creams.
- *Cereal*—if you're still craving the kiddie, sweetened brands, mix with the grown-up, fibre-rich kind for a healthier start to the day.
- *Soy sauce.*
- *Pasta*—look for the whole wheat variety. Skinny noodles are good for thin sauces, while fat shapes (like rigatoni) hold thicker sauces.
- *Chicken and beef stock or bouillon cubes*—stock up on the canned stuff when it's on sale, or make your own. Try Google for recipes; it's not hard to make.
- *Flour.*
- *Honey.*
- *A bottle of hot sauce*—if you like spicy food.

Your Freezer and Fridge

Load the freezer up with:

- Frozen veggies.
- Frozen concentrated juice—calcium-fortified.
- Frozen berries (stir into yogurt, blend into smoothies, toss onto cereal).
- Chicken breasts, lean ground beef or chicken.
- Jars, or frozen cubes, of chopped garlic and ginger. Sure, fresh garlic and ginger are inexpensive and more tasty, but the pre-chopped versions are very convenient.

And your fridge should have:

- Eggs.
- Butter.

- Milk.
- Low-fat cheese or cottage cheese.
- Bagged salad greens (romaine or mixed; iceberg isn't as nutritious).
- Low-fat milk or fortified soy milk.
- Low-fat yogurt.
- Ketchup, mustard.

Spices

It's probably best to wait until you've explored a few recipes and found out what you'll use most before you start loading up on spices. For now, pick up some salt, pepper, red pepper, Italian seasoning, garlic powder, crushed pepper flakes (for spicing up dishes), dill (for salads and roasted potatoes), dried ginger, oregano, basil, thyme, rosemary (great on chicken and fish), chili powder (good on popcorn), seasoning salt, and lemon pepper (also good on chicken and potatoes). You'll find the store-brand spices (in bags) a lot less expensive than the jars.

Once open, store spices in sealable freezer bags, away from heat, moisture, and sunlight. Test them occasionally to see if they still have their flavour. For ground spices, shake them, let them settle, and then take a sniff. If you can't smell much, toss them out.

For more on what spices go with what, visit: www.epicurious.com.

TIP: Don't shake your spices from the bottle directly onto something you're cooking. The steam will enter the container and spoil the spice's flavour. Also, once you've accidentally dumped the whole bottle of cayenne pepper into the stew, there's no going back!

Been there Done THAT

I bought a sad little dill plant at the market. It grew beautifully, so I bought a pot of parsley, then chives, and basil. I got myself a second-hand window box and before long I had the neatest little herb garden. Not only do I grow my own herbs, but I dry and package them up for Christmas, birthday, even hostess gifts.

—TESS, 20

Oils

You might have heard a lot of talk lately about different kinds of oils—which are good, which are bad, and which you shouldn't even allow into your kitchen. If you're confused, don't worry, you're not alone. Even the experts seem a little confused sometimes, because research is constantly coming up with something new. For now, we do know that some fat is good and some is bad. Here's a primer on what to look for— and what to look out for. It's a little complicated, so bear with me. It's worth it.

Fats are divided into *unsaturated fats* and *saturated fats*. Unsaturated fats are the good ones (classified as monounsaturated or polyunsaturated). Saturated fats, like butter and coconut oil, are the bad, clogging-up-the-arteries kind. Trans fats (also called partially hydrogenated oil) are also nasty. Trans fats are found naturally in some animal-based foods, as well as in semi-solid fats like shortening and hard margarine. You want to avoid it. With me so far? Olive oil, on the other hand, is your friend. A little bit each day can reduce the risk of heart disease. But don't go overboard here. It's still a fat, and it will still pack on the pounds.

When you're shopping for olive oil, "light" describes the flavour, not the calorie count. Use all oils sparingly, and instead of just pouring oil directly out of the bottle, measure it first.

- Olive oil burns more quickly than some other oils, so it's not the best for high-heat cooking.
- Canola has a more neutral taste and is a good all-purpose oil.
- Sunflower oil contains vitamin E. It's good for frying.
- Flaxseed oil is best reserved for salads because it burns easily. Keep it refrigerated.
- Sesame oil is not generally used to fry food. It has a nutty flavour and is best added to a stir-fry just before serving.

And then there's walnut oil, and peanut oil …

Okay. Deep breath. Before you go screaming out of the store, relax. You just want to know what to buy. Okay, here it is.

- Buy olive oil for salads or as an addition to cooked foods.
- Buy canola oil for frying. You probably don't need much of the other stuff for now.
- Avoid margarine, vegetable shortening, and all products made with partially hydrogenated oils.

- Steer clear of deep-fried foods that contain trans fats. (Trans fats are usually found in commercially prepared baked goods, margarines, snack foods, and processed foods, but they're gradually being phased out.)
- Want something to spread on your toast? Choose a soft tub margarine that contains little or no trans fat. Butter should be a rare treat.

What is kosher salt?

Kosher salt is used in curing meat. Jewish food laws state that Jews must not consume blood. Because of its size and shape, kosher salt absorbs moisture easily, so meat is soaked and salted in kosher salt to absorb the blood. But you don't have to be Jewish to enjoy it. There are no additives, the flavour is milder, and the size of the grains is larger than normal table salt. Give it a try, you might prefer it. Use it in recipes that call for a salt crust (and on the edge of your margarita glass). It works well on an icy sidewalk, too.

What to Do with All That Stuff You Just Bought

First of all, put it in the right place. You don't want to spend all that money just to watch your food go bad.

Produce Storage

- Apples, citrus fruits, strawberries, raspberries, grapes, pineapples, watermelon, and cherries should be stored in the fridge. Try to keep apples separate from other produce because they emit a gas that spoils other food.
- Buy only as many bananas as you think you'll eat. (You can break off two or three from the bunch in the grocery store.) Keep them on the table or the counter where you'll see them and remember to eat them. They will last longer in a closed bag. When they're a little too ripe for regular eating (spotty but not black), slice them onto yogurt or cereal, or fry them in a bit of oil and serve on pancakes or ice cream. When your bananas are seriously black, peel, wrap, and freeze for smoothies and baking later (banana bread is really easy). They'll look horrid, but taste fine. You can also store them in the fridge rather than on the counter; the skin turns brown but they're fine inside.
- Tomatoes should be stored in a cool location, out of direct sunlight—not in the fridge, which will spoil the taste.

- Potatoes and onions should be kept in a cool, dry place—not in the fridge, not under the sink—but keep them separate, because onions emit a gas that ages potatoes. If you keep an apple with your potatoes, the potatoes can last up to 8 weeks before going wrinkly.
- Plums, peaches, nectarines, pears, mango, and melon will ripen on your counter. When they get too soft, put them in the fridge and they'll last a few more days.
- Store fresh veggies in plastic bags lined with paper towels to soak up excess moisture.
- Garlic—store it in a cool, dark, dry place (it can last several weeks).
- Berries go bad quickly. Only wash as many as you can eat at a time. Washing them all at once speeds up the rotting.

TIPS:

Never store canned foods above the stove, under the sink, or anywhere else they might be exposed to extreme temperature fluctuations.

If you keep your flour in an airtight jar in the fridge it will last longer.

Pantry Shelf Life

- *Canola or vegetable oil*—tightly capped, in a cool, dry, dark place, keeps for 3 months.
- *Cereal*—2 to 3 months after being opened.
- *Chocolate*—in a cool, dry place, 1 year. (Yeah. Riiiight.)
- *Maple syrup*—1 year, refrigerate after opening.
- *Baking powder*—store in an air-tight container for up to 1 year.
- *Canned goods*—for best quality, use within 1 year.
- *Ketchup packets*—you know, the ones you swiped at the fast-food kiosk. They get yucky after 9 months.
- *Cookies, cake mixes, pasta*—up to 6 months after purchase.

The Freezer

Invest in some good sealable freezer bags and a permanent marker. Any time you cook, divide what's left over and label it, along with the date. When you buy things like chicken breasts, separate them into two or three per bag, making the package as flat as possible so that it thaws better, and toss them in the freezer.

What can you freeze?

Pretty much everything, if it's done right. Here are a few ideas:

- *Baked goods:* Wrap them in foil, then in freezer bags. Thaw at room temperature or microwave.
- *Cookie dough:* Mix up your own dough, scoop it out in spoonfuls, freeze on a tray the same way you do fruit, and when it's hardened, pop it into freezer bags. When the mood hits, you can bake them from frozen (add a few minutes to the cooking time) and pretend you're Martha Stewart.
- *Tomato sauce:* To save freezer space, ladle cooled sauce into zippered freezer bags, one to two cups per bag. Press out the excess air, and lay the bags flat to freeze. They'll stack better that way. To thaw, place the bag in a bowl of warm water until you can pour out the sauce.
- *Soup:* Freeze in one- or two-cup portions, leaving room at the top of the container for the liquid to expand. Thaw in the fridge or a bowl of water until the soup can slide out into the pot for reheating.
- *Leftovers:* Scoop into freezer bags, or in muffin tins lined with foil. When frozen, place in bags. Pop them into the microwave at work (without the foil—you know you can't put metal in a microwave, right?) for a nice hot lunch.

> **More than You Really Wanted to Know**
>
> What is "freezer burn"? That's the funny brownish bits that you find on food if you haven't wrapped it properly. Air seeps in and the food dries out. It looks gross but it won't kill you—just trim it off. Next time, re-wrap your food when you get home from the store, squeezing out as much of the air as possible.

TIPS:

Potatoes do not freeze well. They get all dark and mushy. Make sure you remove them from whatever you're freezing. And don't try to freeze lettuce or celery. It won't work.

Keep your freezer full to lower your electric bill.

Slice bagels before you freeze them. They will defrost faster and can even be toasted while still frozen. Remove them from the freezer, spread with cream cheese, and they'll thaw by lunch.

I don't know where that old myth started that you should store your batteries in the freezer. Horsefeathers! It doesn't work, and it might even damage them.

Defrosting

The experts say you should thaw your food in the fridge. That way, bacteria won't have time to grow in your food and cause trouble in your tummy. That, however, requires "advance planning," and darling, that has never been your strong point. You can always nuke the food to thaw it, of course, but if you don't have a microwave, there are other options.

Unwrap a piece of frozen meat or poultry. Place it on a heavy pan (not non-stick) and set it on the counter. The metal should absorb the warmth from the room and deliver it to the meat. In about an hour, it should be thawed. (Munch on raw carrots while you wait.) If the meat is not thawed within an hour, do not let it languish there—bacteria will have a party. Stick it back in the fridge. Or try this. Cut the food into smaller pieces (if you can—careful, it might be too hard. Use a heavy knife). Place in a zippered bag. Submerge the bag in cold (not hot, even though it's tempting) tap water, changing the water every 10 minutes until it's thawed.

The Fridge

Yippee! At last, you've got more than just orange juice and mustard in the fridge! Now doesn't that feel good? Let's see how you can make this work for you.

- Keep your fridge organized. Put similar things together.
- Regularly clear out anything past its prime. Open up storage containers occasionally and see what surprises you.
- Fruit and veggies that are refrigerated should go in the crispers (the two drawers in the bottom of your fridge). They'll stay fresh longer down there.
- Stacking plastic containers saves space.
- Pay no attention to the egg-holders and butter drawers in the door of your fridge. Eggs, butter, milk, and cheese need to be in the back of the fridge, where it's constantly cold.
- Save the door for condiments.

TIP: Lettuce gone limp? Rinse it with cold water, dab it dry with a paper towel, then stick it in the freezer for a couple of minutes. That'll perk it up. (And didn't I want to do that to you some mornings!)

- Opened white wine keeps in the fridge for about four days. If it's unopened, keep it on its side so the cork (if it has a real cork) stays moist.
- Fish and seafood should go in the coldest part of the fridge—at the bottom, at the back—in air-tight containers.

Food Safety

Before I leave you to get on with your cooking lessons, there are a few things that I have to tell you—or I won't be able to sleep tonight. First, do you know what these things mean?

- "Use by"—food tastes and looks fresh until this date.
- "Guaranteed fresh"—usually found on baked goods, targets freshness.
- "Sell by"—this is aimed at stores. You can probably eat it for another week after that date.
- "Expiry date"—after this date, throw it away.

Safe Grocery Shopping

- Buying cold cuts—shop at delis that are busy so the meat doesn't hang around very long. Buy only what you can eat in a few days. Check the best-before date on pre-packaged foods. Try to avoid cold cuts containing nitrates—they've been linked to cancer.
- Steer clear of unpasteurized beverages. Pasteurization is a heat treatment that kills harmful bacteria. Most drinks sold in Canada are pasteurized, but some juices sold at orchards, farmers' markets, roadside stands, country fairs, and juice bars are not, and carry a risk of being contaminated. Some refrigerated display cases or produce sections of stores also carry unpasteurized beverages.
- Look for "best before" dates on foods, and expiry dates on drugs and natural health products. Remember that these dates apply only to unopened items. Once they're open, consume ASAP.
- Buy perishables last so they don't have time to thaw or grow warm in your grocery cart. Keep raw meat separate. If you've got a long trip between the grocery store and home (more than 30 minutes), bring a cooler and freezer pack.
- Never buy food in packages that are torn, leaking, bulging, or past the "sell by" or expiry dates.

- Don't buy eggs from farmers' markets or small grocers that don't have expiry dates on their cartons. Make sure the eggs are in an original carton (some hobby farmers may reuse old cartons).
- Choose well-wrapped chicken from the bottom of the case, where it's coldest. Check the best-before date. At the checkout, ask that the chicken be placed in a separate bag just in case the juices leak.

Safe Produce

- Before cutting or eating fresh produce, wash it thoroughly—even if you're not consuming the peel—with running water, not soap or bleach. (Just imagine all the time those veggies spent lying in a field somewhere ... with all the cows ... on second thought, don't imagine it!) If the fruit or vegetable has a firm surface, like carrots, melons, or potatoes, scrub with a veggie brush.
- Pitch the outside leaves from cabbage and lettuce, pull apart what you need, and bathe the rest in water and a few spoonfuls of vinegar, a few leaves at a time.
- Bacteria love bruised areas on produce. Cut them out.
- Is the tomato sitting on your counter (or buried in the fridge) starting to ooze juice? Toss it.
- Steer clear of raw sprouts.
- Don't eat potatoes that are green.
- Just because the bag of salad mix or pre-cut veggies says "pre-washed" doesn't mean the produce is clean. Many recent outbreaks of illness have been linked to E. coli bacteria in bagged lettuce and spinach. Always wash, and check expiry dates, because E. coli grows quickly in deteriorating greens.

More than You Really Wanted to Know

Raw food can harbor hepatitis A, worms, parasites, viral intestinal disorders, and other diseases. Micro-organisms in raw seafood are hidden; sometimes, even experts have trouble detecting them. Freezing fish will only kill mature parasitic worms. The only way to fully kill worm eggs and other micro-organisms is by cooking. The safest way to enjoy sushi is to choose the fully cooked or vegetarian varieties.

Safe Fish and Seafood

Do you have a yen for raw fish? (Sorry, I couldn't help myself!) Here's something to think about.

Sushi

Sushi is raw fish. Raw means it is not cooked. Buy your sushi from a reputable restaurant or supermarket and eat it the same day. If it smells fishy *don't eat it!* And here's something else to worry about: bigger fish, like the tuna used to make sushi, can contain mercury, which is not good for you—it is linked with temporary memory loss in adults and can permanently damage the nervous system in an unborn child. Shorter-living seafood, like shrimp and salmon, are apparently not so risky. Just something you might want to keep in mind.

Oysters

Oysters are a nutritious food, and are great to include in your diet, but please, cook them first! Raw oysters can carry norovirus, hepatitis A virus, and vibrio bacteria.

Fish

Store fish in its original wrapper. Cook it within 1 to 2 days, or wrap it tightly and store it in the freezer. Wash hands thoroughly with hot, soapy water when handling. Thaw it in the fridge, never on the counter. If thawing fish in the microwave, cook it immediately after. Never refreeze.

Safe Fridge Storage

- Lunch meats—once you've opened them, they only last about 5 days in the fridge. Unopened, they're good for about 2 weeks. Check the expiry date.
- Milk, opened, lasts 5 days. Unopened, it's good for 2 to 5 days past the sell-by date.
- Eggs—these are complicated. Store eggs in their carton in the back of your fridge, not the door. Toss any with hairline cracks. Raw, they last 3 to 5 weeks. Once you crack open an egg, it's good for 2 more days. Hard-boiled, they last a week. Cooked egg dishes are good for 3 to 4 days.
- Leftover pizza is fine in the fridge for 2 days. On the counter, no more than 2 hours—even if it does not contain meat.

- Chinese food—4 days in the fridge.
- Cheese—hard cheeses (Parmesan, Swiss) last weeks if tightly wrapped. Sliced, they keep for 2 days. Processed cheeses—3 to 4 weeks. Soft cheeses should be tossed a week after opening.
- If mould is visible on solid cheese, trim it off, along with 2.5 centimetres (1 inch) around it. Throw out the old wrap and wrap anew. Soft cheese with mould should be tossed.
- If you see mould on more porous foods, like bread, grain, meats, dairy foods, or fruits and vegetables, throw them away.
- Raw meat or poultry should go on one of the lower shelves so that the juices don't trickle down. Cook or freeze within 2 days.
- Sour cream, opened, should last 2 to 4 weeks.
- Yogurt, opened, is okay to eat for 7 to 10 days.
- Butter is fine for 1 to 2 weeks, margarine for 4 to 6 months.

TIP: Obviously, any food that's slimy, discoloured, or "growing" should be pitched. But bacteria don't always advertise. Do not perform a taste test. When in doubt, toss it out.

- Hot dogs, opened, are good for 1 week. Cook thoroughly before eating.
- Cooked rice and pasta should be eaten or tossed in 5 days.
- Use plastic bags, or place meat, poultry, or seafood on plates so they don't drip onto other foods.
- Wipe spills immediately (especially at the bottom, where gunk lands), and every 6 months give your entire fridge a good cleaning with hot water and mild detergent.

Condiments, open in the fridge, are good for:

- Mayonnaise—3 months.
- Margarine—4 months.
- Pickles—6 months.
- Mustard—7 months.
- Ketchup—5 months.
- Cream cheese—2 weeks.
- Ranch dressing—2 months.
- Peanut butter—4 months.
- Relish—6 months.
- Soy sauce—1 year.

Safe Freezer Storage

- Use a freezer thermometer—check that your freezer temperature is no higher than –27 degrees C (–18 degrees F).

- When freezing meat or poultry, wrap it in heavy-duty foil or freezer wrap and put it inside a freezer bag, squeezing out excess air.
- Don't eat, freeze, or cook any food left out of the fridge for more than two hours.
- Never defrost food on the counter.
- If your food has brownish edges or "snow," it could be freezer burn. You can trim and still eat it, but throw it out if it smells.
- Do not freeze raw eggs in their shell.
- Ice cream will last for 2 to 3 weeks after opening.

Here's a chart to help you remember when to empty out your freezer.

Storage Chart (from "packaged on" date or purchase date from butcher)		
	Fridge	Freezer
Ground meats†/poultry, fresh seafood	1 day	2–3 months
Variety meats (e.g. liver, kidney, heart)	1-2 days	3–4 months
Stew meat, ribs, stir-fry strips, kabobs	2 days	3–6 months
Whole chicken/turkey or pieces	2–3 days	pieces 6 months whole 12 months
Steaks, roasts, chops	3 days	8–12 months
Cooked meats/poultry, cold cuts (open pkg)	3–4 days	2–3 months
Vacuum packed roasts/steaks (unopened)	See pkg date	10–12 months
Fresh shell eggs	See best before date	For egg freezing instructions visit eggs.ca

†For ground meats with longer storage time, look for packs that have a "best before date." These usually come in deeper plastic tray packs that are wrapped in a plastic that is not touching the meat. Once opened, use or freeze within one day.

And a few more dates to remember:

- Butter, in a freezer bag, should last 4 months.
- Fish—6 months.
- Shelled nuts—9–12 months (1–3 in fridge).

More than You Really Wanted to Know

A study recently in the *Journal of Food Protection* found 59 percent of fridges are cooled to a temperature above 5 degrees C (41 degrees F). Check that your fridge is at 4.4 degrees C (40 degrees F). Your freezer should be at –27 degrees C (–18 degrees F) or less. You can get a fridge thermometer at most grocery stores.

Resources

For advice on spices

www.epicurious.com

For measurement conversion charts

www.readersdigest.ca/food/metric.html

Food safety

www.foodsafety.gov
www.eatwelleatsafe.ca
www.fsis.usda.gov/OA/pubs/facts_basics.pdf

Tips, tools, and customized food guides to help you make wise food choices

www.dietitians.ca/eatwell
www.canadian-health-network.ca
www.healthyeatinginstore.ca
www.eatrackter.ca
www.eatsmart.web.ca
www.mypyramid.bov/mypyramid/index.aspx

5

Making It Edible—
How to Cook 101

Tell me what you eat and I will tell you what you are.

—ANTHELME BRILLAT-SAVARIN

You've brought home the bacon? Good! Now it's time to fry it up in the pan ... or ... something.

Can't cook? Balderdash! There is no such thing as "can't cook." There is such a thing as "no experience," but that can be fixed, easy. Just ... cook! And cook again. Yes, you will mess up. You will try to make whipped cream and nearly turn it into butter. You will add too much spice, overcook, undercook, and burn your fingers. Who cares? So you try again. And you get better. Whatever you do, don't get discouraged, reach for the cereal box, and call it quits.

Before we give you some recipes to try, let's look at the cooking basics.

Reading a Recipe

Ingredients are the food items that you will need to create your masterpiece. The recipe lists them in the order in which you'll use them. Read through the entire recipe before you start to be sure you have all the ingredients and tools you'll need, and the time to make it.

When you're just learning to cook, it's important to stick with the exact measurements and instructions. As you become more experienced, though, you'll be able to tinker a bit. And remember, when you're

TIP: Pick up a children's cookbook. They explain what all the cooking terms mean, and many include pictures of the pans, utensils, cooking gadgets, and techniques the recipes call for.

cooking, you're cooking. You're not watching TV, surfing the Internet, or hanging out with your friends down the hall. If nothing else, you'll need to stir on occasion and make sure your pot doesn't boil over, so hang around and don't let yourself get distracted.

Cooking Glossary

- *Al dente*—referring to pasta, it means slightly undercooked, chewy. It can also refer to vegetables that are cooked till tender but still crispy.
- *Bake/roast*—to cook in an oven. Roasting is usually done at temperatures above 450 degrees F, while baking is done at lower temperatures.
- *Baste*—slathering a sauce, marinade, or drippings over the food while cooking, to add flavour and moisture.
- *Beat*—mix quickly, sometimes with an electric mixer or beater.
- *Blanch*—immerse in hot water and cook briefly.
- *Boil*—oh come on, you know this! The liquid has to have big bubbles that break the surface. Anything less is a simmer (see below).
- *Broil*—Your oven should have a "broil" setting. Raise the oven rack to the highest, or second-highest shelf, turn to broil, and cook the food close to the heat source. Use the broiler pan that came with the oven (it catches the drips) or use a wire rack on a rimmed baking sheet.
- *Brown*—to cook meat until it's turned that colour.
- *Chop*—cut into coarse pieces.
- *Cream*—usually involves butter and sugar, in baking; beat together until creamy.
- *Cube*—cut into 13-millimetre ($^1/_2$-inch) pieces.
- *Dice*—cut into 4- to 6-millimetres ($^1/_8$- to $^1/_4$-inch) cubes.
- *Divided*—when you see this, it means the ingredient is not added all at once, but rather in portions, as described in the recipe.
- *Dredge*—coat in a dry mixture like bread crumbs or flour.
- *Fillet*—any meat, poultry, or fish that is boneless and cut thinly.
- *Fold*—gently add another ingredient and "fold" it in with a spatula, without over-mixing.
- *Fry*—cook in a pan with little sauce or fat.
- *Mince*—cut into little tiny pieces.
- *Poach*—cook in liquid. This is usually done with eggs or fish. Heat is kept low to simmer (only an occasional bubble appears on the surface).

- *Purée*—blend until smooth. With vegetables, cook until tender, then blend; add a little oil and Parmesan and you've got a nice thick soup.
- *Reduce*—simmer until much of the liquid has evaporated and the flavours are condensed.
- *Sauté*—like frying, constantly stirring until cooked.
- *Scallions*—also known as green onions.
- *Sear*—meat is cooked over higher heat to get a tasty crust and seal in juices.
- *Shallots*—kind of a cross between onions and garlic.
- *Simmer*—cook liquid at just "below the boil"—tiny bubbles, no big rolling motion.
- *Slice*—cutting thinly across.
- *Stir-fry*—Asian method of cooking small pieces of food, stirring constantly over high heat in a small amount of oil in a large, deep, bowl-shaped pan.
- *Steam*—to cook food over (not in) a small amount of boiling water, with a tightly closed lid. A good way to retain nutrients in vegetables.
- *Stock*—the liquid in which meat, poultry, fish, or vegetables are cooked for a long time. You can also buy stock in cans or as bouillon cubes and add to hot water.

Some Basic "How-Tos"

How to Boil Water

Don't laugh. I really am going to teach you how to boil water. We're going to do this right, in four easy steps:

1. You'll need water. Cold water. Not hot. You might think you're speeding things up by getting water hot from the tap, but you could be getting extra sediment from the water heater. Yum. Get the good, clean, cold stuff. Fill your pot—but not to the top, it will boil over.

2. Place the pot on the stove and turn the heat to high. Put on the lid so the heat doesn't escape.

3. When you start to hear noise coming from the pot, check it out. If there are just tiny bubbles forming at the edges of the water at the surface, put the lid back on. It's not ready yet.

4. Check again. When you see steady, big bubbles rolling up from the bottom, you're good to go.

How to Peel Produce

1. Rinse and dry the fruit or vegetable.
2. With thin-skinned food (carrots, parsnips, potatoes, apples) use a swivel peeler. Hold the food on the cutting board and scrape down and away from yourself, turning as you go.
3. Poke out any bruises—or, with your potatoes, the "eyes"—with the round edge of the peeler.
4. Rinse again.

How to Chop an Onion

1. Cut a thin slice off the top (non-root end) of the onion.
2. Make a shallow, vertical cut down one side, and another on the other side. The papery skin should now pull back easily. Peel off any tough outer layers, too.
3. Cut the peeled onion in half, lengthwise from the top toward the root end.
4. Place the halved onion cut side down on the cutting board.
5. Make several horizontal cuts parallel to the board, stopping just before you cut all the way through the root.
6. Make several vertical cuts from the top to root end, again, stopping just before you hit the root.
7. Cut cross-sectionally so the onion falls into small pieces.
8. Repeat with the other half.

More than You Really Wanted to Know

Why does onion-chopping make you cry? Chopping releases the sulfides in onions, which react with your eye fluids. It makes them sting. Your eyes water because they are trying to get rid of the chemicals.

How do you prevent this? Well, you can wear goggles. You can chew bread while you chop, hold a cookie between your teeth, or chew mint-flavoured gum. You can try breathing only through your nose. But don't try holding a lit match between your teeth. Whoever came up with that idea was nuts! My best advice? Keep your onions in the fridge. That, a sharp knife, and lots of practice should keep you dry-eyed.

How to Do Something with That Garlic

1. Garlic comes in "buds," covered in a papery peel like an onion's. You don't eat that peel. Remove it by pulling a "clove" from the bud, placing it on a cutting board, slicing off the tough root, and then pushing down on the clove with the flat surface of the knife near the handle. This should loosen the peel enough for you to pull it away. Now you're ready to slice or mince.

   TIP: To keep garlic from sticking to your knife when you mince, dunk the blade in water first.

2. To slice garlic, cut crosswise in thin slivers.

3. To mince, pile the slices into a heap and rock your knife back and forth through them. You'll need to keep gathering them back into a pile. Repeat until the pieces are fine. Or, if you have a "mincer" or "garlic press" (a gadget available at kitchen hardware stores), place the peeled clove in the box container and squeeze. Scrape the pieces out with the tip of your knife.

How to Chop Bell Peppers

1. Wash and dry the peppers.
2. Cut off the top of the pepper as close to the stem as possible. Trim off the green stem and discard, keeping the pepper parts.
3. Trim out the innards with the tip of your knife. Pull them out of the pepper and discard.
4. Cut the remaining "shell" in quarters, removing any leftover seeds or membrane.
5. With the skin side down, cut each quarter into strips. If you want the pepper diced, line the quarters up and slice across.

How to Peel Tomatoes

1. Put a pot of water on to boil.
2. Wash the tomatoes. Cut a large X in the bottom of each one, just deep enough to break the skin.
3. When the water's boiling, immerse each tomato in the water for 20 seconds, then remove with a slotted spoon.
4. Rinse under cold water to cool the tomatoes. The skin should now peel away easily.

How to Cook Pasta

1. Find the biggest pot you own. Fill it with water, about two-thirds full. Salt is optional.

2. When the water is boiling, add the pasta and cook according to the directions on the package. Keep the pot uncovered, and stir occasionally. Some long pastas might extend out of the pot. As the pasta heats it will bend and you can push it in with a spoon until it's submerged.

3. At around 8 minutes, taste the pasta. First, run it through cold water so you don't burn yourself. If it's chewy, then it's *al dente*, and probably done.

4. Turn on the cold water tap in the sink (make sure there are no dirty dishes hanging out there) and put your colander or strainer in the bottom of the sink. Carefully carry the pot over and dump the contents into the colander or strainer. The cold water should be running down the drain, and not into the pasta—it will keep the boiling pasta water from wrecking the pipes. Don't rinse the pasta unless you're making pasta salad.

About half a kilogram (one pound) of pasta feeds four adults. Don't worry about making too much—you can always use it tomorrow.

Duh moment!

Don't cook drunk. Really. Fires start that way. Big fires.

Putting It All Together

As a fledgling cook, you're probably facing a few particular challenges. For starters, you are often cooking for just one person—yourself. And just to make it more complicated, you probably have a kitchen the size of a broom closet. And it probably doesn't help that you haven't got a clue what you're doing.

TIP: When following recipes, try not to make substitutions—at least not until you've had a few years' cooking experience under your belt. Switching tomato paste for tomato sauce, for example, or garlic powder for garlic salt, or baking soda for baking powder, could turn your culinary creation into something for the trash.

Sure, you can order out. But darling, you are capable of so much more. So rise above. Tackle these challenges. Your belly will thank you.

Cooking for One

You live in a large-scale world, where bigger is better. So what do you do when you face big bags and boxes of everything, recipes aimed at families of four, and veggies that die in your fridge before you have a chance to eat them? Here are some suggestions.

- Many grocers will divide meat purchases into smaller packages if you ask. Buy the family pack of pork chops or ground meat, for example, and ask them to shrink-wrap it into smaller portions for freezing. Smile nicely. Say thank you.

- If you miss big, home-cooked meals, make them anyway, divide them into single servings, and freeze. Rather than try to convert your recipes to serve one, do the recipe up in full. As soon as the meal's cooled, freeze all but one serving. That way you aren't tempted to just dig in and finish the whole batch at once. Or share with friends— maybe you can set up a cooking co-op. Take turns making meals for the night.

> **TIP:** To open tough-to-open jars, use a rubber shelf liner (available at hardware and dollar stores) for a better grip, or lightly tap the edge of the lid with a butter knife handle to break the suction.

- Bored with leftovers? Get creative. You don't have to just keep reheating the stuff until you're sick of it. Fancy it up a bit. Leftover pasta is a good addition to soup, for example. It also tastes great pan-fried in some butter or oil. If you've got a mess of rice and some broccoli sitting around, type both into your search engine along with "recipes" and see what comes up. (For more leftover ideas, see page 155.)

- If you find you're not eating much salad because you never quite get around to tearing up the lettuce, wash and tear it as soon as you get home from the store. (See page 115 to learn how.) You're more likely to eat your salad if it's ready and waiting for you when hunger calls. Store it in the salad spinner (which is a nifty gadget that spins the lettuce dry), or in a zippered bag with a paper towel to absorb the moisture.

- Too tired to cook? Keep healthy snacks around. Admit that you're going to falter some nights and end up grazing, then prepare ahead. Make sure that what's lying around isn't so bad—like cut-up vegetables, dried fruit, cheese strings, and hummus.

- What's the point? If you're not motivated to cook without an audience, make yourself the audience. Throw together something special just for you. Light a candle, pour some wine, eat your favourite home-cooked meal, and savour the fact that you made this because you wanted to.

Single-serving meal ideas

Any one of these is quick, easy, and small. Just make sure you include all four food groups.

- Prepare a grilled cheese with cold cuts tucked inside.
- Fry up some ground beef/chicken/turkey/tofu with herbs, drain the fat, add some veggies, and cook until tender.
- Make scrambled eggs and toast.
- Make mini pizzas on bagels, English muffins, or pita bread.
- Crack open a can of salmon, mix with an egg, bread crumbs or crushed crackers, a spoonful of mayonnaise or milk, and a few herbs. Make this into patties and fry in a bit of oil.
- Try an omelet with whatever leftovers you've got from last night.

TIP: You might be missing out on protein because meat comes in large packages and takes effort to prepare. Keep canned fish and beans in the cupboard as backups.

The "Dos" and "Don'ts" of Cooking in a Cubicle

It is possible to eat grandly while cooking humbly. Some "Dos" and "Don'ts" for your humble hovel.

- **Do** shop more often. You just won't have the space to store up a full week's worth of food along with the staples.
- **Do** organize your kitchen. You haven't got the luxury of wasted space. Be efficient. IKEA has great ideas. (For more on kitchen storage, see Chapter 4.)
- **Do** cook efficiently. Chop everything first. Clear away the peels and discards, wipe the counters down, and start the next task with a clean slate.
- **Don't** think you're stuck with just a hot plate if you've got no room for a full-sized stove. What about an electric griddle? A George Foreman Grill? These plug-ins can be used, then shoved back into a cupboard when you're done. (Cooled off first, of course!)

- **Don't** fill your kitchen with non-food items. That pile of paperwork—file it. The junk drawer—de-junk it. Purse, briefcase, newspapers—put them in another room.
- **Don't** imagine you need every nifty appliance ever advertised on the Home Shopping Network. Save the trendy gadgets for your "I've Made It" mansion.
- **Don't** just stack the dirty pots, pans, and bowls in the sink for later. You'll have a kitchen full of dirty stuff and nowhere to finish preparing the meal. Clean as you go.

TIP: Cooking greasy food can stink up your apartment—and even the hallways outside. Try leaving a bowl of white vinegar on the counter for a few hours. If you can't wash the greasy pan right away, leave it in a sink filled with soap, water, and vinegar to soak up the odour.

Recipes and Meal Planning

When you are planning a meal, don't forget about the Canada's Food Guide Rainbow. You'll want to try to include in each meal:

- Grain products.
- Vegetables and fruit.
- Milk products.
- Meat and alternatives.

But none of this is very helpful if you don't have recipes to tell you how to cook them!

One of the best ways to collect good recipes is by word-of-mouth. Your buddy threw together some weird concoction that you really liked? Ask for the recipe. Auntie Hortense makes a scrumptious plum pie? Get her to tell you how—she'll be delighted. Know someone who's a good cook? Ask for lessons. They'll be flattered! And if the recipes don't turn out, don't throw in the tea towel. Learn from your mistakes.

When you find a recipe you like, save it in one of those photo album binders with the sticky clear pages. You can organize them in any way you like. When you're ready to start cooking, take the page you need out of the binder. The plastic covering will keep it safe from spills. Wipe it clean with a wet washcloth and put it back when you're done.

This is not a cookbook, but here are a few recipes to get you started. Also, check out the Internet—especially www.allrecipes.com, which includes feedback from other cooks and advice on how to make a recipe your own.

A few basic ideas to keep in mind:

- Think about timing. Turn on the oven first so it has time to warm up. Start the water boiling while you chop. Think about what you're preparing, how long each food will take, and how to time it so that everything's done at the same time. This takes some practice.
- The smaller and thinner the food, the faster it will cook. If you're rushed, or just plain hungry, chop the potatoes into quarters, cut up the chicken rather than cooking it whole, choose angel hair pasta rather than penne.
- Use a timer. Sure, you can tell yourself you'll remember to take the dish out of the oven in 20 minutes, but we all know you better than that. Listen for the beep.

TIP: Don't pick a recipe that calls for something you need to buy, use just a teaspoon, then leave it to get mouldy in the back of the fridge.

- Many recipes don't specify how much salt and pepper to add. This is not to annoy you. It's because they assume everyone has individual tastes. Until you gain some cooking confidence, just add a tiny bit. You can always add more when it's on the table—but you certainly can't take it out once it's in. (Although, if you do mess up and dump a load of salt in, you can try adding a raw potato. It might soak up the saltiness.)

Breakfast

You're right—it's crazy to leave the warmth of your cozy bed to start messing about in a dark kitchen when you're not even hungry, much less awake. And yes, it's even crazier if you've got to get dressed for work or an early-morning class as well. But your body needs you! Your metabolism slowed down while you were sleeping. Breakfast is the kick-start it needs, and it needs it fast—within two hours of waking. Otherwise you'll be famished by lunch, pig out, eat way more than your body can handle, and store the extra as fat.

You hate breakfast. You need breakfast. What to do? Make breakfast brainless. Planning is everything.

Make sure your breakfast contains food from at least three of the four food groups—grains (whole wheat toast, cereal, or oatmeal), fruit, some form of protein, and milk or yogurt or cheese. Taking the easy way out—grabbing a diet Coke and a Pop-Tart—will only send you on an energy spike, and then a mid-morning crash.

Some morning ideas:

- An orange, cheese, and a handful of pecans.
- Peanut butter spread on a whole wheat tortilla, with a banana rolled up inside.
- Add skim milk to instant powdered breakfast, some frozen fruit, and yogurt. Blend and go.
- Whole-grain toast or bagel with cream cheese.
- Mix together scrambled eggs, salsa, and grated cheese. If you're running out the door, roll it up in a tortilla or pita.
- Make up some oatmeal—the old-fashioned way takes time but is healthiest, or try the instant oatmeal packs if you're rushed. Add some dried fruit or nuts. Or cottage cheese and cinnamon and nutmeg.

> **TIP:** For super-fluffy pancakes, follow the recipe on the pancake mix but substitute club soda for water.

- Cereal—with milk, fruit, and protein on the side. Look for cereals with less than 12 grams (.4 ounce) of sugar per serving.
- Yogurt or cottage cheese mixed with trail mix, fruit, or bran cereal.
- Nothing wrong with warmed-up leftovers from last night's dinner.
- Toast a frozen whole wheat waffle, spread it with peanut butter, and sprinkle it with raisins.
- If you must rely on an energy bar (it's better than nothing), look for one that has at least 3 grams (.1 ounce) of fibre and 10 grams (.35 ounce) of protein.

How to cook eggs

Cracking an egg: Gently bang the egg on a flat surface to start the crack. (Don't break eggs on the edge of a pan or table; doing that can push the shell inside and break the yolk.) Insert your thumb in the little opening and break the rest of the shell directly above the bowl. Practise when you're not pressed for time.

> **TIP:** If you spill an egg, dump some salt on it for easy clean up.

Boiled: Put your eggs in a pot and cover with cold water. Add a pinch of salt. Bring the pot to a boil. Lower the heat and simmer 2 to 3 minutes for a soft-boiled egg, about 4 to 5 minutes for medium, and 15 to 20 minutes for hard-boiled. Remove eggs with a slotted smooth and immerse immediately in cold water to stop the cooking.

Fried: Put a small amount of butter or oil in a pan and turn the burner to medium. When you can drop a drop of water into the pan and hear it sizzle, the pan is hot enough. Crack the eggs into the pan (or, if you don't trust yourself yet, into a bowl, then gently pour them into the pan). For sunny-side-up eggs, allow them to cook for about 3 to 4 minutes on one side. If you prefer sunny side down, cook for 2 minutes before using your spatula to flip the eggs over and cooking a minute or two more.

Scrambled: Beat your eggs in a bowl. Add a spoonful of milk, and salt and pepper according to your own taste. Heat a small amount of butter or oil in the pan over medium heat. Pour the eggs into the pan and cook, while gently stirring, until the eggs are light and fluffy, about 4 minutes. Or, if you're really in a hurry, dump the egg into a mug, add some salt and pepper and a bit of milk, stir, and microwave for one minute. Remove and stir, then continue to nuke it and stir it in 30-second increments until cooked. (About 2 to 3 minutes.)

Poached: Fill a small pot or pan with about 5 centimetres (2 inches) of water and bring it to a simmer. Add a few drops of vinegar (to help the egg whites hold together). Break an egg into a small bowl. Stir the simmering water like a whirlpool, and while it continues to spin, gently drop the egg into the centre. Immediately reduce the heat so the water barely moves. Cook for 3 to 5 minutes before removing the egg with a slotted spoon.

Here are some new breakfast ideas to try when you've got time to plan ahead:

Mini bread pudding: Before your old bread gets too stale, mix 2 eggs, 125 millilitres ($^1/_2$ cup) milk, and 10 millilitres (2 teaspoons) of honey in an ovenproof bowl. (Check the bottom of the bowl; it should say whether it's ovenproof or not.) If you have berries, add some. Add your leftover bread and let it soak overnight. In the morning, stick it in the oven, uncovered, and bake at 160 degrees C (325 degrees F) for 20 minutes.

Cheese/eggs 'n' ham: Grate 125 millilitres ($^1/_2$ cup) cheddar cheese. Set aside. Heat a small amount of butter in a pan. Add 125 millilitres ($^1/_2$ cup) diced cooked ham or any cold-cut meat to the pan and stir until browned. Add the uncooked scrambled egg mixture. Cook as described above for scrambled eggs. Just before the eggs look done, add the cheese and 25 millilitres (2 tablespoons) of chopped chives.

Mexican eggs: Grate 75 millilitres ($^1/_3$ cup) Monterey Jack cheese. Make basic scrambled eggs. Just before the eggs are cooked, stir in the cheese. Then, when the eggs are fully cooked, add 50 millilitres ($^1/_4$ cup) salsa (drain excess liquid first) and 125 millilitres ($^1/_2$ cup) crushed tortilla chips.

French toast: Melt a small amount of butter in a pan over medium-low heat. In a small bowl, stir 1 egg and 5 millilitres (1 teaspoon) of milk with a fork. Dip 1 piece of bread in the egg mixture, then place it in the frying pan. Brown on both sides. Serve with syrup, jam, or dip in vanilla yogurt.

Muffin madness: To avoid having to butter and ladle muffins in individual tins (when you really have much better things to do), make a double batch of muffins and dump it all into a 20- by 30-centimetre (9- by 13-inch) pan. It might take longer to bake, so keep an eye on it. (It's done if, when you push gently in the centre, it bounces back.) Cut into pieces. Wrap individually and freeze.

Westerns-on-the-run: Spray non-stick spray into muffin tins. Crack an egg into each tin, then sprinkle in chopped veggies and cold cuts. Top with grated cheese. Bake 12 to 15 minutes at 180 degrees C (350 degrees F). When cooled, freeze in zippered bags. Microwave 30 seconds for a quick breakfast with toast.

Lunch

Here are some ideas to make lunch easier:

- Buy a bag of quick-cooking oats. Put 125 millilitres ($^1/_2$ cup) in a plastic zippered bag along with a pinch of cinnamon and nutmeg. Keep it in your desk so that all you need is 250 millilitres (1 cup) of boiling water and a bowl and you've got a hot and filling snack.
- Find an inexpensive local ethnic food restaurant. Order a large serving of your favourite dish, take it home, and divide it into three smaller servings. Freeze and bring to work.
- More things to keep in your desk: peanut butter, English muffins, bagels, crackers, instant soup in a cup, dried fruit, and nuts.

TIP: Once a week hard-boil a few eggs and stick them in the fridge. Then you've got some ready protein for breakfast, a snack for the office, or the fixings for an egg salad sandwich.

Funky grilled cheese: Toast two frozen waffles. Spread one side with mustard, the other side with butter. Place ham and cheese in between. Cook in a buttered pan, pressing to make the cheese melt. It should take 3 to 4 minutes.

Spinach and pita dip: Thaw and squeeze out the water from a 275-gram (10-ounce) box of frozen spinach. Purée with 375 millilitres ($1\frac{1}{2}$ cups) of store-bought hummus. This is good with pita bread cut into triangles and toasted with a bit of olive oil.

Yogurt veggie dip: Take one single serving of plain yogurt and mix in one packet of dried salad dressing (Club House Herbs & Spices or Ranch is great.) Dip. Eat.

How to make your basic, garden-variety salad

Start with the green stuff—otherwise known as lettuce. You can stick with the boring "head lettuce" or "iceberg lettuce," if you want, but that's not the most nutritious, or tasty, choice. Why not live on the edge? Buy some of that weird-looking green stuff sitting on the shelf next to it. You can get mixed greens, romaine, baby spinach … the choices are endless, and they're all packed with vitamins and antioxidants and other good-for-you stuff.

Even if you're buying it in a bag that says "pre-washed," wash it anyway. The best way is to "float" the greens. That means you fill up a clean sink or a big bowl with cold water and swish the torn-up greens around to loosen the dirt. Next, put them in a salad spinner, if you have one, and spin; alternatively, pat them with paper towels until dry. If you won't be eating until later, wrap the greens in a paper towel and put them in a plastic bag in the fridge.

Dinner

The nutritionist Adelle Davis used to say that you should "Eat breakfast like a king, lunch like a prince, and dinner like a pauper." But most of us like to end the day with the most comforting meal, usually (at least for non-vegetarians) including some meat or fish. Here are some ideas that might help.

The basic burger

Buy fresh, or thaw if pre-frozen, some ground beef. (For more on buying ground beef, see page 105.) Add a little pepper, or go a little further and try mixing in some minced onion, barbecue sauce, Worcestershire sauce, garlic, soy sauce, hot sauce, or jalapeños. Use your imagination.

Mix with your well-washed hands until just combined, then gently mould the meat into patties. Don't worry about the perfect shape—you want to handle the meat as little as possible. Just don't make the patties too thick or they won't cook on the inside. Aim for $1/2$-inch thick, and slightly larger than your bun, as the burgers will shrink as they cook. Take any of the patties you won't be cooking today, put them on a baking sheet and freeze until solid, then transfer them to a freezer bag.

Remember: after touching raw meat, wash your hands well.

To cook the patties, you can use the stove or barbecue grill. If you're using your stove, preheat the skillet (cast iron, if you have one) on medium-high. Place as many patties as can fit without crowding in the skillet and cook for a couple of minutes until the top starts to ooze juice. Then flip them with a spatula and continue cooking until browned. They're done when the inside is no longer pink and juices run clear. (If you have a food thermometer, temperature at the thickest part should reach 71 degrees C (160 degrees F).) If you're using a barbecue, spray the grill with non-stick spray or brush with oil before turning it on. Cook on medium heat. Never push down on the burgers with your spatula; you'll press out all the yummy juices.

How to cook with ham

Small cooked hams available in shrink-wrapped packages in the meat department might look bigger than your belly can handle, but leftovers can be done up many ways. Start with this recipe:

TIPS:
To reduce the chance of your burgers being contaminated by E. coli (a really nasty bacteria that can make you very sick), the ground beef should be completely cooked. However, cooking at high temperatures can cause the formation of carcinogens (which cause cancer). It's enough to make a person switch to tofu! But that's not necessary. Just lower the cooking temperature to medium and flip every minute until done. You can substitute healthier ground turkey or chicken in most recipes calling for ground beef.

SPICED HAM

1 ham	

Glaze:	
1/2 cup mustard	125 ml
1/2 cup brown sugar	125 ml
1/4 cup honey	50 ml
1/4 cup orange juice	50 ml
1 tsp cloves	5 ml

Mix ingredients. Preheat oven according to the directions on package. Make some deep slices with a knife across the top of ham. Put the ham in a shallow baking or casserole dish. Pour glaze mixture over the ham and stick it in the oven. Baste occasionally as you bake, according to the package directions.

And now that you have leftover ham:

- Top a tortilla with chopped ham, salsa, and cheddar cheese and warm it up for a hot ham and cheese sandwich.
- Dice and toss it into omelets.
- Cut it up and sprinkle it on your salad.
- Mix it into cooked green beans, scrambled eggs, potato soup.
- Sprinkle it on pizza with drained pineapple from a can.
- Throw some onto baked potatoes with grated cheese.
- Mix with cooked pasta and cream of chicken soup (don't add water). Bake 20 minutes at 180°C (350°F). Sprinkle with grated cheddar cheese and return it to the oven until the cheese melts.

HOW TO MAKE CHICKEN SOUP

Start with 500 millilitres (two cups) of chicken broth. If you don't have any home-made broth, low-sodium canned is fine. Slowly bring it to a gentle boil on the stove. While it is heating, chop some onion and a big carrot, and if you have them, a tomato, potato, and mushrooms. Add 5 to 10 millilitres (one to two teaspoons) of poultry seasoning. (You'll find it in the spice aisle at the grocery store. This is optional, but guaranteed, it'll make it taste better than Grandma's.) When the broth is bubbling, lower the heat to medium-low. Add the veggies. You can also add cooked or raw (diced) chicken and rice, or pasta. Simmer, covered, until the veggies are soft and the chicken is cooked through, about 20 minutes. (To determine if the chicken is cooked, take out a piece, put it on a cutting board, and slice it open. It should be white inside.) Add salt and pepper and serve.

Want to try another soup recipe?

YOUR CHEATIN' SOUP

Crack open a can of veggie juice. Pour it into a pot and heat. Sprinkle with a little basil. If you have some skim milk powder on hand, add a little to make it a more well-rounded meal—you'll get a dose of calcium and vitamins A and D. Experiment to get a taste you like.

TIP: For an easy side dish, try boiling your favourite pasta, drain, then add a bit of butter or olive oil and shake on some grated Parmesan cheese and a touch of Italian seasoning, basil, or thyme.

Vegetables

I know it's not way up on your list of priorities—you've got places to go, people to see. But you need your veggies. For vegetables and fruit, Canada's Food Guide recommends 7 to 8 daily servings for young women, 8 to 10 for young men. Just do it, okay? It's not so hard once you make it a habit.

Remember, just because a vegetable is fresh doesn't mean it's more nutritious than frozen. Vegetables lose their nutrients during shipping and storage, and even more when they sit neglected in your fridge. Frozen vegetables, on the other hand, are usually picked ripe and flash-frozen, so they retain nutrients better.

Greens are something you should eat several times a week. You know about salad, of course, but there are other options worth trying, like cabbage, turnip greens, kale, and Swiss chard. Wash, cut off the stems, and place the greens in a large pan with a few spoonfuls of water and olive oil. Add a little garlic salt and sauté until limp. Leftovers are great tossed in soup.

Don't be afraid of the weird veggies—rutabagas, turnips, beets, parsnips, and yams. They're great for you and usually available when other more fair-weather fare is not. These winter vegetables taste delicious roasted. Just peel them, cut them into cubes (use

TIP: Some winter vegetables, like turnip and
squash, are hard to cut.
To keep from slicing your
hand open, nuke the veggie
whole for a few minutes
to soften it. It should be
easier to cut.

a sturdy knife), toss with olive oil, salt, and pepper
(and thyme or rosemary if you have it), put them in a
casserole dish, cover it, and bake at 200 degrees C (400
degrees F) for 20 minutes. Remove the cover, stir, and
bake for 30 minutes more.

How to cook squash: Look for the butternut or
acorn variety (if you're not sure which is which, ask
your grocer for help). Set the oven to 190 degrees C
(375 degrees F). Cut the squash in half with a sturdy
knife, scoop out the seeds and stringy innards (for the garbage), and bake face down
in a baking dish, with 125 millilitres ($^1/_2$ cup) of water for 45 minutes. Scoop out the
cooked insides (don't eat the peel) into a bowl, add some olive oil or butter, salt, and
pepper.

How to steam veggies: Fill a pot with about 2.5 centimetres (1 inch) of water. (You
can add half a cube of chicken or vegetable bouillon for more flavour.) Put a steamer
basket inside the pot, then put the lid on and turn the stove on to high. When the
water comes to a boil, add veggies (cut-up carrots, broccoli, cauliflower, etc.). Replace
the lid, turn the heat to low, and cook for about 5 minutes, until the veggies are tender.

TIPS:

Add frozen broccoli florets to sautéed onion and garlic. Toss with cooked pasta
and freshly grated Parmesan.
Just about any veggie is great on the barbecue, drizzled with a little olive oil.
You might need to use a special grate to keep smaller fare, like mushrooms,
from falling onto the coals.

You might also want to try:

REFRIGERATOR BEAN SALAD

Drain a can of chickpeas. Add any chopped veggies you have on hand. Pour in some
vinaigrette salad dressing. You can serve as is, or add boiled pasta. This will keep for
several days in the fridge.

Things to do with potatoes

Boiled: If you wash the potatoes really well, it's not necessary to peel them. In fact, the peel is a good source of fibre. Cut larger potatoes into quarters. In a heavy saucepan, cover the potatoes with water. Cover with a lid. Turn the heat to high. When the water boils, reduce the heat to low and simmer for 20 minutes, or until the potatoes seem tender when you pierce them with a fork. Uncover and drain into a sieve. (Just as you did with the pasta, make sure you've got the tap running cold water into the sink so you don't wreck the pipes.)

Mashed: Boil peeled potatoes as described above and drain. Mash them with a masher or beat with a mixer, adding milk until fluffy. Add butter, salt, and pepper. Mashed potatoes can be made with any potato you like, depending on how you like them. Prefer them light and fluffy? Then you'll want to go with your basic old high-starch Idaho or russet potatoes—you know, the big ones with the rough brown skin. Want your mashed potatoes to be creamy-smooth and dense? Go for a higher-moisture potato—like the red-skinned kind. Yukon Golds are good if you don't want to add much butter but want to pretend it's there. (Okay, it works for some.) And if you can't decide, mix it up.

TIPS:
Potatoes cook faster when they're cut in quarters. Peeled potatoes will turn brown if left exposed to the air for a while. No big deal. But if you don't like the colour, place them in a pot of cold water until you're ready to use them.

Microwaved: Pierce the potatoes with a fork. Place them on a paper towel or microwaveable plate. Cook 1 medium potato 4 to 6 minutes on high. Turn halfway through cooking. Let stand 5 minutes.

Roasted: Preheat oven to 220 degrees C (425 degrees F). Cut potatoes into 2- to 3-centimetre (1-inch) pieces. Toss in a bowl with enough olive oil to coat them. Stir in salt and pepper and herbs like parsley, rosemary, or thyme. Arrange in one layer on a baking pan. Roast 20 to 40 minutes until tender, stirring occasionally.

Baked: Best for baking are Idaho or russet potatoes. Preheat oven to 200 degrees C (400 degrees F). Wash unpeeled potatoes and pierce them with a fork to allow steam to escape. Bake on an oven rack or baking sheet for 1 hour until tender.

Feeling more adventurous? Try this recipe:

HEALTHY FRENCH FRIES

1 large russet potato	
Olive oil	
Seasoning salt	

Preheat oven to 450°F. Scrub potato. Cut into strips. Toss with olive oil, then sprinkle with seasoning. Bake 8 minutes per side for thin fries, 15 for fat, until lightly browned.

Chicken

SPICY FAKE CHICKEN WINGS

2–3 chicken breasts	
3 tbsp hot sauce	45 ml
3 tsp honey	15 ml
2 tbsp Worcestershire sauce	25 ml
1/2 tsp minced garlic	2 ml
Small amount of vegetable oil	

Cut chicken breasts into "nugget"-size pieces. Preheat non-stick pan on medium high. Stir together hot sauce, honey, Worcestershire sauce, and garlic. Nuke half the mixture for 10 seconds and set it aside. Pour the other half in a zippered bag. Add the chicken to the bag. Toss to coat, then fry in hot pan 1 to 2 minutes per side until no longer pink and juices run clear. Pour the remaining spice mixture over the chicken to serve.

MARK'S POTATO CHIP CHICKEN

About 1 pound chicken parts (wings, thighs, or breasts)	500 g
1/2 cup ranch salad dressing (or Italian) or sour cream	125 ml
small bag potato chips (plain, ridged, barbecue, or sour cream)	150–200 g

Preheat oven to 190°C (375°F). Cover a baking sheet with tinfoil. Coat with cooking spray or vegetable oil. Dip chicken in the dressing to coat it. If you plan ahead, let the chicken sit in the dressing in the fridge for a few hours (to make it extra moist). Poke a hole in the chip bag with the tip of your knife to allow air to escape, then roll the chips with a rolling pin or juice glass to crush. Roll each chicken piece in chips to cover it completely. Place on tinfoil. Bake 35 to 40 minutes, until chip coating is golden.

MAPLE CHICKEN

1/4 cup maple syrup	50 ml
4 tsp lemon juice	20 ml
1 tbsp butter or margarine	15 ml
4 pieces of chicken (thighs or breasts)	

Preheat oven to 230°C (450°F). Mix syrup, lemon juice, and butter together in a small pot. Simmer 5 minutes. Coat a casserole dish with cooking spray and put the chicken in it. Add salt and pepper. Bake 10 minutes. Remove chicken, pour on syrup mixture, and return to oven. Bake 15 minutes more until juices run clear when you cut a chicken piece in half.

Fish

Here are some recipes to help you graduate from frozen fish fingers.

SWEET SALMON

Salmon fillets
Small amount of maple syrup
Small amount of brown sugar
Salt and pepper

Preheat oven to 230°C (450°F). Place fish on tinfoil-lined pan that has been sprayed with cooking oil. Drizzle with maple syrup, sprinkle with a little brown sugar, salt and pepper. Bake 10 to 12 minutes or until the fish flakes easily with a fork.

JAMMED SALMON

1 tbsp jam (blueberry or raspberry)	15 ml
1 tbsp barbecue sauce	15 ml
2 salmon fillets	

Preheat broiler. Mix the jam with the barbecue sauce. Cover a baking sheet with tin-foil, coat with a non-stick cooking spray. Place the salmon fillets on top, sprinkle with salt and pepper, then spoon the jam mixture over, reserving 10 ml (2 tsp) for later. Place under broiler for 5 minutes or until the fish flakes easily with a fork. Spoon remaining sauce over fish and serve.

MOM'S TUNA CASSEROLE

1/2 pkg pasta, any shape	
1 can tuna (flaked light), drained of liquid	170 g
1/2 cup frozen peas	125 ml
1 can cream of broccoli or asparagus soup	284 ml
Small amount of grated cheddar cheese	
Small amount of crumbled potato chips or crackers (Crumble with your hands, or put chips or crackers in a zippered bag and run a juice glass over them.)	

Preheat oven to 160°C (325°F). Bring pot of water to boil, add pasta, boil 8 minutes. Drain and put in a bowl. Add tuna, peas, soup, and stir. Pour into casserole dish. Sprinkle with cheese and chip crumbs. Bake 25 to 30 minutes.

More recipe ideas

BBQ PIZZA

1 pound ground chicken or beef	500 g
1/2 cup frozen small mixed vegetables	125 ml
1/3 cup barbecue sauce	75 ml
1 package (400 g / 14 oz) pizza crust	
1 package (170 g / 6 oz) shredded mozzarella cheese	

Preheat oven to 220°C (425°F). In non-stick skillet over medium heat, cook ground chicken or beef, stirring constantly to break into pieces, until no longer pink. Stir in vegetables and barbecue sauce. Heat through.

Place crust on a large cookie sheet. Spoon mixture onto crust, sprinkle with cheese. Bake 10 minutes.

GARLIC BREAD

Turn on the broiler in oven. Slice any kind of bread (loaf, baguette, etc.). Place 15 ml (1 tbsp) of butter in a small microwaveable bowl. Microwave for about 30 seconds to soften. Spread on bread. Sprinkle with garlic powder. Toast in oven until brown. (Keep an eye on it—it happens quickly.)

TIP: When you drain fat (that's the greasy liquid that forms in the pan when you cook food like bacon or ground beef), don't pour it down the drain. You'll clog the pipes. Carefully spoon the hot liquid (let it cool first, if possible) into an empty can, and when it's cold, toss it into the garbage. (I know some people use it for cooking, but honey, we know better.)

TANGY/SWEET MEATBALLS

1 can cranberry sauce, or 1 jar raspberry jam or grape jelly	398 ml/250 ml
1 bottle chili sauce	335 ml (approx.)
1 pound ground beef (or frozen pre-cooked meatballs). Substitute ground chicken or turkey, if you prefer.	500 g

Preheat oven to 190°C (375°F). Roll ground meat into balls. Spread on a cookie sheet lined with tinfoil and pop it into the oven for about 20 minutes. (Cut a meatball in half; if it's not pink inside, it's done.) You can skip this step if you're using frozen meatballs—read the instructions on the package. Mix cranberry sauce and chili sauce in a pot. Put it on the stove at medium heat. Add meatballs. Cook for about 10 minutes or until heated through.

NOT-QUITE-HOMEMADE BAKED BEANS

1 can baked beans	398 ml
1/2 cup barbecue sauce	125 ml
1/2 cup brown sugar	125 ml
Worcestershire sauce (optional)	

Empty the baked beans into a medium-sized pot. Put the pot on the stove, turn heat to medium, and add barbecue sauce (hickory flavour is good), brown sugar, and if you have it, a dash of Worcestershire sauce. Stir and cook for 10 minutes.

RAMEN CHOP SUEY

1 package ramen noodles	85 g
Frozen mixed vegetables	
Sauce:	
1/2 cup plus 2 tbsp water	125 ml plus 25 ml
1 tbsp cornstarch	15 ml
4 tbsp soy sauce	50 ml
1/2 pack ramen seasoning (to reduce sodium)	
2 tsp sugar	50 ml

Mix sauce ingredients in a large frying pan. Add 1 handful of frozen mixed vegetables—Oriental, if you have them. Put the pan on the stove at medium heat.

Meanwhile, boil the ramen noodles in a separate pot. (If you've only got a hot plate, you'll have to wait until the vegetables are cooked before you can boil the noodles.)

Cook vegetables and sauce until thickened. Pour over the cooked noodles, stir.

TIP: If you come across a recipe calling for canned diced or crushed tomatoes, you can use clean kitchen scissors to easily chop up whole tomatoes while they're still inside the can.

How to Roast a Turkey

Here it is, the granddaddy of all sit-down dinners. Once you've roasted your first turkey and served it to admiring friends and family, you'll definitely feel as though you've made it to adulthood. A lot of people approach this challenge with fear and anxiety, but it's really a lot easier than you might think!

Been there
Done THAT

A young woman was ahead of me in the check-out line. It was December 23rd. She had an 11-kilogram (25-pound) turkey in her basket—frozen. Should I say something? I tapped her on the shoulder and said, "What a good idea—buying a turkey for Thanksgiving, *now*." She looked at me like I had two heads, sniffed, and spouted, "I am cooking Christmas dinner for ten." For two cents I could have smiled and said nothing, but heck, it was Christmas. "A turkey that size will take four to five days to thaw and another five to six hours to cook. There are some lovely fresh turkeys right beside the frozen ones, though." I think she was about to say, "Mind your own business," but instead she pouted for a minute, then pulled her buggy out of line and stomped away. Later, as I was loading up my car, I saw her prance by. I could clearly see her purchases in her cart. Should I have told her that she had just bought a large chicken that might feed five people? Naw.

—LINDA, 43

Decide first if the plan is to buy a frozen or a fresh turkey. If you don't have freezer space to keep the bird, go fresh and order in advance. That means that you go to your favourite store, tell them what size of bird you want (or tell them how many people you plan to feed and they'll tell you the size), and give your name and number. Simple. Likewise, some stores will store a frozen bird for you. Ask.

The shopping list

- Large turkey pan with cover, or disposable tinfoil roasting pan.
- Tinfoil.
- Meat thermometer, oven-safe (found in any supermarket).
- Butter.
- Poultry seasoning (found in the spice section).
- 2 to 3 boxes of pre-made turkey dressing.
- 4 cans of turkey gravy.
- 2 onions (one very large).
- 2 celery stalks.

- Can of ginger ale or beer.
- Turkey—to make sure everyone has a full serving, with leftovers, allow 675 g (1$^1\!/_2$ lbs) per person.

If you don't own a covered roasting pan (check in the drawer under the stove, you might find one has been left there), then buy a big one. They are usually speckled black or blue and they can be found in the cooking section of any downscale cooking store or large hardware store (think Canadian Tire). They are not expensive—usually under twenty bucks.

TIP: If you opt for a disposable foil pan, place a cookie sheet under it and lift the pan out of the oven with the cookie sheet. If not, the pan will collapse and dinner will be on the floor.

Choosing the turkey: Frozen Butterball is an old fave, and fresh Butterballs are available, too. These turkeys are reliable and almost foolproof, but by all means ask around, see what friends recommend.

How to thaw a frozen turkey

The best way is to allow the turkey to thaw in the fridge. Keep it in its original wrapping, lay it on a newspaper breast side up, and allow one day of thawing for every 2 kilograms (4 pounds).

4- to 5-kilogram (9- to 11-pound) turkey—2 to 3 days
5- to 7-kilogram (11- to 15-pound) turkey—3 to 4 days
7- to 9-kilogram (11- to 20-pound) turkey—4 to 5 days
9- to 11-kilogram (20- to 24-pound) turkey—5 to 6 days
(All times are approximate.)

If you are really short on time, you might try thawing your turkey in cold water. Scrub out the sink, fill it with cold water, and plunk the frozen turkey, still in its packaging, in. Make sure the water covers it, and change the water every 30 minutes. It should take about 1 hour per kilogram (roughly 30 minutes per pound) to thaw the turkey.

4- to 5-kilogram (9- to 11-pound) turkey—4 to 5 hours
5- to-7 kilogram (11- to 15-pound) turkey—5 to 7 hours
7- to 9-kilogram (11- to 20-pound) turkey—7 to 9 hours
9- to 11-kilogram (20- to 24-pound) turkey—9 to 11 hours

Important: Do not thaw a turkey at room temperature or in warm water. The outside skin surface will grow bacteria before the inside of the turkey has thawed.

Once the turkey has been thawed, remove the neck and giblets bag (go ahead, reach inside the place where the poor thing's head used to be and grab hold), then rinse out the cavity. You should also rinse the bird all over, making sure you get in behind the wings and all the other cozy places bacteria might hang out. (Try not to let the water splash all over your sink area. Just imagine all the salmonella nasties splattering around.) There are many recipes for these organs you've removed, and when you feel more adventurous you might want to check into using them for soup, or cooking them to make a very generous treat for your cats, but given that this is your first turkey, just toss them. Note that a thawed turkey can be kept in the refrigerator up to four days before cooking.

Now, preheat your oven to 200 degrees C (400 degrees F).

Important: Never, *ever* stuff a turkey in advance, or partially cook the turkey with the intention of "finishing it up" later.

Stuff it!

Make life easy, buy several boxes of turkey-friendly stuffing. Add chopped onion and celery and mix it in a bowl. (As you become more experienced, you might want to fancy it up with extras like cranberries and nuts.) Add chopped parsley and 25 to 45 millilitres (a few tablespoons) of poultry seasoning. Add 125 millilitres ($^1/_2$ cup) of water, slowly. Mix. Add more water until you can form the stuff into a couple of good-sized baseballs.

Note: If you do decide to get more creative with the stuffing, use only cooked meats or oysters.

You will need 375 millilitres ($1^1/_2$ cups) of stuffing per kilogram ($^3/_4$ cup per pound). Don't get too anxious about this. If you make too much stuffing, wrap it in tinfoil and bake it for half an hour. If you haven't made enough, chop a large onion in half and use it to block the cavity.

Add salt and pepper to the turkey's cavities (top and bottom). You might want to rub a little butter in as well, but in our calorie-sensitive world, maybe less is more.

Stuff the turkey. Really ram that stuffing in, top and bottom. (If this is a big turkey you might need an extra person to hold the turkey while you stuff it.) But be careful not to overpack it—the stuffing will expand during the roasting, and your bird could explode (which is, admittedly, kind of cool, but not very appetizing). Tuck the legs back into the tucked position and pop it into the roasting pan.

TIP: To keep the wing tips from burning, wrap foil around them.

Pour a half bottle of ginger ale or beer gently over the bird. (It is not necessary to baste a bird, but if you do feel the need to do something, pour a little more ginger ale or beer over it periodically.)

If you have a meat thermometer, insert it into the meaty section between the leg and the breast. Cover your turkey with the roasting pan lid or make a tent of foil over it.

Put the bird in at 200 degrees C (400 degrees F) and cook for 15 to 20 minutes. (Set the timer!) Then lower the temperature to 180 degrees C (350 degrees F) and continue cooking.

The guide below is *not* exact. Use a meat thermometer to know when the turkey is fully cooked. The temperature in the deep thigh should reach 85 degrees C (185 degrees F); the centre of the stuffing should be 74 degrees C (165 degrees F).

Approximate cooking time for a stuffed turkey

(If your turkey is not stuffed, you can take 30 to 45 minutes off the cooking time.)

    4- to 5-kilogram (9- to 11-pound) turkey—2 to 3 1/2 hours
    5- to-7 kilogram (11- to 15-pound) turkey—3 1/2 to 4 1/2 hours
    7- to 9-kilogram (11- to 20-pound) turkey—4 1/2 to 6 hours
    9- to 11-kilogram (20- to 24-pound) turkey—6 to 7 1/2 hours

Take the turkey out of the pan and let it sit for a full 15 minutes. Meanwhile, scrape the bottom of the pan to make the gravy. Add a little beer or ginger ale, put it in a small pot, and boil it for a minute or two. Now cheat and add the canned gravy. Mix and heat.

How to carve a turkey

If you want to show off your beautiful bird, bring it to the table on a platter surrounded by nuts and oranges, or whatever strikes your fancy, then clear some elbow room and carve it there, or take it back into the kitchen to carve.

1. Remove the stuffing and keep it warm.

2. Pull a turkey leg out and cut the skin between the leg and the body. Separate the leg at the joint.

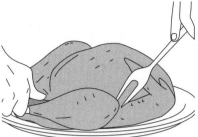

3. Hold the turkey steady with a fork stuck in the wing and, with a knife, make a long, horizontal slice into the body frame. Remove the wing.

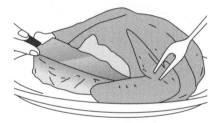

4. Start slicing off the white meat, skin and all, just above the wing joint. Work your way up to the top of the breastbone.

5. Wrap leftovers within two hours of roasting. Cut the turkey from its bones, and store stuffing in a separate container. Refrigerate up to two days, or freeze up to two months.

What to do with the turkey leftovers

"HOMEMADE" TURKEY SOUP

(Better than Mom's homemade soup, unless Mom cheated too.)

4 to 6 10-oz. cans of condensed chicken broth	284 ml
Minute Rice	
Poultry seasoning (in the spices section of the store)	
Parsley	
1 onion (cut in half)	

Remove the meat from the carcass. Freeze what you will not eat within the next 48 hours.

Place the turkey carcass into a large stockpot. Almost cover the carcass with cold water. Add a handful of parsley and an onion. Bring to a boil. Simmer for 4 or more hours.

Strain out the bones and put the soup in the coldest spot in the fridge. (Some people prefer to put the soup in the freezer for a few hours.) When it's cold, remove it from the fridge and skim off the fat with a spoon. This is your broth. Bring the broth to a boil.

Add 2 tablespoons of poultry seasoning, pepper.

And now cheat—add as many cans of condensed chicken broth as you like. Do not add water. (Hide the cans at the bottom of the recycling bin.) Discard onion or keep and chop.

Add a cup of Minute Rice. Bring to a boil, then simmer for 5 minutes until rice is tender. Serve.

TURKEY CURRY

1 large 12-oz. can or jar of your favourite curry sauce	400 ml
2 stalks celery	
1 small onion	
1 large apple, peeled	
1 snack-sized bag of trail mix	

Chop up all the vegetables and the apple. Add cooking spray to a pan and gently fry the apple and vegetables, covered, until all are soft. Add the chopped turkey, trail mix, and curry sauce. Heat slowly until the raisins in the trail mix are plump. Serve on rice with chutney.

Leftovers

So, how great is this? You made a meal so good that you're actually thinking about putting the leftovers aside for later! Well done!

Here are some tips for making the most of what's left.

- Chop up leftover meat and veggies from last night's dinner and toss them into an omelet, or in a wrap with hummus or tzatziki.
- Chicken—chop it and add to salad, pasta (with a bit of vinaigrette), or wrap it in a tortilla with lettuce, tomato, onion, and mayonnaise. You could also mix it with a spoonful of store-bought pesto and add it to salad. (Save the remaining pesto for another meal: serve it with pasta, or on fish. It can be frozen in ice-cube trays.)
- Leftover stale bread? Before it goes mouldy, cut it into cubes, toss it with olive oil, and bake it in a 180-degree C (350-degree F) oven. Makes great croutons for soup or salad.
- Make up a big batch of brown rice (check the package—it should have instructions) and divide it into portions for the week. You can take it for lunch as a side dish, or throw it into soup broth, or add chopped-up veggies.
- Salmon tastes great cold or warmed up for lunch. Try it chopped up with a spoonful of mayonnaise or ranch dressing and chopped celery or green onions as a sandwich filler.
- Cooked ground beef—divide it into individual portions. Place it in containers and freeze. When you're looking for dinner, add it to spaghetti sauce or Kraft Dinner with grated cheese.
- Need to purge the kitchen of strange old condiments, extra herbs, aging veggies, and half-cans of things? Google the ingredients with "recipes" and see what comes up.
- Bit of jam left in the jar? Add a spoonful of water, juice, or Grand Marnier for a delicious ice cream topping.

TORTILLA LEFTOVER SUPREME

Tortilla
Grated cheese, sour cream, or salsa

Place a large tortilla in a skillet and heat on medium. Scrounge up whatever leftovers are in the fridge and spoon them in a strip down the centre. Cook for a couple of minutes. Add grated cheese, sour cream, or salsa. Roll up the tortilla by folding over each of the sides using a spatula. Carefully flip and let it cook for another couple of minutes. Slide it onto your plate.

What to do with the gross stuff: Are there scary things languishing in your crisper? Reach in, pull them out, and try to identify them—they might still be usable. Rubbery celery, limp carrots, puckery peppers—pretty much any vegetable, really, that hasn't started to get mouldy can be thrown into a pot with water to make stock for pasta or soup. If it's just a few spongy apples, you can add them to muffins. Mushy bananas are good for that, too.

Desserts and Snacks

So, you've made the fabulous meal, and now you want to top it off with an even more fabulous dessert. What's stopping you? Is the thought of trying to bake something delicious sending you into a tailspin?

Well, baking is a bit different from cooking. You have to be a lot more precise about your ingredients, and mixing them in the right order. It's all about chemistry, the way those cakes magically rise in the oven. A packaged cake mix takes a lot of the skill out of the equation: just follow the directions on the box. But even baking a batch of cookies is pretty easy. Here's the easiest cookie recipe I know:

PEANUT BUTTER COOKIES

1 cup peanut butter	250 ml
1/2 cup sugar	125 ml
1 egg	

Preheat oven to 160°C (325°F). In a large bowl, mix all ingredients until well blended. Refrigerate for 30 minutes. Roll into 18 balls. Place 5 centimetres (2 inches) apart on ungreased, tinfoil-lined cookie sheet. Using the back of a fork, flatten each ball in a criss-cross pattern. Bake for 18 minutes or until lightly browned. Carefully slide the tinfoil with cookies onto a wire rack to cool. (If you don't have a cooling rack, look inside your oven before you preheat it. Are there two racks in there? Take one out and use it for cooling your cookies.)

If you want to get fancy with this recipe, you can roll the balls in sugar before flattening with a fork, or add a handful of chocolate chips or oats.

If you don't want to heat your oven (or if you're stuck with just a toaster oven for now), there are some yummy recipes that don't require baking.

IMPRESS-YOUR-DATE PEACH DESSERT

Cut four peaches in half. Remove the pits. (Use canned peach halves if you don't have fresh.) Brush each side with melted butter. Grill on the barbecue or indoor grill, covered, until they are softened and grill marks appear (about 3 minutes per side). Put two halves in a bowl and drizzle with honey or dessert wine. Serve alone or with sherbet—by candlelight, of course.

> **Duh!**
> **moment:**
>
> Baking soda and baking powder are not the same thing. There is also a difference between bleached flour, self-rising flour, and bread flour. They are not interchangeable. Stick to the recipe if you want it to turn out.

CINNAMON APPLES

(These are nice for Valentine's Day.)

2 large apples (Golden Delicious or Gala), peeled and cored	
1/4 cup water	50 ml
Heart-shaped cinnamon candies	
1/2 tbsp margarine or butter	7 ml

Place the apples in a medium-sized saucepan. Add water, a handful of small red cinnamon heart candies, and margarine or butter. Cover. Turn heat to high, bring to a boil, then reduce to medium. Simmer 8 to 10 minutes, turning apples occasionally. Serve on a small plate drizzled with the sauce.

TORTILLA AND DIP

Mix equal parts salsa and small-curd cottage cheese. Serve with tortilla chips.

DUMP DESSERT

1 can (600 g / 20 oz) fruit pie filling (cherry, raspberry or apple), or 1 can of peaches chopped, or 2 cups fresh or frozen blueberries	
1 can (600 g / 20 oz) crushed pineapple with juice (do not drain)	
1 yellow cake mix (dry in bag—don't follow directions on box)	
1/4 cup (more or less) chopped nuts (walnuts or pecans)	50 ml
1/4 cup butter	50 ml

Preheat oven to 180°C (350°F). Into a baking pan (33 x 23 cm / 13 x 9 inch), dump pie filling and pineapple. Stir just a bit. Dump cake mix evenly over top, then dump in nuts if you're using them. (Coconut is another option.) You can either cut the butter into pieces and layer it evenly on top, or melt it and drizzle. Do not mix!

Bake 1 hour until browned and bubbly. It will look gooey, but try it warm, with ice cream. Delish! (You can also try this with chocolate cake mix, served with chocolate syrup.)

PEANUT BUTTER BALLS

1 cup icing sugar	250 ml
1 cup peanut butter	250 ml
1/3 cup butter or margarine melted	75 ml
4 cups Rice Krispies	1 L

In a large bowl, mix icing sugar, peanut butter, and butter or margarine until well blended. Gently fold in cereal until well coated. Using lightly dampened hands, form into 2- to 3-centimetre (1-inch) balls by heaping tablespoons. Refrigerate on a baking sheet lined with wax paper for 30 minutes. Transfer to a sealed container. Store in a cool place for up to one week, or in the fridge for up to two weeks.

POPCORN

Oh I know, you've been doing it since public school—just stick the bag in the microwave and nuke it for 3 minutes. But did you know there's another, old-fashioned way that tastes just as good and is a lot less expensive? On the grocery shelf next to the pre-fab bagged stuff you'll find hard kernels that look like uncooked corn (which is what they are, actually). While you're at the store, pick up some paper bags. Back home, pour 50 ml (¼ cup) of kernels into a bag and fold it shut three times. Place in the microwave on its side. Nuke on high until the popping slows—anywhere from 1½ to 3 minutes.

TIP: Instead of making, or buying, expensive, sugary frosting for your home-made cake, (*à la* Betty Crocker), use two cups of single-serving pudding cups—the kind you used to find in your school lunches.

As for toppings, butter's a no-brainer, but you can also sprinkle on:

- Garlic salt.
- Parmesan cheese.
- Dry Italian salad dressing mix.
- Instant lemon-flavoured iced tea mix.
- Dry chocolate milk mix.
- Sugar with a bit of cinnamon.

How to make real coffee

1. Use the right grind of coffee. A medium-ground coffee is pretty safe, but check the instructions that came with your coffee maker.

2. Buy just as much as you need. Don't buy bulk. Exposure to air is not good for the flavour. Vacuum-packed containers are your best bet. Check the expiry date.

3. Once the package is open, store the coffee in an airtight container in a cool, dark place—not the fridge or freezer. Your coffee may take on the flavours of other food in the fridge, and moisture could ruin the taste.

4. Scoop out 25 millilitres or 2 level tablespoons (1 official coffee measure) for every 200 ml (⅓ pint) of water.

5. Add cold water.

6. After 20 minutes on the warmer, it's toast. If you need to reheat it, don't let it boil.

If you enjoy experimenting, try an espresso-cappuccino maker. Follow the directions that come with it, and make sure that you clean it after each use, especially if you are using it to froth up your milk.

How to make good tea

Fill the kettle with cold tap water. Bring it to just boiling. (Don't let it boil too long.) While you're waiting for the water to boil, heat your cup or teapot with a bit of hot water.

TIP: Boiling water makes green tea bitter. Add the water to the tea bag just before it boils.

Use 1 tea bag or 1 teaspoon of loose tea per cup. If you're using an infuser (or tea-ball), make sure you leave some space in it for the tea leaves to expand. Let it steep 3 to 5 minutes for "regular" tea, 1 to 3 minutes for green tea. Some herbal teas come with their own instructions about steeping, so check the box.

When Things Go Wrong ...
Fixing Your Screw-Ups

- Burned the spaghetti sauce? Gently pour the sauce into a new pot. *Do not* scrape the bottom—you'll only mix the burned sauce in with the good sauce. Reheat the sauce in the new pot on low. If it no longer has that smoky taste, you're a hero. Otherwise, you are out of luck.
- Did you get carried away with the spice, and now you have a red-hot chili that is inedible? Add sweetness—honey or brown sugar will do (or try white sugar in a pinch). Wait until the sweet works its way in. Adding water and allowing the chili to *cook down* also helps.
- Burned garlic? There is no salvation. Toss it and start again.

Shortcuts and Lifesavers—Gotta Love 'Em

- *Rotisserie chickens*. If you have leftovers, use them for tomorrow's lunch sandwich, or shred them and add them to soup, salads, pasta.

- *Salad greens, pre-washed in a bag or plastic tub.* Salad that's ready to go. Remember to rinse, in spite of what the label says.
- *Frozen veggies*—for stir-fries, or tossed into a jar of pasta, or an omelet.
- *Frozen yogurt, or single-serving cans of fruit cocktail and applesauce*—nutritious, easy, won't go bad.
- *Store-bought salad dressing*—pour over beef or chicken strips, then put them into zippered plastic bags and freeze. By the time they thaw, they'll be marinated and ready to barbecue or stir-fry.
- *Peanut butter, cottage cheese*—easy source of protein and nutrients.
- *Canned fish*—sardines, tuna, salmon, mackerel—great for protein and other nutrients. Stir into cooked pasta with salad dressing for a quick meal.
- *Nuts*—especially almonds and walnuts. Add them to salads or stir-fries, or grab a handful for a snack.

Going Vegetarian

So you don't want to kill animals. Or you think vegetarian's healthier. Or you have religious or political beliefs. Okay, that's a valid choice—but be smart about it.

Vegetarian diets can be very healthy, offering more fibre and less fat, and reducing your risk of heart disease, type 2 diabetes, osteoporosis, hypertension, and some cancers. A vegetarian diet can also help you lose weight. However, if you aren't careful about getting the right mix of foods, or if you're more concerned about the weight loss than the health benefits (and you're skipping high-fat healthy fare like nuts, seeds, and legumes), you could find yourself saddled with other problems—like an eating disorder.

Becoming a vegetarian involves more than simply telling people you don't eat meat. First, you'll need to determine which type of vegetarianism you wish to follow.

- *Semi-vegetarians* do not eat beef, veal, pork, or other meats, but do eat fish, poultry, dairy products, and eggs.
- *Lacto-ovo vegetarians* eat eggs and dairy, but no other animal products.
- *Lacto vegetarians* do not eat any animal products (including eggs), but allow dairy products.
- *Ovo vegetarians* allow eggs but not dairy or other animal products.
- *Vegans* do not eat any animal products, including eggs, milk, honey, or even gelatine from bone marrow (guess what—no more marshmallows!), relying exclusively on plant-based foods.

Been there
Done THAT

All I wanted to do was have a dinner party with eight people. Two of my friends are kosher. Fine, paper plates, and I'd serve smoked salmon and cream cheese. But wait, another friend has an allergy to fish. Nix the smoked salmon. A third is a vegan, and a fourth actually gave me a list of likes and dislikes as long as my arm. I thought, fine, I'd serve Scotch, jelly beans, and rocks. I turned it into a potluck.

—MAGGIE, 26

TIP: Try tofu. Make a smoothie with soy milk. Substitute soy crumbles for at least half of the ground meat in your recipes. Marinate firm tofu cubes in your favourite salad dressing and sauté with veggies. Look, Mikey likes it!

Whichever kind of vegetarian you are, you should continue to get your food from a variety of different sources, including whole grains, fruits, vegetables, legumes, nuts, seeds, meat alternatives, and some vegetable fats and oils. It's important to eat enough complete protein, which is found in animal foods but not in plants. You might need to combine foods—like grains with nuts or seeds, for example. Also, make sure you're getting enough calories, iron, zinc, calcium, and vitamins B12 and D. Find out all you can about making this a healthy choice: contact a local vegetarian association, take a vegetarian cooking class, or see if you can get a referral to a dietitian who works in a hospital or community clinic. There are some great books available in libraries and bookstores, including *Becoming Vegetarian*, by Vesanto Melina, RD.

And yes, vegetarians can eat animal crackers.

Food Safety

You don't want to get totally paranoid about this, but you don't want to spend the night in the bathroom, either, just because you got a little sloppy with what you wolfed down for dinner.

Here's what you need to know.

- Clean hands and food preparation surfaces.
- Separate raw from cooked.

- Cook foods thoroughly.
- Keep cold food cold, and hot food hot.

If you keep those four golden rules in mind, you should do fine. But there's more I need to warn you about, because I won't sleep at night if I don't.

Safe Cooking

- Cooking with eggs? Wash hands, utensils, food preparation areas, and equipment with hot, soapy water after they come in contact with raw egg.
- Don't eat raw cookie dough—or taste cake batter—when baking with raw egg.
- If you like Caesar salad, look for recipes that don't call for raw eggs.
- Cook eggs until both the yolk and the white are firm—not runny.
- Bacteria in soil can cling to rice, and flourish when the rice is cooked and left at room temperature. Refrigerate your leftover rice immediately.
- Frozen chicken nuggets are usually raw or only partially cooked. Always follow the cooking instructions. Bake them in the oven—don't use a microwave, because nuking won't kill all the harmful bacteria.
- Ground meat, with all that surface area, makes a great big playground for nasty bacteria. Wash your hands before and after handling and dry them with a paper towel. When you make burgers, don't make the patties too thick (they should be less than 1.5 centimetres or half an inch) so they will cook through before they burn on the outside. Cut the burger in half—if it's still pink, cook it some more.
- Wash lids of cans and necks of bottles before opening.
- If possible, wipe counters with paper towels rather than cloth. If you spill juice from meat or poultry, wipe it with a paper towel, then spray the counter with a sanitizing spray designed for kitchen surfaces. Wash lids of cans and necks of bottles before opening.
- If you have a cut, wear a Band-Aid, or rubber gloves, or both when handling raw meats.
- Don't eat food from cans or jars that are leaking, badly dented, or have bulging lids.
- Don't taste-test while you cook. If the food is not thoroughly cooked, you could be exposing yourself to bacteria. And if you taste with the same spoon you're cooking with, you expose everyone else to whatever germs are hiding in you.
- Marinate meat in the fridge, not on the counter. If you want to baste the meat while cooking, make extra marinade; never use the leftover marinade as it will contain juices from the meat.
- Don't put cooked meat back on a plate that held raw meat.

- Even if it's just a can of ravioli, heat your food thoroughly, till it's bubbly or steaming. For sauces, soups, and stews, bring them to a full boil.
- Put leftovers in the fridge right away, in a labelled plastic container.

Safe cooking temperatures

Cook food so it's hot enough to destroy surface bacteria. These are the temperatures you should see when you use your food thermometer:

Temperature Rules for Safe Doneness
(Canadian Industry Standards)

Ground beef/pork	160°F (71°C)
Ground chicken/turkey	175°F (80°C)
Beef, lamb and veal roast and steaks	145°F (63°C) Med-rare
	160°F (71°C) Medium
	170°F (77°C) Well
Pork chops/roasts/fresh cured ham	160°F (71°C) Medium
Ham, ready-to-eat, fully cooked	Cold or 140°F (60°C)
Whole turkey (stuffed) and chicken (stuffed or not)	180°F (82°C)
Stuffing	165°F (74°C)
Whole turkey (without stuffing)	170°F (77°C)
Chicken/turkey pieces	170°F (77°C)
Rolled stuffed beef roasts or steaks (e.g. London Broil)	160°F (71°C)
Minute Steak (or meat labelled Delicatized/Diced/Tenderized or Cubed Steak. NOT Fast-fry Steak)	160°F (71°C)
Egg dishes, casseroles	160°F (71°C)
Battered meat/seafood—Do not undercook. Cook following package directions	
Fresh meats marked "Seasoned" on label	160°F (71°C)
Leftovers, reheated	165°F (74°C)

Safe Fish and Seafood

Fish

- Store fish in its original wrapper.
- Cook it within one or two days, or wrap it tightly and store it in the freezer.
- Wash your hands thoroughly with hot, soapy water when handling fish.
- Thaw fish in the fridge, never on the counter.
- If you've thawed fish in the microwave, cook it immediately after. Never refreeze.
- To cook fish, measure it at its thickest part. Cook 10 minutes per 2.5 centimetres (1 inch), flipping halfway. If it's cooked in foil or sauce, add an additional 5 minutes. When it's done, it will be opaque and flake easily with a fork.

TIP: Out for dinner, then a movie? Don't drag your doggy bag of leftovers around with you. Two hours without refrigeration can make you sick. Even one hour on a hot day can be really bad news.

More than You Really Wanted to Know

Raw food can harbour hepatitis A, worms, parasites, viral intestinal disorders, and other diseases. Micro-organisms in raw seafood are hidden; sometimes, even experts have trouble detecting them. Freezing fish will kill only mature parasitic worms. The only way to fully kill worm eggs and other micro-organisms is by cooking. The safest way to enjoy sushi is to choose the fully cooked or vegetarian varieties.

Sushi: Sushi is raw, uncooked fish. Buy your sushi from a reputable restaurant or supermarket and eat it the same day. If it smells fishy, *don't eat it!* Bigger fish, like tuna, can also contain mercury, which is not good for you—it is linked with temporary memory loss in adults and can permanently damage the nervous system in fetuses. Shorter-living seafood, like shrimp and salmon, are apparently not so risky.

Oysters: Oysters are a nutritious food, and are great to include in your diet, but please, cook them first! Raw oysters can carry the norovirus, the hepatitis A virus, and vibrio bacteria. I won't go into all the nasty details, but believe me, you don't want this. It can be deadly. If you must eat raw oysters, remember that it's buyer beware. Choose a popular restaurant that's been serving oysters for a while—if they were making people sick, they'd be gone by now.

Barbecue Safety

Nothing says *the good life* more than tossing some meat on your own outdoor grill. But whether you're blessed with a state-of-the-art gas barbecue, or a simple Hibachi on the fire escape, remember this: you are playing with fire.

> **Duh** **moment!**
> #1
> *Never* use gasoline to light any fire!

- Keep your gas grill outdoors. No matter how badly it's raining, don't even think about dragging it into the garage. You'll cause a buildup of carbon monoxide.
- Be sure that your barbecue is away from overhangs and low-hanging branches.
- The cylinder that holds the gas should be upright at all times.
- Read the owner's manual before you use your barbecue for the first time.
- To light a gas barbecue, follow these steps:
  1. Open the lid.
  2. Turn on the propane. You don't need to crank it up full. Just open it a quarter- to a half-turn, then if there's a problem you can shut it off more quickly.
  3. Light the match if you're using one. (A long-necked barbecue lighter is better.)
  4. Switch on the burner.
  5. Insert the match flame (or lighter) in the hole at the bottom of your barbecue, if there is one. If not, light through the grate above.

> **Duh** **moment!**
> #2
> Never, *ever* spray lighter fluid on a fire that is already lit. It could stream that fire right back at you, which would really hurt.

- When you're done cooking with your gas barbecue, follow these steps:
  1. Leave the barbecue on for a few minutes to burn off remnants of food and grease. Use a barbecue brush to clean off grate.
  2. Turn off the cylinder valve.
  3. Switch off the barbecue burner so that gas won't get trapped in the hose.

If you're using a charcoal grill, stack the charcoal in a pyramid in the centre and douse with lighter fluid. (Check the instructions on the bag to see how much.) Wait a few minutes for the fluid to soak in, then light with a long-necked match or lighter. Allow the briquettes to burn for about half an hour, until they have a white ash coating. Carefully spread the coals evenly. You're ready to go!

Microwave Safety

- Choose microwave-safe plastic wrap and never let it contact food directly.
- Use only plastic containers that have been designated microwave-safe, or cook with microwaveable glass.
- Never reuse the trays from microwaveable frozen dinners.
- Never zap foods in margarine or yogurt tubs, or Styrofoam takeout food containers.
- After using the microwave to defrost food, refrigerate it or cook it right away.
- Stir food that is being microwaved to be sure there are no under-heated spots where bacteria can thrive. For more even heating, cut food into small pieces, arrange it evenly on a plate, and cover it to trap the steam.
- Never cook whole poultry, including turkey, in the microwave.
- Never use metal, or metal-trimmed plates or glass, in the microwave. Sparks will fly!

Safe Cleanup

- Wash your dishcloth every other day, and hang it to dry when it's not in use. If it comes in contact with any raw meat or poultry, rinse it well and don't use again until it's gone through the laundry at a hot temperature with a bit of bleach.
- A dishwasher is your safest choice, but if you're washing dishes by hand, at least make sure the water is as hot as you can stand.
- Don't leave dishes in the sink to "soak." They won't magically come out clean, and in the meantime, you're basically making germ soup.
- And definitely do not throw sharp knives into the murky water and leave them. The next person to go groping around in there will get a nasty surprise. Instead, completely immerse eating utensils, rub them all over with a soapy cloth, rinse them thoroughly, and let them air-dry. (Hand towels just spread the bacteria around.)

- No need to buy antibacterial dish soap. Regular detergent and hot water does the trick. For best cleaning, look for a detergent that promises to cut grease. For cleanup after working with raw food, use a bleach solution—5 millilitres (1 teaspoon) bleach to 1 litre (4 cups) of water.
- Think a toilet seat is bad? Have a close look at your cutting board. Now that's a truly scary place. Wash your board in the dishwasher or scrub it with soapy water and a brush, then sterilize it with a bleach solution. Let it sit in the solution for about 5 minutes, rinse and dry with paper towels. Make sure cutting boards have a chance to air-dry in between use. When your cutting board is so hacked up that you can't properly clean it, toss it and buy a new one.
- Use different knives and cutting boards when cutting meats and veggies.
- Throw your tea towels in the laundry every other day and wash with hot water. Fridge and cupboard door handles, sinks, and taps are all bacteria hotspots. Wipe them regularly with disinfecting spray, wipes, or hot soapy water and paper towels.

More than You Really Wanted to Know

The dirtiest thing in your kitchen is probably your sponge. You don't want to know how many millions of bacteria are hanging around in there. Your dishwasher won't kill them all, since it usually doesn't get hot enough. Nuking might work, if you zap the sponge on high for one minute (but be sure it's wet and contains no metal, or you'll start a fire). Better yet—just throw it out. A dishcloth that you launder in hot water after every use is probably your safest bet.

What If ...?

Kitchen mishaps do happen. Here's some advice to keep in mind, just in case.

Q: My can of Alphagetti is dented?

A: Don't eat anything that comes from a dented, leaky, rusty, or bulging can. Same goes for any canned food that bursts or explodes when you open it. Air might have entered the can, and the food could make you sick. When shopping, inspect cans before you buy.

Q: Something on the stove catches fire?

A: Before you run out of the kitchen screaming, try dumping a box of baking soda on the flames. If you can, top it with the pot lid to starve it of oxygen. Don't try to carry it to the sink. Don't try to douse it with water. If it's grease, the fire will only spread. Better yet, buy a fire extinguisher. Put down this book and go buy one. Now!

Q: The power goes out?

A: Keep the refrigerator and freezer doors closed as much as possible. Note when the power goes off. A chest or upright freezer should keep food frozen for 48 hours if it is full, 24 hours if it is half full. A fridge should keep food cool for 4 to 6 hours. If you are lucky enough to have a thermometer in the freezer (you did buy one, didn't you?), check the temperature when the power comes back on. If it's 40 degrees C (104 degrees F) or below, the food can be refrozen. If you don't have a thermometer, check the food; if it still contains ice crystals it can be refrozen. Breads and pastries can be refrozen. If fruit or juice smells funny after thawing, toss it. Frozen veggies should be tossed if they have been warmer than 40 degrees C (104 degrees F) for 6 hours. If you're in the middle of cooking when you lose power, throw out the partially cooked food.

Q: Forgot the pizza on the counter?

A: If it's been sitting there while you watched a DVD, you're probably okay. Two hours at room temperature is the limit. In the fridge, it's good for two days, then it's time to say goodbye.

Q: I ignored all this advice and now I have diarrhea, a fever, and I think I'm going to … going to …

A: Throw up? You could have food poisoning. Or it could be the flu—the symptoms are very similar. In fact, it's estimated that for every food-borne illness that is diagnosed, 20 go unreported. But food poisoning can be very serious, leading to chronic conditions like arthritis, paralysis, even death. If you think your tummy troubles stem from bad food, see your doctor, or call the local public health department. Mild cases can be treated at home. Don't eat solid food; just drink

More than You Really Wanted to Know

It can take 24 or 36 hours, even up to several days, for you to get sick from some of the pathogens (disease-causing micro-organisms) that cause food-borne illnesses.

lots of liquid, including some salt and sugar to replace what you're losing. In most cases, recovery occurs within 12 to 24 hours. But if you collapse, or suddenly develop extremely severe diarrhea and vomiting, get a ride to a doctor right away. Also, contact a doctor immediately if you have any of the following symptoms: a fever higher than 38.5 degrees C (101 degrees F), diarrhea that lasts more than 24 hours, vomiting that lasts more than 12 hours, severe cramps, bloody diarrhea, reduced saliva or urination, dizziness, confusion, increased heart rate, trouble breathing, an inability to keep liquids down for more than 12 hours, or if you suspect botulism.

How Not to Kill Yourself in the Kitchen

Here are the safety tips that, to date, you have ignored. Please note: you are alive and reading this because somebody *did* know these tips.

- **Do** have a fire extinguisher handy in the kitchen—and read the instructions *before* you need it.
- **Do** be careful around steaming pots and kettles. When you lift the lid off a boiling pot, point it away so that the steam doesn't burn you.
- **Do** unplug and tie up appliance cords so they're not left to dangle.
- **Do** replace any appliance that keeps blowing a fuse or tripping a circuit breaker.
- **Do** find out which of the back elements on your stove gets hot when you turn the oven on. (One of them—often the back left—is also a vent for the oven.) Don't rest your plastic spatula, milk bag, or grocery list there.
- **Do** use a proper oven mitt—not a dishtowel or that dirty shirt you just tossed on the chair. Both are slippery and won't keep out the heat.
- **Do** beware of anything cooked in the microwave. Open it slowly, and be careful of the steam.

- **Don't** leave a pot handle sticking out over the edge of the stove.
- **Don't** put dirty knives into a sink full of soapy water.
- **Don't** store alcohol near the stove. It's flammable.
- **Don't** leave the kitchen when frying anything. Oil is extremely dangerous.
- **Don't** let grease build up on the stove; it can ignite.
- **Don't** store things over or above the stove. When reaching, dangling sleeves can catch fire.

- **Don't** use the stove as a countertop or the oven as a storage cupboard. You'll forget. Keep paper towels, tea towels, and wooden or plastic spoons well away from the stove.
- **Don't** wear loose sleeves or flowing clothes when cooking—they can brush against a hot burner and catch fire.

Important: Make sure your smoke detector is working. If your cooking skills are a little lacking and the smoke detector keeps going off (sometimes heat alone is enough to make it wail), wave a magazine nearby and open the windows. If it keeps happening you can remove the batteries briefly, but put them back as soon as you are done burning—um, I mean *cooking*. Some house smoke detector systems are wired in and controlled through the circuit-breaker box. They're easy to turn off, because you just flip the circuit breaker. But don't forget to turn it back on when the smoke has cleared.

Fire!!

- *If it's grease in a pan:* Don't use water. That will cause it to spread. Instead, smother it with a lid. (Remember science class? It needs oxygen to burn.) Leave the lid on until you're sure it's cooled. Or dump baking soda into the fire, and turn off the stove.
- *If it's in the oven or microwave:* Leave the oven or microwave door shut and turn off the heat. If it's still burning, get out and call the fire department.

Resources

Canada's Food Guide

www.hc-sc.gc.ca/fn-an/food-guide-aliment/index_e.html

Conversion charts

www.readersdigest.ca/food/metric.html

Substitution tips

www.foodnetwork.com (look under "cooking")
www.foodsubs.com

Food safety

www.foodsafety.gov
www.eatwelleatsafe.ca
www.fsis.usda.gov/OA/pubs/facts_basics.pdf

Tips, tools, and customized food guides to help you make wise food choices

www.dietitians.ca/eatwell
www.healthyeatinginstore.cawww.eatracker.ca
www.eatsmart.web.ca
www.mypyramid.gov/mypyramid/index.aspx

Cookbooks

Starting Out: The Essential Guide to Cooking on Your Own, Julie Rosendaal

Cookbook for College Kids: Revised Classic for the Novice Cook, Sheila McDougall

Clueless in the Kitchen: A Cook Book for Teens, Evelyn Raab

The Bachelor's Guide to Ward Off Starvation, Clarence Culpepper

Serves One: Simple Meals to Savor When You're on Your Own (2nd Edition), Toni Lydecker

Help! My Apartment Has a Dining Room Cookbook: How to Have People Over for Dinner Without Stressing Out, Kevin Mills

Going Solo in the Kitchen, Jane Doefer

6

Taking Care of Your Stuff

You can't get spoiled if you do your own ironing.

—MERYL STREEP

Washing Clothes 101

You are about to discover an aisle in the grocery store that you never knew existed—the cleaning products aisle. Big, huh? You can spend a fortune here, so consider first some natural alternatives (see Chapter 3: Housekeeping 101), and then buy only the basics.

First things first: laundry soap.

Regular detergent will do for most of your laundry. Start with a good house brand and switch if you are not happy with the results. If you have tough stains to go after and you think it might help to use bleach, buy a bleach that is colour-safe. (If regular bleach splatters on your dark pants, you'll be wearing polka dots.) If you are washing in hard water you might want to add a water softener. You'll know you have hard water if it's hard to get a lather in your shampoo. If you have a ring around the inside of your toilet, that too might mean hard water buildup. (It could also mean someone doesn't like to clean toilets much.)

Been there
Done THAT

For my money, a little water softener goes a long way. I only use half as much detergent now, and the lime scale that comes from having hard water doesn't build up nearly as quickly.

—MERCY, 22

The Washer

So, now you've got your detergent and your pile of stinky clothes. What's next?

First, separate your laundry into four piles: colours (especially oranges, pinks, and reds), darks, lights, and delicates (linens, silks, wool, etc.). Wash each pile separately. The delicate pile might be hand-washed, or, at the very least, run through the washing machine on the *delicate* cycle.

As you separate, read the labels (usually found on the back of the collar, pants, or in a side seam). Lycra, for example, goes in a cold wash.

What do the pictures on the labels mean?

Here's the most important label you have to look for, and you should be thinking of this when you go shopping. It's the one that says "Dry Clean Only." When you see this label, you have two options:

1.   Don't buy it.

Or:

2.   Buy it, and dry clean it—every time.

Note: The chemicals used at the dry cleaners are hard on clothes and on the environment, not to mention your wallet. Clothes you can launder at home really are best—Mother says so!

As for the rest of the labels, photocopy the list on the next page and post it above your washing machine. You'll be checking it often.

Loading

Check the pockets of all your clothes before washing and drying. (Leave your lipstick, pen, or Kleenex in a pocket just once and you won't do it again.) Load clothes into the washing machine till it's about three-quarters full, never to the top. Fill with water and add soap. Cold or lukewarm water is easier on your clothes than hot. Gentler detergent is easier on them, too. To prevent spotting (you will know it when you see it), don't overfill your washing machine. If spotting does occur, rub the damp material with liquid detergent and rewash.

Laundry Labels

Wash

Cold-water wash

Gentle wash

Hot-water wash

Do not machine-wash

Hand-wash

Do not bleach

Do not wring

More than You Really Wanted to Know

Fabric Softeners are an optional thing.

Pros: Besides giving fabric a softer feel, fabric softeners help reduce static cling and are really useful on synthetics and permanent-press materials. For best results, add liquid fabric softeners to the final rinse cycle, or add softener sheets on top of wet laundry in the dryer cycle.

Cons: Fabric softeners contain potentially hazardous chemicals like chloroform, benzyl acetate, and pentane—chemicals that can be even more hazardous when heated in the dryer and released, airborne, into the environment.

On the bright side: It's an urban myth that fabric softeners, or dryer sheets, cause fires. They don't clog filters, either. Clean out the lint tray every time you use the dryer and you will be fine.

TIPS:

- Wash your towels every five days or after two to three uses, especially if it's hot and humid out.
- Clean your sheets once a week, every second week in hot water to kill off dust mites. (They are the little creepy-critters that feed off dead skin cells.)
- Take large blankets and comforters to the laundromat. A home washing machine is usually too small to do a good job.
- Loofahs, synthetic sponges, cotton washcloths, and anything that might qualify as a body scrubber can become a breeding ground for bacteria. Rinse after each use and allow time for drying between uses. To wash it, add the body scrubber to your usual hot-water wash or dishwasher load. If it has no metal components, you can pop a dry body scrubber in the microwave for 1 to 3 minutes.
- Wash your baseball cap by running it through the dishwasher on the top rack.
- Does your teddy bear need washing? Stick him in a pillowcase and close it up with a ponytail holder. (Same goes for anything delicate.)
- To get the smell of smoke out of clothes, add a cup of vinegar to a steamy, hot bathtub of water and hang the clothes above the steam.

More than You Really Wanted to Know

You will carry more excrement on your hands while doing the laundry than you might in the bathroom. Wash your hands after switching loads.

The Dryer

Time to check those labels again.

Here are some additional hints:

- Hang slightly damp permanent-press shirts on an unrusted or wooden hanger. Button buttons, then straighten the shirt and gently brush out any wrinkles.
- In a hurry and your stuff is still wet? Stick a large, dry bath towel in the dryer with whatever you need dried fast. The towel will absorb some of the moisture.

Dryer Labels

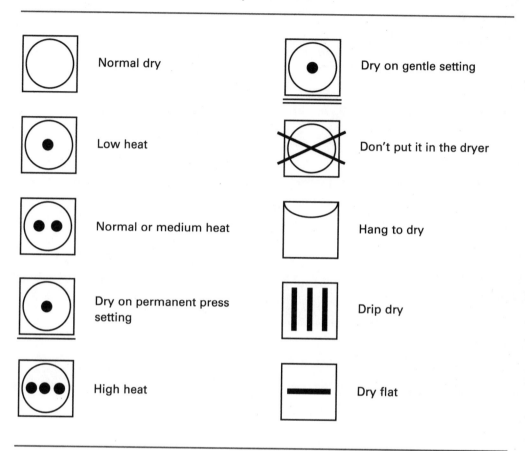

- Remember to clean the dryer filter by hand every time you use the dryer. If the lint is allowed to build up it might catch fire.

How to wash a sweater: Cotton sweaters can usually be machine washed on delicate and in cold water. Wool sweaters should be hand-washed using a mild detergent and lukewarm water. Before laying them flat on a smooth surface to dry, roll them in towels to press out excess water.

Been there
Done THAT

I recycle everything, even dryer lint. I hang it on an old clothesline, but tossing it on a bush works, too. Birds use it to build their nests. No kidding!

—STEVE, 23

TIP: To unstick a sticky zipper, rub the teeth of the zipper with a pencil. Graphite works as a dry lubricant.

How to clean a leather coat or jacket: Mix dishwashing liquid with water (one part liquid to five parts water) and stir it up until it's foamy. Lay the coat on a flat surface and gently rub it with the solution. Do not soak the coat. Wipe it with a clean, damp cloth. To remove a grease spot from suede, dip a toothbrush in vinegar and brush it over the spot.

Stains

Oh no! You're wearing your favourite shirt/skirt/dress/sweater/pants, and you've just splatted something nasty on it! If you are serious about getting it looking as clean as the day you bought it (or anywhere near that condition), you'll have to bring in some heavy guns to treat stains. Your first ally in this battle is the sun—if you have a clothesline or any place to hang your clothes outside, you might find that the sun's natural bleaching powers will solve a lot of your problems, while UV radiation also kills bacteria.

For more help, try these stain-removal weapons.

- Bleach.
- Cornstarch (absorbs stains).
- Liquid enzyme detergent (available in grocery stores). Examples are Biz or Axion.
- Meat tenderizer (breaks down proteins in stains).
- Hydrogen peroxide (a mild form of bleach, easily available).
- White vinegar (small bottle, add 150 millilitres (²/₃ cup) water to 75 millilitres (¹/₃ cup) vinegar).
- Lemon juice.
- Soap (in bar form, without perfumes or additives). Example: Ivory.
- Toothbrush to scrub strains (an old one).
- Cheap shampoo (removes body oils—i.e., ring around the collar).
- Borax, which is also known as boric acid. (It's a poison: keep out of reach of small children.)

And if you are really serious about this stain business, dry-cleaning fluid is usually available at hardware stores.

Important: *Read the instructions for use that come with these products and take any necessary precautions. And if there are children in your life, even just as visitors, remember to keep cleaning products* out of sight and reach. *And mixing products like ammonia and bleach can create toxic results. Just don't.*

Here are some stain "Dos" and "Don'ts":

- **Do** act immediately.
- If the *splat* is goopy, **do** scrape up as much as possible with a spoon or blunt-edged knife.
- **Do** blot up liquids with warm water and an absorbent material, such as a white paper towel or tissue.
- **Do** test all stain treatments on a small bit of the material before charging full steam ahead.
- **Do** use cold water instead of hot, unless instructed otherwise.
- **Do** rinse the stain from the back of the material first, then try out the recommended stain treatment.
- **Do** use an eye-dropper to drip detergent or solvents onto the stain.

- **Don't** rub the stain.
- **Don't** use bleach or liquid enzyme detergents on wool or silk.
- **Don't** dry it out by applying heat, including a spin in the dryer.
- **Don't** use solvents or turpentine.

TIP: To remove ring-around-the-collar, squirt a little liquid dishwashing soap on the offending areas. Let it soak, rinse, rinse again, and wash as usual.

TIP: Call in professionals for stains from permanent markers, wood glue, hair dye, shoe polish, and most oil paints, to name just a few. Keep the stain moist with a damp cloth and head for the dry cleaners.

Red wine: Rinse the stained cloth from the back. Turn it over and pour club soda, white vinegar, and cold water (in equal parts) on the stain. Sprinkle on salt to absorb the liquid. Rub gently, rise in cold water. Repeat.

Try, try again: Pour white wine over the red wine stain, then rinse.

White wine: Rinse the stained cloth from the back. Apply an enzyme detergent. Let stand for a few minutes. Rinse again and wash in cold water.

Coffee and tea: Rinse the stained cloth from the back. Apply an enzyme detergent. Let it stand for a few minutes. Rinse again and wash in cold water. (If the stain has dried, rub the stain with the detergent, then soak the material in cold water for 30 minutes.)

Try, try again: Mix borax and water, apply to the stain, and let it stand for 30 minutes. Wash. (Borax is usually found in the laundry aisle of your local grocery store.)

Still trying? Dip a cloth into a beaten egg yolk. Rub the yolk into the stain. Then rinse with clear water.

Milk or cream: Treat it as quickly as possible. Soak in cold water or sponge the stain with club soda.

Try, try again: Add liquid enzyme soap to tepid water and soak for 30 minutes.

Oil (including butter or margarine): Blot with a paper towel, then treat the stain with a grease solvent or detergent that says "enzyme" on the label. If it won't harm the fabric, wash it in really hot water.

Blood: Pour hydrogen peroxide directly onto the stain, and when it stops bubbling, blot it up with a rag soaked in cold water. (This also works on leather.)

Try, try again: Sprinkle the stain with salt and rinse with cold water. Soak in cold water for 30 minutes. Apply spot remover and wash with liquid enzyme detergent.

> **Been** there **Done** THAT
>
> Best stain remover I ever used are those little hand-washing-up packets they give you at chicken restaurants. A little dab will do ya.
> —BECKY, 24

Sweat: If you have underarm perspiration stains, scrub the area with lemon juice and water. Add bleach to the wash if it won't harm the material.

Try, try again: Scrub the stain with one part white vinegar to four parts water. Rinse. (Do not add bleach to the wash after using vinegar! It creates a toxic gas.)

Vomit: The acid in vomit can permanently damage fabrics. Remove as much of the gross stuff as possible. Presoak in cold water using an enzyme detergent for 30 minutes. Soak old stains for several hours. Launder in warm (not hot) water, rinse, and inspect.

Try, try again: If the stain remains, soak for an additional 30 minutes, then rewash.

Still trying? Launder using chlorine bleach that's safe for the fabric.

Urine: To remove urine odours from mattresses, dampen the smelly area with water, then sprinkle with borax. Rub the borax into the mattress well. Let it dry. Vacuum or brush off any remaining powder.

If the dog has peed on the rug, soak it up immediately, then clean the area with dish detergent and water. (If you have a pet and pee-pee is a problem, visit the pet store. There are any number of products that may dissuade Fido from returning to his favourite spot in the house.)

Mud: Scrape dried mud off the material with a dull knife. Rub liquid enzyme detergent into the stain, then soak it for 20 minutes in lukewarm water. Wash as per instructions on the label.

Try, try again: Apply a spot remover or blot the stain with white vinegar, then wash as usual.

Gum: Warm some white vinegar in the microwave, then pour it over the gum. Gently scrape the gum off with a butter knife. Repeat. (Vinegar must not be too hot.)

Try, try again: Stick the clothing in the freezer for a few hours. Scrape the gum off with a dull knife. Dab the area with spot remover and wash.

Grass: Grass stains are green chlorophyll mixed with protein and other organic matter. Dab hydrogen peroxide directly onto the stain, then launder as usual.

Try, try again: Rub the area with a liquid detergent that contains enzymes. Wash with fabric-safe bleach.

Bike-chain grease: Soak the material in grease-cutting dishwashing liquid, then wash.

Candle wax: Rub the wax with an ice cube, then scrape off as much as possible. (If it's a tablecloth or placemat, toss the material in the freezer to harden.) Blot the remaining stain with rubbing alcohol. Wash.

If the wax is on a carpet, or a cloth chair, lay a brown bag over the wax and run a warm iron over it. The bag will absorb the wax.

If the wax is on a wood floor, use a hair-dryer to warm the wax, then remove most of it with a dull knife. Heat again and blot with a paper towel. Wash with vinegar and water.

Tomatoes: Run cold water over the back of the stain. Rub liquid enzyme detergent on the area and let it stand for a few moments. Wash. Repeat, and let it dry in the sunlight.

Try, try again: Put the garment in a laundry presoak and let it stand for 30 minutes, then wash as usual.

Still trying? Sponge the stain with dry-cleaning liquid, then rub in laundry detergent. Wash.

TIP: There are some stains that you just won't get out: old pee stains, pesticides, bleaches, and acne medications and some skin creams (they may contain benzoyl peroxide), to name a few. If you have given it the old college try and still want to try, try again, take it to a really good dry cleaner and ask for their advice.

Carrots and sweet potatoes: Run cold water over the back of the stain. Rub in liquid enzyme detergent and let it stand for a few moments. Wash as usual.

Try, try again: Put the garment in a laundry presoak and let it stand for 30 minutes, then wash as usual.

Eggs: Run cold water over the back of the stain. Rub in liquid enzyme detergent and let it stand for a few moments. Wash as usual.

Try, try again: Put the garment in a laundry presoak and let it stand for 30 minutes, then wash as usual.

Mustard: Run cold water over the back of the stain. Rub it with liquid enzyme detergent and rinse again in cold water. Repeat a few times, rubbing the stain as you go. Apply spot remover and wash as usual.

Try, try again: Rub with glycerine.

Tea: Dilute lemon juice with an equal amount of water. Pull the material tight and, using a Q-tip, dab the stain with the solution. Flush several times with cool water. Repeat.

Mascara: Rub the stain with dishwasher soap (the undiluted kind is best), and wash as usual.

Perfume: Rinse the area with water, then blot with a paper towel. Use the eye-dropper to apply a little enzyme detergent. Rinse with water and wash as usual.

Try, try again: Dab on a little alcohol, rinse, wash.

Nail polish: Blot away as much of the stain as possible while it's still damp. Soak it in an oil-free nail polish remover that contains acetone. Wash. Careful: do not use nail polish remover that contains extra ingredients such as moisturizers. And read the fabric label carefully: nail polish remover will damage fabrics with acetate or triacetate.

Lipstick: Blot with a paper towel. Rub the stain with a bar of non-perfumed soap. (Dishwasher soap, colourless, might substitute.) Rinse. Repeat if necessary. Wash as usual.

Try, try again: Sponge with alcohol and wash.

Still trying? Soak in milk for 30 minutes and rinse in hot, soapy water. Wash.

Ink: Dab rubbing alcohol on the stain. Repeat.

Try, try again: Spray the stain with hairspray and let it sit for a few minutes, then hand-wash. Repeat.

Ironing

You have a choice. You can learn to iron your clothes, or you can take everything to the dry cleaner. The dry cleaner will set you back between $20 and $50 a week.

Right.

Buy an iron and an ironing board. (Yes, you can double a towel on the table and iron the odd small thing, but you won't be able to handle a shirt that way.) The thicker the pad on the ironing board the better, so buy a cheap board and a good pad.

Read the label to find out what the item's made of. Delicate fabrics require a low setting. Cottons and linens can handle steam, and woollens can take medium heat and steam.

Test the heat of the iron on a small patch of fabric (e.g., the tail of a shirt). A too-hot iron will stick to the fabric.

Do not iron velour, suede, ultrasuede, leather, or velvet.

When ironing wool, place another material (a cloth napkin, perhaps, or a tea towel) between the iron and the material to keep the wool from turning shiny. When ironing corduroy, put a terrycloth towel between the iron and the fabric so you don't crush the "ribs."

How to iron cotton shirts

1. Sprinkle all the shirts you plan to iron with water and roll them to keep them damp. (Or pull them out of the dryer when not quite dry.)
2. Undo all the buttons, including buttons on the cuffs.
3. Iron the collar first, then the yoke (the top of the shirt's back).
4. Lay the shirt out with the back down so that you are looking at the inside of the shirt.

TIP: You can reduce the amount of ironing you need to do by leaving your clothes in the dryer for only 15 minutes, then hanging them to dry.

5. Iron the back of the shirt starting at the top and working to the bottom.
6. Bring the right side over and press.
7. Bring the left side over and press.
8. Lay out the sleeves and press.
9. Iron pleats by pointing the tip of the iron into the pleat.
10. Hang up shirt.

Oh, you are brilliant!

How to iron a tie: Lay the tie, on a towel, good side down, wrong side up. Cover the tie with a dry cloth or pillow case. Press. If the tie is still wrinkled, then sprinkle a little water on the pillow case (not the tie) and press again.

Taking Care of Your Clothes and Accessories

Now that you are buying your clothes with your own wallet, you might feel more inspired to make them last. Here are a few tips to help you make the most of your wardrobe:

- Fold your sweaters, don't hang them.
- To get rid of wool balls (or "pills," those bumpy little things on your once-smooth sweater), don't pick—swipe them with a disposable razor. Place your hand beneath

the sweater to flatten it, then gently press and flick with the razor. Or use a fabric shaver. You'll find them in the gadget stores. And while you might not want to advertise this, lice shampoo often comes with itty-bitty combs. If you happen to have a lice kit hanging around, you can use that.

- Do not store clothes in dry-cleaning bags. They need to breathe.
- Ditch the wire hangers—they leave marks on the clothes and may bend them out of shape.
- And forget storing clothes in cardboard boxes. The boxes might leach dyes onto your clothes. Fork out a few bucks for polyester storage bags or plastic bins.

TIP: Cedar blocks or cedar sachets placed in your drawers will greatly reduce the risk of moths and will keep sweaters smelling crisp. But don't let cedar actually touch your clothes as it might cause yellowing. Orange peels work, too.

Been there
Done THAT

When I am cruising a department store, I take home some perfume samplers and tuck then away in my drawers, to keep things smelling nice. They work well in the linen closet, too.

—SARAH, 19

How to sew on a button

1. Match the thread with the button, not the fabric.
2. Take a length of 50 centimetres (20 inches) of regular thread and pass it through the eye of the needle. Tie the two ends of the thread together and snip off the ends. (Easy way to tie ends: wet them, then twist them back and forth between your thumb and forefinger.)
3. Check that the button is centred on the material. If you need to, mark the material with a tiny dot. Place the button over the dot.
4. Stab the material from behind and push it through one of the buttonholes. Fun huh? Pull until the thread is taut.
5. Here's a professional trick. Place a matchstick between the button and the fabric. Continue to stitch the button onto the material using all the buttonholes. Each

TIP: The next time you are
in a hotel, pocket the freebie
sewing kit and bury it in
your shaving/cosmetic bag.

hole should have four stitches. Remove the matchstick. Lift the button and bring the needle down through one buttonhole but not through the material. Wrap the thread around the stitches that hold the button to the fabric four times to create a shank. This will serve as a knot. There will now be space between the material and the button, allowing the button to lie flat when buttoned.

Taking Care of Your Good Shoes

They cost *how* much? Well, then, you'd sure better take care of them.

- Polish your shoes before wearing them for the first time.
- If they really are expensive, don't wear them two days in a row. Leather needs to rest.
- Use a shoe horn to get them off, and repeat after me, "I will not flip off my shoes by putting one toe against the heel and yanking."
- Cedar shoe trees should be put into the shoes at night, and any time the shoes get wet.
- He is called a cobbler, like in the fairy tales. Visit him when the heels of your shoes wear down.
- If the heels are scuffed, match the shoe colour with a marker and draw on.

Shoe-polishing 101

Buy yourself a little shoe-polish kit. It comes with two brushes and a cloth. When polishing shoes, cover your hands with rubber gloves or plastic sandwich bags. Getting shoe polish off your hands is a pain.

TIP: To store boots for the summer and keep them in shape, take two empty plastic water bottles and poke holes in them. Fill with potpourri and tuck in boots. Too complicated? Stuff your boots with newspaper. If you are concerned about the newsprint rubbing off, jam the newsprint in plastic grocery bags first. And wipe road salt off your leather boots immediately.

Remove the laces and use a cloth to get rid of the dirt. Rub hard polish (the stuff that comes in a flat can) in a circular motion and let the polish dry for five minutes. Now go to it with the big buffing brush until it's shiny. Next, wipe with the cloth. Wax-based polishes last longer. Store shoes on shoe trees to prevent them from getting all bent out of shape.

How to Clean Your Jewellery

Beads: Water might damage or rot the thread, so clean your beads with baking soda and an old toothbrush. Sprinkle the baking soda over the beads, brush, and dust off with a cloth.

Pearls: Do not immerse them in water. You might harm the thread. Instead, just polish them gently with a soft cloth.

TIP: Clean a hairbrush by running a comb through it, then sprinkle on baking soda and rinse in hot water.

Diamonds: Grandma's diamonds likely should be cleaned by the pros. Go to a well-established store to have precious stones cleaned. If you want to give them a touch-up, do not wash them in the sink, or you might have to call the plumber in to fetch them out of the drain. Wash the diamonds in a bowl of soapy water. Use a soft toothbrush to get rid of the dirt, then dry with a soft cloth.

Emergency Fixes!

Try these ideas before you panic and throw out your expensive electronic equipment. You might be surprised.

Skipping CD or DVD player: Remove the disc and dust. Try it again. If it is still skipping, remember not to leave your discs in a freezing car or under the hot sun—that can affect performance.

Your cellphone fell into the toilet: It's not over yet! Take the battery out and dry the inside of the phone with a blow-dryer. Dry the battery off, too. Put the battery back in and test. If it doesn't work, leave it for a few days to really dry out. Or, battery removed, submerge it in a bowl of dry rice, not cooked rice! Leave it for a few days. Test. If it still doesn't work, take it to a call centre and try a new battery.

Your new digital camera fell into the lake: Do not open the camera or the exposure to oxygen will begin the process of rusting. Instead, take it to a good camera store post-haste.

TIP: Clean your cellphone with a damp cloth or a pre-moistened towelette. Do not spray it with a cleanser.

Coffee on the keyboard: Unplug the keyboard from the computer. Tip the keyboard upside down—or, if it's a laptop, the whole unit—to drain out every last drop, then take a blow-dryer to it. Brush the keys with a dampened cloth. Do the same for a laptop, except shut down and disconnect as step one. Take the computer in for a check if you think that moisture has leaked into the main part of the unit. (And if you take your coffee with cream and sugar, likely you're out of luck.)

Damaged personal computer: Techies have rescued files from computers that have been through fire, fluid, and run-amok three-year-olds. No matter what the condition of the computer, take it in to a service centre. Don't give up too easily. Most data can be rescued.

Resources

Laundry symbols

To get a good look at these, go to
www.tide.com/en_CA/articles/read.jsp?topic=laundry_symbol

Body Basics

7

Your Body—
An Owner's Guide

Every patient carries her or his own doctor inside.

—ALBERT SCHWEITZER

I know, it's just not fair. You've finally got the freedom you've been waiting for, and now suddenly people are expecting you to be, like, *responsible* and everything. You've got to get up in the morning—all by yourself! And lately, all you want to do at the end of the day is crash on the couch. You can't even party like you used to!

Darling, I hate to be the one to break it to you, but you are not invincible. You can't burn the candle at both ends without eventually feeling the heat. So stop. You've got at least three-quarters of your life to go. You're going to need your body for a good long time. And when that high-performance vehicle of yours breaks down, you'll want to at least have read the owner's manual, because there's no trading it in for a new one.

Fact is, you are going to get older; we all do. It starts the day you're born. While you can't stop the wrinkling or the greying, you can put an end to the habits that will

More than You Really Wanted to Know

The National Institutes of Health recently studied young people as they moved out of their family homes and entered young adulthood. What they found was alarming. Diet got worse. People exercised less, had less access to health care, and were more likely to drink, smoke, and take drugs. The study concluded that the transition to adulthood is a very vulnerable period, with huge health consequences.

make you look, and feel, older than you really are. What you do right now—what you put in your body, what you do with it, and how you treat it—has a direct bearing on how healthy you will be in the future. From now on, you are in charge of you.

Taking charge of your health is not complicated, really. You just need to know the basics. Eat right. Don't smoke or do drugs. Limit salt, caffeine, and alcohol. Get enough sleep and physical activity. Don't get too much sun. And practise safe sex. There now. You'll do just fine.

Fighting the "Freshman Fifteen": Eating Right

Something happens to your body when you enter your twenties, and it isn't always nice. Whatever habits you've established start to reveal themselves. Often, the first sign is the top button of your jeans. (And no, they haven't shrunk *again*.)

> ### *Been* there
> ### *Done* THAT
>
> I'd always been so skinny. But I started coming home just bagged and I'd end up eating "Mr. Noodles" for dinner. I picked up this nasty habit of eating dry Jell-O powder as a snack while I studied. By spring, all I could fit in were my stretchy yoga pants.
> —KELSEY, 23

Because young adults famously gain some extra weight in the first year after leaving home for college or university, this phenomenon is often called the "Freshman Fifteen" (which I guess sounds friendlier than the "Freshman 6.8 Kilograms"). Recent studies quibble with that a bit. Researchers at the University of Guelph found only a typical 2.25-kilogram (5-pound) weight gain between high school and the end of first-year university. Whatever. The sorry fact is, all that freedom to eat what and when you want means your jeans might no longer snap shut.

So you've suddenly got an extra 3 centimetres around the waist. Blame the beer-quaffing at night, the M&Ms while you study, the inability to fit exercise into a busy day—or maybe just dealing with the stress and loneliness of living away from home. Whatever the cause, you need to do something about it, now, before 3 centimetres turns into 30. Pants with elastic waistbands are just not your look.

The big difference between life as a kid and life as an adult is planning. Healthy grown-ups have to think about what they are going to eat before it goes into their mouths. And they have to schedule their days to include exercise. If you just "go with the flow," you'll be "going with the flab" in no time.

That doesn't mean you need to give up snacks and sit down to three full meals every day. Snacking is probably a good idea; it keeps you from gorging at mealtimes. But honey, *think*. Get yourself out to a real grocery store (not a convenience store) and buy some healthy snacks. Then stash them wherever the munchies tend to hit—in your desk, your glove compartment, your kitchen cupboards. (Keep them out of sight, though, so they're out of mind.) If you've got a long commute, pack something healthy to eat on the way so you don't get ambushed by vending machines or drive-throughs.

Here are some more plan-ahead ideas for healthy snacks.

Stock up on: Yogurt, cut-up fruit or veggies (the more colourful, the better), nuts, whole wheat crackers or pita bread, hummus, cheese strings, low-fat popcorn (snack-size bags), mini cans of salmon or tuna, flavoured sparkling mineral water, grapes, dried fruit, granola bars (without trans fats and low in fat and sugar), high-fibre cereal, cocoa and small packets of sugar to make your own chocolate milk, single servings of unsweetened applesauce or fruit, whole-grain crackers, and nut butters.

Give up on: Pop (even diet pop—the sweetener can cause a surge of insulin, triggering cravings for more sweets), any pasta or bread that isn't whole wheat, sugary cereal, and the usual, obvious, evil things, like potato chips, french fries, and candy.

> **TIP:** Got a craving? Don't give in to the call of the cake or ice cream or can of Pringles! Distract yourself. An absorbing activity like a crossword or Sudoku puzzle can help you withstand temptation. Or call a friend, because you wouldn't, of course, want to talk with your mouth full.

"Dos" and "Don'ts"

- **Do** avoid late-night eating.
- **Do** stick to a regular eating schedule.
- **Do** start your meal with a soup or salad. Even a big glass of water can help fill you up.
- **Do** eat because you're hungry, not because you're bored, upset, or procrastinating.
- **Do** make your own popsicles by freezing real fruit juice concentrate (only add half the water) in paper cups or plastic popsicle forms.
- **Do** quell your munchies with a cup of hot soup or tea.
- **Do** create your own single-serve snacks by buying large bags or boxes and dividing them into small baggies or containers. Hide the rest to be eaten later.

- **Do** buy pudding mix, make it up with low-fat milk, and ladle it into smaller, single-sized servings.
- **Do** eat whole fruits and vegetables instead of just the juice. Whole foods take longer to eat than a gulped-down liquid version, they tend to be lower in calories, and they contain more fibre (which can make you feel full).
- **Do** brush your teeth after you eat. You won't want to muck them up again.
- **Do** keep healthy snacks and bottled water at your desk so you won't be tempted by the vending machine.
- **Do** try making your own dips for veggies (try powdered soup mix stirred into light sour cream or plain yogurt).
- **Do** put a bowl of fruit by the door so you can grab an orange or banana on the go, rather than be tempted when you're out.
- **Do** stick to just four bites when you indulge in "forbidden" foods, and try to really savour them.
- **Do** make sure your meals contain protein to make you feel fuller longer.
- **Do** brown-bag it to school or work. You can control the portions, calories, and fat that way. Or eat half your lunch at noon, the other half when you get the mid-afternoon munchies.
- **Do** enjoy foods that fill: oatmeal, apples, lentils.

- **Don't** skip breakfast. You'll end up overeating later.
- **Don't** skip meals. Your body goes into "starvation mode," which leads to weight gain.
- **Don't** snack out of the bag or box. It will be empty before you know it. Pour the snack into a bowl, then seal the bag and put it back in the cupboard.
- **Don't** go for more than four hours without eating.
- **Don't** be fooled by "light" on the label. Look for something with 3 grams (.1 ounce) or less of fat, and watch that the reduced fat doesn't come with higher calories.
- **Don't** swear off ice cream—just don't bring it home. Go out and buy a cone when the urge hits you.
- **Don't** swear off pizza, either. When you've just got to have it, choose lower-fat toppings or at least blot off the fat with a paper towel.
- **Don't** be tricked by foods sweetened with fruit juice. Their nutritional benefit is nil.
- **Don't** eat your meals in front of the computer or TV. Set the table. Sit at it. Let your brain know you're filling your tummy.

- **Don't** wolf down your food. It takes fifteen to twenty minutes after you begin eating for your body to notice that it's had enough. Studies show the faster you eat, the more calories you consume. Put your fork down between bites and chew slowly.

What Is a Serving, Anyway?

Don't be surprised if "supersize syndrome" has messed up your concept of what a real "single serving" looks like. You're not alone. Restricting your portion sizes to something more realistic is an easy way to make friends with the bathroom scales. Here's a helpful way to keep it in perspective.

Portion sizes

Grains or starch. One fist. Two, if you've been very active.
Poultry and meat. The size of your palm or a deck of cards.
Fat. The size of your thumb-tip.

More than You Really Wanted to Know

One can of pop contains about 50 millilitres (10 teaspoons) of sugar. Drinking a can a day could mean a weight gain of 7 kilograms (15 pounds) a year. Harvard School of Public Health researchers reached this conclusion after reviewing forty years of nutrition studies. Part of the problem may be because soda pop, and other sugary drinks, are sweetened with high-fructose corn syrup, or HFCS. Some experts believe our bodies do not absorb HFCS the same as other sugars—basically, tricking us into not feeling full, while at the same time, causing us to store more fat. Drinking lots of pop is also not good for teeth or bones. Drinking the occasional pop as a treat won't kill you, but if you're thirsty you would be smarter to guzzle down that fantastic-tasting, low-calorie, low-fat, additive- and caffeine-free beverage: water.

The Challenges

Feeling sad? Don't turn to the ice cream tub!

- Call someone who makes you feel good—Mom, Dad, your sister, a friend.
- Rent a funny movie.
- Cuddle up with your blankie and a good book.

- Borrow someone's dog and take him for a walk.
- Have a bath by candlelight.
- Meet a good friend for coffee.
- Fake it. Smile in the mirror. Sing in the shower.

Party Temptations

You might do well with your healthy habits during the week, when you've got your nose to the grindstone. But when your mind wanders to more interesting things on the weekend, it's easy to forget. Want to stay out of trouble at parties? Try sucking on a breath mint or lozenge so you're not tempted to nibble. Keep your hands busy—hold a clutch purse or camera in one hand, a drink in the other. If you're craving something crunchy, bypass the chips and grab some cut-up veggies or a pickle instead. Drink water between beers to limit the calories—and the hangover.

Weighing yourself weekly can help you stay on track, but think about the best time to do it. If you weigh in on Friday afternoon and don't like what you see, it might be a helpful reminder to lay off the Lays on your party weekend. On the other hand, a weigh-in after five weekdays of good food behaviour might encourage you to throw caution to the wind—*Party!!!* In that case, a better time to weigh in might be Monday morning, when you can see what real damage the weekend parties have done. Whatever you choose, stick to a regular weigh-in routine, so you can really compare results honestly.

Eating Out

A pox on supersizes! Whoever started that trend should be deep-fried in trans-fat–laden hot oil! But believe it or not, it is possible to dine out without pigging out. It just takes some advance planning.

First, collect the takeout menus from your favourite restaurants. Circle the healthiest options. Stash them in your glove compartment or desk. You'll never be tempted by supersizes again.

More dining out ideas:

- Good: entrees that are baked, broiled, steamed, roasted, or grilled. Bad: foods that are battered, fried, or served in cream sauces.
- Ask for sauces or dressings on the side.

- Eat only half your meal. Either share it with a friend, or ask for half in a doggy bag before you start. If you are at a sit-down restaurant, forgo the appetizer, or order a salad or a non-creamy soup.
- Have the waiter remove the bread basket.
- Try ordering an appetizer for your main course.
- Opt for baked potato instead of fries.
- Don't call it a coffee break when you order one of those fancy frappe-latte-cino things with whipped cream. Who's fooling whom? That's dessert, darling, and your waistline knows it.
- Remember, just because the supersize is cheaper, that doesn't make it a better deal. It's a very bad deal for your waist, hips, and thighs.

Don't be fooled by these goodies. They're just junk food in disguise:
- Oversized store-bought muffins and carrot cake.
- Sun Chips, Crispers, and other snacks that boast they're "baked, not fried" (they're still loaded with fat).
- Taco salad.
- Granola (when it's full of sugars and fats).

Putting More Movement into Your Day

Remember the days of pickup hockey and dancing till dawn? Have they gone the way of recess? Is the grown-up you sitting in a lecture hall? Chained to a computer or filing cabinet by day, TV by night? Has your body forgotten how to move? That's not good. You want to be expanding your horizons—not your backside. Time to get up off your butt and remind it what it's good for.

- *Walk while you work.* Book it round the block on your coffee break or lunch. Walk to work, or if it's too far, catch the bus midway.
- *How far can you park?* If you have to drive, pick the farthest spot in the parking lot.
- *Get some face time.* When you need to talk to a co-worker, don't e-mail or phone— walk across the office and do it face to face.

- *Take the stairs.* Elevators are for wussies. If you're in a dorm, use the bathroom on another floor.
- *Raking leaves, shovelling, or housecleaning?* Do it vigorously enough to break a sweat.
- *Do your errands on the run.* Instead of relying on your car, take off on foot during your lunch hour.
- *Swear off drive-throughs.* Always get out of the car at a fast-food place, at the cleaner's, the pharmacy, or the bank. Wash the car by hand.
- *Replace your desk chair with an exercise ball.* It'll keep you moving and your abs engaged.

At some point, you'll probably need to do more than simply squeeze more movement into your day. Good health depends on getting your heart rate up for a minimum of 30 minutes per day.

Exercise—the Basics

- Exercise three to five times a week.
- Warm up for five to ten minutes.
- Maintain your exercise intensity for at least half an hour. (If you want to lose weight and not just maintain it, you'll need to do this at least five times a week.)
- During the last few minutes, stretch to cool down.

TIPS:
- Drink water and eat two to four hours before your workout. Make your meal one that is high in carbs, low in fat, and offers moderate amounts of protein, about 400 to 800 calories altogether.
- A recent university study proves listening to your favourite music makes exercise more bearable. Tunes with more than 135 beats per minute may motivate you to push harder.
- Use peer pressure to your advantage. Join a sports league or a gym with a buddy. You're more likely to stick with it if others are counting on you.

More than You Really Wanted to Know

You already know how important it is to drink lots of water when you're exercising, but did you know it's possible to drink too much? A 28-year-old California woman was found dead recently, a victim of "water intoxication." She had taken part in a radio station contest to see how much water she could drink without going to the bathroom. Apparently, she didn't realize that when you take in too much fluid too quickly, it pushes the body's electrolyte balance past safe limits—a deadly mistake. Stay hydrated—just don't drown yourself.

Cost Cutters

- Contact the local Humane Society to see if they need dog walkers.
- Use the local community centre for swimming, gym, etc. It's much cheaper than exclusive fitness clubs.
- Exercise for free. Skip the health membership and hike, walk, bike, or blade.
- Rent exercise videos to find one you like, then buy it and exercise at home.
- Look for drop-in basketball, volleyball games, etc., at your local community centre.
- Sports equipment—buy it used, especially if you are just starting a sport and don't know if you will commit to continuing.
- Gyms often waive enrollment fees or give discounts in January, so that's a good time to join. They'll be busy then, though, so you'll have to schedule your visits on weekends until the newbies bail. Another good time to join: June, when some clubs reduce fees to drum up business during the slow season.
- Local YMCAs can be less expensive and less intimidating than gyms for novices, and they usually offer a wide assortment of activities.
- Check out www.sparkpeople.com instead of pricey weight-loss programs for advice, calorie counters, recipes, and workouts.

Cheating

At some point in your crusade for health and fitness you might get discouraged. At some point, you might even be tempted to take some shortcuts. There are plenty of crazy weight-loss schemes out there. And thanks to the free-market economy, there are loads of "miracle" products that people would love to sell you, as well. Here's why you should take a pass.

Energy in a Bottle

There are lots of beverages out there that promise to help you lose weight, boost your energy, or lower your cholesterol. Just guzzle this magic brew and presto—you're all pumped up and revved up, ready for sports, all-nighters, dancing till dawn. Uh, hello? Liquid energy? Sorry to break it to you, but there really isn't much evidence this stuff actually works.

Some of these drinks contain ginseng, for example, but the amount is minimal and therefore ineffective. Some drinks, like "Cocaine Energy Drink," contain 280 milligrams of caffeine—compared to the average 80 milligrams in a cup of coffee. And caffeine, when it's combined with other stimulating herbs, as it is in some drinks, can be dangerous. Even worse is combining caffeine with alcohol, which might mask danger signs like dizziness or a racing heart. In Sweden, "energy drinks" are under investigation after being cited as a possible cause in three deaths. Not a good idea, dear.

Artificial Sweeteners

Think you can get away with guzzling diet pop all day? Sugar-free equals guilt-free, right? Wrong—there's no such thing as a free ride. Turns out artificial sweeteners may actually increase caloric consumption. Consuming sweets without calories seems to disrupt the body's regulatory control system. It's also possible that diet drinks trick people into thinking they can indulge elsewhere. And if you're filling up on the empty stuff, you're missing out on the benefits of plain water, milk, or juice.

Meals in a Can

Meal replacement drinks are okay once in a while, but don't rely on them. If all you do is crack open a can, you'll never learn how to work real, healthy food into your life. You'll get better long-term results by finding out which real foods are good for you.

Energy Bars

Don't they look yummy? And they can burn fat, build muscle, improve your sports and your love life and your living room décor and your math marks …

Yeah, right. Many of these bars contain hundreds of calories, and offer no more energy than you'd get from a granola bar and a glass of milk. Some do contain vitamins, minerals, and other nutritional extras, but there's little in the way of natural fibre, phytochemicals, and the good protein you'd find in real food. Some are no better than a chocolate bar and a multi-vitamin. Ignore the hype—stick with the real thing.

Supplements

Most "fat-burning" supplements are designed to make you urinate—which causes a weight loss, but not the kind you want. The fat's still there. Manufacturers often tell you to take their product while also exercising and cutting back calories. Well, of course you'll lose weight if you exercise and eat less. Don't give the supplement credit for that!

Some supplements can be downright dangerous. Skip supplements that contain ma huang (ephedra) and guarana (caffeine). They can damage your heart. Products containing bitter-orange extracts (citrus aurantium) may be risky for those with hypertension or other heart problems. HCA—short for hydroxy citric acid—is another common supplement with dubious claims. We still don't have proof if it's safe, or if it even works for weight loss. Until we know for sure, it's best to steer clear. Creatine, an amino acid supplement, is a big thing with guys looking to bulk up. High doses can also cause nausea, diarrhea, indigestion, cramps, and strains.

Laxative Abuse

This is another no-brainer. The risks, as follows: chronic constipation, abdominal cramping and pain, diarrhea, and vomiting. Overuse of laxatives can also impair absorption of certain vitamins and minerals, which leads to bone disease. It will impair absorption of fat (thus the greasy diarrhea and weight loss), and can also cause damage to the gastrointestinal tract, permanent bowel damage, and liver disease.

TIP: Watch out for something called PPA (phenylpropanolamine). It's found in over-the-counter diet products and it can increase blood pressure if taken at too high a dose. In fact, it can cause problems for some people at the recommended doses, as well. Some cold and allergy medicines also contain PPA, so read the labels to be safe.

Weight Loss Magicians

Some pills and diet patches promise to "burn," "block," or "flush" the fat from your body. Is it really possible? Is there a magic pill that can make it all just go away? Well, remember how I had to tell you about Santa and the Tooth Fairy? Guess what? No magic pill, either. So far, anything that looks like it has any effect also has serious side effects too. The latest warnings concern ephedrine and caffeine—bad idea. Taken together, they can cause dizziness, tremors, headaches, heart-rate irregularities, seizures, psychosis, heart attacks, and stroke. As for those eyeglasses that claim to decrease appetite and earrings that control hunger with acupressure—oh, come on!

Just for fun, check out this website: www. wemarket4u.net/fatfoe.

More than You Really Wanted to Know

Nearly 20 percent of girls aged 19 to 20 use diet pills to try to lose weight, according to a recent study at the University of Minnesota. Really dumb idea, girls. Not only did the pills used by the girls in the study fail, but by the time the study was completed, those who used the pills (and other "cheats" like fasting and purging) ended up three times more likely to be overweight. Repeat: dumb.

Fad Diets

Come on, dear, you're smarter than that. Losing weight is hard work. There are no quick fixes. Steer clear of any diet that:

- Promises more than a 1-kilogram (2-pound) weight loss per week.
- Requires you to buy special products, foods, or supplements.

- Forbids entire food groups.
- Requires you to follow a strict set of dietary rules.

Radical dieting and rapid weight loss really mess up your body. No matter what the weird diet claims, an artificial approach to food is not good. When you starve your body, your body changes. When you return to what's normal, your body thinks it's still being starved and stores the calories as fat—thus you get the yo-yo effect. You feel like a glutton with no control, binging and starving and rebounding back again. Your immune system is weakened and your morale is low. Stick with the good old Canada's Food Guide and regular exercise. It's not sexy, but it works.

More than You Really Wanted to Know

Sure, Gwyneth Paltrow, Angelina Jolie, Beyoncé Knowles, Cate Blanchett, and Kate Moss all swear by it—but does that mean it's right? Think about it. According to the celebs, if you fast and take laxatives, special herbs, and cleansing foods, somehow your body's going to be perfect, just like theirs! Thanks to detox, you too can flush poisons from your body, clear your complexion, improve your immune system, your mental state, and your digestion, and of course, lose weight.

Okay, now listen to the *real* experts. Detox diets are *dangerous*. Doctors and nutritionists warn that prolonged or repeated fasts can lead to vitamin deficiencies, muscle breakdown, blood-sugar problems, headaches, lethargy, lack of focus, and irritability. The crash diets can cause bone loss and weaken the body's defences against inflammation and infection. Laxatives and frequent liquid bowel movements offer even more unpleasant effects, like dehydration and skin irritation on your bottom.

The fact is, your body does a perfectly fine job of flushing toxins all by itself, thanks to your large intestine, liver, and kidneys. A more sensible approach is to improve your eating habits in a way that you can maintain over time, by eating high-fibre fruits, veggies, whole grains, and beans, avoiding processed food, and washing it all down with lots of water.

I joined one of those medically supervised weight-loss plans. I lost weight, all right. My blood pressure also started going up and down, I felt dizzy half the time, and when I complained they said that the diet was "not for me." I think they fired me! I didn't get my money back because I had lost a few pounds. That little experiment must have set me back $600.

—NAME WITHHELD

Purging

Otherwise known as sticking your fingers down your throat and watching your meal come back up. Bad idea, on several fronts. When you do this regularly, the stomach acid that flows through your mouth can cause irreparable damage to your teeth. They might become sensitive to heat, cold, and acids, and eventually they could decay and fall out. Your salivary glands might swell, too, because of irritation from the vomit. You might suffer from stomach ulcers and bleeding in your esophagus. You'll be tired all the time and your throat and stomach will hurt, constantly. Eventually you'll start throwing up blood, your hair will fall out, you'll end up with burst blood vessels in your eyes and face, and you'll suffer damage to your heart, liver, gastrointestinal tract, and brain. And you're doing this ... why? To look good? Yeah. That's attractive.

Steroids

Guys aren't exempt from this messed up view of the healthy body. Washboard abs, tanned and hairless chest, sculpted pecs—you gotta have it all, no matter what the cost. So while girls are binging and purging and going for the lipo, guys are guzzling protein drinks and shelling out for tanning booths and laser body-hair removal. Nothing like equality of the sexes, eh?

And then there are steroids—the gym rat's "dirty secret." Anabolic steroids—or "juice"—are manufactured variations of the male hormone testosterone. They can be taken orally, injected, or used in gels or creams rubbed on the skin. Most people who use steroids use needles. Users like juice because, when combined with intense workouts, it gives them increased muscle mass and strength. But there's a whole lotta bad that goes along with that.

- Acne.
- Secondary male sex characteristics, such as increased sweat gland activity, aggression ("roid rage"), excessive hair growth, and deepening voice (especially bad if you happen to be female).
- Male-pattern baldness.
- Gynecomastia, or "gyno"—growth of breast tissue in men.
- The injection site may become sore or develop an abscess or infection.
- Cellulitis—a painful, spreading inflammation of the skin.
- Shrinkage of the testicles and decreased sperm production, sterility.
- Enlargement of the heart muscle.
- Increased blood pressure.
- Liver and heart disease.
- Increased size of prostate gland.
- Hepatitis B, hepatitis C, and HIV from contact with infected blood through needle sharing or sharing steroid vials.
- Addiction—withdrawal symptoms include mood swings, fever, depression, fatigue, restlessness, insomnia, sweats, reduced sex drive, and loss of appetite.

Honey, be careful. People might boast in the gym about what steroids have done for them. They might try to talk you into it, saying it's only risky for those who haven't done their research. They might say that only those who aren't cycling on and off the drugs have problems. The fact is, steroids are risky for everyone. And if they are purchased off the street, they're not monitored, so you could be getting the wrong strength or a fake product. If you're seriously tempted, at least contact your local public health department or kids/youth helpline. They'll give you free and confidential information.

Risky Business

You're all grown up. You are making your own decisions, and some of those decisions will have life-altering consequences. It's like skating on a frozen lake. Sure, the ice is bumpy in parts, and the snow drifts over in others, but really, nothing feels quite like it. Then you come across a patch where the ice thins.

Skate, by all means, but know when to stop and look around. Take risks but not mindless ones.

Body Art

Nix the piercing and tattoos. Yeah, everyone is doing it, but darling, you will regret it. Your tastes will change. Don't believe me? Remember that mushroom haircut you had in Grade 6—you loved it! Imagine being stuck with *that* for the rest of your life.

Tattoo artists, and those who specialize in tattoo removal, say it takes about three months for people to have second thoughts about their body art. Know who's most inclined to regret it? The poor bloke who, thanks to booze or love or both, had his sweetie's name engraved on his flesh. Second most common reason why people want the tattoo removed is the up-and-comer who needs it gone for career reasons. One more thing, removal can cost ten times what you paid in the first place. Then there is the likelihood of scarring. I'm thinking skin grafts. Sound good to you?

Before you roll up your sleeve, sailor, consider this. A tattoo is a wound—multiple punctures deep into your skin that are filled with ink. And like any wound, it is vulnerable to infection and disease—bacterial skin infections, dermatitis (severe skin irritation), flare-ups of eczema. If it's not done safely, viruses such as HIV and hepatitis B and C can sneak into your body.

As for piercing. Consider these tongue-piercing risks, from the University of Manitoba:

- Hepatitis, HIV, herpes simplex virus, tetanus.
- Extended bleeding if blood vessels are ruptured.
- Blocked airways if the tongue swells.
- Loss of taste.
- Numb tongue.
- Constant soreness in mouth and throat.
- Speech problems (Donald Duck sound sexy to you?).
- Difficulty with chewing and swallowing.

Okay, so maybe you're fine with your tongue as it is; you have another body part in mind. Mouth? Nose? Not a great idea. They're susceptible to infection because of the millions of bacteria that live in there. Cheek, tongue, or lips? That can land you nasty gum problems. And as with any piercing of the skin, there are always the risks of uncontrolled bleeding, scarring, abscesses, inflammation, and nerve damage.

All right, if you're still stuck on that idea of a Celtic something-or-other drawn on your ankle, or a fetching ring for your lip (don't say I didn't warn you), then here's how to go about it safely.

The most important thing is to find an establishment that is clean—where equipment is either disposable (needles, gloves, masks, etc.) or sterilized. Be sure that it's reputable and licensed to perform the procedures. If you see needles being used on

---

Been there
Done THAT

I just picked the Japanese symbol out of a book. I assumed that it was the symbol for world peace. I mean, how was I to know the word meant "house"?

—ERIN, 19

Been there
Done THAT

A girl, let's call her Sally, had her tongue pierced. Soon she developed the nasty habit of flicking her tongue against her upper teeth. It wasn't long before she flicked away the delicate skin on the roof of her mouth. Try as the dentist might (and after Sally's parents spent thousands of dollars) new skin could not be grafted over the exposed roots. Alas, Sally lost her front teeth and ended up wearing old-lady dentures. And for what?? The adventure cost her $4,000.

more than one patient, ink sharing, or technicians not wearing gloves, run in the opposite direction.

Make sure your immunizations (especially hepatitis and tetanus) are up to date. If you have any medical problem (heart disease, allergies, diabetes, infections, or impaired immune system, for example), or if you're pregnant, talk to your doctor first. Think long and hard about piercing or tattooing unusual and sensitive areas. Never, never try to pierce or tattoo yourself (or let a friend do it). That would be the ultimate in stupid.

And keeping in mind that you might one day be a soccer mom or corporation president, the American Society for Dermatologic Surgery recommends you choose something simple. If you're going for a tattoo, opt for something small with fewer colours—it's easier to remove. Ear piercing is a more conventional choice than eyebrow. Confine your body art to a place that can be covered by clothing in the workplace.

Finally, take care of your wounds as they heal. Follow the instructions from the tattoo or piercing technician and watch for signs of infection—redness, swelling, pain, prolonged bleeding, pus, or changes in skin colour. If you're at all concerned, call your doctor right away.

By the way, remember that mushroom haircut? It grew out. Your tattoo? Not so easy. If you want to get rid of it, you'll require a number of visits over several weeks with a tattoo remover who will use a laser to zap through the top layers of your skin. It can be "uncomfortable" (a.k.a. *painful*), just like getting a tattoo was. And just like when you got your tattoo, you will have a new wound that needs special care. Sometimes the area gets infected or scarred or the skin changes colour. As for tattoo removal cost, start saving now. It'll cost lots more than you paid in the first place.

Resources

Healthy eating

Enter your food choices and activities to find out how you're doing. Also offers health tips: www.dietitians.ca/eatracker

Canada's Food Guide to Healthy Eating: www.hc-sc.gc.ca/fn-an/food-guide-aliment/index_e.html

Helpful information about eating disorders

www.nationaleatingdisorders.org

Advice, calorie counters, recipes, and workouts

www.sparkpeople.com

8

Preventing Illness—And What to Do When You Can't

If you woke up breathing, congratulations! You have another chance.

—ANDREA BOYDSTON

Hate to break it to you, honey, but in Canada, "sick season" is a part of life. From November to March you're a walking target for germs. Maybe it's because we all tend to hole up indoors, rubbing shoulders (and other things) for months on end. No, I'm not suggesting you move to California. I'm just saying you've got to protect yourself. Eating right and exercising regularly are your first line of defence. The second line is way easier: WASH YOUR HANDS!

Germ Fighting

Most people think you catch illnesses from people coughing or sneezing in your face. But the truth is, the main way you get sick is by touching things that have been contaminated, and then touching your eyes, nose, or mouth. Don't blame flying germs—blame your roving hands.

Where the Germs Are

Studies show these are the grungiest places to touch:

- Bus and subway armrests, hand straps, and rails.
- Public washroom surfaces (especially bathroom door handles and the middle stall).
- Shopping cart handles (some stores now supply wipes).
- Computer mouse at Internet cafés.
- Shared customer pens (keep your own in a pocket or purse).

- Elevator buttons (first floor especially). Use the knuckle on your pinky.
- Escalator handrails.
- Vending machine buttons, including ATMs.
- Public phones.

Hands, Meet Soap ...

Eeew! Guess what, Cindy? "Icky" can be "invisible"—as in, you don't always see the germs—as in, there's nobody in a black hat shouting, "Yoo-hoo, bad guy over here!"

Say you're in a public washroom. Say you're not the first person on earth to have ever used that public washroom. Say whoever used it before you used the toilet and left behind a few little gifts—pathogens, bacteria, viruses, other micro-organisms—on the door or toilet handle. Guess what you're walking away with? And germs don't just lurk in washrooms. Think about what you touch all day—elevator buttons, stair railings, doorknobs, the cash machine, telephones, money … Doesn't that make you want to wash your hands?

Duh |
moment **!**

How to wash your hands:

1. Scrub the entire hand—front, back, nail bed, beneath rings—vigorously for at least 20 seconds (or, if you don't mind looking really silly, sing "Happy Birthday" twice). Use water as warm as you can stand.
2. Rinse, pointing your fingers down to wash off germs.
3. If you're in a public washroom, use a paper towel to dry, then use the same towel to turn off the tap and open the door.
4. At home, use your own personal hand towel. Got a houseful of people? Colour-code your towels.

So now you know how and why you should wash your hands. How about when? Well, you don't want to become obsessive about it. Most bacteria need a warm, moist environment to survive; they won't live long on hard, dry surfaces. Still, you should wash whenever you can. Try to get into the habit of washing your hands as soon as you return home. Also:

+

More than You Really Wanted to Know

A survey of washrooms in public places found that only 83 percent of adults actually wash their hands after using the washroom, even though 91 percent say they do.

- Before eating.
- After using the bathroom.
- After blowing your nose.
- After coughing or sneezing into your hands.
- Before inserting or removing contact lenses.
- Before and after handling food, especially raw meat, poultry, or fish.
- Before and after treating wounds or cuts.
- Before and after touching a sick or injured person.
- After touching animals or animal waste.
- After handling garbage.

Hand sanitizers

You can't always find running water to wash your hands, so it's smart to keep some alcohol sanitizers handy. They don't require water, and they are an excellent alternative (although only soap and water will get rid of dirt, blood, and other gunk). Keep small containers in your glove compartment, pocket, or purse. The best is a thick gel or foam that won't drip off your skin. Look for at least 60 percent alcohol. Put a dime-sized amount in the palm of your hand and rub all over. You've used enough if your hands still feel damp after twenty seconds of rubbing.

TIP: Washing hands can lead to dryness—especially in winter—and germs can hide out in cracked skin. Use hand cream often.

Since hand sanitizers are flammable, store them away from high temperatures. If you're surrounded by people who don't hand-wash as often as you'd like, try leaving a few containers of sanitizer where they'll notice—at the office kitchen counter, next to the buffet table—or use yours in front of them, and maybe they'll get the hint.

Antibacterials

You may have noticed that a truckload of antibacterial products have flooded the market in recent years, in everything from toothpaste to baby toys. Should you use them? At this point, experts think not. They are concerned that antibacterials kill most, but not all, bacteria. That means the toughest are left behind, which might encourage the evolution of drug-resistant bacteria. It might even weaken our natural ability to fight infection. Take a pass. Stick with soap.

Germs in the Bathroom

Do you wonder what despicable germs are lurking about in a public washroom, waiting to jump up and nab you the minute you sit down? Relax. You're not likely to pick up a disease—sexually transmitted or otherwise—when you lounge on the loo. Your thighs and buttocks just aren't that enticing to germs. If it sets your mind at ease, cover the seat with a bit of toilet paper. If it's really gross, find another stall. Worry about your hands. That's where you're more likely to pick up nasties—and carry them up to your mouth, nose, or eyes.

Germs at Work

Beware the dreaded PowerPoint remote! Studies show it's the germiest thing in a typical workplace. But there's lots of competition: the telephone, computer keyboard, mouse—just about anything that gets a lot of handling. During flu and cold season you can stay healthy if you:

- Keep a dispenser of disinfecting wipes in your desk, and wipe your workspace daily.
- Bring a mug to work and clean it yourself. Don't drink from the office collection. You don't know how well they've been cleaned.
- Beware the door handle on the microwave in the office kitchen.
- Remember to wash your hands frequently throughout the day and keep your hands away from your face.

TIP: Think twice about plunking your purse, gym bag, or backpack on the washroom floor. Remember, not everyone shares your stellar aim, so your bag might be sharing the floor with whatever missed the toilet bowl. You get home, throw your bag on the bed or kitchen counter and ... well, yuck!

More than You Really Wanted to Know

- On your keyboard: 3,769 bacteria per square inch.
- On your desktop: 5,015 bacteria per square inch.
- On your phone: 5,585 bacteria per square inch.

If you're eating at your desk, you might want to wipe your hands and workspace with disinfectant.

More Ways to Combat Germs

- Buy liquid hand soap rather than bars, because germs remain on bars. Clean the dispenser every day or so.
- Don't leave wet towels in a clump. The longer they sit around wet and dirty, the more likely germs will set up shop.
- When cooking, don't taste-test food with the same spoon you use for stirring.
- Don't share forks, spoons, glasses, or water bottles.
- Being cold won't give you a cold—but it can make you more vulnerable to whatever germs are floating around out there. Whenever you head outdoors, hear that little voice of mine calling out, "Where's your hat?" You can lose more than 30 percent of your body heat through your head. Oh, and cover up that neck, too.
- Keep your body strong with exercise and rest.
- Don't smoke. Smoking makes you more vulnerable to colds. Avoid smoky areas, too. Smoke can dry out your nasal passages.
- Drink lots of fluids—but not the alcoholic kind. Water flushes out your system; booze dehydrates you. Sorry.
- When using a public phone, keep your mouth far from the mouthpiece, and wash your hands afterwards. If someone's sick in your home, ask him/her to wipe the phone receiver after using it. If you are sick, don't share your cellphone.
- Don't pump gas, then drive and snack. Do you know how many grubby hands have touched the gas nozzle, the debit machine, the change from the cashier? That's why you put the hand sanitizer in your car, remember?
- Eat lots of brightly coloured fruits and vegetables.

- Buy a bunch of pens and stash them everywhere—purse, pocket, glove compartment—so you never have to use someone else's. Cold germs survive on surfaces for hours. Just imagine what's partying on the pen in your doctor's office.
- Avoid shaking germy hands with someone who might be sick.
- Close the toilet lid when you flush to prevent germs from spraying into the air.
- Use public washroom stalls that are closest to the door—they are usually the cleanest because they are least used.
- Shake water from your shower curtain and leave it open to dry when you're done. This helps to prevent mould or mildew. Mould and mildew are more than gross, they're actually unhealthy and can cause lung infections.
- Stay at least one metre away from anyone who is coughing, sneezing, or nose-blowing.
- When a sickness outbreak hits the news, avoid big public gatherings for a while. Rent a movie instead.

TIP: At a buffet or salad bar, don't use plates that are still wet from the kitchen—they may be breeding bacteria.

More than You Really Wanted to Know

Avoid makeup counter samples. You can catch conjunctivitis from mascara or eyeliner, or pick up herpes from a lipstick sampler. If you can't resist checking out the wares, use the back of your hand rather than eyes or lips. Shop during the week when there are fewer shoppers contaminating samples, or ask for sealed samples. And while we're at it, don't share makeup, tweezers, nail files, or brushes.

Eating to Stay Healthy

Certain foods are more helpful than others in supporting your immune system. If your diet is rich in the following foods, you might be less likely to get sick, and if you do, you might recover more quickly.

TIP: Don't forget your apple a day—it really does keep the doctor (and dentist) away.

- Leafy green vegetables: spinach, dark-green lettuce, broccoli.
- Carrots, pumpkin, butternut squash.
- Yogurt.
- Fruits: citrus fruits, kiwi fruit, blueberries, raisins, dried cherries.
- Red peppers.
- Potatoes.
- Turkey and other meats.
- Eggs.
- Legumes.
- Garlic.
- Smoked oysters, crab meat.
- Tea.
- Soy.
- Almonds and sunflower seeds.

Sleeping to Stay Healthy

I've been trying to wake you up for the past ten years. Well, now I am telling you to sleep—but *at night*. Look, sleep is to the brain what food is to the body. You want to wake up and take on the world? Stop it with the all-nighters; they screw up your sleep patterns, and the next day you can't think. (Yes, that's why you failed Physics.) You should be getting seven to eight hours a night.

When you wake up, get out into the light. Take the neighbour's dog for a walk, go buy a newspaper or a coffee, do what you have to, just get up and out, even for ten minutes. Now you are ready to take on the world.

Are you still struggling with this one? Let's break it down a bit more.

Getting to Sleep

- Give yourself one to two hours free of worry before bed. If all the things you've got to do keep rolling around in your head, keep a pen and paper by the bed. Write those things down, then forget about them. You may find, as John Steinbeck said, that your problem is resolved after "the committee of sleep has worked on it."
- Stay away from the computer at night. Don't check your e-mail before you turn in.
- If you can, keep the TV in another room.

- Turn the clock so it's facing the wall. You'll be less tempted to check the time all night long.
- Stick to a regular schedule with a consistent bedtime.
- Steer clear of anything with caffeine after 2 p.m. Even decaffeinated drinks can contain a bit of caffeine. Drinking five to ten cups of decaf a day could jolt you with the equivalent of a cup or two of regular java.
- Don't pig-out before bed, and definitely stay away from the wasabi and anchovies. If your tummy's growling, settle it with a little turkey or warm milk.
- Don't wolf down your dinner and hit the sack. Leave a couple of hours between dinner and bedtime.
- Skip the nightcap—it can disrupt your sleep.
- Keep your room dark and quiet—use blinds, white-noise machines (buy one, run a fan, or tune the radio between stations with the volume low), or calming music.
- Exercise during the day—but at least three to four hours before bed, to give your body time to gear down.
- Just before you hit the sack, pull on a pair of socks. Studies show it might help you fall asleep faster.
- If you can't sleep after twenty minutes, don't just lie there staring at the ceiling. Get up and do something else—read in another room, watch TV, or do a Sudoku puzzle. Same thing if you wake up in the middle of the night.

A word about napping and sleeping pills

Both are tempting. Both can backfire.

If you've had a bad night and can manage to squeeze in a quick nap, go for it. It might revive you. The best time to catch some zzz's is around 2 p.m. But lounge in bed for any longer than ten to twenty minutes, and your body will slip into a deeper sleep, leaving you feeling yucky for the rest of the day. Don't make a habit of this nap thing, or you'll never teach your body that day's for wake, night's for sleeping. If you find you're drowsy midday, try exercise instead. Just twenty minutes can wake you up and send oxygen to your brain.

Another thing not to make a habit of: sleeping pills. They're just a quick fix. Sure, they'll help you doze off, but you could end up feeling just as dozy in the morning. And if you rely on them too much, you could end up with "rebound insomnia" when you stop.

Getting Yourself Awake

Here's the bad news (which you have, hopefully, already figured out): Mom is not your alarm clock any more.

And here's the good news: no more detentions for being late to class.

But that doesn't mean you get to slack off. In university, late sleepers miss important information that's doled out to the keeners at the start of class. In the working world, the boss can simply fire you. So you know what that means? Wakey-wakey … all by yourself. Too tuckered to toddle out? Here are some suggestions:

- Hide the alarm clock. You won't be able to just smack the snooze button. In fact, set two alarm clocks at opposite ends of the room.
- Don't set the alarm clock to pleasant music. Try a talk show that gets you riled, or the buzzer, or opera, or Celine Dion, or simply static between stations. Think *annoying*.
- Before you go to bed, put a glass of ice cubes on the nightstand. By the time morning comes it will have melted into ice-cold water that you can splash on your face. A spray bottle works well, too. (Don't try this on your roommate.)
- If you tend to doze off in the shower, get a waterproof alarm clock and set it for mid-shower time.
- Don't close the drapes at night. Let the morning light waken you. Move your bed to face the window. Or set a timer to turn on a light that is on the other side of the bedroom.

TIP: Don't even think about popping a caffeine pill. Sure, it sounds like a simple solution when your energy is flagging, but these zingers often contain more caffeine than coffee. Over the long term they can cause weight gain, cardiac disease, kidney and liver irritation, and inflammation. You'd be smarter to focus on healthier—and more long-term—ways to stay alert. That might include better eating (more protein, veggies, and grains; less sugar), reducing stress, more exercise, more fluids (since dehydration can reduce energy), and, duh, more sleep at night.

- Tag-team with your roommate: you watch his back, he'll watch yours. (That only works if you *both* have to be up. If not, it's nasty.)
- Drink a glass of water before turning in. Your bladder will force you out of bed. (Not too much, though, or you'll wake up in the middle of the night.)
- Stay away from the computer. Don't even go near it in the morning. You know why.

Check out some of the funky new alarm clocks: some play your iPod, simulate the sounds of nature, or offer aromatherapy. And if you're truly desperate, there's a flying alarm clock called Blowfly that buzzes around the room like a giant mosquito, or one called "Clocky" that has wheels that roll it off your nightstand. It will hide somewhere in your room—a different place each day—and keep beeping until groggy you get up and crawl around looking for it. (No fair whipping it against the wall.)

Note: If you are skipping sleep regularly, be sure to take a multivitamin to keep yourself from getting sick. If the problem persists, talk to your doctor. Insomnia can be related to medications, hormones, or an underlying physical or mental health problem.

TIP: Canadian houses dry up in the winter. A dry nose is more vulnerable to germs. If you have a humidifier, use it, but keep it properly cleaned. No humidifier? Boiling water adds humidity to a small apartment. Or try putting bowls of water on the radiators or in front of the heat registers. When you have a shower or bath, leave the door open afterwards to let the steam circulate through your home. And don't drain the tub until the water cools down.

When Sickness Comes Calling

You hurt all over. You've got a runny nose, a nasty headache, you can't stop coughing, and one ear really hurts. You're wicked sick. Is it the flu? A cold? Are you dying?

Cold or Flu?

It's not easy to tell the difference, but usually, the flu is more severe than a cold—and it hits you like a Mack truck.

	Cold	Flu
Starts with:	Creeps up on you; you feel a little worse each day	Sudden; yesterday you were fine, today you suck
Is there a fever?	Rarely. If you do, it's low-grade (100–101°F)	Usually, lasting 3–4 days
Is there a cough?	Yes—mucusy or dry	Yes—usually dry
What else?	A cold usually sets up shop in your upper respiratory system: runny nose, sore throat, watery eyes, congestion in chest, sinuses, and ears.	A miserable mixture of aching joints and muscles, extreme fatigue, nausea and pounding headache
Duration	Worst is usually over in 72–96 hrs (can linger low level for weeks)	7–14 days, 2–3 severe
Peak period	All winter (adults get 2–5 per year on average)	Winter and early spring, occurs in outbreaks

TIP: Some over-the-counter meds might help, but choose only products that treat the symptoms you have. (This will save money, too.) Antibiotics won't help either colds or flu. Antibiotics kill bacteria, not viruses, and are no help to you when cold or flu viruses show up.

Should I get a flu shot?

Even though it's not 100 percent effective, it's not a bad idea—especially for health care workers, and anyone with chronic heart or lung disease, diabetes, kidney disease, anemia, or immune-system problems. If you're thinking of getting the vaccine, and don't fall into one of these categories, ask your doctor. Don't get a flu shot if you're allergic to eggs or have a fever. Best time to get the needle? October to November. You may experience some adverse effects, a little soreness where the needle went in, or aches and fever, but the vaccine does not *cause* the flu.

How to Take Your Temperature

You've got a thermometer in your medicine cabinet / first-aid kit, right? If not, go buy one. Your best bet is probably a digital thermometer—flat, plastic, pencil-shaped, with a display window at one end and the temperature probe at the other. Make sure it has working batteries.

More than You Really Wanted to Know

More than 200 different viruses can cause colds. The flu, on the other hand, is caused by just a few different viruses. That's why there's a vaccine for flu but not for colds. Unfortunately, there is no cure for either.

Get it out, read the instructions, and take your temperature now so that you're not trying to figure out how it works when you're sick. You can take a temperature via the mouth, ear, armpit, or rectum. Mouth is preferable (I'm sure you'll agree), but if your head's stuffed up and you can't breathe through your nose, you might have to take your temperature in your armpit. The results won't be as accurate, and it might read .6 degrees C (1 degree F) lower than an oral temperature.

Wait at least 20 to 30 minutes after eating, drinking a hot or cold liquid, or smoking, and at least an hour after exercising or taking a hot bath. Stick the thermometer under your tongue, just to one side of the centre, and close your lips. Leave it there for however long the instructions say, or until it beeps. Pull it out and see what it says. It should read 37 degrees C (98.6 degrees F)—give or take .6 degrees C (1 degree F). Your normal body temperature changes slightly throughout the day, depending on your activity level, time of the month (females), and time of day. When your temp reads 38 degrees C (100 degrees F) or higher, you're running a fever.

TIP: Clean your thermometer with cool soapy water and rinse it off before putting it away.

Fever in itself is not bad; it's how your body defends itself against infection. Unless you're instructed otherwise by your doctor, it's not necessary to treat a fever. Just don't overdress, and if you're really uncomfortable, you can take a coolish bath or acetaminophen (like Tylenol) or ibuprofen (like Advil)—but, if you're under twenty, not Aspirin. Children and teens can contract a serious and sometimes fatal condition called Reye's syndrome when Aspirin is taken for flu symptoms.

What to Do

If you're sniffly and sneezy and your head's all stuffed up

- Elevate your pillow to help the mucus drain.
- Run a cool-mist humidifier or breathe in the steam from a shower or a pot of boiling water. (Careful, don't get too close!) Do this for at least 10 minutes. Or fill a bowl or sink with steaming water and bend your head over the bowl with a large towel over your head to trap the steam.
- If the congestion makes your head hurt, apply an ice pack over the sinuses for 20 minutes.
- Drink plenty of non-caffeinated liquids.

TIP: To keep from getting a raw nose from constant blowing, try just "honking," rather than rubbing. If it's too late, and the skin around your nose is tender and sore, try massaging it with Vaseline.

- Use a saline spray or a saline nasal rinse, which can flush out the mucus but is not, like nasal sprays, potentially addictive. (See page 238 for more on this addiction.)
- Try an antihistamine to help dry up some of the mucus. (Although they're really only useful if you also have allergies.) Warning: antihistamines often cause drowsiness.
- Oral decongestants can shrink the swollen passages of your nose. Talk to the pharmacist about whether these would help.

If you can't stop coughing

- Drink plenty of clear fluids.
- Inhale steam, either with a humidifier, a vaporizer, a pot of boiling water, or by sitting in a bathroom and running a hot shower.
- Use more than one pillow to prop your head up while sleeping.
- For a thick cough, or if you're having trouble coughing the mucus up, an expectorant cough syrup might help.
- For a dry, hacking cough that keeps you awake at night, a suppressant cough syrup might help. (Warning: this can make you sleepy, so use it only when you are able to rest.)

- Remember, though, that you *want* to get rid of that gunk in your chest. A good approach might be to use a cold remedy that combines antihistamine and decongestant. It will treat the congestion that's causing the cough. Look for something that contains chlorpheniramine and pseudoephedrine.

If your throat hurts

- Gargle for five seconds with 250 millilitres (1 cup) of warm water mixed with 5 millilitres (1 teaspoon) of salt.
- Drink sour fluids (like lemon tea) to get your saliva flowing.
- Gargle with 1 millilitre (¼ teaspoon of salt or baking soda in a glass of warm water a few times a day.
- Lozenges and hard candy can be soothing.
- Take Aspirin or Aspirin substitutes.

*In any of the above situations, if you're feeling achey or your head aches, it's okay to take ibuprofen or acetaminophen.

TIP: Some decongestants can cause blood pressure to rise. If you have high blood pressure, talk to your doctor or pharmacist before taking cold remedies.

Duh|
m o m e n t !

Aspirin, Tylenol, and Advil are *not* all the same thing. They work differently. If you're not sure which you need, ask your doctor or pharmacist.

Eating to Feel Better

Feed a cold, starve a fever? Neither, actually. Both colds and fevers do best with fluids. I know you'd love to huddle under the covers while Mommy serves you hot chicken soup, but kiddo, you're on your own.

And in case you thought your mother was crazy, a hot bowl of chicken soup really does help a cold; it hydrates you, gives you nourishment when you may not feel like eating, and helps clear up the mucus and block the inflammation that makes you cough. You can make your own (see page 140 in Making It Edible: How to Cook 101 for a recipe) or heat up some canned soup—it's almost as good. Add extra veggies to boost its healing power.

With any luck, you've got some groceries in the fridge and can throw together some homemade remedies from the kitchen to make you feel better. Not quite the same as Mom, I know …

Feel a cold coming on? If you can stomach it, try munching on raw garlic or a Spanish onion. If you catch the cold early enough, you might stop it in its tracks. If not, read on.

Sore throat? Suck on a sucker, sherbet, popsicles. Eat soft foods. Try a dollop of honey stirred into warm lemon water, juice, or herbal tea. You can buy ginger tea or make your own by grating a piece of ginger root into boiling water, adding a cinnamon stick, and letting it steep for 20 minutes.

TIP: How do you know if you're dehydrated? Your urine is dark yellow. If you're getting enough fluid, your pee should be almost clear. (Your pee can also change colour if your diet has changed—a neon yellow if you're taking certain vitamins or you've gorged on asparagus, for example.)

Stuffedupedness? Drink plenty of clear fluids. Add some chilies or cayenne pepper to your soup. Try horseradish or wasabi. Mix a dash of hot sauce in a small glass of water and gulp it down.

Upset tummy? Peppermint tea. Plain toast or crackers with flat ginger ale. Ginger tea (grate some ginger into boiling water, add a little honey or lemon). Drink a cup of water mixed with 10 millilitres (2 teaspoons) cider vinegar. Avoid greasy or acidic foods, and dairy products.

Nagging cough? Try a cup of hot water mixed with a spoonful of honey and lemon. Suck on cough lozenges or hard candy—low in sugar, since sugar can make illness worse.

Diarrhea? Think *BRAT*: bananas, rice, applesauce, and toast. You can also try chicken soup with rice. Calcium tablets might help. Or mix 2 millilitres ($1/2$ teaspoon) each of salt, baking soda, and sugar in a glass of water. Sip through the day to replace fluids lost.

How to Tell If It's Something Else Altogether

See a doctor if:

- You start spiking a fever and experience increased pain in your head. You could have bacterial sinusitis, which calls for treatment with an antibiotic.
- You notice mucus that is yellow or green rather than clear, white, or grey. This could indicate a bacterial infection, which calls for treatment with an antibiotic.

- You have frequent sneezing jags, itchy eyes, or dark circles under the eyes. This suggests an allergy.
- You seem to have a cold every couple of months. This could suggest chronic sinusitis.
- You're experiencing severe dizziness.
- You have a fever that's higher than 38 degrees C (100 degrees F) for more than 48 hours.
- Your cold doesn't go away after 10 days.
- You are having trouble breathing, you are wheezing, or you feel short of breath with normal activity.
- You have dark green, very thick, or bloody phlegm.
- You notice a strange rash.
- You have an earache, fluid draining from your ear, loss of hearing, or severe facial pain.

How Do I Know If It's Strep?

Yes, the big bad strep. How do you tell if you're just being wimpy about a garden-variety sore throat, or if it really is strep and antibiotics will make it all go away? Here are some signs to watch for:

- Big-time pain when you swallow.
- Swollen, sore glands.
- Fever.
- Headache.

More than You Really Wanted to Know

- If you're carrying the flu bug you can infect someone else 24 hours before you even show symptoms. Most people fall ill within one to three days of becoming infected.
- You might still be contagious up to a week after symptoms first appear.
- You can pass on a cold several days after being exposed to the virus—before you show symptoms.
- Alcohol, cigarette smoke, and sugar can make your illness worse.

Peer into the mirror—do you see white patches on the back of your tongue, or does it look red? An angry red look suggests strep.

If you suspect strep, see your doctor or drop in to a walk-in clinic, just to be sure. Not to scare you, but untreated strep infections can sometimes result in rheumatic fever—not a good thing for your heart or other organs.

Very important: If you're prescribed antibiotics, *always* finish the bottle, whether you're on the mend or not. And never "borrow" from someone else's prescription, even if you're convinced you have the same problem. What, you've got your medical degree all of a sudden?

Should you skip your workout?

It depends on how hard you're working out. If symptoms are above the neck (a simple cold) you're probably okay for a light workout. But a tough workout can stress your body and weaken its defences against the illness. You'd be smarter to take a break until you're better. Give yourself a few extra days after you recover from a cold, and a week after the flu. When you do go back, only go half as hard until you regain your strength.

Headaches—When to Worry

Sometimes headaches are more than just an inconvenience. Call the doctor if your pain:

- Is sudden and severe.
- Follows a head injury.
- Keeps you from functioning normally.
- Occurs more than two days a week.
- Is accompanied by a stiff neck, fever, and vomiting.
- Is making you feel confused.
- Is also disrupting your vision, or you feel weakness or numbness.

TIP: At the first sign of a tension headache, press a cold pack on the part of your head that hurts. If that doesn't work, try a microwaveable hot pack.

Meningitis

Spit happens. It happens especially when you're living in a dorm, or when you're cozying up to strangers—sharing cups, cigarettes, food, or lips. And believe it or not, spit can kill you.

Meningitis C is caused by bacteria carried in the throat and nose of up to 30 percent of healthy people. When you share their saliva, you can catch this serious infection of the blood, lining of the brain, and/or spinal cord. Because of your tendency to live "up close and personal," young people are more at risk than others—especially those who are living away from home for the first time in first-year university or college dorms.

Symptoms to watch out for:

- High fever.
- Severe headache.
- Stiffness of the neck.
- Sensitivity to light.
- Vomiting.
- Red, blotchy rash.
- Dizziness and confusion.

If you or someone you know shows these symptoms, get medical attention as soon as possible. Seriously. Meningitis progresses quickly. Treatment with antibiotics is most effective during the early stages. If you don't catch it soon enough, you could lose your hearing, vision, an arm or leg—or you could die. The disease kills one in ten.

Scary stuff.

How can you protect yourself? Keep yourself as strong and healthy as possible by eating right, sleeping well, and getting fresh air and exercise. Not so smart: hanging out at bars, drinking, and breathing in cigarette smoke. Sharing utensils, cigarettes, food, team water bottles, or band instruments can also put you at risk. Free vaccinations are available. Talk with your doctor about getting a vaccine, visit www.meningitis.ca or contact Health Canada at 1-866-225-0709.

How to Keep Germs from Spreading Throughout Your Home

- Wipe down all shared hard surfaces with disinfectant wipes.
- Make sure whoever's sick covers his/her mouth when coughing or sneezing (using the inside of your elbow is best).

- Throw away tissues and wash hands after blowing.
- If you are sick with diarrhea, don't prepare food for others. No matter how well you think you washed your hands, it's incredibly easy to pass on these pathogens.

How to Keep Germs from Spreading Throughout Your Workplace

Should you stay home from work? It's probably a good idea to call in sick on the first day or two of symptoms: that's when you're most contagious. A non-stop runny nose or cough isn't nice for anyone to be around. Same goes for vomiting and diarrhea. And stay home if you have a fever.

TIP: Never share your toothbrush, your hairbrush, your mascara, or your lip balm. Even if the lip balm says "medicated," viruses can still be passed on. Wiping the tip doesn't help, either.

But lying around watching *Jerry Springer* doesn't do you any good either—it prevents the fluids from draining from your sinuses and ear canals. As soon as you can, get your butt moving. Just do your best to keep your germs to yourself—especially if you work in health care, in a school, a nursing home, or in food preparation.

- Get a flu shot to protect yourself and prevent contagion. (More on this, page 220.)
- See your doctor within 48 hours of getting the flu to find out if antiviral medications might shorten the illness.
- Don't leave your used tissues in a pile—that's just gross! And don't act like Michael Jordan with the garbage can, either. We really don't want to see those cruddy things.

How to Find a Doctor

Good luck! No, really—good luck. You're going to need it. Canada is currently experiencing a shortage of physicians, and almost four million Canadians are without a doctor. If you've just moved to a new town, it might not be easy to find someone accepting new patients. It is very important that you do, though, *before* you get sick, so that you have a caregiver who knows you and your past history.

Some ideas:

- Start by looking in the Yellow Pages for doctors near you. Call and ask if they're accepting new patients. If the answer is no, ask whom they'd recommend you call.

- Ask friends and relatives for recommendations—pass the word on that you're looking.
- If you're a student, check with student health services.
- Contact your provincial College of Physicians and Surgeons.
- In a university town, call the family medicine training program to find out if there are available residents.
- Ask at the local walk-in clinic. To find a clinic, check the Yellow Pages or phone your local municipality.
- Ask the local hospital if they have a list of which family doctors are taking new patients.
- Try a nurse practitioner—nurses with additional training who can do almost everything a family doctor can do, including prescribing drugs and ordering tests.

> **TIP:** If you must go to work, put a lid on the chitchat, reschedule meetings, wash your hands frequently, and use disinfectant wipes on your desk, phone, and door handle.

If you find someone you'd really like, but who is not taking patients, ask to be placed on the waiting list. Until you find someone who will take you on, you will have to use walk-in clinics. Try phoning ahead, if possible, to see what the wait is. Avoid emergency departments unless you believe your problem is life-threatening and can't wait until tomorrow. (Find more on visiting Emergency on page 243). If you're not sure how seriously to take your health concern, call your provincial health phone line. (For more information, see the Resources section at the end of this chapter.)

What to Look for in a Doctor

There's always the off chance that you'll luck out and actually have more than one doctor from which to choose. If that happens, sit down and figure out which you prefer. You've probably got preferences on basics like age and gender, but beyond that, some things you should consider:

Location: If you can, choose a doctor who is equidistant between home and school or office. If you take public transit, make sure the office is easy to reach. If you drive, scout out parking.

Wait times: Ask the receptionist how long patients typically wait for appointments, and how far in advance they are booked. Months? Not good. Ask how the doctor deals with patients when they need urgent care. Can he squeeze you in when you're sick?

Availability: Can you reach the doctor off hours? Is there a number you can call, or does she e-mail?

Don't worry about scheduling annual physicals just yet. After your first visit, the doctor will decide how often you need to see him for regular checkups based on medical history, health habits, your risks for disease, and other health concerns. If you encounter a health problem, don't cross your fingers and hope it goes away. Keep track of your symptoms, and if you're experiencing a lot of pain or you're particularly worried, for heaven's sake, call the doctor!

Doctor's Appointments

You're in the doctor's office, a little nervous, maybe worried about something and not sure how to ask the right questions without looking stupid. You're afraid you'll forget everything you're supposed to tell the doctor, afraid you'll forget everything you're supposed to remember that the doctor tells you, secretly scared the doc's going to ask you to strip down, or pull out a big needle and tell you, boy oh boy, are you ever behind in your vaccinations. And you've got about ten minutes to deal with all this before you're ushered out to make way for the next patient.

No wonder your blood pressure's up! Visiting the doctor can be a stressful event—or not, depending on how well prepared you are. Before you go:

- Tell the receptionist why you are making the appointment.
- Get familiar with your own medical history—previous reactions to medications, allergies, chronic illnesses, dates of major illnesses, operations, hospitalizations. And know your family health history, including cancer, heart disease, high blood pressure, diabetes, genetic disorders, and alcohol or other drug abuse.
- Gather any information you think might be relevant to this visit—health changes, tests, the date of your latest period, special diet. Be informed about medications and remedies you are taking (including over-the-counter vitamins, herbs and minerals, nutritional supplements). Bring the bottles or labels with you.
- Make a list of questions and concerns.

When you're in the doctor's office:

- Explain clearly to the doctor why you're there. Tell her your physical symptoms, your thoughts, feelings, and what you're worried about. Be specific. Inform him of any changes in your life—they might affect your health.
- Ask the questions you consider most important first, before you forget.
- Take notes—when to take medications, what to do before medical tests. This will help you remember what your doctor said.
- Don't be upset if the doctor asks embarrassing questions. The doctor is supposed to ask about domestic abuse, weight gain, drug abuse, and sex. Be honest. If you hide things, she can't help. Besides, she's heard it all before—and is sworn to protect your privacy. Don't hide your body, either. She's probably seen all that before, too.
- Talk about your feelings. If you're sad, or you've lost your energy or appetite, it could be a sign of other disorders or physical illnesses.
- Be honest. If you smoke or do drugs, tell the doctor. Talk about your drinking; it could interact with your meds. If you are on medications, let the doctor know about any side effects you're experiencing. And if you're skipping your meds, 'fess up.
- If you don't understand something, speak up. Ask the doctor to "say it in plain English," or if he can, show you a diagram. If you're expecting to hear a lot of information and not sure if you can take it all in, bring a relative or good friend. You could even bring a tape recorder.
- Repeat what the doctor tells you back to the doctor in your own words, to be sure you've understood.
- Review your list of questions—forgotten anything?
- Ask if there is a way you can ask her additional questions you might have forgotten later, by phone or e-mail. Is there a website you can go to? (Remember that websites affiliated with a university or medical society are most accurate.)

Before you leave: Do you understand what the main problem is? Do you know what you need to do—and why?

Back home, record any further symptoms or side effects of the medications.

There. That wasn't so bad, was it?

TIP: Keep your shots up to date. You need a tetanus-diphtheria booster every 10 years. However, if you have had a severe wound with a rusty nail, you should get a booster within 48 hours. You might also need vaccinations against measles, mumps and rubella, pneumonia, or hepatitis B. Don't be chicken. Ask your doctor.

Reducing wait time

No one likes cooling their heels in the doctor's office, surrounded by ancient, irrelevant magazines and screaming, snotty toddlers. How do you avoid this special hell? The later in the day you book an appointment, the greater the chance it will be delayed, so book an appointment at the beginning of the day, or the first appointment after lunch. (If you want extra time, on the other hand, try booking the last appointment of the day.) Call before you leave to see if the doctor is running behind. If you've had consistently long waits, ask the doctor (not just the staff) what you can do to avoid the problem.

Scared of the needle?

I could say "Don't be such a wimp"—but I won't. And I certainly won't say "Oh, grow up." That just wouldn't be nice. Instead, let's call it what it is—trypanophobia—and look at some solutions. Because like it or not, grown-ups need to get needles just like kids do.

If the idea of a needle (a vaccine or blood test) has really got you freaked, tell your doctor. She may offer a "cooling spray" or anaesthetic cream that will numb the skin. Remember, tensing your muscles can make the pain worse, so try deep breathing. Just before the needle goes in, blow out hard through your mouth. Look away. No need to see it enter your skin. You could also try coughing—German researchers have found that can lessen the pain. And, if all else fails, bring your stuffed bunny—we won't tell.

Looking for Medical Advice—Online

When it's the middle of the night and you're worried about a health problem, it's tempting to boot up the computer and look for answers. It's also dangerous. Google "prostate cancer" and you'll get 55 million matches. "Headache" gets you almost 60 million. Is all that information really going to set your mind at ease? Not likely!

There are a myriad of websites out there that offer inaccurate advice, or are there only to promote their products. There are also plenty of sources of useful information.

The trick is in knowing which is which, lest you turn yourself into a "cyberchondriac." Here are some tips to make you a wiser, more skeptical Googler:

- Non-profit organizations, universities, governments, and hospitals are usually good places to start your search for information. Government website addresses end in ".gov" and nonprofits end in ".org."
- Credible websites offer an "About Us" link, telling you who owns the site. If it's a company trying to sell you something, be aware that they may be plugging their treatment or product.
- Look for websites that make it easy to determine who is providing the information. The best identify the physicians or other health professionals, or provide the names and credentials of the editorial board members who review the information.
- Beware of websites that provide out-of-date links or that aren't updated at least annually. The information might be outdated too.
- It's a good sign if the website reminds you to check with your own doctor before acting on the information it offers.

Never self-diagnose based on information you learn over the Internet. Bring the information you've found to your doctor. But don't bring in a stack of printouts to discuss. Your appointment time is limited—so limit your Internet-based questions to a reliable, clearly identified source. (See the Resources section at the end of this chapter for recommended websites.)

Taking Medication

At some point or another, you are going to need medicine. It might be something simple, like Aspirin for a headache, or something more complicated, prescribed by your doctor. Medicine should never be taken lightly, no matter what kind of spin the marketing guys give it (bubble-gum flavours have always seemed so wrong to me).

Duh moment!

Never use someone else's prescription.

Taking Doctor-Prescribed Medications

Before you walk out the office door with that little piece of paper clutched in your hand, make sure the prescription makes complete sense to you. After all, it's your body it's going in! Discuss with the doctor why you need the prescription, what the side effects are, and how long you should be taking it. Find out what the risks of taking the drug are and if they outweigh the benefits. Make sure you're clear on the drug's name, the dosage, and purpose. (You're not the only one who struggles to read the doc's chicken scratch on the prescription. The pharmacist might have trouble too.) Find out if there is a less-expensive, generic version she would recommend. Armed with all this knowledge, you're now ready to venture into the pharmacy.

Try to use the same pharmacy whenever you fill a prescription. The pharmacy will be able to keep a record on its computer of all your prescriptions and warn you of any possible drug interactions.

To be sure you're getting just what the doctor ordered, confirm your own name and address on the label to make sure you haven't been handed someone else's medication. And here are some questions to ask the pharmacist:

- What's the name of this medicine? (Make sure it's the same name the doctor used.)
- What can I expect this medicine to do? (Will it cure your illness, or just alleviate the symptoms?)
- How long will it take to work? How will I know it's working? What if it isn't?
- Will it interact with any other drugs, vitamins, or herbal remedies I'm taking?
- What's the best time of day to take this medicine?
- Should I take it with food, or on an empty stomach?
- Should I avoid certain activities while taking this medicine? (Driving, operating machinery, or exercise might be affected.)

TIPS:
- Some citrus juices (like grapefruit) can make you absorb toxic amounts of certain medications. Find out from your doctor or pharmacist what is safe to combine.
- Don't chew or crush pills unless instructed to do so. Some long-acting medications are absorbed too quickly when chewed.
- Don't stop taking a medication without discussing with the doctor first. If you're experiencing side effects that bother you, there might be alternatives, and some meds must be stopped gradually.

- Is there anything I need to avoid eating or drinking (especially alcohol) while taking this medicine?
- Can the medicine be crushed (and mixed with something) or split?
- What should I do if I forget a dose?
- What side effects should I look for? What should I do if this happens?
- Where should I keep this medicine? (Fridge, bathroom?)
- Is there any written information about this medication that I can take with me?

More than You Really Wanted to Know

All drugs have two names—one is the "generic" name (what the medicine is called—like ibuprofen) and the other the brand name (the name a manufacturer has given it—like Advil).

Label Lingo

Your prescription meds will come with labels. They're not decorations. They're important warnings and instructions. Here's what some of them mean:

- *May Cause Drowsiness or Dizziness:* It might also upset your sleep—check with your pharmacist.
- *Refrigerate:* If it says this, keep it in the fridge door, away from food.
- *Avoid Sunlight:* Not the meds—you! Some drugs make you extra-sensitive to sunlight.
- *Shake Well:* Not you—the meds! The contents might settle on the bottom and you won't get the right dose. Shake at least 20 times.
- *Avoid Alcohol:* Drinking can affect how well the meds work.
- *Do Not Take Antacids, Dairy Products, or Iron Preparations:* They can prevent the medication from being absorbed.

TIP: Keep your drugs in their original container. If you put them in another container (old film tube, for example), it's too easy to get mixed up or keep them past their expiry date.

Taking Over-the-Counter Drugs

Just because they're easy to get doesn't mean over-the-counter medications are as harmless as that pack of gum you picked up at the same time. You need to be just as careful with these meds as you are with the meds your doctor prescribed. Here are some reminders:

- *Treat just the symptoms:* Rather than grabbing the first cold or flu drug you see, take your time, think about what symptoms you're experiencing, and buy only the products that target those symptoms. Some remedies try to treat several symptoms at once—but more ingredients is not necessarily better. In fact, taking a product with a long list of ingredients can be risky; you might be taking extra drugs that you don't need, and they might have negative side effects.

- *Don't mix drugs:* If you're using herbal supplements or alternative treatments, or if you're already on drugs for something else, check with the pharmacist to see what happens when they're combined. In fact, you should ask the pharmacist for advice before taking any over-the-counter product you haven't used before.

- *Read the label:* Be aware of what is in the product. Sometimes there's a combination, and if you're taking more than one drug with that ingredient, you could be getting too much. For example, some cold medicines contain the same ingredient found in diet pills. Also, pay attention to potential side effects and warnings about who should not be using the product.

- *Look for generic brands:* Some drugstores place generic brand drugs next to the advertised brand. Compare the active ingredients on the two packages. They are probably the same, with differences only in the "inactive ingredients" (like flavouring). You can save about 25 percent by buying generic.

- *Think before taking drugs for fever:* It's not always necessary. Anyone 19 and under should not take products containing Aspirin when he or she has chickenpox, flu, or symptoms that might be the flu. They might develop a rare but life-threatening condition called Reye's syndrome. If your fever is lower than 38 degrees C (100 degrees F) you might not need to take anything. It won't help you get better faster, though it might make you more comfortable. If the fever is higher, or lasts longer than a day or two, talk to your doctor. It might be caused by a bacterial infection. (For how to take your temperature, see page 220.)

- *Consider the different cold medications:* Be careful which you take. Some are more for allergy relief than colds. Some contain both antihistamine (which dries up a

runny nose) and decongestant (to loosen stuffiness). There might also be some Aspirin or
acetaminophen in there. Some work right away,
while others are time-released to last up to
12 hours. Antihistamines can cause drowsiness;
decongestants can have the opposite effect. Cough
medicines are equally tricky—some suppress
coughs, while others loosen the phlegm. Many
have the same ingredients as cold medications
so it's easy to double up. The pharmacist can
help you.

> TIP: Use the dosing cup or spoon that comes with the medicine, or buy one at the pharmacy. Don't use a measuring spoon from the kitchen—they're not accurate.

Note: If you're too sick to deal with all this, ask a friend to help you—but give him
the above information, first.

What to Keep in Your Medicine Cabinet

Actually, that dinky little cupboard in your bathroom should not be called a "medicine
cabinet." Not only is it too darn small (making everything tumble out when you open
it, bleary-eyed, in the morning), but most medicine should not be kept in the
washroom anyway—it's too humid. A cupboard or closet would be better. Save the
medicine cabinet for the extra toothbrushes, condoms, floss, and all those skin creams
you thought would produce some magical effect on your already gorgeous face.

Here's what you should put in your Not the Bathroom Medicine Cabinet:

- Antihistamine (in case of allergic reaction).
- Analgesic or anti-inflammatory (ibuprofen) medicine (for pain or fever).
- Antibiotic ointment (fights off infection).
- Antacid (relieves upset stomach).
- Syrup of ipecac (induces vomiting—don't use unless you've checked with a doctor).
- Decongestant (for stuffy nose).
- Fever reducer (acetaminophen or ibuprofen).
- Hydrocortisone (relieves itching and inflammation).
- Antiseptic (helps stop infection).
- Throat lozenges.
- Thermometer.

Note: Keep all items in their original containers so you don't take the wrong one. Any ointment whose tube is cracked should be pitched. At least once a year (your birthday? when you change the clocks?) go through your medicine cabinet and chuck out all old and unused drugs. Once it's past its expiry date, medication is not as effective. To avoid a lot of waste, don't buy those extra-big packages. Don't just toss or flush the meds, though, because they could be toxic. Check to see if your pharmacy has a drug recycling program, or if your municipality incinerates drugs.

Your first-aid kit should have: Tweezers, disinfectant, bandages, cold pack (or label a bag of peas in the freezer "first-aid pack"), scissors, large sterile gauze and adhesive tape for large wounds, safety pin and large cloth triangle to use as a sling, cleansing solution, antibiotic cream, calamine lotion, cotton swabs, hydrogen peroxide, flashlight, eye patch.

A Different Kind of Drug Addiction

Honey, I know you'd never consider yourself an addict, but check your pockets, would ya? Or your purse? How many ChapSticks have you got in there? How about nose spray? Headache pills? *Busted!*

Some over-the-counter remedies can actually be, if not addictive, then at least "habit-forming." They can cause rebounds or reliance problems. Before you know it, you're stuck in a vicious cycle. (Are you reaching for your lip balm right now?)

If you take pain reliever more than twice a week, for example, you could end up with rebound headaches. Other products cause similar problems.

Nose Drop / Nasal Spray Addiction

Believe it or not, Oprah Winfrey once devoted an entire show to people who can't live without their nasal spray. And if Oprah's talking about it, it's got to be serious! Nasal decongestant sprays and drops shrink nasal passages. If your stuffed nose is keeping you from breathing, then this is a good thing. The problem is, if you use it too much, your nose can become tolerant to the decongestant's effect. You end up needing more and more to get rid of your stuffiness. This is called "rebound swelling." Prolonged use leads to nose stinging and burning, chronic swelling and irritation of the lining of your nose—and more mucus.

Been there
Done THAT

I used nose drops for a cold that just would not go away. It eventually did but I still couldn't breathe. Anyway, I kept using the nose drops. I had no idea that they were addictive. I switched to "pediatric nose drops" (the kind for kids). I used them for a while, but frankly the only way to get off of them was to quit cold turkey. It took three miserable nights and that was that.

—LINDSAY, 18

So how do you fix the problem? Stop using the stuff! You should never use a spray or drops for more than three days in a row. If you have, and you're "stuck," then you've got to quit. Sorry, but that's the way it is. You'll feel worse for a while. But after a few weeks your breathing should return to normal. In the meantime, you could try an oral decongestant, or ask your doctor for a prescription that would help you breathe freely again.

Lip Balm

If you never go anywhere without your lip balm, if you turn around and go home again when you've forgotten it, if you've got multiples lying around in your desk, your purse, your bedside table—then, darling, you might have a problem.

You might have heard the rumours swirling around concerning lip balm addiction. Some claim that manufacturers use addictive chemicals. Others say they add fibreglass to the product to prolong chapped lips. There's never been any proof of that. But the fact is, lots of people are hooked on the stuff.

The problem starts with "lip-licking." You might live in a dry climate, which wicks the moisture away from your lips. You lick them. Licking wipes off the natural oils on your lips. They feel dryer. You lick them again. You buy lip balm to solve the problem. Balms help because they contain petroleum or wax—but it's a quick fix, and a temporary one. The lip balm makes your lips feel moist—so you apply it again. You get used to that nice softness and moisture, and worry that your lips will dry if you stop.

Honey, your lips won't dry up and fall off. They might feel a little uncomfortable for a while, but this too shall pass. So put the stuff away. If you feel the urge to lick your lips, try using your knuckle to transfer your own body oil from your forehead to

My lips were always dry. I should have taken shares out in the company that makes that lip balm stuff. It was my doctor who said, "Check the house humidifier. It's usually part of the furnace." He said there are different settings on it and it should be switched to suit the seasons, that my place was too dry. He also said I should leave my window open a bit at night. It worked.

—JAY, 23

your lips. Or use a little Vaseline—once a day. If it's unbearable, try an over-the-counter prescription cortisone ointment to reduce the inflammation long enough to help you break the habit. You could also add some humidity to your place with a humidifier or a pan or pot of water on a radiator. Make sure you're drinking lots of water a day. Don't smoke. Check to see if your acne medication might be exacerbating the problem. And if all else fails, move to the rain forest.

Eye Drops

Get-the-red-out drops can temporarily alleviate the problem of bloodshot eyes, but they won't treat the cause. Why are your eyes red? Could it be because of an environmental irritation—like dry air, sun exposure, dust, allergic reaction, smoking?

If it's something in the environment, wear sunglasses when outdoors to reduce exposure to dust, sun, and wind. If you think it's the heat or air conditioning, don't sit near a vent or fan, and be sure your car's vent isn't blowing on your face. Blink lots while at the computer. Make sure you're eating lots of fish or flax, or taking an Omega-3 supplement to keep your eyes moist. Eye drops shouldn't be used with contact lenses because the lens can absorb the drops, leading to a buildup of solution.

Laxatives

Some people turn to laxatives with the mistaken belief that they should have a bowel movement every day, and if they're not pooping that much, they must be constipated. In fact, that's not true. (See Constipation, page 267). Others rely on laxatives as a diet tool—which is really stupid. The problem is, if you start using laxatives too much, the colon begins to rely on them to bring on bowel movements. Over time, the nerve cells in the colon can become damaged and lose their natural ability to contract. Regular use of enemas can have the same effect. If you do use a laxative, make sure you follow the manufacturer's instructions, which usually advise seeing a doctor if you need to use it for more than a week.

Resources

Provincial Health Phone Lines

British Columbia
BC NurseLine
Greater Vancouver: 604-215-4700
Toll-free: 1-866-215-4700

Alberta
Health Link Alberta
Calgary: 403-943-5465
Edmonton: 780-408-5465
Toll-free: 1-866-408-5465

New Brunswick
Tele-Care 1-800-244-8353

Saskatchewan
HealthLine 1-877-800-0022

Manitoba
Health Links / Info Santé
Winnipeg: 204-788-8200
Toll-free: 1-888-315-9257

Ontario
Telehealth Ontario 1-866-797-0000

Quebec
Info-Santé CLSC: www.Msss.gouv.qc.ca/reseau/info_sante.html—type in your postal code for a local number.

Newfoundland and Labrador
Toll-free advice line from the Janeway Children's Health and Rehabilitation Centre, for
children and young adults up to age 18. 1-866-722-1126

For a list of regional clinics that provide health education counselling and services, go to:

http://chp-pcs.gc.ca/CHP/index_e.jsp/pageid/4005/odp/Top/Health/Clinics_
and_Services

Meningitis vaccinations

Talk with your doctor about getting a vaccine, visit www.meningitis.ca, or contact
Health Canada at 1-866-225-0709.

Recommended websites for health searches

www.hc-sc.gc.ca
www.webmd.com
www.nih.gov
www.mayoclinic.com
www.pubmed.gov
www.onhealth.com
www.canadianhealthnetwork.ca
www.cma.ca
www.canadian-health-network.ca
www.mydoctor.ca
www.medlineplus.gov
www.healthfinder.gov
www.intelihealth.com

9

When You Need Medical Help—Fast!

I told the doctor I broke my leg in two places.
He told me to quit going to those places.

—HENNY YOUNGMAN

What if you can't get in to see your doctor—if it's after hours, or the doc's unavailable? If your doctor's answering service can't direct you to an alternative service, you might have to visit a community or hospital health clinic, which are open most evenings and weekends. (Put this book down right now and find the hospital and nearest health clinic in the phone book. Write down the address in your address book. Memorize it.)

It's an Emergency!

If it's the middle of the night and it just can't wait, you'll have to head to Emergency. How do you know if it's serious enough? Are you experiencing chest pain, shortness of breath, sustained high fever or abdominal pain, slurred speech, sudden change in vision, broken limbs, or severe cuts? These all warrant emergency attention. If you're not sure, call your toll-free provincial health hotline (see pages 241–242).

What should you bring to the emergency department?

- Your health card.
- A copy of your medical history—allergies, surgeries, meds and alternatives. (If you can't manage to write them down, bring the bottles with you.)
- A friend/relative/driver, if possible.
- Contact information for your family doctor.
- A book or magazine. (You'll probably have a long wait, and waiting room reading material is likely germy.)

While waiting to be seen

- Wash your hands with the disinfectant when you enter, and keep your hands away from your face. Touch as few hospital surfaces as possible.
- Be as calm and clear as you can when describing your symptoms to the hospital staff.
- Be patient—the ER staff will assess you and see you according to urgency.
- Tell the triage nurse if you develop a higher fever, new symptoms, or your condition changes in any way.
- Don't consume anything. If it turns out you need surgery, a full stomach could be a problem.

When you do finally see the emergency doctor, stick to your current health crisis. Don't swamp him/her with too much information. Take notes on what you are told, or ask a friend to. Do you understand what you've been told? Do you know what you should do next, and with whom you should follow up?

First Aid

Let's hope you never have to deal with any of this. But, life being what it is, you should be prepared. Here's a quick first-aid primer. Read it now so that you're prepared. You don't want to go frantically searching for first-aid advice while someone's bleeding all over your carpet!

How to Deal with Cuts

If blood is spurting out, if it's quickly soaking the bandage, or if there is a body part amputated or almost cut off, elevate the wound, put pressure on it, and get the heck to Emergency—*now! Go!!* Better yet, call 911.

If the wound is not too deep, you can probably treat it at home. Wounds should be cleaned as quickly as possible to promote healing and reduce the risk of infection and scars. Here's what to do:

1. Find a clean pad (washcloth, paper towel, gauze, bandage, sanitary napkin). If you have sterile gloves in your first-aid kit, use them. If not, use layers of the cleanest material available, like cloth or plastic bags, for your own protection.

2. Apply pressure continuously for about 20 to 30 minutes. Don't keep checking to see if it's stopped. If blood soaks through, place another bandage over the first and continue applying pressure.

3. Raise the injured body part to slow bleeding. (Don't tourniquet.)

4. If there is an object in the wound (and you can't gently remove it with clean tweezers), apply pressure around it—not on top.

5. When bleeding stops, rinse the wound well with clear water. You can use soap and a washcloth to gently clean around the wound. If you have a sprayer in the sink, use that to get the dirt out.

6. After you clean the wound, apply a thin layer of an antibiotic cream or ointment to help keep the surface moist, and put a sterile bandage on it. (Don't glob it on—the bandage won't stick.)

TIP: If your wound is infected or pus-filled and gets worse (red, swollen, and increasingly painful) over the course of a few days, get yourself to a doctor. Even a small scratch can pick up an antibiotic-resistant infection.

Don't: Splash the wound with hydrogen peroxide or iodine. You will regret it. Not only does it destroy skin cells, but it hurts like heck!

If the cut is deep and won't stop bleeding, you'll need to get medical attention. See your doctor if:

- The edges are widely separated.
- The wound is caused by a bite.
- The cut is jagged.
- The wound is on your face.
- There is dirt in the cut that you can't get out.
- The area around it feels numb.
- You haven't had a tetanus booster in the last 10 years (5 if it's really deep).

Does this look infected?

Yup—if:

- It drains a thick, creamy, greyish fluid (pus).
- There is swelling, heat, pain.

- There is a red circle or streaks around the wound.
- You start to run a fever.

How to Deal with Minor Burns

Don't put butter on a burn. That's an old wives' tale and could just lead to infection. Hold the burned part under cool running water (not cold), or soak a towel in cool water and wrap it. Dab some antibiotic ointment on if you have some on hand. After a few days, if you happen to have an aloe vera plant on hand, you can squeeze the juice onto the burn to help healing too. If blisters form, don't break them.

How to Deal with a Head Injury

It's serious, and you need to get medical attention, if:

- You see stars.
- You develop a headache that won't go away.
- You experience nausea and vomiting.
- You can't remember basic things.
- There's a change in your body temperature, pulse, and breathing.

Make sure you have someone with you at all times if a head injury is suspected.

How to Deal with Frostbite

Darling, I'm not going to ask what you were doing out there on a day like that. I'm sure it was terribly important and did not involve schnapps, a cardboard box, and a big hill …

Frostbite is like a burn, but it's actually frozen, sometimes dead, skin. You're at risk of frostbite anytime the temperature falls below –10 degrees C (14 degrees F). Your toes, nose, fingers, earlobes, feet, and chin are most susceptible.

The first thing that happens is "frostnip," in which the outer layers of the skin turn white and numb. If the skin remains exposed to the cold, the deeper layers and tissue are affected. That's frostbite. If the skin is white or blue and feels frozen, it's second-degree. Third-degree is when the skin is white, blotchy, or blue, with damage beneath the surface. If you suspect frostbite:

1. Get into a warm place.
2. Loosen or remove wet, tight clothing and jewellery and wrap yourself up in a blanket.
3. Warm the area by soaking in warm water. Don't heat it too quickly or you'll end up with pain and blisters.
4. When the skin becomes red, stop (about 45 minutes).

If you can't get warm water, cover up with whatever you can find—blankets, coats, sweaters—and warm the area with your breath. Or tuck the frostbitten part in someone's warm armpit or on the tummy. Don't use direct heat, and never rub or massage the area. Don't break blisters.

How to dress warmly—and not get frostbite in the first place

- Wear tightly woven clothing (like wool) or one of the new synthetic fabrics that wick moisture from your skin. Layer your clothing. Wear two or three pairs of socks instead of one heavy pair. Don't wear cotton next to your skin because it stays wet. Always wear a hat and make sure it covers your ears.
- Don't expect that flask in your pocket to warm you up. Booze just causes blood to lose heat faster. Drink lots of warm fluids but steer clear of coffee or tea since caffeine has the same effect as alcohol.
- You might think that cigarettes provide heat, but in fact smoking slows down blood circulation to the extremities.

How to Deal with a Nosebleed

Most nosebleeds look much worse than they really are—they're not serious. If you get a nosebleed, here's what to do:

1. Sit down and tilt your head slightly forward. Breathe through your mouth.
2. Pinch the soft part of your nose (the area between the end of your nose and the bone that forms the bridge above it).
3. Try not to talk, sniff, swallow, cough, or move your head.
4. Keep your nose pinched for 5 minutes. If it's still bleeding, repeat for another 10.

5. When the bleeding stops, don't do anything that will make it start again—no bending over, blowing, and for heaven's sake, no picking!

6. If the bleeding has not stopped after 30 minutes, if you're feeling faint, or if the nosebleed is the result of injury, see a doctor.

How to Deal with Splinters

To remove a splinter, first wash your hands. Don't let the splinter get too wet, though. If it's wood, it will swell and be harder to remove.

Using clean tweezers, gently pull the splinter out in the direction in which it entered. If you can't grip it with tweezers, try this. Mix 500 millilitres (2 cups) of Epsom salts (available at the drugstore or the health food store) to 4 litres (1 gallon) of water. Soak a washcloth in the solution and apply it to the splinter. The salt might shrink the moisture around the splinter and push the sliver a bit toward the surface of the skin. Then you can try again to use the tweezers.

Still not working? Take a deep breath: it's time for—*da-dum*—the needle. Sterilize a needle (in boiling water, rubbing alcohol, or over a flame—wipe the blackened part with sterile gauze afterwards). Gently pick at the skin above the end of the splinter to expose it to the tweezers. If you still can't grip it, soak the skin around the splinter twice a day in a solution of 5 millilitres (1 teaspoon) baking soda, 250 millilitres (1 cup) warm water. After a few days, it might slip out.

Make sure the entire splinter is out. Clean the spot, blot dry, and bandage.

How to Deal with Sprains and Strains

If you've twisted or sprained a body part, just remember *RICE*:

TIP: Fill a freezer bag with ice cubes to create a cold compress, or use a bag of frozen veggies. Wrap a thin towel around it to protect the skin.

R—Rest the injured area.
I—Ice it for 5 to 10 minutes every hour.
C—Compress the area by wrapping it tightly with an elastic bandage for 30 minutes, then unwrap it for 15 minutes.
E—Elevate the area to reduce swelling. Prop it up to keep it elevated while you sleep.

If the problem is in your finger or hand, remove any rings right away, before it swells. And it's okay to take Aspirin or ibuprofen for pain and swelling.

It's serious, and you need to see a doctor, if:

- A bone sticks out, or the limb looks crooked.
- The injured body part feels numb, or the skin around it turns blue.
- You can't move or put weight on it.
- It hurts to press along the bone, or the pain keeps getting worse.

How to Deal with Bee Stings

Here's what to do:

TIP: If a bee gets in your car, stop the car, roll down the windows, and gently "encourage" it to fly out.

1. If the stinger is still in there, get it out fast— whether by scraping with a fingernail or pulling.

2. Immediately apply ice for 10 to 20 minutes.

3. Dab on some calamine, or a paste made with baking soda and water, to soothe and relieve the itching. Redness and swelling are normal and can last a few days.

4. If you're bothered by pain, take Aspirin, acetaminophen, or ibuprofen. An antihistamine can help with excessive itching.

5. If you have been stung more than 10 times, or inside the nose or mouth, you'll need emergency medical attention.

It's serious and you need to see a doctor, if:

- Within an hour after an insect sting or bite, you develop hives anywhere, swelling in the face, shortness of breath or wheezing, difficulty swallowing, or if you feel dizzy.
- The area around the sting swells or hurts enough to disrupt your normal activities or keep you awake.
- There is pus, or the redness and swelling get worse after 24 hours.

Next time, don't get stung. Try to keep your shoes on outside, and don't wear perfume or brightly coloured clothing in bee territory. Don't aggravate bees and wasps by swatting or running. If one lands on you, stand still. It should fly away on its own. Or, if you can't handle that, gently brush it away with a napkin or something light.

How to Deal with Something in Your Eye

Here's the number-one rule: Don't rub! You'll make it worse. Instead, remove your contact lens, if you're wearing one. If the object is on the white part of your eye, or inside the lower lid, moisten a Kleenex and gently remove it. If it's on the dark part of your eye, lean over the sink and splash tap water into your open eye to try to flush it out. If that doesn't work, cover it up with a patch or dark glasses and see your doctor. If it's embedded in your eye, lightly cover it and get to the emergency department.

How to Deal with Tooth Troubles

- *If your teeth are sensitive:* Tooth whiteners might be to blame. Stop using whiteners, tartar-control toothpastes, and toothpastes containing baking soda. Brush gently.
- *If you knock out a tooth:* Rinse it and put it back in, quickly. Bite down on a wet cloth or teabag to hold it in place and get to a dentist right away. If you can't reinsert, put it in a cup of milk.
- *If you crack a tooth:* See a dentist; a chipped or cracked tooth can become infected.
- *If your jaw is aching:* It could be temporomandibular joint disorder, or TMD. You might be grinding your teeth at night, or moving your jaw around as you sleep because it's improperly aligned. Try sleeping on your side or back (rather than face down). If the ache doesn't go away, see a dentist.

What If Someone Keels Over in Front of You?

You can recognize a stroke by asking the person to do three things (remember them by thinking of the first three letters in "stroke"):

S—SMILE. Look for weakness in the face.
T—TALK. Can she say a simple sentence?
R—RAISE both arms.

If the victim can't do these things, dial 911 immediately and describe the symptoms to the dispatcher.

Important numbers you should have

- Emergency services (likely 911, but check).
- Poison control.
- Your doctor, dentist.
- Any available hotline or mental health crisis line.

Note: Emergency numbers are often listed at the front of your phone book

10

Healthy Sex
and Sexual Health

Sex is a bad thing because it rumples the clothes.

—JACQUELINE KENNEDY ONASSIS

Yes, you knew it would come up sooner or later. We've got to deal with it, but we'll keep it brief, okay?

I'm sure you know all about the mechanics, so we'll skip that part. But birth control is a biggie. I'll assume you're using something—unless you're planning on making me a grandma sooner than I thought?

The Best Birth Control Is the Method You'll Actually Use

Let's make sure what you're using is best for you. This is serious stuff—for men and women—so give it some thought. Here's the first question.

Do you want to:

1. Prevent pregnancy, or
2. Prevent pregnancy *and also* protect yourself from diseases that can be transmitted through sex?

At this stage in your life, you'll probably want to pick Door Number 2. A whole host of sexually transmitted infections (STIs) can be "caught" through unprotected sex, including AIDS, herpes, genital warts, and chlamydia.

Here are some more important questions to ask yourself when deciding on a birth control method:

• How well do you know yourself? Are you good at being prepared, organized, responsible, "in-the-moment"? (Think about that pile of incomplete high school assignments, forgotten notes, and misplaced gym shoes. Have you outgrown that?) How are you at remembering things like daily vitamins and medications?

TIP: Taking St. John's wort can make birth control pills less effective.

- What's your budget? Do you have the money for something pricier than a condom (e.g., birth control pills)?
- Do you really think you're going to be able to say "No" when you're in the heat of the moment? If not, abstinence or the rhythm method might not be best for you. (And don't even think about "pulling out." That's just stupid—and it doesn't work.) Are you going to have it together enough to keep a barrier method (like a condom) with you at all times?
- Are you okay with needles? If not, you'll want to skip shots and implants.
- What about side effects? Some methods carry side effects that might or might not be important to you. Some women can develop urinary tract infections with the use of spermicides.

You have way more choices available to you than we did way back in prehistoric times. You can choose from hormone-related methods (including the pill, patch, and injections), barrier methods (condoms, sponge, IUD, cervical cap, etc.), and even emergency contraception (see below). All that choice is great for you—more options, less chance of disease or unwanted pregnancy. But it can also be a problem if you're overwhelmed by what to pick.

Don't rely on what your poker buddy tells you—talk with your doctor. (For more information, see the Resources section at the end of this chapter.)

Condoms—Your Best Friend

The condom should be your best friend, no matter what you do about birth control. That's because it's one of the best ways to protect yourself against sexually transmitted disease, and an excellent way to keep yourself from getting HPV, a virus that causes cervical cancer.

Duh | moment!

Going for an encore? Don't try to reuse your old condom. Crack open a new one.

Be sure to use condoms made of latex (rubber). The AIDS virus can get through condoms made of animal membranes. Don't use lotions or petroleum jelly (such as Vaseline) as a lubricant because they can cause the rubber to break. Water-based

TIP: Condoms don't last as long if you keep them in your wallet or car, where heat and cold might break down the latex. Keep some there, just in case, but replace regularly.

lubricants (like K-Y Jelly) are the best choice. Follow directions carefully. And don't get all fancy with the colours or taste—that kind doesn't protect as well. Condoms expire after three to five years, so unless you're planning on being extremely busy, don't buy in bulk.

Condoms are most effective when combined with spermicides. Spermicides should be placed in the vagina (not just on the condom).

The Morning-After Pill

Did the condom break? You got carried away? Or, for some other reason, did you end up having unprotected sex? Don't panic. Get an emergency contraceptive pill (also known as the "Plan B pill") from your doctor or pharmacist right away. If you're lucky, there's a 24-hour pharmacy nearby. If you're luckier (smarter), you've planned ahead and stashed a package for just such an emergency. After 72 hours, it's too late.

The Plan B pill is not the same as RU-486, or the "abortion pill," which contains chemicals to end a pregnancy. Plan B works by preventing a possible pregnancy in the first 72 hours, before sperm and egg have met.

Worried about possibly having contracted an STI? You'll have to wait for two weeks before a test can determine that.

For more information on emergency contraception, try www.not-2-late.com.

TIPS:
- If you are travelling, bring along your own condoms. Depending on the country you are visiting, the quality can differ substantially.
- And watch out for knock-off condoms—no pun intended. Produced in far-flung countries, these condoms are cheaper (often too cheap) but packaged as your favourite brand. They offer little to no protection. Buy your condoms in a trusted store and pay up. The cost of a knock-off condom is way too high.

Sexually Transmitted Infections (STIs)

Q: What's the most common symptom of sexually transmitted infection?
A: No symptom. That's right. Nada.

So how do you know if that hot date has a hot virus of some kind? You don't. Anyone who's ever had sex is at risk of carrying something nasty. You can ask, of course. That's assuming you want to break the "mood." And that's assuming you can trust him/her, assuming he/she knows, assuming he/she is thinking clearly and not thinking about something a little more, um, pressing. That's a lot of assuming—and you know what they say about assumptions, don't you?

That's why it's smart to make condoms a habit. You don't need any big discussion, just pull it out. No condom, no go. Use them every time you have sex, and use them

More than You Really Wanted to Know

The Centers for Disease Control and Prevention says syphilis cases have increased among Americans for the fourth straight year, in part because of the rise in Internet-solicited sex.

during all types of sex, including vaginal, anal, and oral sex. For oral sex with a woman, you can use a condom cut open to place between her body and her partner's mouth, or even grocery-store plastic wrap. Spermicide nonoxynol-9 can help kill some of the germs.

After sex, pee right away and wash your genitals with soap and water—it's a simple way to help stay healthy.

See the doctor if you notice:

Duh moment!

One in 10 men thinks chlamydia is a flower.

- Unusual discharge from the penis or vagina.
- Rashes around the genitals, itchiness around the genitals, sores around the genitals, blisters and bumps around the genitals, pain in the genital area, burning sensation when peeing or having sex, peeing more than usual.

Sometimes there are no signs at all. If you are worried, you should see your doctor. For more on sexually transmitted infections (STIs), go to: www.tellsomeone.ca.

Visiting the Gynecologist—Oh Yay!

Or should that be "Oy vey"? I have to admit, going to the gynie doesn't rank among my favourite pastimes. Unfortunately, it is part of being a grown-up.

Most women start seeing a general practitioner or gynecologist for pelvic exams during their teenage years, and return for checkups every few years after that. If you haven't yet had the pleasure, then you're probably a little bit freaked. But don't be. These docs have seen it all before; this is their job. And remember that this "chore" might keep you from getting very sick with sexually transmitted diseases and even cancer. Here's what you can expect.

When you arrive, you'll let the receptionist know and give her your health card number. Then you'll sit in a waiting room that may be packed with pregnant women, newborns, and parenting magazines. When you are called into the examining room you might first be asked to pee in a cup. You'll need to tell the nurse the first day of your last period, what meds you're on, if you've had any spotting or pain. Then the nurse will leave while you get completely undressed and cover yourself with a paper gown or sheet.

TIP: Get notes that pop up on your computer desktop to let you know when it's time for a breast self-exam or a mammogram at www.post-it.com/research. When you do a self-exam, apply lotion—it will be easier to feel changes.

When the doc arrives, she will examine your breasts and abdomen for unusual lumps (ask how to check your breasts yourself). Then you'll be asked to lie on the examining table on your back, with your legs apart and your feet in supports called stirrups. The doctor will look at your external genitalia, then insert a lubricated instrument called a speculum into your vagina. It might feel a little cold, but it lets the doctor see inside. Next she will insert a wand-like thing to get a sample of your cells to test for cervical cancer—this is known as a Pap smear. You shouldn't feel any pain, just some pressure. If it does hurt, speak up. It could indicate a problem. The doctor will also insert a lubricated finger into your vagina and press gently on your tummy to feel your ovaries and uterus.

That's it. The doctor leaves while you get dressed. When you're done, open the door slightly so the doctor knows when you're ready. She will likely return to talk about your sexual history, the examination, and when you should come back.

Piece of cake, right? So do it—every year, even if you think you're healthy. It could save your life. 'Nuff said.

About the exam:

- Get a Pap smear once a year for three years, beginning at age 18 or when you start having sex. If the results have been normal, then get one every two years after that. Ask your doctor to be sure.
- Try to schedule it for a time when you won't have your period.
- Don't douche, have sex, or use spermicide or vaginal medication for 48 hours before the test.
- If you have a question that makes you nervous or shy, admit it. Say, "Doctor, I'm really embarrassed to ask this, but …" The doctor will be extrasensitive.

Premenstrual Syndrome

While we're at it, let's talk about PMS. Changing hormone levels and brain chemistry can really mess you up—moodiness, cramps, acne, swollen feet, headaches, insomnia, and an overwhelming wish that your boyfriend would get hit by a bus. But you don't have to turn into the Wretched Witch of Wherever. Sometimes, lifestyle changes can help. Try:

- Reducing caffeine and alcohol consumption.
- Cutting back on salt, sugar, fatty foods, and red meat.
- Increasing calcium, magnesium, fibre, and foods containing vitamins B6 and E and D.
- Getting some exercise on a regular basis.
- Reducing stress, especially at that time of the month.

TIP: If your period cramps are really bad, saturate a flannel rag with castor oil and lay it on your abdomen. Cover that with plastic wrap and a towel, then put a heating pad on top. Leave it there for 15 minutes. The extra warmth will feel great!

If that doesn't help, and you are having extreme pain or depression, see your doctor. There are medications that can treat the problem.

Resources

Birth control choices

Try the questionnaire created by the Association of Reproductive Health:
www.arhp.org

Check out the website for Sunnybrook Women's College Health Sciences Centre:
www.womenshealthmatters.ca/centres/sex/quiz/birthcontrol.html

For more information on emergency contraception, try www.not-2-late.com.

Sexually transmitted infections (STIs)

Go to: www.tellsomeone.ca

11

When Good Bodies Go Bad ...

Man is the sole animal whose nudity offends his own companions,
and the only one who, in his natural actions,
withdraws and hides himself from his own kind.

—MONTAIGNE

Embarrassing Body Questions

I won't be able to catch everything that's secretly bothering you, but maybe this will answer some of those concerns that you daren't ask anyone else.

Bad Breath

Do you find yourself secretly cupping a hand over your mouth, trying to figure out if you've got bad breath? Ever wonder if yours could be as bad as Cindy's in the next cubicle? Or if that fettuccini you had for lunch will lose you friends?

You're not alone. Many people struggle with this one, which is why there are so many breath-freshening products on the store shelves. But those just mask the problem. Bad breath stems from two sources—the mouth, or the stomach—wherever bacteria have decided to set up shop. Breath mints and gum won't do anything about that.

Been there
Done THAT

Bad breath is just the kiss of death for me. We can be out on a date, doing great together, he seems really nice, we're getting along, and then all of a sudden—eeew! And the worst is when you find out while you're kissing. That's when everything stops! I mean everything. I'm looking for the exit.

—CHRIS, 19

First of all, how do you know if you do have a problem? You can ask a close, honest friend or relative. Barring that, try this: lick the back of your hand and give it a sniff. Reeks? Deal with it. Here's how.

- First of all, make sure your gastrointestinal tract is healthy. That means eating a balanced diet with plenty of fluids.
- It goes without saying (but I'll say it anyway) that you have to brush, for at least 2 minutes, and floss after every meal. Don't forget your gums and tongue. Try an infant toothbrush to get the back of your tongue.
- Avoid garlic, onions, red wine, coffee, meat, and any other food or spice that you think wrecks your breath. Try munching carrots instead—some people swear by it.
- See your dentist regularly.
- Don't smoke.
- Breathe through your nose—a dry mouth can lead to bad breath. Don't talk too much (keep your mouth closed). Sugarless lozenges can also keep your mouth moist.
- Avoid alcohol—it dries out the mouth too (and there's nothing worse than a drunk with bad breath). If you think postnasal drip is to blame, try an over-the-counter saline nasal spray.
- Keep breath-strips or a mini bottle of mouthwash handy. (Gum chomping looks tacky and can hamper your speech.) If you do use gum or mints, go for the sugarless brands, because sugar creates smelly plaque.
- Use a bent spoon to gently scrape the back of your tongue.

Some food culprits to avoid

Dairy products, especially cheeses; coffee, and other acidic drinks like tomato and citrus juices.

Some food "helpers" to try

Chew on herbs like coriander, tarragon, spearmint, rosemary, or cardamom. (Or steep them in hot water and sip.) Try yogurt with active cultures (not the sugar-laden variety); crunchy, fibre-rich foods, like carrots or apples, to cleanse the mouth after a meal; food with vitamin C to discourage bacteria growth and prevent gum disease.

If none of this seems to help, and people are still flinching and backing away, then you should contact your dentist. There are prescription antibacterial rinses and germicides that can help.

Ear Wax

Do not use Q-tips to clean out your ears. Ear wax is ear sweat, and when you use a Q-tip you are effectively jamming the wax into your ear. Not a good plan.

Ear wax is good. It keeps water away from your eardrum when you shower or swim. It discourages bacterial and fungal growth. Most people don't need to clean their ears at all; ear wax is part of your very own self-cleaning system. Some people, however, do produce a little more than normal. If you find your ears are continually being clogged, you might want to see your doctor occasionally to have it removed.

Leaky Bladder

Otherwise known as "incontinence," this problem can crop up any time in life. Sometimes it's caused by pregnancy or childbirth, sometimes by injury or weak pelvic-floor muscles—and it's more common than you might think. "Stress incontinence" occurs when you cough, laugh, sneeze, jump, or lift; a little pee leaks out. "Urge incontinence" causes an immediate need to "go." It can be triggered by chocolate, caffeine, booze, or spicy food. If you've got this problem—and before you invest in Depends—try:

- Skipping the "triggers" (like caffeine, booze, and certain spices).
- Pelvic-floor exercises (Kegels)—tighten up the muscles as if you are stopping the pee mid-flow. Hold as long as you can. Do up to 10 contractions at a time.
- If you're in a mad dash to the washroom, put mind over matter. Don't panic. Look anywhere but the toilet you're racing to and sing a favourite song in your head to take your mind off your destination.
- If you simply can't make it and are about to have an accident, try stopping and squatting until the urge passes. Pretend you are tying a shoelace.

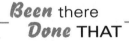

Been there
Done THAT

I used to have this sort of "giggle dribble" when I was younger, but it got really bad in university. I had these sudden uncontrollable urges to go to the toilet—so strong that "holding it" was not an option. As soon as I needed to go that was it—I had to drop everything and run to the can. I didn't tell anyone, though, because I was too embarrassed.

—MELANIE, 22

Smelly Poop

Do people evacuate the building after you've hit the dorm washroom? Have you noticed others rushing out of the office john after you've been in there? Spraying air freshener? Opening windows? Setting up fans? Darling, that *is* a problem. Everyone's excrement smells. Some just smells more. This can be even more embarrassing, now that you're doing your business in washrooms that other people share rather than the privacy of the family home. But how do you know what's normal? It's not exactly something you can discuss around the water cooler.

Normal poop is the consistency of peanut butter—brownish, sausage- or S-shaped—and it slips quietly into the toilet. It doesn't plunk out like bullets. (That's a sign you need more fibre, fluid, or exercise.) If it's super-stinky, that could be a result of a high-fat diet—especially if your "caca" floats in the toilet bowl. (Oh come on—have a look! Nobody's watching.)

If odour is a new problem for you, think about what you've been eating lately. If you're really concerned, you might even want to keep a "Stool Journal" to keep track of what effect your diet is having. Sometimes, though, stinky poo is a symptom of a physical problem. You should be concerned when it coincides with other symptoms, like stools of an abnormal colour (pale is not good), mucus or blood, cramps, fever, or weight loss. If you notice any of these things, see a doctor.

If you're otherwise healthy, though, and smell is the only problem, you'll just have to work on covering up the smell. Bring a little can of air freshener into the washroom with you, or discreetly hang some air fresheners, or set up a bowl of potpourri as part of your new bathroom "redecorating" scheme.

Duh moment!

How to Wipe Your Bum

Wipe front to back. Why? Your bottom is full of bad bacteria. If you wiped from back to front, the bad stuff gets into the vagina and causes all sorts of nasty problems. And while we're at it, pee before and after sexual intercourse, and don't douche. It will lower your odds of getting a urinary tract infection.

Indigestion

Aww, it used to be so cute, that little burp of yours. Pat your back and out it would come. But you're not little and bald any more, and when the burps come, nobody cheers. In fact, when your belly's overfull these days, we call it indigestion, and it's kinda gross. You don't need the empty Cheesie bags and burger wrappers to tell you when you've got it. You know the signs:

- Burning sensation in the back of the throat.
- Pain in your upper belly.
- Uncontrollable burping.
- Nausea.
- Bloating.

If you've pigged out and are feeling it, you can pop the button on your jeans, vow never again, diet tomorrow—but what can you do to relieve the discomfort?

- Go for a walk—hoofing it can help get your gastrointestinal tract working.
- Try sipping mint tea, or add some grated ginger or a teaspoon of powdered ginger to hot water.
- And don't forget to say "Excuse me."

Next time, avoid the culprits—skip whatever foods you're sensitive to, slow down, calm down, and quit pigging out. Eat smaller meals. Avoid greasy, fatty foods, don't smoke, wait for your food to digest before you run out to catch the bus, and go easy on the chocolate and citrus fruits.

If you get indigestion even when you're eating right, or if it's combined with weight loss, extreme stomach pain, loss of appetite, sweating, or shortness of breath, see a doctor.

Cold Sores

Cold sores are annoying, unsightly, and can wreck a great date. That's the good news. Bad news: they are contagious, incurable, and unpreventable.

You can, however, reduce their frequency and shorten their lifespan. Here are some tips for dealing with cold sores.

- Keep yourself as healthy as possible. Eat well, sleep right, and manage stress.
- Be aware of "triggers"—stress, fever, and menstruation are common ones.
- Avoid skin contact with anyone who has a cold sore.
- Keep your lips moisturized in winter and covered with sunscreen in summer.
- Don't share eating utensils, towels, or bath items with someone who has one.
- Wash your hands frequently, and especially before touching anyone else.
- Ice or warm compresses may help ease the pain.

- Don't touch the sore. Squeezing or picking at it will just make it worse.
- Try not to touch your eyes or genitals when you have an outbreak—you could infect other body parts.

If you get cold sores often, see your doctor. You may be able to get a prescription that will shorten the duration and decrease the pain.

Stinky Feet

Oh that smell! There's nothing quite like it. It comes from the heady mixture of perspiration and bacteria. Squish it all into a warm, moist place like your shoes and it cooks up foot odour. If you've got bad luck and bad genes (um, that wouldn't be from me), then you've got feet that can wilt flowers.

As soon as you get home, doff your shoes and wear flip-flops. Wash your feet daily. If normal soap doesn't work, try an antibacterial soap. Try soaking your feet in warm water with vinegar or Epsom salts, or spray them with rubbing alcohol every morning. You can also try wiping white vinegar on your feet and letting it dry before putting on cotton socks. Or dust cornstarch or baby powder on your feet before putting on cotton socks.

Never wear the same shoes two days in a row. Let them air out between use. Use odour-absorbing insoles in them, stuff them with newspapers or scented dryer sheets when you're not wearing them, or spray the inside with disinfectant. Curse your genes. Go barefoot.

Been there
Done THAT

When we went on long trips I remember my parents used to make me lie across the back seat, across the laps of my brother and sisters, and stick my feet out the window as we drove. When I got older, I'd never remove my shoes. Ever. On dates, I did everything I possibly could to avoid it. When we went bowling, I'd back off into a corner and quickly switch shoes so my girlfriend wouldn't know.

—BRAD, 29

Body Odour

Sweat's a fact of life. Odour—not so much. That's because, normally, perspiration doesn't smell. But when it mixes with the bacteria on your skin and clothing, stinkiness can result. Hormones, dehydration, sexual stimulation, and fear can also raise a stink.

What helps? Showering more often, changing clothes, and using deodorant, of course. A quick shower splash in the armpits won't do it—you'll need to really soap, lather, and dry well. You can ramp up the protection further with antiperspirant, which actually reduces the amount of sweat (as well as counteracting odour, which is what a deodorant does). For women (and, who knows, some men?), keeping the underarms well shaved can help. Antibacterial soap under arms and feet or deodorant with baking soda are also worth trying. Sometimes taking zinc supplements (30 mg a day) can reduce the odour. Also, try drinking more water.

If body odour is really interfering with work or social life, a doctor can prescribe a heavy-duty antiperspirant, or even suggest treatments like Botox, surgery, or electrical stimulation of the skin to reduce sweat.

If it's not *you* who smells, but a buddy, co-worker, or significant other, you want to be tactful about it. Anonymous notes are not nice, dear. There's a better way.

First, make sure his/her mental health seems okay. (Depression can make a person forget hygiene—and that's a bigger issue, by far.) Then, speak up. He might really not know he's turning others off. Speak plainly— you're telling him this in kindness because you like him and want to enjoy his company. If he's got practical reasons—a broken washing machine, for example— point out the closest laundromat. And if you're too chicken for a face-to-face, offer your friend a gift basket that "happens" to include bath bubbles, deodorant, scented soap, etc. Make it look spa-ish. Maybe your friend will get the hint.

> ### *Been* there *Done* THAT
>
> Aaack! Help! You would not believe how bad my roommate stinks! The smell of B.O. is starting to soak into everything in our little apartment. I don't know how to tell her, but I've got to do something. I can't live like this much longer!
>
> —EMMY, 18

Acne

Not fair, is it? You've got this far in life, made it through puberty and beyond. What's with the pimples—still?

Actually, it's not unusual at all for people in their twenties, and even thirties and forties, to struggle with acne. Sometimes, acne doesn't pop up until after you've reached adulthood. It can be related to stress, fatigue, hormones, or just plain bad genetic luck.

What should you do? First of all, *don't* pick at them. Squeezing can force the infected stuff deeper into the skin, making it worse. The sun does more harm than good, so don't bask in the sun, thinking it will help. There's no proof that particular foods cause acne, but if you notice "triggers," you'd be wise to avoid them, and try to eat healthy foods as much as you can. Wash your skin twice a day with a fresh washcloth and gentle (not antibacterial) soap. Don't scrub. Shampoo your hair at least twice a week, because the greasies can travel to your face.

One of the best ways to clear up blemishes is with an over-the-counter product containing benzoyl peroxide (BP). Start with a product with a relatively low dosage—it might be enough. Benzoyl peroxide might dry out your face and make it extra-sensitive to sun exposure, so if you're using it, try to cover up, use sunscreen, and stay out of the sun. If BP doesn't help, see your doctor. Birth control pills are one thing that can reduce the number of outbreaks.

TIP: Big zit, big date? Dab some toothpaste (not gel) on it to help shrink the blemish.

Troubled skin?

Don't:

- Load on the makeup.
- Expose your skin to extreme temperatures.
- Rub your skin.
- Wear irritating fabrics (if it's "bacne"—back acne).
- Let Rover lick your face.

+

More than You Really Wanted to Know

The most common type of acne is *acne vulgaris*. (How's that for a pretty name?) Acne affects about 90 percent of adolescents, and 20 to 30 percent of those aged 20 to 40. It accounts for more doctor visits than any other skin problem.

Warts

Try duct tape. Studies show it works better than the drops of liquid nitrogen that you can buy over the counter at the drugstore. Put duct tape on the wart for six days, then remove it for one night. Soak the wart in warm water for ten minutes, then rub with emery board. Cover again for another six days. It should disappear in about six weeks.

Remember, you can pick up plantar warts and athlete's foot from walking barefoot on the gym floor or in the locker room. The floor is a perfect breeding ground for viruses and fungi because it's warm and damp. Keep flip-flops on your feet for protection.

Constipation

Think you're constipated just because you don't have a bowel movement every day? Oh come on, honey! There is no "right" number of times—you could go three times a day or three times a week. Everybody's different.

However, it is possible that you're a bit "blocked up" if your poop is hard, dry, lumpy, or difficult to pass. You probably don't need to worry much; usually, constipation is temporary and not serious. Lack of fluid, fibre, or exercise is often to blame. If that's the case, there are solutions.

Don't automatically reach for laxatives. They can cause your body to become dependent on them, and make your food move too quickly through your system to absorb nutrients. Instead, try drinking more water and avoiding caffeine. Get at least 30 minutes of exercise each day, and beef up the fibre in your diet. What's fibre? You'll find it in these foods:

- beans
- asparagus
- Brussels sprouts
- carrots
- cabbage
- whole grains
- bran
- prunes

TIP: If you notice blood in your stools, if you have frequent diarrhea, or if you have pain with bowel movements, see the doctor.

Steer clear of fatty fare like chips, cheese, chocolate, fries, and burgers, and white foods like bread, rice, pasta, and dough. Cut back on refined sugar, candies, cookies, pop, salty snacks, and processed foods. Eat more slowly. Make some time for quality time in the can. And when you gotta go, for Pete's sake—go!

Farting, Bloating, Tummy Issues

What are we talking about here? Silent but deadly, or loud and long? No big deal when you are all alone in the middle of the night, but out in public, it's another story. Can't blame it on the dog any more—especially if you're sitting in a meeting or at your girlfriend's parents' house for dinner.

Maybe it was the pizza and beer or the party platter of nachos. Something isn't right.

So what do you do? You hold it in. Your stomach whines back. You glare at someone—anyone. It was them, not you. Well, we've all been there, done that, and blamed it on someone else. Studies show (yes, believe it or not, they have actually studied this) the average person passes gas 10 to 14 times a day. If you're lucky, it's not all at once and it's not in the office elevator.

If your tummy's troubling you a little more than usual, you might want to look at your diet—both how you eat, and what you eat. If you've been wolfing down your food, or stuffing your face, that might give you gas. Make sure you're chewing your food well and eating slowly. Booze, smoking, and stress can all make your stomach fussy too. You know about the magic of beans, of course, but you should also watch out for (and possibly eliminate, one by one, to find out which is to blame):

- pears, peaches, apples
- whole grains
- asparagus, onions, cabbage, cauliflower, broccoli
- milk and dairy products
- carbonated drinks
- sugar-free food and drinks, xylitol, sorbitol, or fructose
- gum

Been there
Done THAT

I often wondered why farting was embarrassing but burps—not so much. I was an assistant teacher for kindergarten to Grade 3. In kindergarten the kids never thought anything of farting, and if they were sitting cross-legged on the floor they'd even fall onto one cheek to let it rip. Things changed a little towards the end of Grade 1, became funny in Grade 2, but by Grade 3, farts were embarrassing.

—WINTER, 19

If you're eating a high-fibre diet (which is good, by the way), then make sure you're drinking plenty of water. If you're about to eat a high-fibre meal, try popping a gas-reducer like Beano (available at drugstores) beforehand. And if you can't help it, you've just got to let one out, well, dear, just go find a well-ventilated room. And say, "Excuse me."

Something Fishy?

Women are supposed to have a slight vaginal odour; it's also normal for it to change during the monthly cycle. But it shouldn't be strong, unpleasant, fishy, or ammonia-like. If it is, you might have an infection, and require a doctor. Similarly, if you're itchy and have a discharge that looks like cottage cheese, you could have a yeast infection. An over-the-counter treatment can help. (Don't use for more than a week, or more than two times a month.) If the problem continues, or if you have burning or pain when you pee or have sex, see your doctor.

For good health below the belt:

Don't:

- Wear pantiliners all the time (causes irritation).
- Douche (kills healthy vaginal flora).
- Wear thong underwear (transmits germs from back to front).

Do:

- Wipe front to back after using the toilet.
- Pee before and after sexual intercourse.
- Wear undies with a cotton crotch.
- Eat lots of yogurt containing *Lactobacillus acidophilus.*
- Eat acidic fruits like mango and cranberry.
- Wash with a gentle, scent-free soap (like Dove).

Tip: A shower a day—absolutely. But once a week give your privates a treat. Give them a good soak in the bathtub. They will love you for it.—Sue Johanson a.k.a. The Sex Lady

And men, semen usually has a vinegar or chlorine-like smell. If yours smells strong, or nasty, you might have a bacterial infection. Get it checked out by a doctor.

Diarrhea When Menstruating

Relax. Doesn't mean a thing. It's totally normal, relatively common, and is related to hormonal changes. Exercise, good eating, and avoiding stress, alcohol, and caffeine can help. If it's really bad, try taking ibuprofen the day before your period starts.

Baby Powder for Your Not-So-Babyish Body Parts

Summer can make you feel hot and sticky—especially "down there." If you're thinking that baby powder might dry things up, think again. Talcum powder has been associated with ovarian cancer in women when it's used in the genital area—even when it's sprinkled on underwear or sanitary napkins. If the heat makes you feel yucky, wear cotton undies instead. In fact, why not wear them all the time? Doctors say underwear made of synthetic material traps heat and moisture. That can lead to bacterial growth and urinary tract infections.

Lost Tampon

It's possible to forget a tampon, but not really possible to lose one. There's nowhere for it to go! If it went in and didn't come out, then it's still in there, possibly hiding around the little nooks and crannies inside you. If you can't find the string, it might be tucked up inside. You do need to get it out, though, or you're at risk for serious infection. Can't really remember? I know, life gets busy. One signal that you've forgotten something: an unpleasant smell or discharge. If you can't find the string and pull it out, get to a doctor.

Canker Sores

Canker sores are small, painful sores in your mouth, on the inside of your lips, your cheeks, or under your tongue. There are a number of possible causes, including deficiencies in iron, vitamin B12, calcium, and folic acid. Sometimes they'll flare up with hormonal change or stress.

If you seem to be getting a lot of canker sores, make sure you're eating a well-balanced diet with lots of veggies. Try consuming more milk or yogurt. Avoid spicy, salty, or acidic foods, and stay away from anything "abrasive," like potato chips and nuts. Use only soft-bristle toothbrushes, and brush your teeth and gums gently. A couple of home remedies might help:

More than You Really Wanted to Know

What grosses women out:

1. *Dirty Nails.* You think a woman is going to let you near her, let alone touch her, with dirty nails? Think again. If your nails are in terrible shape, hit any mall and find a manicure service. Now buy a nail-care kit to keep your nails trim and neat.

2. *Nose hair.* Remember creepy Uncle Pete with the bushy nose? Say no more. Buy a nose-hair trimmer, available in gadget shops, and use it.

3. *The Unibrow.* This hairy stripe across the forehead doesn't even look good on Bert from *Sesame Street.* Even worse, your new girlfriend's grandma might be Irish: "Beware the man whose eyebrows meet for in his heart there lies deceit." Get rid of it! Pluck it out with a pair of tweezers, shave it off, wax it off, talk to your barber. Do whatever it takes!

4. *Ear hair.* Talk to your barber about this one too. Really. And since we are in the area, ear wax has gotta go, but do not jam a Q-tip into your ear. Not only will it push the ear wax in but you might end up with an ear infection. Your doctor will need to clean out your ears. Your pharmacist might also have some suggestions. Drugstores carry products that can help clear away wax. Not sure if you've got a problem? (After all, it is hard to see your ears in the mirror.) Ask a trusted, preferably female, friend.

5. *Dry skin.* Use face and body moisturizer and ditch the alcohol-based aftershave products. If you have a dry face or are prone to rashes, get to a dermatologist!

6. *Dandruff.* It doesn't matter how expensive your new suit is, if it's dotted with flakes you're out. If dandruff shampoo doesn't work (read the directions on the bottle), add this to your list of things to talk to the dermatologist about.

7. *Bad breath.* Replace your toothbrush often, and use a tongue cleaner, too. (Some brushes have them on the back side of the toothbrush, or they can be found in the pharmacy next to the toothbrushes.) Floss! Use mouthwash and carry heavy-duty mints designed to help with stale breath.

8. *B.O.* Deodorant. 'Nuff said.

- Apply vegetable oil to a cotton ball and hold it against the sore several times a day.
- Rinse out your mouth with salt water.
- Suck on a zinc lozenge.
- If the pain makes it hard to eat, take some ibuprofen or acetaminophen. There are also topical medications like Anbesol, Oragel, and Orabase that you put right on the sore.

If your sores last longer than a week, or if you have other symptoms of illness, have the doctor check you out.

Taking Care of Skin

A tanning booth? Are you crazy? You think you look gorgeous with a healthy glow? That a sun lamp's safer than the sun? Wrong, wrong wrong!

First of all, you don't look healthy with a "glow." You just look cooked. And in just a few short years, you'll look all saggy and wrinkly. Second, skin cancer is a very real possibility. Hate to burst your bubble, but you are not immortal. Skin cancer has been skyrocketing among those under forty. And while we're talking bubbles, let's burst a few more:

- Getting a gradual tan will not protect your skin.
- A tan is not attractive. A tan is a sign of damaged skin.
- Wearing makeup with SPF 15 will not provide enough protection. You still need sunscreen.
- Clouds and car windows don't protect you either. You can still soak up wrinkles and skin cancer through either.
- Even though it says the sunscreen is waterproof, you must still reapply after swimming.
- Even though it says "all-day protection," you are not protected all day. Reapply often. Cover up.
- Dark skin is not safe from skin cancer. It might be less likely, but it is still possible.
- Tanning beds are not safe. It's still a UV ray, and it's still bad news.
- Even swimming, or sitting in the shade on a sunny day, leaves you exposed. The sun will find you there, too.
- Skip the sun lotion that promises to keep mosquitoes away at the same time. The DEET that repels bugs should not be reapplied often, but the sunscreen that repels the sun's rays *should* be reapplied frequently. It doesn't make sense to combine the two ingredients in one product.

Before you join a monastery in rainy Scotland, there are alternatives.

- Try to plan outdoor activities for early or late in the day. The sun's rays are strongest between 10 a.m. and 4 p.m.

- If you're going to be in the sun for any length of time, wear clothes made from tightly woven cloth.
- Wear a broad-brimmed hat to protect your face, neck, and ears—start a new fashion. (Baseball caps don't count.)
- Apply a shot-glass full of sunscreen—broad-spectrum with a SPF of 15 or higher—15 to 30 minutes before you head out, and reapply every 2 hours (more often if you're sweating or swimming).
- Spread the stuff on gently; if you really rub it in, it won't be as effective. Make sure you cover all exposed skin, including ears, back of neck, and lips. If you can, use spray-on sunscreens; they may give you better coverage because they go on more evenly.
- Don't forget your eyes. Choose sunglasses that filter out 100 percent of UV light.

TIPS:

- To keep sunscreen from running into your eyes, apply wax-based lip balm around your eyes.
- Sunscreen should be good for a year, but it shouldn't last that long. If you're putting on enough, you should be going through a bottle a week.
- Winter can be wicked on skin—especially if you're out unprotected in fresh snow. And if you're hitting the slopes, at a higher altitude, your skin can fry in less than an hour.
- Tanning booths might be a more dangerous way to tan, because they usually use the longer-wavelength ultraviolet A, which penetrates much more deeply. And there's research showing you can actually get addicted to sunlamp tanning, with withdrawal symptoms like nausea, shaking, and dizziness.
- If you drive a lot, wear sunscreen on your left side because the sun can penetrate car windows. North Americans get skin cancer more on that side, Brits on the right.

Some people are more at risk of developing skin cancer than others. Be extra-cautious if you:

- Have fair skin, red or blond hair, light-coloured eyes.
- Sunburn easily.
- Have many freckles or moles.
- Spend a lot of time outside—now and when you were a child.
- Have had a serious sunburn.
- Others in the family have had skin cancer.
- Sunbathe—either in the sun, or with a sunlamp.

TIP: If you blew it and got sunburned anyway, try soaking for 15 minutes in a lukewarm bath with half a cup of baking soda. Or spread yogurt on the sunburn, let it sit for 20 minutes, then rinse clean with lukewarm water. Say 10 "Hail Mary"s and don't ever let it happen again.

Check Your Skin

Every couple of months, examine your body from head to toe in a well-lit room—ideally after a shower or bath. Use a hand mirror and full-length mirror to see your scalp and back. You want to become familiar with what's normal for your body, so that you catch anything unusual early on. The earlier skin cancer is found, the better the chance it can be cured. Don't forget to check between your toes, under your nails, the bottoms of your feet, your back, scalp, and all those other spots where the sun don't shine. (You know what I'm talking about—skin cancer can happen down there, too.)

Most skin cancers develop on parts of the body that are regularly exposed to the sun. When you're checking your skin, pay close attention to:

Cancer hotspots

- head
- neck
- face
- tips of ears
- hands
- forearms

- shoulders
- back
- on men: chest and back
- on women: back of neck, back of calves, and hands

What are you looking for?

A for asymmetrical shape
B for irregular borders (edges blurry or jagged)
C for colour changes
D for diameter greater than the size of a pencil eraser
E for evolving—changing shape, size, colour, or symptoms (itching or bleeding for example)

See a doctor if you notice any of those signs, or a fast-growing mole, a scaly or crusted growth on the skin, or a sore that won't heal.

Taking Care of Your Eyes

Here's something else to put on your to-do list: along with the dentist and doctor, you should see an eye doctor regularly to have your eyes checked. Why? Because regular eye exams can pick up things like diabetes, high blood pressure, high cholesterol or stroke, and serious eye disease. Any one of these things can develop without any warning or symptoms.

You do not need a referral to see an optometrist (a referral is required for an ophthalmologist, who deals with more serious issues and performs surgery), but your provincial health care plan may only cover one appointment every two years once you are over the age of 18. Today, anyone can pop into a store that sells glasses and get "a free eye examination." Careful here. The reason you must go to an optometrist is that he or she will check for eye diseases, among other things. If glaucoma runs in your family, and even if it doesn't, an eye exam every two years is mandatory.

Another reason to have an eye doctor on your medical team is to have somewhere to run to if your eye is scratched.

TIPS:
- Donate your old glasses to Lions Clubs International. They clean and repair glasses and give them to patients around the world.
- Try not to squint when you're using the computer. Long-term squinting can cause you to blink less often, which can lead to eye strain, dry eye, and presbyopia.
- Replace your mascara after an eye infection so you don't reinfect yourself.

TIPS:

- Keep a pair of prescription glasses on hand in case you get an irritation in your eye. That way you can give your eyes a break from contacts until the irritation goes away. If you don't, the irritation could turn into an ulcer—which is far more serious.
- General lens care: wash hands with soap and dry with a lint-free towel before handling lenses or touching your eyes. Make sure your cleaning solution hasn't expired. Replace your storage case every three months.

Contact Lens Emergencies

Sleeping with your lenses in

Honey, I don't care how tired you are—do not go to sleep with your contacts in. Studies show that people who sleep with their contacts in are more likely to develop eye problems, and if you wear your lenses for longer than the doctor has suggested, you could end up with eye irritation, scratches, or an infection. If you find you're often too wiped to deal with it at the end of the day, make a point of removing them an hour or two before bed, when you've still got a bit of energy.

If you do blow it one night and crash without removing them, get them out ASAP, and give your eyes a break for a day or two by wearing eyeglasses instead. Keep extra contact lens carrying cases and mini bottles of cleansing solution in your purse, backpack, or glove compartment (and at your friend's place, if that's a regular crash-pad for you). In a pinch, you can put them in a cup filled with clean water so that you give your eyes a rest. Make sure you do a proper cleaning before you put them back in your eyes. And don't even think about sticking them in your mouth to clean them.

Can't get your lenses out?

Sometimes your eyes and lenses get too dry and they stick. A squirt of saline can loosen things up enough to remove the lens. If the contact seems "lost" in your eye, don't panic. Sure, it feels uncomfortable, but just relax, put a few drops of saline in, blink, and keep your eyes closed a while. Don't poke around at it. If it doesn't "show up" on its own, go to your doctor, or to a walk-in after-hours clinic, for help. Get a ride there.

Coloured contacts—what, are you crazy?

I'm not going to flip out on you if you decide to change the colour of your hair. And go ahead, smear on fake tan if you think you need to change the colour of your skin. But darling—your eyes? What are you thinking?

Cosmetic lenses might look cool, but they're not risk-free—especially when you buy them from salespeople who aren't qualified in eye care. Before you get any lenses, you should have your corneas checked out to be sure they're suitable for contact lenses. It's important, too, that the lenses are fitted properly, because no two eyes are exactly the same size. A bad fit can mean permanent eye damage. And of course you can really mess up your eyes when you leave the lenses in for too long, wear them after their "expiry date," sleep with them in your eyes, or don't clean them properly. Just because they are not considered a "prescription" device doesn't mean you can just pop them in like you do fake nails and earrings. Take these things seriously—if you take them at all.

Taking Care of Your Teeth

Rule Number 1

Floss. Every day. If you can't floss after every meal, then do it at least once, at night, before you brush. In fact, flossing is more important than brushing because it gets to places your brush doesn't reach. When you brush alone, you leave as much as 40 percent of your tooth surfaces untouched.

TIP: Keep some floss in your pocket or purse— it's smaller than a toothbrush and toothpaste.

Don't go crazy with the yanking and the rubbing—you're not shining shoes. Curve the floss around each tooth in a U-shape and gently scrape up and down toward the gums. It should take about two minutes. A little bit of bleeding is normal if your teeth aren't used to it, and that should stop after a few days. If you do this regularly, you'll protect yourself against bad breath, gum disease, cavities, and even heart disease.

Rule Number 2

Brush your teeth after every meal or snack—or at the very least, at the beginning and end of the day. Brush for two minutes. A battery-powered brush might do a better job at removing plaque than a manual brush, and some even include two-minute timers. Every once in a while, check out the inside of your mouth for sores that won't heal or red or white patches that could indicate oral cancer. Any swelling, numbness, or difficulty chewing should also be brought to your dentist's attention.

TIP: Sports drinks are one of the worst for teeth, followed by pop. When drinking these beverages, make sure the straw is near the back of your mouth so that the sugar in the drink doesn't spend so much time near your teeth.

Rule Number 3

Watch out for these cavity-prompting habits:

- Acidic foods like pickles, citrus fruit, and juices—they can erode enamel.
- Citrus-flavoured pop and sports drinks—use a straw to avoid contact with teeth as much as possible, and chug, don't sip.
- Candy, of course, but also beware of dried fruit, doughnuts, muffins, and cookies, which stick to teeth.

Duh moment!

How to Brush Your Teeth

- Use a toothbrush with soft, rounded-end bristles and a head that's not too small to reach way back. Consider an electric toothbrush (the kind with rotating and back-and-forth movement is best). Look for the Canadian Dental Association (CDA) Seal of Recognition.
- With the brush at a slight angle, gently stroke teeth with round movements where teeth meet gums. Don't scrub—you'll wreck your enamel.
- Move from one end of your mouth to the other, both sides.
- Brush surfaces of back teeth where you chew.
- Brush your tongue.
- Spit. Rinse.
- Rinse your brush and shake gently until it's dry. Leave in upright position to air-dry.

TIP: More of a good thing is not necessarily better. Brushing and flossing harder won't get your teeth any cleaner—but it could cause dental problems. You don't want your brush bristles to be splayed after a few months' use, and you don't want to saw through your gums with the floss. Easy does it.

More than You Really Wanted to Know

Your toothbrush can be a breeding ground for bacteria. Any germ you once harboured can fester there quite happily. And every time you flush the toilet, millions of germs are tossed into the air, some landing on your toothbrush. A dark medicine cabinet or enclosed plastic case are no better, because bacteria and mould like the dark and lack of air circulation. Replace your brush as often as you can. Buy cheap brushes so you don't mind chucking them after a couple of weeks. Find someplace else to store the brush. Close the toilet lid when you flush. And don't even think about reusing your brush after it lands on that miserable bathroom floor.

Cost Cutters

If you live near a university with a dental faculty, you can save significantly on dentist fees—although you may have to wait a while for an appointment. To find out how to become a patient at a faculty dental clinic, go to www.acfd.ca and click on Links to Dental Schools.

Fear of Dentists

Fear of dentists is right up there next to fear of flying and public speaking. Maybe it's the idea of being helpless, unable to speak, with big needles and grindy torture noises all around. Or the dentist looking all horror-showish with the mask and gloves and the chemical smells.

But guess what? You gotta go. Every six months to a year. So get over it. How? Here are some suggestions:

- Talk about it with your dentist. If you let him know you're nervous, he'll do everything possible to help you relax. Some will show you hand signals so you can communicate when you're in pain or

Duh moment!

Don't share or borrow a toothbrush.

TIP: Out of floss? Swish water around in your mouth after brushing. Then go buy floss.

I always hated the dentist, but my mom used to make me go. When I moved out, I just put that nasty idea right out of my head—until my teeth started to hurt. I knew I had to go. But the fear was *huge*. I finally signed up for a research study at the university that was looking at how to overcome phobias. It took another year of visualizing therapy before I finally got up the guts. By then I had a mouth full of cavities—and who knows how bad my breath was!

—JILLIAN, 26

need a break. Others might walk you through the procedure, step by step. Many now provide music and headphones—or you can bring your own.

- Use visualizing and relaxation techniques. Breathe deeply and slowly while picturing a favourite place.
- Make your appointment on the weekend or late in the afternoon, when you're more relaxed and not stressing over missed work.
- Remember that you can have your gums numbed before your teeth are cleaned, using a gel. Ask the hygienist.

TIP: If you're having dental work done, schedule it for later in the day. That way you won't be getting the feeling back (and the pain) just when you want to go to sleep.

- If you're still not comfortable with your current dentist, ask your friends if they're happy with theirs—and switch. There are all kinds of ways dentists today are trying to make your visit "pleasant"—from virtual-reality goggles to spa services, like patient-controlled massagers, aromatherapy eye pillows, facials, and reflexology. (The latter choices may still be available only in California, but rest assured, they'll find their way to Winnipeg soon.)

Vanquishing Your Vices

I'd like to think that you made it all the way to adulthood without picking up any vices, so you needn't burst my bubble by telling me otherwise. But just in case I'm wrong, may I suggest you pick your vices carefully? At the very least, avoid the ones that can kill you, get you arrested, or end up with you being tossed out of a frat house.

Smoking

This is a tough one to tackle right now. It's in your face all the time, at parties and clubs, coffee breaks, between classes. What with the move out, the pressure of new jobs, exams, roommate hassles, or money woes, this is a tough time to kick the habit. And if you've never smoked, you're going to be facing all that peer pressure all over again!

So let's try a little visualizing instead. Erase those sexy smoking images the marketers have burned into your mind and replace them with this: you, twenty years from now, all wrinkly faced, with yellow teeth, smelly clothes, and bad breath, huddled outside your office building in a bitter winter wind with the other smokers getting their "fix." You're hacking. You're unhealthy. You're wishing you'd quit when you had the chance. Or never started in the first place.

With each puff, envision these risks:

- Stroke, asthma, cancer, and heart attack.
- Links to Sudden Infant Death Syndrome.
- Lower estrogen levels and a risk to fertility.
- Respiratory problems. (Supermodel Christy Turlington, a smoker for 10 years, reportedly suffered from chronic bronchitis and strep throat due to her smoking habit. Yeah, and you thought she was perfect.)

More than You Really Wanted to Know

- 24 percent of those who've kissed a smoker said it "tasted like an ashtray," 17 percent said "it was a bit of a turnoff," and 15 percent said it was "completely disgusting," according to a recent Ipsos-Reid/Pfizer poll.
- The net worth of the average nonsmoker is 50 percent higher than a light smoker, and twice that of a pack-a-day smoker, according to Ohio State University researchers.

- Death—smoking causes 47,500 a year, according to the Canadian Cancer Society, and there's a pretty good chance that death will come not when you're an old geezer, but rather in middle age (between 40 and 70).

TIP: Throw out your lighters and ashtrays—out of sight, out of mind.

If you light up only once in a while—when you go out to clubs, say, or at the odd party—experts say you are still at risk. Just smoking a pack a week can still cause serious damage.

And here's one more thing to think about: your wallet. What if, every time you bought a pack of cigarettes, you put the money aside instead? Even if you just put the money into something conservative like government bonds, you'd still accumulate a tidy sum. Want to know how much? "Health tools" at www.mediresource.sympatico.ca will calculate it for you.

Studies show that the average smoker tries to quit 10.8 times over a period of almost 20 years before finally breaking the habit for good. You might as well get started now, while you're young enough to have 20 years left! I'm not going to tell you how to do it. Obviously, it won't be easy. You're going to need a plan, and you'll want to tell your friends because you'll need their support. You might need something to help you deal with the withdrawal, like the nicotine patch, inhalers, spray, or gum. Talk to your doctor. Check out www.quitneg.org or www.smokershelpline.ca. And if you've got this far, give yourself a pat on the back. Just deciding you're going to quit means you're partway there.

Duh moment!

So you don't smoke cigarettes? You just enjoy a cigar, or pipe once in a while? Or you only indulge in smokeless tobacco or the occasional snuff? Don't fool yourself. Tobacco is tobacco. Tobacco is bad.

Hooked on Hookahs

Speaking of tobacco and bad …

The hookah fad seems to have a lot of young people fooled. It seems so harmless, this Middle Eastern turn-taking tradition. After all, it's just a social thing, right? You're

More than You Really Wanted to Know

Hookahs, which are smoked for about 45 minutes, deliver 36 times more tar than a cigarette, 15 times more carbon monoxide, and 70 percent more nicotine, according to Thomas Eissenberg, a psychology professor at Virginia Commonwealth University and co-author of a study on hookahs.

just chillin' round a fancy vessel filled with fruit-flavoured tobacco, sharing sucks on the snake-like hose, ripe odours wafting about you. You feel mellow and cool, chic and global. How could anything so romantic and seductive possibly be bad?

Well, first of all, hookah smokers are inhaling a mixture that is 70 percent fruit and molasses, 30 percent tobacco. Tobacco is bad, remember? Your body does not like it. Just because you're not actually burning tobacco (you're inhaling the smoke from heated moistened tobacco) doesn't mean you're not doing damage. Although it has been filtered through water, the toxins are still there, as is nicotine, the addictive substance in tobacco smoke. Any exposure to nicotine is dangerous. Some studies have shown there's just as high a concentration of cancer-causing and addictive substances in hookahs as in cigarettes. And you hang around a hookah a lot longer than you hang on to a cigarette, so you're increasing your exposure. Do it often enough and you could end up with mouth cancer, lung disease, stomach and esophagus cancer, and coronary heart disease. Doesn't sound so romantic any more, does it?

If you're looking for a way to mellow out, you might want to look into yoga or meditation instead.

Caffeine

Are we going to call this one a vice? Oh heck, why not? It is a drug—an addictive one. Consumed in excess, it affects your body in the same way an upper does. Just like cocaine, heroin, and amphetamines, caffeine stimulates your brain, using the same mechanisms. So yes, it is probably something you should be careful with—whether you get it in cups of coffee, in your energy drinks, pop, cold meds, or some combination thereof.

If you feel you can't get through the day without your coffee hit, then you are probably addicted. And what's wrong with that? Maybe you think it helps you get through the day. Researchers at Duke University Medical Center have found that it does exactly the opposite—it exaggerates stress. And its effects tend to spiral. Once the energy surge wears off, you're hit with tiredness and look for more caffeine to get you going again. That's not good, because it means your body is being pumped all day long. You end up jittery and irritable, your blood pressure elevated, increasing your risk of heart attack and stroke.

And then there's the whole issue of sleep—or lack thereof. The effects of caffeine float around in your body for about six hours. That coffee you sipped all afternoon could still be coursing through you when you hit the hay. You might fall asleep fine, but you could be missing out on the benefits of deep sleep. That means you wake up groggy, needing another hit in an awful way.

So go easy on the caffeine, okay? Try to keep it to no more than three to four 250-millilitre (8-ounce) cups of brewed coffee a day, and pay attention to the effects on your body. You've had too much if you notice you're:

- Irritable.
- Anxious.
- Restless.
- Dizzy.
- Unable to concentrate.
- Jittery.
- Crampy.
- Headachey.
- Suffering from insomnia.
- Experiencing abnormal heart rhythms.

If you think you've been overdoing it, cut back. Don't touch caffeine after noon. Be aware of other sources of caffeine, like tea, pop, energy drinks, chocolate, and some medications. Some sources might surprise you—cold relief medicine can contain caffeine, for example. Mountain Dew's way up there, with more caffeine than Coke, and 7-Up's way down, with zero. Even orange pop might be spiked with the stuff. Check the labels.

Don't try to quit cold turkey, or you'll suffer from withdrawal. Try to cut back by half a cup per day. If that's too hard, replace one of those cups with regular tea, which has less caffeine. Then move to herbal tea, which is caffeine-free.

But don't assume you're safe guzzling decaf. Recent studies are finding that almost all decaffeinated coffee contains some caffeine, and drinking five to ten cups of decaf a day could jolt you with the equivalent of a cup or two of regular java. Just remember, "decaf" is not the same as "caffeine-free." Stick with the latter if you're extra-sensitive.

Drinking

Look around you and see what drinking does to individuals, families, and careers. Now add up the cost of, say, a bottle of wine a night. Make it a cheap bottle, $10. That's $70 a week. Now toss in a case of beer for, say, another $25 a week. And once in a while add on a bottle of gin at $35. The total is almost $500—a month! That's a huge car payment, a trip to Europe once a year, clothes to die for. You could support a small African village on that.

There are a lot of good reasons to just stay away from alcohol altogether. You might enjoy it, but you certainly don't need it. But if you do decide to drink, keep in mind that saying: "All things in moderation." You already know the reasons why, but I'm going to tell you again anyway. Too much alcohol can damage your liver and contribute to some cancers, such as throat and liver cancer. It is also linked to depression, heart disease, peptic ulcers, and addiction. Drinking alcohol during pregnancy is also a risk, as is driving or operating machinery while under the influence. If you're going to drink, put a limit on it. Moderation is key. Experts say that means no more than nine drinks a week of:

- 12 oz. bottles of beer.
- 4 oz. glasses of wine.
- 1 oz. (or jigger) of liquor.

Remember—that's per week. Try not to exceed two drinks per day. There should also be at least one day per week when you do not drink any alcohol at all.

Hangover Hell

Darker, sweet liquors seem to produce the worst hangovers. Brandy is the biggest culprit, followed by red wine, rum, whisky, white wine, gin, and vodka. There have also been studies showing bourbon is twice as likely to cause sickness as the same amount of vodka.

Then again, you can get hungover drinking any kind of alcohol if you gulp it fast enough. So don't. Take a pass on the shots and the drinking games, sip slowly, dilute your drinks, and fill your belly with non-alcoholic drinks and food. And, because drinking alcohol is dehydrating, when you get home, gulp down a glass or two of water before you crash into bed.

Some more hangover helpers:

- Peppermint or ginger tea. (Toss a bit of peppermint or a slice of ginger into boiling water, simmer 10 minutes. Ginger tea can be sweetened with honey.)
- Tomato juice, orange juice, or a banana milkshake. (Blend a banana with soy milk and honey.)
- Might as well take a vitamin with these morning-after drinks.
- For the headache part, try raw cabbage or sauerkraut juice. (No kidding! Naturopaths swear by it.)

How to keep from getting drunk

Getting tanked on the weekend is really stupid. How stupid? Well, you look stupid, for starters. You know what I'm talking about—that dopey, gropey, clumsy look just does not work for you. And when you're hammered like that, you know how easily you can end up doing things you'll really regret. Rug burns on the forehead are never an attractive look, but beyond that, there are the more serious risks: car crashes, fights, drowning, alcohol poisoning, and falls. And new studies show that binge drinking is especially dangerous for young people whose brains are still developing. Too much booze can lead to lasting brain damage. So doing something stupid can make you even stupider.

TIP: Mixing alcohol with diet pop could make you drunker quicker. Studies show diet drinks cause more alcohol to be absorbed by the bloodstream, possibly because of the lack of sugar, which tends to slow down absorption.

That doesn't mean you can't party. The key, once again, is moderation. You want to slow down how quickly the alcohol is absorbed by your body. That's why it's a good idea to have a big meal before you head out, preferably something high-carb like pasta or bread. Don't drink faster than one drink per hour. It might help if you alternate non-alcoholic drinks with alcoholic, or add some sparkling water to dilute your wine. Be conscious of how much money you want to bring with you—that will limit your trips to the bar. If you're having trouble figuring out whether you're sticking to your limit, then you've had enough. If you're having trouble saying no to high-pressure "friends," have an excuse prepared: you're in training for a marathon; you're auditioning for that intern job at MuchMusic tomorrow.

More than You Really Wanted to Know

When you mix energy drinks with alcohol, you're less likely to know when you're drunk—and more likely to do stupid things. That's according to investigators at Wake Forest University School of Medicine in North Carolina. Their study found that those who "mix" are twice as likely to:

- be injured during a bout of drinking.
- need medical attention.
- ride with a drunk driver.
- take sexual advantage of someone or be taken advantage of sexually.

If you're dating, it's especially important to stay under control. That can be difficult when you're nervous and want to make a good impression. You think a few drinks will loosen you up, make you more interesting, make your date more interesting. But remember, you're using booze as a crutch. You don't want your date to like the drunk you—you want him or her to like the real you.

Drinking and drugs

Don't—repeat, don't—mix booze with drugs. At the very least, it can seriously slow down your nervous system, and can stop medications from working or alter their effect. Drinking and taking a drug like ecstasy together can make you much more likely to dehydrate and overheat. Using alcohol and drugs together can heighten the effects of both, with serious consequences. And some combinations of alcohol and drugs can be deadly.

Duh moment!

Want to sober up? Don't rely on coffee, sleep, a cold shower, or making yourself throw up. They won't work. Only time takes alcohol out of your system—and sometimes it takes more time than you think. If you've really gone overboard, you might still be drunk when you wake up in the morning. Give your body 48 hours to recover.

How to Know If You've Got an Alcohol Problem

Are you controlling your drinking—or is your drinking controlling you? How do you know? Well, if you are wondering, then there's a good chance that you already have a drinking problem.

Some other signs:

- Drinking more than you planned at social events.
- Feeling guilty about the amount you drink.
- Drinking when you know you shouldn't—like at school or work.
- Taking time off because of hangovers.
- Getting into trouble, fights, or accidents because of booze.
- Thinking a lot about the next drink.
- Spending more than you can afford on alcohol.
- Drinking alone or in secret, or hiding your booze.
- Needing to drink increasingly greater quantities to get a buzz.
- Losing interest in things you used to enjoy.
- Getting annoyed when someone suggests you cut back on the booze.

If this describes you, or someone close to you, then look for Alcoholics Anonymous in your local phone book. Or talk to your doctor (or local health clinic) about what other types of services are available to help. See the website for Alcoholics Anonymous at www.alcoholics-anonymous.org/.

How to Help a Friend Who's Been Hitting the Booze

Sure, it's kinda funny when your buddy's walking into walls and saying really stupid things. Probably, it's funnier if you're a little wasted, too. But what if your friend needs help? How do you deal with a party pal whose face is in the toilet, or in the mud—passed out puking and not funny any more?

First thing you should do is remove the source of the problem. That means no more to drink—for you or your buddy. You're going to need all your faculties if you're going to be of any help. Don't try to get him to "walk it off"—his coordination and reflexes could make that dangerous. Instead, get him to a quiet place, keep him warm (since alcohol can lower body temperature), and help him get comfortable. If he wants to lie down, make sure he's on his side with something behind his back to prevent him from rolling over onto his front, where he could drown in vomit, or onto his back, where he could choke on it. Offer him water—it won't sober him up, but it will help him feel a little better the next day. Forget trying to get him to eat. By this time, it's too late for food to slow the absorption of alcohol, and it could further upset his stomach. Coffee will not help and may make it worse, because the caffeine will just pump him up even more, when he may be better off just mellowing until the booze has run its course.

If he needs to throw up, accompany him to the washroom so he doesn't slip and fall on the hard floor. He might want to sleep, but watch that he doesn't fall unconscious. How will you know? He might be unconscious if he doesn't respond to a gentle shake, if he's breathing slowly or shallowly, feels cold to the touch, or has bluish lips. If that's the case, call 911. Also, get emergency help if he is severely ill or having trouble breathing. A person whose body is overloaded with booze can suffer alcohol poisoning, choke on vomit, or fall into a coma. We're talking life-threatening here.

Signs that your friend is in dire need of help:

- Mental confusion, stupor, coma.
- Vomiting.
- Seizures.
- Slow breathing (fewer than 8 breaths per minute).
- Irregular breathing (10 seconds or more between breaths).
- Low body temperature, bluish skin colour, paleness.

If you suspect alcohol poisoning, even if all the symptoms are not present, don't guess—call 911. If you don't, your friend could choke on his vomit, stop breathing, and suffer seizures, permanent brain damage, or death. Don't worry about whether he'll be angry or embarrassed. You cared enough to save his life.

Now, assuming you've helped your friend out of his fix, think about it. Is this the first time this has happened? Is it an ongoing problem for your friend? Do you consider yourself a good friend, and want to give him more lasting help? Then maybe you should try to talk with him about his regular visits with the bottle. People who have trouble controlling their drinking are often defensive, so you'll want to proceed carefully. Some suggestions:

- Pick your time. Do it when your friend is sober, and away from the booze.
- Pick your place. Do it in private, so he's not worried about eavesdroppers.
- Pick your message. Plan ahead. Find out if there are resources, websites, or counsellors available. Write this information down so that you can hand it to your friend if he seems open to it. Practise what you're going to say with another friend, making sure that you are criticizing the specific behaviour—not the person.
- Tell your friend how his actions are hurting your friendship. Empathize if he seems to be having trouble coping with other stresses in his life, and offer some new ways to ease those problems.

- If he says he wants to cut back on the booze, work together to come up with ways that you can support him.
- Check out the website for the Centre for Addiction and Mental Health (www.camh.net). It has terrific information about alcohol and other addictions.

Marijuana

So maybe you're not as likely to overdose on this one, but there are other ways that pot can wreck your life. Even if you're just a "light" smoker, you might be doing long-term damage to your body. Did you know that marijuana can:

- In the short term, cause chronic congestion, sore throat, and dry mouth?
- Immediately impair your thinking and motor-skill abilities, cause fatigue and anxiety, and mess up your judgment so that you make stupid, risky decisions?
- Harm your reading comprehension, problem-solving, and short-term memory?
- Lead to throat and lung cancer, and serious respiratory problems?
- Contribute to mental health problems such as depression and anxiety, and personality change?
- Be more harmful to the lungs than cigarettes (since usually joints are smoked unfiltered and inhaled deeply)?
- Damage male and female reproductive systems, and affect fetuses during pregnancy?

How to Get Home—Alive

Q: How do you know if your driver is too high or impaired to get you home?
A: Don't even try to figure out whether your buddy has had one drink or toke too many.

If at any point during the night you saw your friend with a drink or a joint, then find another way home. Never go out in the evening without phone money (if you have someone you can call to pick you up), or money for bus or taxi fare. Worst-case scenario—walk home. Really.

The problem here is experience, or lack thereof. You might have reached adulthood, but you still lack experience driving, and you lack experience drinking. That means you have a four-times greater risk of getting in a fatal accident. Think about it. It took a lot to get you to this ripe old age and we don't want to lose you now.

And what about your friend, the one who was supposed to be the designated driver, but blew it? Be the best friend a person ever had and get those keys off him.

Don't leave him to slip behind the wheel. It could be the last you see of him. Try to persuade him to come with you in your alternative mode of transport. Let him know that you will accompany him to pick up his car tomorrow, or arrange for someone who's sober to drive it home. Let him know you're not being a party-pooper—you're just being a good friend.

Resources

General information about health and taking care of your body

www.goaskalice.columbia.edu

Help with quitting smoking

Check out "Health tools" at www.mediresource.sympatico.ca to calculate how much you'd save by quitting.
Also go to www.quitneg.org and www.smokershelpline.ca.

Help with alcoholism

Go to the website for Alcoholics Anonymous at www.alcoholics-anonymous.org/ for more information and resources.

Centre for Addiction and Mental Health: www.camh.net

The Big Picture

12

Your Job, Your Career

As you climb the ladder of success,
be sure it's leaning against the right building.

—FROM *P.S. I LOVE YOU*, COMPILED BY H. JACKSON BROWN JR.

Making Decisions

It probably seems to you as though everyone you know has been asking you, at least since you started high school: "What do you want to do with your life?" Lucky you if you have that answer. If not, instead of getting tangled up in The Big Question, take a breath and figure out what you don't want to do with your life. Let's rule out the easy stuff. I am assuming that you don't want to become a monk or nun. (At least not now. Once you have a stressful job and a houseful of kids these options might become very appealing.) What else do you not want to do? Can't imagine working behind a desk? Wouldn't teach high school if your life depended on it? Come on, put some effort into this. Make a list. Call it "The No-Go List."

And now, here's the million-dollar question. Ask yourself this: *When and where am I happy and most content?* Don't get goofy. This is hard stuff. Make it into your second list. Call it, oh, I dunno, "The Happy List."

If that isn't working for you, make a list of jobs that you *think* might make you happy. We're hoping here that you'll hit upon that old Do-What-You-Love-and-Money-Will-Follow method. Don't get hung up on the idea "I'm choosing the job or career that will be mine *for the rest of my life.*" It probably won't work out that way. You only have to look down the road a little bit … not all the way to the end!

More than You Really Wanted to Know

The average person goes through eight jobs before the age of 32.

Another option is to take a career assessment test. If you're a student, start with the one offered at your college or university (check with the student placement office). Hey, it's free! Or take a career assessment test online, like the one at www.myplan.com.

There are lots of so-called experts who will offer career help for a fee. Many are great, but a lot of them have no special qualifications to call themselves career counsellors. If you decide to use a professional service, before you slap down the money ($600 and up), get references. Now, actually *call* those references.

First Steps

Okay, have you narrowed down the possibilities, at least to a manageable list of options? Good! Now, you need to get some experience—mostly to find out if this job you have in mind is really what you think it is. So, how do you do that?

Job Shadow

Let's say you have just sprained your ankle, badly. It's off to the physiotherapist. Let's assume that you are interested in some aspect of sports medicine but don't see yourself as a doctor. As you are lying on the table having your ankle examined, ask the physiotherapist about his job. Tell him that you are interested in becoming a physiotherapist. Ask if it would be possible to job shadow him for a day—which means sticking with him as he goes about a normal working day.

Find yourself sitting beside a cop/lawyer/soldier/designer/whatever on a plane? Aw, go on, say: "I've been thinking about going into the police force." You'll find it's the rare person who will not babble on about his or her job, and you'll get the scoop on yet another career option.

In other words, look around. Ask. What's the worst thing that can happen? Someone says, "I don't want to talk about my job." So what? Just don't take it personally.

And if someone does say yes and you do spend a day, or week, job shadowing, don't forget to send a thank-you note. If you develop a good relationship, then he or she has become a new contact in your chosen field. Keep in contact. (Just don't go overboard here, or this giving soul will feel as though he or she has inadvertently adopted you.)

Volunteer

If you think you might want to work in sports, magazines, television, or in a hospital, get some on-site experience. There are many fields that will take volunteers. Load up your CV with different kinds of volunteer work. Interested in Africa? Cancer? Call up a volunteer organization and ask to help. Maybe you could help out on a political campaign.

Take a minute for an attitude check before you head down this road. Be humble. You are volunteering whatever small skills you have in the form of menial labour—you are not stepping in to take charge or save the day. There's a reason they won't be paying you—you might or might not actually be much help. You are there to learn, so keep your eyes and ears open. And just because this is volunteer work, that doesn't mean you don't have to adopt a committed attitude toward it. Treat it as seriously as any paying job. If you show a real dedication to the work, the organization might be able to provide a valuable reference.

Intern

Many organizations offer internships, particularly those that run a tight ship and appreciate the cost-efficiency of free labour. Magazines, television networks, and newspapers typically offer internships; so do large corporations, law offices, and banks. Work your connections—your parents' friends might know of something, or ask a professional in the field. Think outside the box. What about the White House, the House of Commons, the Forestry Service? Do you already have specific skills to offer? Is there an internship related to your educational background? No employer has room in the workplace for an intern whose only useful skill is making the coffee run.

And the warning about attitude above applies here, too. If you used a family connection to land an internship, you'd better give it your best shot, because if you screw up, that contact won't be helping again. And a successful internship can end with a very valuable recommendation, while a bad-attitude internship will hang around your neck in that field of work for a long, long time.

Since most internships are part-time, you might have to supplement your income with a paying gig—think Starbucks. Better yet, go to bartending school and check out Safe Serve certification at www.safeserve.com. Or take on two internships at the same time. Welcome to the world of the twelve-hour workday. You can do it; it's not forever.

+

More than You Really Wanted to Know

Temporary Placement Services: Find a listing on the Internet or in a phone book. Call to find out what the firm does and about the application process. Most temp agencies deal in specific areas—e.g., office workers or hospital staff, construction, and so on. Some temp agencies hand out daily jobs; others are longer-term or project-driven.

When you sign on with a temp agency, you are an employee of the agency. The placement service pays you. Ask about how and when you will get paid. In most cases the company you are temped out to will sign off on your time card. At the end of the workweek you will take your time card into the office and pick up a cheque.

Been there *Done* THAT

I got a summer job at a huge family playground as a ticket-taker. It wasn't as dead-end as you'd think. In the evening they hosted all these musical bands. I stayed around to help for a couple of nights running. One of the roadies quit suddenly. The manager turned to me and said, "You want to work here?" It was the best summer of my life. I'm producing those shows now.

—BRYAN, 26

Temp Work

Sounds awfully, uh, *temporary*, but you'll get a bird's-eye view of different firms, you'll earn a few bucks while looking for a job, you can try out different positions within a company, and you'll get to meet people. Contact a temp agency and give it a shot.

Finding Work

Honey, just get a job. Any job will do to start with. You never know where it might lead you. But sitting at home with Oprah, you know where that will lead you. As long as you're out there, you're learning new skills, gaining experience that you will transfer to your dream job one day.

Imagine that you are working as the towel boy at a Hawaiian resort. With a glorious sun beating down on white, sparkling sand, and shiny, sunscreen-slathered bodies lining the beach, you start thinking: Is this all there is to life? Must I be a boy-toy forever? Might I do something with that engineering degree my parents spent their retirement fund on?

You can do something. Contact the old alma mater, specifically, your college or university's student placement office. Its sole raison d'être is to help you get a job. Isn't that amazing? If the school has a resumé feedback service, use it. Inquire about vocational testing, practice interviews, and job listings. They might also have a mentor program and career workshops. Corporate recruiters might make visits. And if you have been out of school for a few years, don't sweat it—the office can help even wayward alumni!

TIP: Stay in touch with professors who have good connections with the industry you're interested in—they may be able to help you.

Freelance

Building a freelance career can take time, and the rewards will be quite meagre for a while. But with more and more work being done electronically, from any location, the possibilities for a freelance career are greater than ever. You might want to try working in an office at first, to learn from others and make professional connections, and then launch yourself as a freelancer when you feel you have the necessary background. If you are interested in writing for magazines, for instance, be open to taking a non-writing job in a magazine office. You'll meet some useful people and find out how the business really works.

Many freelance jobs have a creative aspect. But if you want to build a portfolio in writing or illustration, for example, you must start small and local. Don't expect more than a few bucks for your first cartoon/article. If you need the byline (your name on the article) to build your portfolio, you might have to work for next to nothing for a while. Do your best work. Don't hold back.

Job Surfing

Check out these websites for job possibilities. Search the world!

- *General:* careerbuilder.com; monster.com; jobs.com; hotjobs.com; mediabistro.com; hireminds.com; jobsinthemoney.com; craigslist.com; jobhuntersbible.com; rileyguide.com; youth.eeoc.gov
- *Education:* teacher.net
- *Engineering:* engineeringjobs.com

- *Entertainment/broadcasting:* entertainment-jobs.net
- *Freelance/project work:* eLance.com; guru.com
- *Journalism and writing:* newsJobs.net; journalismjobs.com; freelancewriting.com
- *Law and government:* lawjobs.com
- *Medical:* md-jobs.com; medicaljobline.com
- *Publishing, media, and design:* mediabistro.com; hireminds.com
- *Not-for-profit and environmental:* nonprofit.com; opportunitynocs.org; environmental-jobs.com
- *Tech and dot-com:* hireminds.com; techies.com

TIP: Go to company websites. Many of these firms post jobs on their websites and nowhere else! You can register and post your resumé. If jobs open up that fit your specifications, you can receive e-mail alerts.

A warning: finding a job this way will probably be hard slogging. The glamorous days of skyrocketing dot-commers are way behind us. You are competing with many more highly qualified young people, and thanks to the Internet, the job search is depersonalized and often discouraging. Just remember—you are about as likely to get the job you want right now as you are to win the lottery. That's normal. Don't despair. Accept that you will have to start small (you might not even *like* your first job) and take baby steps to get to where you want to be. Hang in there and remember: slow and steady wins the race!

Guerilla Job-Hunting Tactics

Do you prefer a more traditional job-search style? Nothing beats an in-your-face approach. Here are some tips:

- Start by collecting letters of recommendation from past employers, teachers, and successful friends (this is why you never want to burn any bridges).
- Drop off your resumé in person. You might not make it past the gatekeeper (otherwise known as the receptionist), but you can always try. Smile lots. Politeness counts.

Job fairs

University and college employment offices have listings of upcoming job fairs. Go, armed with a stellar resumé and decent writing paper. Don't just rifle through the pamphlets, talk to people. Make a connection. If you see a job or a company that you really like the look of, and if you do make a connection, ask for the person's card. If they are collecting CVs, hand over your pristine resumé. Now be creative. Walk away from the booth, sit down, and pen a nice thank-you note. If spelling is a challenge for you, consider composing the note on your laptop, running it through your spell-checker, and then writing it out, correctly, by hand.

Dear Mr. Guy-Running-the-Booth,

Thanks for spending time explaining the inner workings of Big Boy Inc. I am interested in the job and hope we will meet to continue our conversation.

Sincerely,
Rob Hire-Me

For goodness sake, don't forget to include your contact info.

Many job fairs will be held at hotels, and most companies that set up booths will stay overnight there. Go to the front desk and find out if your target employer is registered. If the answer is yes, hand over the thank-you note. If that doesn't work, tip a bellhop a few bucks to deliver the note. Oh, and stay out of the hotel bar. If you finally do meet the guy, and you're wasted, he'll hardly be impressed.

Help Wanted classifieds

While the want ads probably seem very *last century*, they can still be helpful. Most newspaper ads appear on Sundays, Saturdays, and Mondays. Wednesday and Thursday papers have the fewest.

Read the ad carefully and tailor your cover letter to suit the job. If you can, research the company on the Internet or phone the firm and get the name of the person making the hiring decision.

Wait two days, then phone to see if your resumé has arrived. Doubtless they will say "Yes," because no one wants to search through the pile of CVs. Now, ask for the fax number and fax a copy of your letter and CV. Call back to see if it has arrived. Speak nicely. The objective is to get an interview. Even if it's not your dream job, you'll have made a new contact and practised your interviewing skills. What the heck!

Making Contacts

If you are going to carry around that hippie-ish "everyone over thirty is stupid" attitude you will miss out on opportunities. Maybe it's time to start attending your parents' (did I hear you say "boring"?) parties. Let people know that you are looking for a job. Listen and look for opportunities everywhere. It's called networking. That *old* forty-three-year-old man Dad introduced you to at the beer store might be a senior partner at his law firm soon. Be nice. Be open-minded.

And even if you don't have helpful family connections, that doesn't mean that you can't meet people on your own. Working part-time at a golf club, for example, will allow you to rub shoulders with all kinds of people. And again, this is where volunteering can work for you. Potential employers who spot a hard-working, motivated, capable volunteer will remember that person when they have an employment vacancy to fill.

Tell your employed friends and neighbours that you are looking for a job. If a job comes up in their company, they will know about it before the vacancy is announced to the outside world. Spreading the word should be part of your job-search campaign.

Think about your passions. Do you care about a cure for cancer? The rainforest? Attend professional seminars, or join a volunteer committee, and meet people. Often

Been there
Done THAT

My daughter graduated with a Fine Arts degree and a minor in advertising. Through a family friend I got her a job interview in a top advertising firm. She went through the interview process, got the job, then decided that she *needed the summer off*. No amount of talking could convince her that this was an incredible opportunity. She didn't have a great summer since most of her friends were working and she didn't have any money to travel very far. Come September she was jobless. I had used up my best contact, and ended up looking like an idiot in the process. My friend really didn't want to talk to her either. To make Christmas money she took a job in a liquor store and then found temporary work after that. It took her two years to find a job that was similar to the one she'd been handed on a silver platter. Maybe it will make her a better or more appreciative person, but I still think she really blew it.

—MARTA

volunteer committee work includes social evenings—take advantage of these opportunities, but be on your best behaviour and don't drink.

If you develop good, dare I say *great*, contacts, hang on to those relationships. Don't use them before you are ready to take full advantage of their support.

If you are ready to take a job, and you have family friends who are willing to put your name forward among their professional peers, by all means accept their help, but be appreciative. You might need their help again later, and if you drop the ball, they are going to end up looking like fools. Thank the people profusely and provide them with all the ammunition you can muster—a stellar resumé, list of references, portfolio, and so on. If you do land a job, a thank-you note is mandatory!

TIP: Expect to start at the bottom of the totem pole and work your way up, and no matter how small the task, give it your all. Starting at ground level is the best way to learn about your profession.

More than You Really Wanted to Know

Headhunter companies are not employment agencies. They hunt for the heads of companies, not the tails. (Um, that'd be you, dear.) It just wouldn't be cost-efficient for a company to fill a lower-level spot that way.
In some cases a firm will go to a headhunter and ask that a specific position be filled. This costs the firm big bucks, usually a large percentage of the hiree's first-year wage. A second kind of headhunter might work on commission on a contingency basis. They get paid only when they actually place an employee in a company. In either case, a young celebrity such as yourself would not likely be of interest to a headhunter.

The Cover Letter

You've decided what kind of job you want to have and you've narrowed the field to several companies. Now it's time to write a kick-ass cover letter.

A cover letter is a sales pitch, a taste of what's to come. It not only highlights your strengths, it also demonstrates that you can organize your thoughts and express yourself clearly—and, most importantly, it tells the employer what you think you can

Template for a Cover Letter

Your name
Address
Phone and e-mail

Date

Company name
Address

Attention: Mr/Ms Interview Person, title

RE: Name of position you are applying for

Dear Name of person (not "Dear Madam/Sir")

First paragraph: *The Opening.* Introduce yourself with a brief phrase such as "I am a senior at Brightboy University and will graduate this spring with a major in Fine Arts." Mention the positionn you are applying for—e.g., junior copywriter in the advertising department. Be sure to note how you heard about the job.

Second paragraph: *The Sales Pitch.* Give an overview of your qualifications, then go into them more specifically, using a few brief examples.

Third paragraph: *The Subtle Schmooze.* Make nice. Tell them why you want to work there.

Last paragraph: *Closing.* Request a follow-up to your letter and ask if a meeting can be arranged.

Sincerely,

SIGN HERE
Type your full name

do for the company. It must not be a clone of all other cover letters. Each job you apply for needs a new letter.

Keep the cover letter short—three to four paragraphs, max. A prospective employer will read and review dozens, nay, hundreds of letters and CVs (curriculum vitae—another word for resumés). The ones that are short, in an easy-to-read script and in a respectable font size (10–14), will have a better chance of landing in the to-be-interviewed pile.

Use a laser printer, heavy bond paper, and a sturdy envelope. Remember, the recipient of your brilliant letter and resumé is looking for reasons to reduce the pile in front of him. Spelling or grammar mistakes will land you in the reject pile right away.

Resumé or CV (Curriculum Vitae)

A resumé or CV is your first, and maybe only, contact with the employer, so get it right. Keep it short and concise. One page should do it. If you look for the term "resumé sample" using a search engine, you will find several good CV samples on the Internet.

Your resumé is a selling product, and the product is you. It is a summary of your education, experience, and skills. The purpose of a CV is to get your foot in the door. It will get you the interview, not the job. Having said that, do not ever lie on a resumé. It only takes a minute to find out if you really did graduate from Trent or Harvard. If a lie is found out later, it constitutes legal grounds for dismissal.

Most companies initially cut down the pile of resumés with "hurdles." In other words, they'll look briefly at a resumé to see if the applicant is missing a key requirement—an MBA, for example, or a professional certificate. If it's not there, the resumé goes in the trash. Make sure you've figured out what the likely hurdles will be, and highlight them.

An employer might review a hundred or more resumés in an hour, spending only twenty to thirty seconds on each one. Therefore you want to stand out, without making yourself look like a goof. That doesn't mean you should use a glow-in-the-dark pen on fluorescent pink paper. Forget the fancy fonts. And be very careful about including a photo. A photo can be used to screen you out on the basis of your age, sex, or ethnic origin. However, in cases where an employer is looking for a particular look (perhaps at a store or restaurant) it might work in your favour ... assuming that you have the look they're looking for.

You will want to customize or tailor your resumé to the job that you are applying for. Watch out for clichés like "people person" and "strong communication skills." Be specific.

What not to say

"I am a well-organized person seeking a challenging position that will enable me to contribute to an organization's goals while offering an opportunity for advancement and self-development."

What? Say that again? No, don't. This is over-the-top fluff that doesn't say anything.

Instead of saying, "I am hard-working and manage people well," say, "Within a six-month period I produced six university theatre productions, each production consisting of three to twelve onstage actors, with twenty-six backstage and support staff." Instead of saying, "I am a team player," say, "Throughout high school and university I played on three rugby teams. In 2007 the Malborough University team made it to the All-World Championship."

TIP: Don't include personal information like marital status, age, race, or hobbies.

Words to avoid: aggressive, ambitious, competent, creative, detail-oriented, determined, efficient, experienced, flexible (unless referring to flexible hours), goal-oriented, hard-working, independent, motivated … you get the idea.

Words to use: achieved, awarded, collaborated, consulted, coordinated, delegated, designed, developed, edited, established, illustrated, implemented, initiated, managed, planned, produced, promoted, scheduled, supervised, wrote.

Been there
Done THAT

I mailed what I thought was a pretty fine resumé off to the one of the largest newspapers in the country. I had great hopes. Then I realized I had addressed it to the "Assistant Editor," as opposed to the "Associate Editor." I was aiming for a job as a reporter. Big mistake. Reporters can't get names wrong. I'm sure that's why I was never called for an interview.

—MELANIE, 29

Template for a resumé

Once you have your draft, get your CV proofread by a professional. Spell-check is not enough. What's your old English professor or high school English teacher doing these days?

Many companies scan resumés into their database, so make your resumé scannable. Keep it brief, and use only good-quality white or off-white letter-size paper. Avoid fancy fonts, exotic coloured papers, photographs, and graphics. To trigger key search words that the company might use, repeat the words used in the job description. For example: if the company ad says "development of marketing plans," repeat those exact words in your resumé.

Fast tips

- Spell out numbers—"eight," not "8"—up to and including "ten."
- Put your name at the top of page two (if there is a page two).
- Have a conventional e-mail address. What does "susie@kissyface" say about you?
- Give the month and year of previous jobs.
- You don't need to put "Resumé" or "Curriculum vitae" at the top of your document. They get it already. Your name is enough.
- Avoid gimmicks. Human resource employers have seen it all. Just the facts, please.
- Don't lie or exaggerate.
- Keep the tone upbeat. No need to be controversial or negative.
- Don't include ethnic status, religion, or political affiliations, unless they are relevant to the job. Same goes for personal information like height and weight.
- Don't just passively send out your applications and wait for something to happen. Follow up appropriately.
- Don't name-drop. If Donald Trump really thinks you are hot, he'll deliver the resumé to the recruiter on your behalf.
- Don't overuse highlighting techniques such as <u>underline</u>, **bold**, and *italics*.
- Avoid the words I, me, my, and we.

> ***Been*** there
> ***Done*** **THAT**
>
> I liked his resumé, but when I called him at home at three in the afternoon it was apparent that I had just woken him up and he hadn't a clue who I was or what company he had applied to.
>
> —RECRUITER

Template for a Resumé

Your name
Address
Phone and e-mail

Objectives
Two lines (optional)

Career history
Beginning with most recent

Company #1
City, Province/State
Dates worked
Job title
Responsibilities/Achievements (start with most recent, most impressive)

Company #2
City, Province/State
Dates worked
Job title
Responsibilities/Achievements

Education
Start with the best and latest (e.g., university/college, then high school). List special awards and honours (start with the most impressive).

Skills
Tailor this to the job you are applying for, e.g., computer skills, language skills. Think about your extracurricular activities—clubs, teams, fundraisers, school projects—as having taught you valuable skills you might bring to the job.

References available upon request. (There is no need to include references on your resumé. Rather, have a separate list ready at the interview to give to employers upon request.)

- You don't need to give your reasons for quitting or leaving your last job, though this will likely come up in an interview.
- Don't offer wage or salary information about your past jobs.

Submitting a Resumé Online

You're young. That can be an advantage when it comes to applying online, since you are probably far more familiar with the World Wide Web than any generation before you. Take advantage of that. Job-hunting on the Internet is fast and cheap.

But be warned. The sheer volume of job-seekers on the Internet means it can be hard to catch a potential employer's attention. As a result, many companies today use an Applicant Tracking System (ATS) which uses keywords and phrases to weed out applicants. Don't get discouraged; just keep these points in mind:

- If you want to use more keywords—and decrease your chances of getting deleted by the ATS—write more than one opening or closing sentence.
- The technology used by many companies now searches by nouns, not verbs. So instead of writing "managed projects," write "project manager."

> **TIP:** Keep a log sheet of where, and to whom, you have applied. Date it. If you haven't heard back in ten days or so, follow up.

- Pay attention to the instructions for submitting your resumé. What format does the company want? Should your resumé be embedded in an e-mail, e-mailed, sent as an attachment, faxed, or snail-mailed? Are there any reference numbers?
- Don't get cute by applying for the same job at different times.
- Watch out for resumé distribution services that blast your resumé to tons of potential employers. Most recruiters don't bother with them.
- When your resumé is read by the potential employer on a monitor he or she can only see the top of the page. Put the really important stuff there. Skip the title "Objectives" at the top and briefly summarize your objectives instead. That way the person reading it will not have to scroll down.
- Some e-mail programs don't have spell-check, so write the text in a word-processing program, spell-check it, then copy and paste it into the e-mail message.
- Do not send an unsolicited resumé as an e-mail attachment. Many companies warn employees not to open attachments from unknown senders to avoid potential viruses.

- Keep it simple and nix the designs, graphics, shading, and indents. Use a standard typeface, and to enhance readability make sure you left-justify all text.
- Use strong verbs like "managed," "created," "developed"—keywords the employer is likely to scan for.
- Use a standard application such as Word to ensure your file can be easily opened.
- Preview your resumé before it is submitted.
- Follow up in a week with a well-worded reminder. Say something like, "I trust you received my resumé and I look forward to hearing from you." And give your potential employer an out. If you hear a pause in his or her voice, consider adding, "I know how many resumés you must have received and how easily things get misplaced. Would it be okay if I just sent along another resumé?"

Job Scams

"Want to make easy money at home? For just a few hours a week you too can make millions of dollars a year."

GEE—DO YA THINK?

Be super-cautious when job-searching online. Your antennae should go up when you see an ad like this.

Here's how a typical money-laundering scam can work. It begins with legitimate-looking contracts, false documents bearing company letterhead, and even false letters of credit, payment schedules, and bank drafts mailed to your house. You, as an employee, are asked to cash cheques with a request that the money be returned via Western Union, for example. You, the victim, will eventually discover that the cheque, certified cheque, or money order was fraudulent. You are liable for the lost money and could even be charged with money-laundering.

Then there are the re-shipment scams. You receive a package and are asked to repackage it and send it on. The package is usually full of stolen goods. Sooner or later the goods will be tracked to your address, and you will be charged with receiving stolen property. Do not cash a cheque for anyone.

Job scams—red flags

- An interview conducted solely by phone. A legitimate employer will not hire anyone without a face-to-face interview.
- Being asked to pay for an interview.

- Being asked for your social security or social insurance number, or any other sensitive information. That should not happen until after you've been hired.
- Vagueness. If a prospective employer does not give you a specific job description for the position, you probably don't want the job.
- Meeting in a coffee shop because "the office is under construction" or "we are just moving our offices." Check it out yourself.

TIP: Use this "untethered" time in your life to search for a job away from your hometown. Nothing helps you grow up faster than moving far away—especially if you're experiencing a new culture.

For more advice on this subject, go to LooksTooGoodToBeTrue.com.

The Interview

You get a phone call with a date and time for an interview. Yippee! Take a minute to get the details right and ask for a call-back number. Emergencies happen. Get the name of the person you are to meet and write it down. Plan out your clothes, make your travel plans for getting to the interview (call the train/bus and get directions and price, check public transit connections, or fill your car with gas). Print out several clean copies of your resumé to take with you.

What to Wear

What do a dishwasher, theatre director, veterinary apprentice, and sales associate all have in common? They must all be squeaky clean. Fingernails, hair, body, clothes. Clean. Most interviewers form their impression of a person in the first seven seconds of a meeting. That early judgment is based strictly on appearance.

Duh moment!

You have just stepped off the elevator and noticed that you have cat hair on your outfit. Smile and ask the receptionist for some Scotch Tape. Head off to the bathroom, wrap Scotch Tape around your fist, sticky side out, and run it up and down your skirt or pant leg.

Beyond that, remember this one key rule: dress one, some say two, steps up from the job you are after. Say you're hoping for a job as a veterinarian's apprentice. You know you'll be cleaning out dog cages, and jeans would be fine for the job, but for the interview, aim one step up—nice dark pants and polo shirt, for example. You might want to invest in a lab coat.

About accessories: How is an interviewer to concentrate if she keeps thinking about how much your pierced tongue must hurt, or how you blow your nose with that nose-ring? And you're not going to like this, but honey, body piercing is yesterday's news. Tattoos too. Hide what you can.

A man applying for a conventional job

- Conservative two-piece business suit (solid dark blue or grey), well-fitted, wrinkle-free.
- Long-sleeved shirt, white or pastel.
- Boring, polished shoes.
- A *nothing-too-fancy* belt. Save the cowboy buckle for Friday night.
- Well-groomed hairstyle.
- A necktie with a conservative pattern, tied properly.
- No jewellery beyond a watch.
- Dark shoes and dark socks.
- Empty your pockets. A clanking key-ring or tinkling coins is distracting and might give away your past profession as janitor.
- Carry a light briefcase or portfolio case. No school bags.
- Earrings are negatives too if you normally wear two, three, or more! Take them out.
- Facial hair is a possible negative, but if you must, make sure beards and moustaches are well trimmed.

A man applying for an unconventional, artistic job

If you are applying for a financial or executive job in the arts community, then you'll still have to go the conservative route. However, if you are looking to be one of the stylish *artistes*, then pick a solid, two-button, navy-blue blazer that fits beautifully. (You can have a cheap one altered.) When standing, always keep the top button buttoned. If this is the first interview, and you are a little unsure of just how artsy this particular place is, wear solid grey dress pants with the blazer, an open-neck shirt, and a V-neck sweater. Great jeans (dark), a polo shirt or white shirt with a V-neck sweater, and casual shoes can work too, if you're certain that co-workers dress casually. But watch the hem of your pants. Frayed jeans that drag just don't work.

Unacceptable, even for an artsy job interview

- Sweatpants.
- Flip-flops.
- Muscle shirts.
- Brand-name–emblazoned shirts.
- Stained or rumpled clothing.
- Bermuda shorts.
- Low-rise pants (spare us the crack in the back).
- Blue, yellow, or magenta hair (or other colour not found in nature).
- Grungy beard.
- Athletic socks with street shoes.

Duh moment!

The only reason for wearing a T-shirt with a brand-name beer on the front is if someone is paying you to wear it, you got it for free, and it's moving day!

A woman applying for a conventional job

Confident women who are in control of their destinies do not dress like teenyboppers. They dress like grown-ups, if they want to be taken seriously. Think conservative. Repeat to yourself—*class beats flash.*

TIP: Yes, black is slimming, but you don't need to fade into the chair. A little colour goes a long way—makes you look more dynamic. Just keep it subtle.

- Pantyhose—off-black or nude—and nix the patterns and racing stripe down the back. No open-toe or sling-back shoes.
- A conservative suit. (Jacket does not have to match the skirt.) Watch the fabric. Wool might be too sweaty, linen too wrinkly.
- Jangling jewellery is about as annoying as a giggle. Leave both at home.
- Take a pass on the shimmery makeup and funky nail polish. And don't try a new hairstyle the morning of your interview.
- Your purse tells all. No matter what the fashion trend, do not carry an over-the-top bag with cowboy fringes and/or bobbles hanging off it.
- Carry a separate briefcase if warranted, or if you are carrying around files.

Duh moment!

Sometimes when you buy an expensive suit jacket there will be a label on the sleeve near the wrist. This is not a decoration or a way to broadcast your good taste. Carefully remove it *before* you head out the door. Oh—and your shoes—there is nothing funnier than watching some impeccably dressed person crossing his legs to reveal a sale sticker still stuck to the sole of his shoe. Don't make that mistake.

Unacceptable, even for an artsy job interview

- Sweatpants.
- Flip-flops.
- Muscle shirts.
- Belly shirts.
- Bra-free.
- Spandex anything.
- Too-short skirts.
- Brand-name–emblazoned shirts.
- Stained or rumpled clothing.
- Bermuda shorts.
- Low-rise pants.
- Blue, yellow, or magenta hair (or other colour not found in nature).
- Long, fake, or wildly coloured nails.
- And ditch the cologne. If the interviewer has an allergy, then this game is over.

TIP: Find out what the company's employees wear. You don't want to show up in a suit if everyone else—including your interviewer—is in jeans. How? Drop off your resumé in person and check them out. Aim for similar, but slightly overdressed.

The job was for a music techie. Musicians don't exactly wear ties. I dressed for the interview like, well, like a musician. Guess I should have paid attention to the "children's musical theatre" part in the ad. The guy doing the hiring didn't exactly appreciate my X-rated T-shirt.

—BRETT, 22

Do Your Homework

Do an Internet search of the company and read past newsletters, published articles, annual reports, and press releases. Find out what they want in the new position, and figure out how your job history matches—with lots of anecdotes to show that you've got what they want.

You might want to dodge the salary question initially by saying, either in the cover letter or in person, "Will accept established range of salary." Do some checking anyway—try speaking to friends in roughly comparable jobs, or you might find some help at www.salary.com. It's wise to have some idea in your own mind of an acceptable salary before you walk in, though, in case they really put you on the spot.

Prepare your very own infomercial. Keep it to thirty seconds. But a warning: if you sound overly rehearsed you might appear to lack sincerity. If you appear overly sure of yourself you might seem smug. And watch the Chatty Cathy stuff, you'll just look nervous.

TIP: You might be tempted to down an extra cup of coffee before your interview just to get yourself pumped up. Don't. And stay away from the sugary cereal and doughnuts. You'll be jittery enough as it is. No need to get yourself wired.

Acing the Interview—Quick Tips

- **Do** arrive early enough to use the restroom first.
- **Do** remove your hat, always.
- **Do** announce yourself to the receptionist. Don't get too personal, but be really nice to this person—he or she often has more power and influence than you might suspect.

- **Do** take a look around you for artwork on the wall, a book on the coffee table—anything you can use to break the ice when you first enter the interview room. If you're lucky, you might see a framed certificate or a press clipping or something else the company is particularly proud of.
- **Do** shut off your cellphone.
- **Do** stand up when the interviewer comes out to meet you.
- **Do** make eye contact when you shake hands.
- **Do** refuse a coffee, unless the interviewer is getting one for him- or herself.
- **Do** sit up straight and pay attention to your body language. Lean toward the interviewer when he or she speaks. Nod every now and then. Take notes—you will look earnest and interested in what they're saying.

- **Don't** flop down into a chair.
- **Don't** launch into small talk. Wait for the interviewer to take the lead.
- **Don't** tell too much. How you *really* feel about your mother is too much … *way* too much.
- **Don't** bring a friend or child to the interview.
- **Don't** flatter or flirt, even if the interviewer flirts with you.
- **Don't** use the word fired, or mention that you didn't get along with a past supervisor. And don't make negative comments about the last company you worked for.
- **Don't** start with questions about your salary or vacation time.
- **Don't** smoke, slump, yawn, chew gum, play with your hair, tap your toes, click your pen, or bite your lips during a job interview.
- **Don't** attempt to look "deep" or "cool." You'll just look bored and arrogant.

A good interviewer spends more time listening than talking. Sometimes, he or she will leave pauses in the conversation to see how you babble to fill in the quiet. *Don't.* If you've answered the question and the interviewer is still staring at you, say, "Have I answered that clearly or do you have another question?"

If you goof verbally or feel that you have been misunderstood, say, "Perhaps I misspoke, what I meant to say was …" If you stumble or drop something, stay calm and show how cool you are under pressure. Always be gracious. If the interviewer is late, has lost your resumé, or mispronounces your name, be understanding, always.

Upon arrival some companies will hand you a form to fill out. Handwritten forms are a nightmare. (This is yet another reason why you should carry your CV with you.) If your handwriting is bloody awful, you're in for a hard time. In a word, *print!* Cross your "Ts," and write legibly and in a straight line. If you are asked to write in longhand you are within your rights to ask why. If you are concerned about what others may make of your handwriting, pick up a book on handwriting analysis. The *science* of it might be questionable, but it can't hurt to know.

> **Duh|**
> **moment!**
>
> Do not, I repeat, do *not* fill out a job application with a pink, green, red, or other colourful pen. It's the kiss of death. Make sure you have with you a blue or black fine-tipped pen. Use that and only that.

Read the entire application before you start filling it out. Pay attention to those sections that say "Do Not Write Below This Line" or "Office Use Only." (Don't fill out those sections, obviously, but read them; they will give you a clue as to what the employer is looking for.) Watch for mistakes in grammar or spelling. Use "N/A" (Not Applicable) if the section doesn't apply to you. Under Salary Requirements, say "Open" or "Negotiable," even if the wage the employer plans to pay is listed or known. You might be able to negotiate a higher wage.

Every interview has a unique focus, but there are some questions asked so often that you can prepare for them. It helps to write out potential answers or practise saying them out loud. Careful, though, you don't want your answers to come off sounding too well rehearsed. And remember to pause before speaking to give yourself a moment to gather your thoughts, otherwise you will sound *too* prepared.

Many interviewers are not trained and fall back on the old chestnut, "Tell me about yourself." It's an easy question to ask but hellish to answer and can be a trap. Reread the "Words to avoid" in the resumé section. Don't wander all over the place, don't recite your life history, and don't tell too much. Try to keep bringing your answer back to a focus on employment goals, to avoid getting overly personal. Your best approach is to prepare a sixty-second answer ahead of time.

More questions to prepare for

- *What are your goals?* Don't go with owning a beach bar in Hawaii.
- *What do you plan to be doing in five years?* Same as above.
- *Why do you want to work here?* Do not say, "You're just around the corner from where I live."
- *What are your greatest strengths?* This is not in reference to weight-training.
- *Tell me about a past mistake and how you turned things around.* Trick question. Do not mention that night in jail and finding religion at four in the morning.

- *What do you like to read?* If you answer "Dickens" it's game over. What you really just said was, "I don't read. His is the only author's name I can think of."
- *Why did you leave your last job?* Say only good things about your last boss (a.k.a. Attila) and the company you worked for (Enron).

Nutbar questions—be ready for them

- Who's your hero?
- What's your favourite …? (television show, book, colour)
- If you could be any animal, what would you be?
- If you won a million dollars, what would you spend it on?
- Would you rather be rich or famous?
- Whom do you admire?
- If you were marooned on a desert island and you could only bring one thing, what would that be? If you could bring only five books onto that island, what books would they be?

Finding the real you (at least that's what they think they're doing)

- What intimidates you?
- Tell me about a time when you have been really frightened?
- How do you decide what is important?
- How do you choose your friends?
- What do you do for fun?
- What on your resumé differentiates you from everyone else?
- What do you do with your spare time?
- If you could travel anywhere in the world, where would you go?

Technical questions (don't try to fake this stuff)

Marketing/advertising questions: Tell me about your favourite advertisement. How would you market lawn ornaments? Disposable shoes? What role does advertising play in society?

Banking examples: A bank is initiating an Internet banking service. Should they use their own name or a third-party brand? A health insurance company lost $60 million last year, and will lose $60 million this year. What are the four key things you will present to the CEO? A coffee retail store is successful in Canada but unsuccessful in the United States. What is the key item for research, and why? Describe one way to approach the problem.

Finance questions: In a portfolio, explain the meaning of diversification and risk. What is the impact of changing interest rates on different portfolios? What criteria will you use in deciding among investment banks? Explain the meaning of interest rate risk and duration. What questions would you ask a CEO of a company to determine the state of his/her business?

The interview is not over until you are out of the building and on the bus. An old trick for the interviewer is to click the pen, close the notebook, and while walking you to the elevator ask personal questions. Careful.

Questions to ask the interviewer

When the interviewer says, "Do you have any questions?" he or she is testing you. If you don't have any questions you might come off as dopey or uninterested. Remember, this is a two-way street. You want to know if this is a good fit for you, too. Here are some good questions to ask.

- Can you tell me what my day would be like?
- Do employees often come in on weekends?
- How would you describe the management style of this company?
- What was the last seminar/workshop offered to your employees?
- What computer equipment and software do you use here?
- When can I expect my first performance review? By whom?

At the end of the interview give the interviewer your card. A simple card with all your relevant information on it (your name, address, phone number, e-mail address, professional website) will do. Ask for his or her business card. Now that you have the correct spelling of the interviewer's name, his or her formal title, and mailing address, send a thank-you note immediately. In the note, thank the interviewer for his

TIP: Keep a stack of plain, classy note cards and envelopes on hand along with a roll of stamps so you're always ready to follow up.

TIP: You will get rejection letters. Expect it—but don't take it personally. Take it as a challenge. You are strong in the face of adversity! Remember Winston Churchill's words: "Success is the ability to go from one failure to another with no loss of enthusiasm."

or her time, restate your qualifications and interest in the job, and remind him or her of your intent to follow up. Mail the letter ASAP.

You will also want to create a file index at home. Take the business card, make short notes on the back, and file it. Keep the box beside the telephone in case the person phones and you develop brain-freeze.

You've Got a Job Offer—But Wait!

Yes—they want you! They are making you a formal offer! But before you sign on the dotted line, step back and think about it. Presumably this is a career move (and not just a paycheque to keep you off the streets). Be prepared to take this very seriously.

Were there any special offers or promises made to you during the interview process? If they're not written down, they don't mean anything. Talk to the hiring manager and the personnel office to have the written job offer amended. If it is not corrected, then rethink the offer carefully. Look at the entire package. *Think* before you sign. Analyze any potential drawbacks, and pay particular attention to these points.

- Is there a written job offer? A written offer ensures that you and the employer are on the same page. You want to get the following in writing: your job title, wage, and the name and title of the person to whom you will be reporting. Are there any special agreements, such as reimbursement for moving costs, car expenses, vacation pay, union dues, retirement contributions, or a signing bonus? Will you be required to travel? Will you use a company credit card or your own? Who collects the air miles, you or the company?
- Performance reviews. Who will be giving them, and when? What about a bonus? How are they given out, and when?
- Watch out for pressure tactics: "Are you in or out?" Don't let them rush you. It takes time and money to train you, no matter how well suited to the job you are. No hiring manager wants to make a bad fit. Mull things over. There is something

wrong if you are pressured to accept an offer on the spot. Besides, if you are already employed elsewhere, you must give proper notice—two weeks. Your new boss should understand that.

TIP: If you're hoping to negotiate a better deal, at this early stage in your career you have a better chance of getting perks (gym membership, more vacation time) than a higher salary.

- If you're offered a job in a new town, research the town thoroughly before you accept. This will be your new home. Do you love it as much as the job—or can you at least stick it out long enough to make your mark, career-wise?

- How long can you expect to wait between receiving a job offer and starting your new job? If you are desperately looking for work, twenty-four hours will seem too long, but in reality it can take at least a month, or longer if you are taking on a higher-level role. However, if the process drags on for months without an explanation, it might be time to move on. There could be lots of reasons why, but you have a life to lead. Get on with it.

- Watch out for *the fit*. Hopefully the hiring manager has walked you around the office. He or she is watching you to see how you get along. You, on the other hand, should be sizing up the staff, too. Getting along with your co-workers is crucial. We all have our quirks, but fundamental differences could mean trouble down the line. Take a look at the bulletin board in the lunchroom. Are there sign-up sheets all over the place? Would you rather chew glass than golf every Saturday? Are staff expected to join the company bowling league? What is the corporate culture like? How are people dressed? Is the place too quiet? Will you be expected to work in an airless cubicle?

First Day on the Job

It's all gravy from here on in—*not!* In fact, this is where things might get tough. In many areas of your adult life, you can pick and choose who you spend your time with. If you don't get along with someone, you can pretty much just move on. But your workplace is a lot more like grade school, where even if you didn't like someone, you were stuck together in the same class all year. In the workplace you are going to come face to face with a whole lot of different personalities, and, like it or not, these are people you are going to have to work productively with.

TIP: Unless it's an integral part of your job, turn off your cellphone while you are at work. At the very least, keep it on vibrate.

If you have a problem situation at your new job, assess whether it's short-term or long-term. Is the troublemaker soon to retire, or is this a young hotshot likely to torment you indefinitely? It's possible that staffing changes in the near future will come to your rescue, and you can put up with the personality clashes for a while. If not, then you'll need to tackle the problem using the people skills you've honed over the years. (If they're not so honed, check out "Staying Put (For a While)" on page 326.)

Don't expect to know everything the first day. The best you can hope for is that you'll find a few kind faces, and the bathroom. Concentrate on learning your co-workers' names, along with their positions and responsibilities. Remember, be very nice to the receptionist. He or she is usually in charge of office supplies, and you'll need some of those. Get to know the tech guys, too. Think you can fix your computer by yourself? Think again. And dodge the office gossip. It is not a good way to fit in, and you might find out that you have aligned yourself with the wrong side.

You will probably be nervous for a long while. You might doubt yourself and worry about making mistakes. Don't be afraid to be afraid. It's normal. Remember, you were hired because the company likes you and has faith in your abilities. Your employers won't expect you to start producing top-notch work right away. They won't expect you to be perfect. They'll expect you to learn from mistakes, ask lots of questions, listen, and observe. So be enthusiastic and optimistic. Volunteer for new opportunities. Smile.

Duh moment!

Learn to make coffee (even if you don't drink coffee). You are part of a team now. Besides, the water cooler and coffee machine are two places where you might meet people who are not in your department. The rule of thumb is a tablespoon of coffee to a cup of water, then one additional tablespoon for the pot. However, coffee systems differ, so ask and pay attention. While you are in the staff kitchen, take a look at the coffee cups. Should you bring your own from home? If not, then make sure you take your turn washing the dishes.

Dressing for Work

Does your workplace have a written dress code? Just follow it. Shop with the dress code in hand. If you are working in a bookstore, for example, and must wear a recognizable shirt or vest, make sure it is spotless. It's your responsibility. Casual shouldn't mean slovenly.

TIP: Buying a T-shirt featuring an off-colour remark is bad judgment; wearing it is poor taste.

Here's the scenario. You spot a beautiful jacket in an upscale second-hand store (that is not an oxymoron). It's a bit big but the material is in perfect condition and it's a classic. Besides, it's worth a fortune and selling for fifty bucks. What to do? Get yourself to a tailor. (Find them in an upscale clothing boutique. Most tailors freelance. Dry-cleaning stores will have recommendations too. The lady at the mall behind the sewing machine likely does not do fine tailoring but you can ask.) If you find someone who can really sew, then write his/her number down, in pen, in your address book.

A good second-hand clothing store (or consignment shop) can help you look like a million bucks on a rookie's salary. Here's a primer on picking through second-hand clothes.

- Fabrics that are delicate (velvet, lace, transparent, top-stitched) are typically difficult to work with. Pass.
- Don't try to alter an outfit more than a size up or down. The garment will lose its shape and you'll likely end up with a whole new look.
- If the pants need to be lengthened, check the hem for extra material.

TIP: Shopping for clothes for work? Take a handful of material in your hand and squeeze. That's what it will look like on you by the end of the day.

Been there
Done THAT

A word about flip-flops. The Northwestern University's champion women's lacrosse team brought the issue out into the open. A contingent within the team wore—*gasp*—flip-flops when meeting the President of the United States in the White House. Flip-flops, even the ones that cost $150, do not belong in the White House or the office. Seriously!

- The waist can be pulled in and the length can be shortened but the butt must fit.
- If the fabric drapes around the chest, have a tuck made at the shoulders. It's a cheap and easy fix that improves a top immensely.

Men

Building a wardrobe costs money, so do it over time. If you land a job in an office then here's what you should buy:

- An excellent quality suit *off the rack*. A custom-made suit is just too expensive. Have the suit tailored to fit. A good men's store will have a tailor on staff. Now buy two pairs of pants to match the jacket.
- A blazer and two pairs of grey flannel pants. If you only have one suit, a blazer can squeak you through a whole lot of events.
- Five shirts. At least one should be white. Keep this one as your "dry-clean–only" reserved for special events.
- A V-neck preppy sweater can extend that preppy blazer look at work, and it can also be worn with jeans.
- Three pairs of shoes (black dress, brown or black casual, deck or sports shoe), a dozen pairs of black socks, plus running shoes.

TIP: Gentlemen, please, hats off when inside. And never, ever, wear a hat to the table.

There you go, honey—you have a wardrobe.

Cost Cutters

You can only afford one suit? Until you get a raise or win the lottery:
Men: Change the look with interesting ties.
Women: Try accessorizing differently with jewellery, scarves, or blouses.

Women

If you're working in the business world, you, just like the boys, will need a suit—although it doesn't have to be a monochromatic, uniform sort of thing. Mixing and matching is perfectly acceptable.

Now is the time to buy sensible, but beautiful, shoes that are—wait for it—*comfortable*. Quality is important here. High heels are fine, as long as you look as though you were born in them and they don't look too much like the stilettos on a corset-clad mannequin. But note: if you find yourself lurching, swaying, or walking as if your head will arrive in the room before the rest of you, then flats might be a better alternative for now. Take a high-heel walking class at night.

TIP: Invest in pantyhose. Yes, we all hate them; get over it.

To make the right impression at work, remember that it's about the whole package. If you're wearing a lovely suit but your hair looks like Marie Antoinette's after her beheading, then you might want to rethink your look.

Workplace Safety

Let's get serious. You can get killed in the workplace, and death has interrupted many a promising career. Young workers are injured by falls, by overexertion, by flying objects, by being caught in or compressed by equipment or objects, by exposure to hazardous chemicals and materials, and by simply not wearing protective equipment or following the rules. In 1999, in Canada, fourteen young workers were killed, the majority in small businesses with fewer than twenty employees.

Then there are the injuries. The most common injuries to young workers between 1996 and 1999 were sprains, strains, and fractures, loss of body parts, abrasions, blisters, contusions, and fraction burns. In 1999, 254 young workers suffered the loss of a body part. Told you this was serious.

As an employee you have three fundamental rights:

1. The right to know how to do the job safely and what the risks are.
2. The right to participate in training and safety precautions.
3. The right to say no to dangerous work.

It is the employer's (i.e., your boss's) responsibility to:

1. Provide a safe and healthy workplace.
2. Train employees concerning potential hazards and ensure that designated employees have required and updated certification.
3. Correct unsafe behaviour and unsafe conditions.

4. Provide personal protective equipment and see that it is properly stored, maintained, and used.

5. Report and investigate all accidents and incidents.

It is an employee's (i.e., your) responsibility to:

1. Work safely.

2. Know and comply with all regulations.

3. Protect yourself, your co-workers, and members of the public who might be affected by your actions.

4. Report unsafe acts and unsafe conditions to your employer.

5. Use personal protective equipment as required by the employer.

For more information, see the Resources section at the end of this chapter.

Duh | moment!

Beware. Managers are increasingly cracking down on employees' personal use of the Internet. More and more are enforcing strict policies with software that prevents staffers from accessing certain websites, reads their e-mails, and monitors Internet surfing. They can do this. You are using their computer—and their paid time.

Staying Put (For a While)

Deciding on a career, preparing a resumé, finding a job, and getting the job—all that's terrific, but can you actually keep the job? If you don't want to go through the whole job-search process all over again, then watch out for the following common pitfalls that can land you back in unemployment.

- *Gossiping.* You will find one or two office chums that partake in this soul-destroying occupation, but most co-workers will run for cover. Gossips do not get the corner office.

- *Not taking responsibility.* Okay, you made a mistake. Everyone does, once in a while. Say you're sorry, fix what you can, and move on.

- *Being bossy* is a sure way to lose friends and make enemies. Do your own work, help out where you can, but avoid dominating or controlling the staff around you, or reporting their behaviour to a superior at every opportunity.
- *Extremists* sap everyone's energy. The negative thinker and the overly positive thinker are so busy either pulling people down or trying to motivate the crowd that they never actually get anything done.
- *Chatterboxes* are irritating at the best of times. These people tend not to listen well, and they chew up working time. Be sensitive to the warning signs (co-workers are always making excuses to get away from your conversations; you find you are talking way more than you are listening) and try to be a better listener.
- *Don't expect the boss to give you an "A" every couple of weeks.* Yes, feedback is a good thing, but in the grown-up world, no one applauds when a job is done right. You have been hired to do it right. A pat on the back might feel great, but seeking approval at every turn just looks childish.
- *Don't expect everyone to like you.* You're not at a social event; you are there to do a job. It's important to establish trust with your co-workers on a personal and a professional level. Try to have lunch regularly with your co-workers, and if there's an office softball team or other after-hours activity that everyone partakes in, be sure to join in. That's not the same as making them all into your new best friends.
- *A thief is a thief.* It's Christmas and there isn't a roll of tape in the office to be found. Funny, huh? How can you be trusted with the Big Chair if you can't be trusted with a roll of tape, or a box of paper, or a calculator, or …?
- *No one likes a devil's advocate.* Why do you feel compelled to take the other side of every argument? Nothing is more exhausting for your co-workers than knowing that you're always ready to challenge them, no matter what they say. After a while, people will just stop talking to you.
- Are you making a few bucks on the side selling vitamins/plastic containers/soap? *Don't even think about using your co-workers as potential clients.* And just because you are selling chocolates/wristbands/wrapping paper for a cause does not give you permission to go desk-to-desk selling your wares.
- *Be careful about calling people at home on work-related issues.* The rule of thumb is, unless it's an emergency, it can wait till working hours.
- *Never ever ever say, "This might be a stupid idea …" or "This might be a stupid question …"* It might not be a stupid question, but you've just persuaded everyone else it is. And if it is a stupid question, then why the heck are you asking it?

Here are some positive things you can do:

- *Show a little common-sense respect for others.* Don't leave your coffee mug and/or dishes in the sink. And if your phone conversations can be heard in the next office, you are speaking too loudly. Be aware that you're not the only one in the office.
- *Watch out for office romances.* They might seem like a great idea when they are going well, but you've watched enough TV to have a pretty good idea just how disastrous it can be when an office romance goes wrong.
- *Do your share.* Everyone eventually notices the Shirker and the Buck-Passer. The former knows how to duck out of work, while the latter cites his or her job description as if it were written in stone. Then there is the Procrastinator, who puts things off till the last minute and then says he didn't have enough time to get the work done. The thing about work is—it's work. None of these people will succeed.
- *Present yourself in a self-confident, mature manner.* That means standing up straight, for one thing. Your posture reflects confidence. Maintain an even tone of voice, with a low pitch, and resist the temptation to speak faster when feeling nervous or flustered. Remember that "like" is not a form of punctuation, so don't sprinkle it throughout all your sentences. And don't end statements on a high note. You'll sound as though you are asking a question, or are unsure of what you are saying. Finally, whatever you do, stop giggling.
- *Quit smoking.* Sure, it's bad for you, and do you know how annoying it is for your boss or co-workers to always have to go searching for you when you're off on a cigarette break?
- *Keep a lid on your personal chat.* Engagements, weddings, breakups, sports triumphs, a new arrival (baby or puppy)—these are all life-altering events … for you, not for the rest of the world. Share your good or bad news and stop there. The same goes for sharing your religious beliefs—not during office hours.

TIP: Don't blow your cool. No matter how frazzled and stressed you are, keep it to yourself. Better yet, deal with the stress in a grown-up way—go for a run, call a friend, take a hot bath. Want to yell at someone? Pick a sport that helps you to let it all out.

Public Speaking

There are few careers in this world that do not require *public speaking*. Novelists read their work out loud, researchers present their findings at seminars, everyone pitches his or her ideas to someone. If you are having trouble with this one, don't sweat it; you're not alone. Speaking in front of groups is the number-one fear in North America. Find a public speaking course. It's all about practice.

You have been asked ...

Whether you've been asked to introduce a guest speaker at the company sales conference, give a toast at a wedding, or deliver the eulogy at Grandpa's funeral, the operative word here is *asked*. Someone else, maybe lots of people, value your thoughts. You are starting out from a place of strength. Be confident!

Know your audience

There are no hard and fast rules here. A eulogy can be funny, while a speech at the sales conference can be deadly serious.

Ask questions

- *How many people will be in the audience?* If over fifty people, you might require a microphone.
- *Where will the speech take place?* A school gym might require a microphone, while a sermon from the pulpit might not.
- *How long have you been given to speak?* If you are making an introduction (i.e., you are not the main event), you should never take longer than five minutes, unless you have been asked to address other matters.
- *Is there anyone you should thank?* The host? The lady who did the flowers? The caterer?

TIP: Don't use any new, splashy words that you do not use every day. Now is not the time to say "Molotov" (think "Molotov cocktail") when you mean "Mazel Tov" (as in "congratulations").

Once you have gathered all the information about the topic you are to speak on, write out the speech. In a fifteen- to twenty-minute speech you should cover about three points. Keep them in mind as you write and you'll stay focused.

Give your audience what they want—something of value. No matter how many times you screw up, if your audience walks away feeling better about themselves, their jobs, if they have learned something new or even been entertained, then you are a success.

Read the speech out loud—to the dog, to your life-size cutout of Captain Jean Luc Picard, to anyone or anything. Read it several times. Do not memorize it, just know it. By all means, put the speech on cue cards (just like you did at school), but if you're more comfortable with longhand on a piece of letter-sized paper, that's fine too. (Just don't fold it several times and stick it in your pocket.)

This is it. Your heart is pounding, throat's dry, legs are twitching, can't recall your name, white spots in front of eyes. Breathe in through your mouth to the count of four, hold for four seconds, breathe out to the count of four. Plaster a smile on your face.

Project your voice to the back of the room. Look for your supportive fans, otherwise known as the head-bobbers. Do not hang your head over your speech. Look up! Keep breathing. You will not die!

Gifting at Work

Careful here. If you are asked to do the Secret Santa thing, stick to the tried and true—chocolates, gift cards, and other generic gift items. But if you insist on being creative, then:

- Know the rules. Is there a dollar-value limit on the amount you can spend? If it's $10, then you can go as high as $15.
- Think elegance: portfolios, coffee table books, picture frames, food baskets, holiday ornaments or decorations if your co-worker celebrates the holiday at home.
- Be charitable. Make a charitable donation in your co-worker's name and give the recipient the tax receipt.

Stay away from anything religious (skip the "What Would Jesus Do?" bracelet), in questionable taste (that means no to the strip club gift certificate and the candy-cane underwear), the second-hand, and especially the gag gift (forget the voodoo doll with your boss's face photocopied on it). Careful with "regifting," too. And if you plan to regift a present in the future, make sure you put a sticky on it reminding you who gave it to you and when.

Boss Troubles

The best way to prepare for a difficult boss is having experienced a difficult teacher. Like that sixth-grade teacher who never gave you a break, your boss is someone you pretty much have to put up with. Here are some of the difficult types:

Mr. Moody

One day he's all chatty, next day he's cold as ice. Maybe this guy/gal can't handle stress. He/she might be a bully, or just an idiot. How do you deal with that?

Survival strategy: Stand your ground. If he is yelling at you, stay very, very quiet. When he has finished his tantrum you might say, "I am here to do my job as best I can. I will try to do better. However, I …"

The Slave-Driver

It's all work and no play with this one. Before you are finished with one assignment you have two more. Overtime is a given.

Survival strategy: Talk to your boss about how often you might have to work overtime and come to a very specific understanding about what is acceptable to both of you.

The Know-Nothing

This woman pretends to know everything when in fact she:

a. doesn't know a thing but thinks if she speaks loudly and long no one will notice;
b. does know, but hasn't got the skills she needs to communicate;
c. is in over her head, scared out of her mind, and faking it.

Survival strategy: Public confrontation doesn't work with this type. You have to talk to her privately with suggestions. Don't be surprised when she implements your suggestions and takes the credit. Next time, write your suggestions down.

"Be My Personal Servant"

This guy hires you as, let's say, an office assistant. The next thing you know you are picking up his dry-cleaning while taking his car in for a wash.
Survival strategy: Ask for a list of your duties, preferably before you accept the job. That way, you're both clear on what is—and isn't—expected of you. If you've already put some time in on the job and can't quit, pick a quiet time and say, "I seem to be spending a great deal of my time on personal errands. I'd like to talk about what your expectations really are."

The "Just Do It" Boss

She hands you jobs left and right without any instructions. When you do it to the best of your ability, she seems to take pleasure in criticizing your work.
Survival strategy: The next time she gives you a job, say, "I know you want this done right, so how about I go and write up what I think this job needs to be

More than You Really Wanted to Know

Did you know that the workplace has its own particular language? (Hint: "touching base" has nothing to do with baseball, and neither does "dropping the ball." And "closing the loop" isn't something you do with a crayon.) As a newcomer, it's okay to ask if you don't understand. For more on office jargon, check out: http://www.theofficelife.com/business-jargon-dictionary-A.html.

completed. If you like what I describe, I'll go ahead. If you don't, you can tell me what you *do* want." This often works, because bosses like this don't know what they *don't* want until they see it. You are also creating a paper trail in case you need to defend yourself somewhere down the line.

Should You Stay or Should You Go?

How long should you give a job before you decide that you hate it? Some say six months, others say a year. The point is, don't jump ship before you have really given the job a chance.

You should stay if …

- Other than one issue (the hours, for example) you like the job and the people, and the company is well managed.
- This is the start of your career, and the job is important for your resumé. (Stay at least a year.)
- The job offers good opportunities for growth and career movement.

You should go if …

- The company is badly managed (e.g., a number of bad managers) and the staff are all in a state of near-mutiny.
- You have at least three months' salary saved up.
- You or your ethics are being compromised (e.g., you are asked to perform unethical or illegal tasks, or you are being subjected to sexual harassment).
- You're in a rut—you've been given no indication that a promotion is anywhere in your future, and your job has hit a dead end.

If money is an issue, you will have to stay until you have found another job to move into. If you can't look for a real job while you are employed, then quit and get yourself a part-time or evening job while you look for work during the day. Think carefully this time about what did not work for you in the first job. Was it that particular work environment, or something about the profession in general?

Until you leave your post, continue to give 100 percent to the job. When you do leave, do so politely by thanking the company for the opportunity and for your newly acquired skills. Put your resignation in writing but deliver the letter in person. Look people in the eye. Give at least two weeks' notice.

Resources

Preparing a cover letter and resumé

Worksearch—A guide to online resumé resources:

www.garywill.com/worksearch/reswrit.htm

CareerLab—Sample cover letters: www.careerlab.com/letters/link001.htm

JobStar—Resumés and cover letters: http://jobstar.org/index.php

Resumania—how not to write a resumé, real errors made by applicants on resumés: www.resumania.com

Showcase Your "Home Run" Accomplishments—how to differentiate yourself from your competitors: www.careerlab.com/art_homeruns.htm

U Waterloo Career Development Manual: www.cdm.uwaterloo.ca

Job scams

www.lookstoogoodtobetrue.com

Workplace safety

Canadian Centre for Occupational Health and Safety (CCOHS): www.ccohs.ca

www.passporttosafety.com

youngworker.ca

prevent-it.ca

Workplace Safety and Insurance Board: www.wsib.on.ca

Office jargon

http://www.theofficelife.com/business-jargon-dictionary-A.html

Career resources, online

Career advice—Brazen Careerist blog: http://blog.penelopetrunk.com/

Articles for job hunters by author and career coach Mark Swartz: www.careeractivist.com

Networking site for job-seekers and employers: www.linkedin.com

Free online career manual, including self-assessment and job-search strategies: www.cdm.uwaterloo.ca

Human Resources and Skills Development Canada, with links to free job counselling/search programs: www.hrsdc.gc.ca

Youth Employment Information: www.youth.ga.ca, or call 1-800-935-5555

Information about workplace rights: www.workrights.ca

The Canadian Employment Lawyers Network has information on employment law and contact information: www.celn.org

Career exploration and job search information and links: www.canadiancareers.com

A place to start looking: www.monster.com

Career Resources, books

What Color Is Your Parachute, Richard Bolles.

What Next? Barbara Moses.

Your local library will have a book called *YouthLink*, a Government of Canada publication.

Sites aimed at students

www.youth.gc.ca

www.jobband.gc.ca

www.workopolisCampus.com

www.JobPostings.ca

Ads from a wide range of sources

www.wantedJobs.com

www.Nicejob.ca

www.eluta.ca

Finances

If you want to know what God thinks of money,
just look at the people he gave it to.
—DOROTHY PARKER

Admit it. You want to skip this chapter. Your eyes are glazing over. You want to read more recipes. You want to find out about decorating your new place. Who the heck wants to talk about *finances*?

You do—if you want to make it on your own.

Let's say you are newly graduated, newly hired. You're earning more than you ever have—finally "in the money"! Of course, there's the small matter of that little $18,000 student loan to pay ... And then, suppose, just *suppose*, you want a roof over your head, food to eat, clothes to wear, transportation to work ...

Before you start scrounging for empties, let's look at how you can get this money stuff under control. (And if you're not there yet, if you're just now heading out to college or university, well, there's no time like the present to start prepping for the future.) We'll start by tackling the money you do have—where to put it, and how best to spend it.

Been there
Done THAT

I feel such a burden on my shoulders due to mismanagement of money: overspending, compulsive sprees on lattes and cigarettes, on things I don't need, late fees, and parking tickets—all leading to debt, lots of debt. And that doesn't include monthly bills and rent. Oh, and car expenses: gas, oil changes ...

—RICK, 26

What to Do with All That Money

Forget the word *budget*, it's negative (like "diet"). What you need is a Spending Plan. A Spending Plan is a strategy that helps you figure out how to live within your means and make your money work for you.

Your first step in developing a Spending Plan is to keep track of your expenses and income for at least one month.

Basic Expenses to Consider

Housing: You need a place to live, whether it's a room in a house, an apartment, or a condo. In nearly all cases, you'll pay rent. *Experts suggest that rent should amount to about 25 to 35 percent of your income.*

Utilities: Some rental plans include the cost of these basic utilities, while others don't. Basic utilities include electricity, water, heat (natural gas, etc.). There are extra utilities you will probably want to budget for, such as telephone and Internet service. *Utilities should amount to about 4 to 10 percent of your income.*

Food: You might want to break this expense into two categories—groceries and dining out. *Aim for about 10 to 30 percent of your income.*

Personal items: Clothing is often a big expense. Haircuts and other personal grooming costs (can you really afford manicures?) fit into this category too, as do services like dry-cleaning. *Experts suggest 3 to 10 percent of your income is a reasonable range.*

Transportation: You need to get to work somehow to pay for all of the above. That means budgeting for gas, oil, and other expenses for your car. Or, if you take public transportation, you'll need money to pay the fares. Depending where you live, a bicycle might actually be a realistic option, for at least part of the year. *Expenses here should take up about 6 to 20 percent of your income.*

Insurance: If you own or lease a car, you will need to budget for insurance (see Chapter 14). Don't forget renters' or house insurance, and life, health, and disability insurance. *Aim for 4 to 6 percent of your income.*

Savings: You should budget to set aside money for emergencies (like losing your job), retirement, or perhaps another goal, such as buying a car or saving for a house or vacation. Ideally, you'll want at least three months' pay set aside. *Aim for 5 to 10 percent of your income.*

Debt payments: If you have a car, chances are you have lease or loan payments. You might have a student loan to repay, or money owing on a credit card, and you will have to make monthly payments. (See page 370.) *Limit this to 20 percent of your income.*

Other costs that will eat into your paycheque:

Taxes: Sure, they might have started life as a temporary wartime measure, but honey, face it, taxes are here to stay. You might be surprised how little you really bring home after income tax and other items are deducted. You also have to learn to file a strange yearly document called a tax return. (More on this fun activity on page 377.)

Start-up costs: If you're moving out on your own for the first time, you'll be facing some one-time expenses—first and last months' rent, damage deposit, moving fees, utility hookup (phone, Internet, etc.), paint, furnishings, kitchen tools, storage equipment, linen, cleaning supplies, household tools, medical supplies.

Luxuries: Cable TV, entertainment expenses, gifts, magazine subscriptions, CDs.

Maybe that all sounds a bit vague. Let's attach some imaginary numbers to it. Yours won't be exactly the same, but it will paint a general picture.

Imagine spreading all the money you bring home in one month (after taxes) onto the kitchen table. That's called your "net spendable income." If we make a wildly optimistic guess here and say you've graduated and are now making $26,000, that means you're bringing home about $20,000, or $1667 a month. From that pile of cash on the table, remove:

$750 for housing	$115 for eating out
$100 for electricity	$200 for personal expenses
$40 for water	$325 for transportation
$150 for heat	$110 for insurance
$170 for groceries	$165 for savings

Can't do it, can you? You're $458 short—and we haven't even included things like cable TV, Internet, or phone fees. If this were real life, you'd be up a creek.

So what do you do (besides calling home)? You can start cutting costs. Maybe you don't need a car and can get by on public transit. Maybe you can find a roommate to share the rent, or eat at home more often, or shop at Goodwill. That's what a Spending Plan is all about. It helps you figure out how to make what's coming in outweigh what's going *out*.

Creating a Spending Plan

T.G.I.F.—it's payday! Wait, can you afford that $7 martini? How many have you budgeted for? Before you hit the town, pull out your notebook and draw up a Spending Plan. (And no, moving back home is not a real "plan.")

A Spending Plan consists of two categories: income and expenses.

Income is money you earn from a job (as opposed to occasional handouts from Mom and Dad). This is called "cash inflow," because it flows in to your control. However, the other side of the equation is expenses or "cash outflow," and unfortunately all too often this leads to *debt*. We will talk about that later, and if you manage your money wisely, it will be the one item in this chapter you will *not* need to read.

Get control. Determine how much cash is flowing in, and how much is flowing out.

If you are regularly employed, then "income" is easy to determine by looking at your paystub. Your net spendable income is what you have as "take-home pay" after deductions (tax, employment insurance, benefits, pension plans, etc.). This is the actual amount that goes into your bank account and is available for you to spend. You might have sources of income other than your job (investments, occasional income, etc.) and these should be included in the final tally as well.

Your "expenses" might be a bit more difficult to determine. You need to analyze your spending.

- First, calculate your fixed monthly expenses: rent, utilities, perhaps tuition fees, car lease payments, cable or Internet costs, basic phone services, cellphone services, anything that is regularly billed on a monthly basis.
- Next, estimate your variable expenses, such as food, laundry, clothing, entertainment, gas and vehicle maintenance, or public transit costs, etc. Include small expenses such as your daily coffee, snacks, magazines, and so on, as well as one-time expenses such as gifts, books, etc.

TIP: If you don't want to cart a notebook around with you, keep all your receipts in a file folder and record them weekly.

This will give you a general idea of your expenses, but to set up a Spending Plan you will need to determine your expenses more accurately. That's why you're going to spend the next month keeping track.

Here's the hard part. Carry that little notebook with you all day long and make a note of *everything* you spend—even the $1.15 coffee you buy each day, or (Heaven forbid) that $2.45 latte! Remember the money you spent on a cab that day you didn't want to wait in the rain for a bus? Remember the ton of toonies you left for that hottie waiter? Mark it down. Yes, this is tedious, but if you can manage to do it for at least a month, you will have an accurate picture of your spending.

Set up your notebook with the following chart:

Daily Budget Tracking Worksheet

Date	Item	Income	Expense	Balance

At the end of the month, group all your daily expenses and total them into categories as shown on the next page.

Now, compare your expenses for the month to your income. If you are spending more than your income, something will have to change. Likely, that will mean cutting back on some costs—otherwise known as "trimming the fat." Gotta warn you, it won't be easy. As a veteran of many diets, I can tell you, trimming fat is hard. But just as a good diet does not forbid all treats, a good Spending Plan leaves room for a little of life's chocolate. The trick is finding just the right balance between needs and wants, between the bran flakes and the chocolate.

Income and Expense Worksheet

INCOME FOR THE MONTH OF	AMOUNT	
Gross monthly income	$	
Other income	$	
Tax	− $	
C.P.P.	− $	
E.I.	− $	
Other deductions	− $	
Net monthly income	= $	

EXPENSES	AMOUNT PLANNED	ACTUAL COST
Savings (at least 10% of net income)		
Emergency fund		
RRSP		
Household		
Rent or mortgage payment		
Utilities (hydro, heat, etc.)		
Home maintenance		
Property taxes ($1/12$ of annual)		
Furniture		
Phone/cellphone		
Internet		
Other		
Food		
Groceries		
Dining out / Takeout		
Transportation		
Vehicle payment		
Auto Insurance		
Gas, parking, tolls		

Registration / licence fees ($^1/_{12}$ annual)		
Public Transportation		
Debt		
Loans		
Credit cards		
Personal items		
Clothing		
Dry-cleaning / laundry		
Grooming (hair care, toiletries, etc.)		
Child care expenses (babysitting, daycare ...)		
Other		
Health		
Dentist		
Eye exame / glasses / contacts		
Prescriptions		
Other		
Recreational / Entertainment		
Vacation ($^1/_{12}$ annual amount)		
Movie rentals / shows, etc.		
Cable or satellite TV		
Club fees (gym membership, etc.)		
Other		
Miscellaneous		
Gifts (birthday / Christmas / other)		
Unexpected		
TOTAL MONTHLY EXPENSES		
Net Monthly Income	$	
Less Total Actual Monthly Expenses	– $	
Net Cash Flow	$	

Here are some suggested monthly allocations for three lower-income budgets. Remember, these figures are not written in stone, only offered as a guideline.

Sample Spending Plans for Lower Monthly Incomes

Expense Category	Net Pay		
	$1500	$2000	$2500
Housing (35%)	$525	$700	$875
Utilities (10%)	$150	$200	$250
Food (10%)	$150	$200	$250
Transportation (15%)	$225	$300	$375
Clothing (5%)	$75	$100	$125
Personal Items (5%)	$75	$100	$125
Savings (10%)	$150	$200	$250
Debt (10%)	$150	$200	$250
TOTAL	$1500	$2000	$2500

Don't expect it to work out the first month. You'll probably have to tinker with your Spending Plan a bit until you hit on one that works. But when you do, reward yourself. (Just make sure it's in the budget!)

Here are some basic strategies to keep you on your feet financially:

- Spend less than you earn. Obvious, but rarely followed.
- Stay on top of your plan and keep it simple. Be honest and realistic about your spending.
- Keep records and receipts.
- If your actual spending doesn't match up with your planned expenses, or exceeds your income, make adjustments as needed.
- Keep accurate records of your credit card purchases, debit card transactions, ATM transactions, and cash purchases, and remember to balance your bankbook regularly (see page 361).
- Pay your bills immediately to avoid late fees—and to avoid having your phone or utilities cut off. (Do you know how *cold* showers can be without hot water?)

TIP: Check the mailbox every day. Pay each bill the day you receive it—phone and Internet are probably the quickest methods. Or, if you can, arrange to have the bills paid automatically from your chequing account. Just be sure you leave enough in the bank, and keep track of what's been paid.

- There are software programs available, such as Microsoft Money or Quicken, that can help you track your cash flow. These programs will also allow you to allocate funds to set aside for savings or set repayment goals for debt.
- Remember to save! You not only need to save for periodic expenses, such as car and home maintenance, you also should strive to accumulate 3 to 6 months' salary for an emergency fund. (By "emergency" we of course mean major repairs to the car, or basic living if your income drops—*not* a trip to Cancun.) You will also want to set aside money for long-term savings (maybe even retirement), as well as a Special Purchase Fund (here's where the Cancun money goes).
- Set financial goals: long-term (retirement) and short-term (a goal to save for in 5 years, for example).

What to Do When Your Spending Plan Doesn't Work

Still can't make it work? If you're running out of paycheque before you run out of month, then you'll need to become a little more "financially creative."

Ways to increase your income

- If you get paid hourly at a job, determine whether you can work more hours each week.
- Look for training programs that your boss will pay for to increase your value as an employee—and hopefully your salary.
- Sell unwanted clothing and other merchandise on eBay.
- Turn a hobby into income. Sell your crafts, or if you play an instrument, maybe you could find a way to perform for money. Can you blow up balloons and make kids laugh? Maybe you can swing a job as a children's party clown.
- Hold a garage sale.
- Start a home business—childcare, music lessons, sewing, typing, lawn care, housecleaning, pet-sitting, maybe even personal shopping.

- Get a second part-time or seasonal job. Post offices and local retailers often hire extra staff at Christmas.
- Were you a whiz at high school math or English? Try tutoring. You can work privately, usually at the student's home, or through a company, which will likely pay less but will provide you with the up-to-date curriculum and the space. Tutors make about $20 to $45 an hour.
- Instead of dining out at your favourite restaurant, get an extra job there as a waiter, bartender, or host. Make some money and have a great dinner on your break for free! (And meet that hot waiter you've been heavily tipping.)
- Instead of shopping at the mall, get a part-time job as a salesclerk at your favourite store—earn money and get a discount on purchases.
- Start a dog-walking service. Make money while you exercise.
- Do you do a lot of partying? Offer to clean up afterwards. While you're at it, offer to return the empties in exchange for the refund.
- Like the outdoors, gardening? Many people will hire others to purchase and plant their annuals each spring, or plant bulbs in the fall.
- Need a change of scenery but can't afford a vacation? Try house-sitting.
- Do direct sales. Try Avon, Mary Kay, Tupperware.
- Neat freak? Start your own sideline business as a professional organizer or "clutter-clearer."

TIP: Beware of "work at home" scams. Check out the following website for details: http://www.workathomecareers.com/scams.shtml.

Ways to reduce your expenses

Never pay the full retail price. Shop at:

- Discount stores.
- Consignment shops.
- Goodwill, Value Village, etc.
- Garage sales—but be careful. Don't just buy something because it is a "good deal." Make sure it is something you actually need and will use.
- Clothing swaps—plan one with your friends who wear the same size.

If you must shop retail, never pay full price:

- Go straight to the sale rack first.
- Shop the clearance section of online stores.
- Shop at dollar stores—they have a wealth of stuff for a buck, and you can stock your entire kitchen and bathroom.
- Time your purchases. The store merchandise cycle is 6 to 8 weeks. After about 4 weeks on the floor, stores often rotate full-price items to discount tables.

The library—your town's best-kept secret

There's far more than books inside today's libraries. To take advantage, you'll need a membership: bring two pieces of ID and your address. Once in, you get to take advantage of some great services, free or for a very small charge. Depending on your library, you might be able to find:

- Computer and Internet access.
- Magazines and newspapers to borrow or buy used, cheap.
- CDs, DVDs, and cassettes.
- Movies.
- Video games.
- Books on CD or tape.
- Free downloads of books are available at some libraries. You can listen to them for about a week on your MP3.
- Photocopy and fax machines.
- A "coupon swap box."
- Cameras to borrow.
- A wide selection of workshops and seminars.

Find your "Latte Factor"

Lattes are the latest scapegoat for money woes. How'd they get such a bad rap? Simple math. Say you buy a latte a day at $3.50 each. In one month, you've spent $105; in one year, $1260. Ten years later, your belly full of latte, you've spent a whopping $12,600.

I'm not saying you've got to give it up. Just be aware of all the little "lattes" that are nibbling away at your paycheque—like newspapers, magazines, bottled water at the convenience store, snacks from the vending machine. Cut these out and you could save up to $300 a month. Or look at it this way: spending $5 less a day will grow to $948,612 over 40 years at a 10 percent annual rate of return when the magic of compound interest goes to work. (More on this on page 363.)

Where to Put Your Money

Assuming that you have some money now—where are you going to stash it? You'll need somewhere safe: bank, trust company, co-op, or credit union. Shop around. They all offer different types of accounts, interest rates, and service fees. Intimidated? Don't be. Just walk into a few and look for the office or sign that says "New Accounts" or "Customer Service." It's their job to answer your questions. You should also check with the human resources department at your place of work to see if they have any no-fee relationships with banks.

At this stage of your life, your best bet might be a basic or no-frills chequing and savings account for your everyday transactions. Investigate which type of institution and account best fits your needs. Will you be writing only a few cheques (for instance, if you are paying your bills with automatic withdrawal, or using a phone or Internet banking service)? Then it might be cheaper to find an account that charges by the cheque. Do you use the ATM a lot? Watch for banks that limit the number of no-charge ATM withdrawals you can make. Also, find out about minimum balance, overdraft (bounced cheque) fees, and fees for cash back from debit cards. Make sure the bank's ATMs are near your home, school, or workplace so that you aren't always paying extra to use some other bank's machine.

> **Duh moment!**
>
> "Interest": When you borrow money, you pay interest to whomever lent it to you. When the bank "borrows" your money (which is what they do when you give it to them in a savings account), the bank pays *you* interest. Interest is usually a percentage amount of the money being borrowed.

TIP: Once you have your Spending Plan established, make a vow to yourself that you will visit the ATM only once a week to withdraw all the money you will need for that week. You'll avoid ATM fees that way, and it might even help you stick to the plan!

+

More than You Really Wanted to Know

More than half (53 percent) of young Canadians aged 18 to 34 now have an RRSP (Registered Retirement Savings Plan)—up from 44 percent two years ago.

You might also want to set up separate accounts for savings. (Yes, you are expected to save at your age, too.) A daily interest savings account might be the best place for your Emergency and Special Purchase funds. If it's the kind of account that requires you to visit the bank to withdraw money, the inconvenience might discourage you from "dipping in." If you're really ambitious, you can set up yet another account for long-term savings. Choose the account that will get you the best rate of interest.

Handling Your Money—the Basics

Remember the piggy bank? Passé. Cash too. Soon you'll be relying on only credit and debit cards, and the occasional cheque. Now's the time to learn about the perils and powers of plastic.

What is the difference between a debit and a credit?

- "Debit" means "subtract." When you use a debit card, you are subtracting your money from your own bank account.
- "Credit" is money made available to you by a bank or other financial institution. It is a loan to you for money you do not have.

Debit Cards

What is a debit card?

A debit card is a plastic card that can be used to withdraw funds available in your bank account using an automated teller machine (ATM). Many merchants also accept debit cards, treating them the same as cash, without added fees.

How does it work?

- A debit card draws money directly from your bank account when used at an ATM.
- A debit card transaction pays the merchant by taking funds directly from your account.

- When you insert your card at an ATM or swipe it at a checkout, you must punch in your Personal Identification Number (PIN).
- The system checks your account to see if it has enough money available to cover the transaction (including your available overdraft, if applicable).
- If there are sufficient funds, there is an immediate electronic transfer of money from your bank account to the merchant's bank account.

What are the pros and cons of using debit cards?

Pros:

- Obtaining a debit card is often easier than obtaining a credit card.
- A debit card offers the convenience of a credit card while allowing you to spend only what you have in your account. It's a great way to avoid racking up credit card debt. Unless, of course, you have overdraft protection, which covers you if you withdraw too much but charges a fee. Not a wise move. (More on this later.)
- Using a debit card instead of writing cheques saves you from showing identification or giving out personal information at the time of the transaction.
- Debits show up when you download your chequing activity and can be easily categorized and tracked.
- Using a debit card frees you from carrying cash or a chequebook.
- The debit card makes trips to the bank less necessary, and allows you the safety of carrying less cash.
- Debit cards might be more readily accepted by merchants than cheques, especially in other states or countries where your card brand is accepted.
- As with credit cards, you may dispute unauthorized charges or other mistakes within 60 days. You should contact the card issuer if a problem cannot be resolved with the merchant.

TIP: Ask your bank about setting a daily limit on your debit card withdrawals. That way you won't be tempted to splurge, and you'll be somewhat protected from theft. Many banks automatically set a daily cash withdrawal limit.

Cons:

- If you make a large purchase, the debit card doesn't offer the same protections as a credit card (see Credit Cards, p. 351) for items that are never delivered, or were misrepresented.
- Since you are spending only what you have and are not using credit, a debit card will not help you build a credit history, whereas a credit card, used properly, will.
- The debit card makes money readily available for you and might encourage impulse buying. If, on the other hand, you are using only cash, you are less likely to buy on impulse because you have to find a bank to make a withdrawal. This gives you time to rethink the purchase.

How to safely use a debit card

- If you have a Personal Identification Number (PIN), memorize it—don't write it down, and definitely don't keep your PIN with your card.
- Don't choose a PIN that can be easily figured out, such as your phone number, address, or birthday.

TIPS:

- Check with your bank to find out what types of service you have and how many transactions you are allowed on your account before you are charged.
- Check with your financial institution about your liability. Many offer consumers better protection than what is required in government regulations.
- Steer clear of ATMs that do not belong to your bank. You'll pay about $1.50 each time. No-name machines at convenience stores are even worse. They might charge an extra $1.50, so you're paying $3.00 every time you make a withdrawal!
- When travelling abroad, check ahead to find out what service charge you'll be paying to make ATM withdrawals. It is often $3.00 for withdrawing any amount from your account.

- Never give your PIN to anyone. If something catastrophic happens (two broken legs and a lengthy stay in hospital qualifies) and you must give your best friend the PIN and card, change the number ASAP.
- Always cover the keypad when you punch in your PIN.
- Hold on to your receipts from your debit card transactions to compare to your bank statement, in case you forget some transactions.
- Always know how much money you have available in your account. (See Keeping Track of Your Money, page 361.)
- Keep track of outstanding cheques, too. It's easy to forget and withdraw more money than you should—which is how bounced cheques happen.

What if my debit card is lost or stolen?

- Report the loss or theft immediately so that you're not stuck paying the bills.
- To protect yourself, photocopy all your cards—credit and debit—and keep the copies in a file with emergency numbers to call to report loss or theft. This way, you'll have the information on hand to make the calls right away.

Credit Cards

Q: What is a credit card?
  a. An all-access pass to the mall.
  b. A way to buy more than you could without the card.
  c. A cool thing to flash in your wallet to attract girls.
  d. Evil.

No, no, no! A credit card is an I.O.U.—nothing more, nothing less. And if you don't give it the respect it deserves, it can be a ticking time bomb waiting to go off in your pocket, future money gone bye-bye. A credit card means debt—and debt is definitely *not* a chick magnet.

A credit card is a bank-issued card that allows you to buy something on credit. It's backed by a contract that requires you to pay a specified interest rate. In other words, it's a plastic card that gives you an on-the-spot loan.

Like a loaded gun, credit cards can be devastating in the hands of someone who has not been trained to use them properly and responsibly. They can ruin your credit, rack up your debt, cause you to lose your job. But credit cards are not inherently *evil*. They can be a lifesaver in case of emergency, a great convenience, and an excellent way to obtain a good credit rating. It all depends on your reason for using them and how responsible you are.

How does a credit card work?

A credit card is like a loan. The amount of credit (how much you can borrow) is determined by your credit history, income, debts, and ability to pay. When you use the card, you are agreeing to repay the amount you've borrowed, plus interest if you do not pay in full each month. You will receive a monthly statement detailing your charges and payment requirements.

If you pay less than the full amount—you can pay as little as a minimum required amount—interest can be charged on whatever you owed initially until the entire thing is paid off. (In other words, if you have a $2000 debt and pay off $200 a month, you could still be paying interest on the $2000 even though you've paid most of it off.) Some cards might instead charge you interest on your highest balance during a month, but if you've paid some down over several months, interest is charged on the declining balance.

Beware private retail cards that boast "No payments or interest for a full year." If you have not paid the entire amount before the twelve months is over, then they will often charge you interest on the full amount, even if you've paid *some* off.

Credit card myths and misconceptions

Don't believe for a minute:

- "Paying the minimum on the credit card is the smartest way to pay because then I can buy a lot and only have to pay a little." Note! See section on credit card interest.
- "If I get a credit card in the mail it means that the credit card company has checked out my finances and I can afford to pay for what I charge." Sure, just like the pet store checks to see if you'd make a responsible pet owner. They don't check, they don't care, they just want your money.
- "I should charge it to the max so they will send me another one." Uh-uh. They might increase your limit, though, and then you can get even further in debt to them.
- "If I get a bad credit rating, it doesn't really count unless I apply for another credit card." Not a chance. If you don't believe me, just try to get a loan, mortgage, or line of credit with a bad credit rating. It counts.

- "It's good to use a cash advance on my credit card and invest it in the stock market or at the races." Heck, why not go for the more attractive odds of winning the lottery? Get a cash advance for that, too. Hope you like the company of collection agency folks.
- "If I go over the limit, it's the card company's fault for not checking, so I am not responsible." What—you didn't read the fine print? The credit company people are not stupid. Maybe someone else here is?

Pros and cons of using a credit card

Pros:

- It's a convenient and flexible payment tool accepted worldwide.
- It provides access to unsecured credit (no collateral required).
- It offers interest-free payment from the time of purchase to the end of the billing period.
- It allows instant payment for purchases.
- It helps you to establish good credit (so that you can make larger purchases, like a car).
- It's handy for emergencies. It's like having a little safety net so you don't ever have to worry about being stranded with no cash (although you'd be smarter to set up an Emergency Fund in a savings account).
- Some credit cards will insure whatever you buy with them.
- Most offer fraud protection.
- Other rewards and benefits, such as air travel points, car insurance, damage and loss insurance, and extended warranty programs, are often available.
- Some cards allow you to accumulate credits toward the purchase of a car, or to support a favourite charity.

Cons:

- You can spend the full amount of your credit limit and get in way over your head.
- Credit card debts are more easily made than paid.
- If you can't pay your bill and you mess up your credit rating, the information stays on your credit file for 7 to 10 years. Even if you pay the debt back,

TIP: You've promised yourself to use your credit card only for emergencies. Midnight munchies and a cashless wallet do not qualify as emergencies.

the information remains on file unless you get the entity that had the debt collection filed to agree to let the collection company delete it.

At first glance, the pros outweigh the cons by a mile. But don't be fooled. If you fall into the credit card debt trap, all the pros are wiped out immediately.

So now that you're well versed on the subject of credit cards, you might be ready to sign up—if you haven't already. Credit card companies waste no time tracking young people down; you might have been approached already. The credit card market in Canada is highly competitive: 600 institutions in Canada issue Visa, MasterCard, and American Express products. According to Bankrate Inc., the average college student gets 12 solicitations from credit card companies per week. Yes, it's flattering to be wanted. But remember, it's not you they want—it's your money. Do your research before you sign.

How to shop for a credit card

- Read the fine print!
- Look for a no-fee card with a rewards program. Possible rewards include:
  —Cash back—you get back a percentage (usually between 2 and 5 percent) of what you spend in a cash rebate.
  —Frequent-flyer miles—receive frequent-flyer miles for every dollar spent using the credit card, and earn extra points when you purchase a flight using the card.

Been there Done THAT

The card company contacted me. I didn't even have to apply for a card. They gave me a free T-shirt for signing up and 0 percent interest. Of course, I didn't read the fine print. That was for the first month. Now I'm paying 21 percent interest. At that rate, my interest will soon be as bad as my bill!

—JEROD, 20

—Hotel points—receive a point for every dollar charged, then redeem points for free hotel stays.

—Merchandise and travel rewards—earn points to purchase merchandise, groceries, gasoline, travel vouchers, etc.

- Don't be tempted by cards offering perks that are more than offset by the fees they charge.
- Check the interest rate, and whether there is an annual fee (a fee charged for use of the card—this can be as high as $130 per year).
- Look for the card with the lowest fixed rate of interest.
- Find out what the grace period is—how many days is it before the lender starts the interest meter ticking. Look for a card with a twenty-five-day grace period.
- Watch out for hidden fees, such as fees for going over your credit limit, late payment fees, and extra finance charges.
- Do they charge a transaction fee for cash advances on the card over and above the interest rate?
- Don't fall for the whole "introductory rate" scam. Companies often lure students with the "bait and switch." After your first year at a low rate and no annual fee, the company increases the rate to a ridiculous amount. And if you don't read the fine print, you might be surprised by a little rule that says the low interest rate is available only with a minimum annual income. If you don't earn that minimum, you're stuck with a much higher rate.
- Don't get sucked in by ridiculously high credit limits. It will just tempt you to spend more than you can afford.

Protecting your credit cards

- Sign the back of your card as soon as you get it.
- Destroy unwanted cards so that no one else can use them.
- Never leave your cards unattended at work. There are more credit card thefts in the workplace than in any other single location.
- Never leave your card, receipts, or statements lying around.
- If your credit card is also programmed for access to an ATM, memorize your PIN and do not write it down anywhere.
- Never lend your card to anyone, and never give anyone your PIN.
- Always check your card when it is returned to you after a purchase.
- Report stolen or lost cards immediately.

- Never give your card number over the phone or the Internet unless you are dealing with a reputable company. The only time you should give it is when you have called to place an order.

How to use a credit card responsibly

Credit card companies love it when you pay only the minimum payment. This is how they make money. Remember, your goal is not to have the credit card company *like* you. Find your friends somewhere else!

- Always keep this fact in mind: this is *not* your money.
- Keep your receipts, and always check these against your statement to make sure your charges are accurate.
- If a card is lost or stolen, report it as soon as you notice it is missing.
- Stick with one or two cards. The fewer the cards you own, the better your credit rating looks.
- Pay the full amount each month. If you can't afford to do that, then you can't afford the purchases you have made. Pay the entire balance when it's due. If for some

Duh moment!

The Lost Wallet

So you blew it; you left your wallet … uh, somewhere. Or maybe someone lifted it while you weren't looking. Now what?

1. Report the missing cards—credit cards, ATM cards—immediately, before they are used by someone else. Most institutions will courier you replacements.
2. Contact the motor vehicle licensing office and any other government identification office to warn them and to get replacements.
3. If your gym pass or parking or work ID or anything else was in your wallet, contact those organizations.
4. Make a plan for next time: photocopy all important documents in your wallet and keep the information in a safe place. Don't keep reminder notes of your PIN in your wallet because no matter how well coded you think you've made it, someone will figure it out, and if they've got your ATM card, they'll have your PIN too.

reason you can't pay the bill as soon as you get it, then at least pay more than the minimum amount due—and then review your spending habits to cut unnecessary purchases.

- When you use credit to pay for an item, write down the amount and subtract it from your funds to ensure you can pay the amount at the end of the month.
- Put your credit card away—far away—if you've had a couple of drinks.

What to do if you lose your cellphone

Why is this in the finance chapter? Well, partly because we didn't know where else to put it, and partly because your cellphone is becoming more and more like a wallet. Think about it. You've stashed all kinds of important information in there—your phone book, calendar entries, photos, songs, maybe even important data from work. And if you lose it, you've lost a lot more than the cost of a cellphone. And not only will you have the hassle of finding your phone or getting a new one, you'll also have to pay for whatever calls are made on your phone by the person who finds it and decides to track down some long-lost friends in Auckland or Peru.

So what do you do?

Your first step is obvious—call yourself. But if you've misplaced the phone in a noisy bar, or if it's turned off, or if the battery has run down by the time you've realized it's gone, then of course that won't work.

Your second step is to contact your wireless service provider—immediately. Until you tell them you've lost your phone, you're responsible for any calls made on it. If you're lucky, you might be able to get a temporary suspension of service while you look a little harder.

The next step is to buy a new cellphone—and take some steps to prevent this hassle from happening again.

If you're prone to losing things, (and you know who you are), it might be worth it to pay a few dollars extra each month for insurance. You might also want to lock your phone to prevent others from accessing it—this function is usually found under "Phone Lock" or "Keypad Lock" under "Settings." And from now on, use passwords to protect your phone book, and don't store anything that you wouldn't want anyone else to see—no credit card numbers or bank account information. Try to keep your phone in the same place all the time—on a strap around your wrist, or the same pocket or section of your purse.

How to Recognize Financial Warning Signs

- You are living from paycheque to paycheque.
- You don't balance your bank accounts and don't even know how much money you have.
- You have no savings.
- You owe more than you own.
- You are an impulsive or compulsive shopper.
- You are gathering debt using credit cards and loans and only paying the minimum balances.
- You have spent your income tax refund even before you have it. And you've spent your pay raise already to pay off debts.
- You are falling behind in utility or rent payments.
- You think that retirement planning is for old people.

You can bury your head in the sand. You can buy lottery tickets, marry an accountant, or better yet, a millionaire. Or you can face the music. You know you have to sometime. Yes, credit card debt is a serious problem. But it doesn't have to be the end of the world if you recognize the problem and start dealing with it now.

1. Immediately stop charging anything additional on credit cards.

2. Find out how much is owed.

3. Pay more than the minimum payment.

More than You Really Wanted to Know

- Credit cards date back to the 1920s. They were first issued by companies to allow purchases made on credit, similar to modern department store charge cards.
- The average Canadian owes $1269 to credit card companies. At 18 percent interest, that's about $230 a year you could save if you paid off the balance.
- If you stick to the minimum amount due to pay off a balance of $1000 on a card with an 18 percent annual interest rate, it would take you more than 12 years to pay it off. During that time, you would also pay $1115 in interest charges.

4. Send in payments as soon as the bill is received. (Every extra day you carry a balance, your interest charges accumulate.)

5. When one card is paid off, *cut up the card* and start making the same payments on another.

6. Do not accept the credit card issuer's offer of a minimum payment of zero or skipping a payment for a month.

7. Consolidate cards. This means transferring balances on high-interest cards to low-interest cards and cutting up the high-interest ones. Better yet, transfer the debts to lower-interest loans. Talk to your bank.

8. Learn from your mistake. When you are out of debt, make sure you don't fall into the trap again.

Cheques

Another method of payment that you'll need to be familiar with is the cheque. Here's how you fill one out:

Sample Cheque

NAME Joe Independant	001
ADDRESS Your own apartment	
CITY/TOWN New City, Far From Home	DATE _____
PAY TO THE ORDER OF _____	$
_____	100 DOLLARS
FRED'S BANK FRED'S BANK ADDRESS	
MEMO _____	_____

⑈004⑈ ⑈12345⑈004⑈ 1234⑈1234567⑈

- *Date:* Write the date you are writing the cheque (unless you are postdating it—we'll get into that later). Format is usually dd/mm/yyyy.
- *Pay to the order of:* Write the name of the person or company you are paying with this cheque.
- *Amount:* Write the amount of the cheque in numerals as well as in words. For example, for a cheque for $114.79 you would write 114.79 after the dollar sign, then you would write out in words "One hundred fourteen and 79/100" on the line below. If there are no cents, write "xx/100." Caution: A common mistake is to mix up dollars and cents. For example, $100.20 written as "One hundred twenty" instead of "One hundred.....20/100." If you do this you might have the larger amount of $120 deducted from your account instead. And make sure that the numbers written out in long-hand match the numerals written on the cheque. Often, bank employees only look at the long-hand numbers, and ignore the numerals.
- *Memo:* No—this is not for your to-do list! Write a brief description of what the cheque is paying for. (Example: "Beer money for Bob.")
- *Signature line:* Sign your name (yes, in cursive writing!).
- *Numbers at the bottom of the cheque:* A secret government code to trace your every purchase? No. The numbers usually represent, from left to right, the branch number, institution number (for example, 004 is the institution number for TD Canada Trust), and your account number. The dots and lines? Um, ask a banker.
- Remember to record the cheque in your Cheque Register—you know, that funny little pad that came with your cheques. (See next page.)

Caution:

- Make sure you fill out the "Pay to the order of" line, or anyone could add his/her name and cash the cheque.
- Do not sign the cheque before you fill it out entirely. This is called a "blank cheque," and anyone could fill it out however he/she wanted, for as much as he/she wanted, and cash it for him/herself.
- Always write in pen and leave no blanks. Draw a continuous line to fill in any remaining blanks.
- Leave your cheques, deposits, and cancelled cheques in a safe place. If you make a mistake, tear up the cheque and make a note in the Cheque Register (see next page).

Keeping Track of Your Money

In your box of unused cheques you should find a Cheque Register (sometimes called a Transaction Record). If you've lost it or actually filled one up, you can ask any teller at your bank for a new one. This book is for keeping track of chequing account transactions (recording what money goes in and out of your bank account). It should look something like this:

Cheque Number	Date	Description of Transaction	Payment Debit (–)	Fee	Deposit Creit (+)	Balance
	2/20	Opening Deposit	$		$200.00	$200.00
105	2/26	Coffee Mart	19.75			19.75
						180.25
	3/12	ATM	100.00			100.00
						80.25
	3/22	Deposit			30.00	30.00
						110.25
	3/23	Deposit			50.00	50.00
						160.25
	3/23	Cash Back from Deposit	25.00			25.00
						135.25
	3/18	Monthly Fee		5.55		5.00
						130.25

In the Cheque Register, write down all the transactions that occur in your account, such as cheques you write, money you withdraw, and—something you might not be overly familiar with—money you deposit. Record all transactions (money in and out) immediately. The longer you put it off, the more likely you will be to forget. If you forget to record a cheque or withdrawal you might end up with less in your account than you think. This can lead you to write cheques for money that is not in your account. This is called "bouncing a cheque." It might sound like fun, but darling, it's not. It costs you money. And the bankers don't like it.

TIP: Keep all your receipts for as long as you can. Train yourself always to put receipts in the same place in your purse or wallet (rather than stuffing them in a pocket), and put them in a shoebox or something when you get home. That way you'll know where they are when you need to make a return or claim an expense.

The very first thing that must be recorded in your new Cheque Register is the present balance of your account. Record this amount (which can be found on your bank statement or ATM record) at the top of the "Balance" or "Balance Forward" column. Write "Opening Balance" in the "Description" column and then the dollar amount in the "Balance" column. Do this every time you start a new Cheque Register. With each transaction (change to the amount you have in the bank), you must:

1. Write the cheque number. (This is usually in the top-right corner of your cheque), or write "Cash" here if you have simply made a cash withdrawal, or "ATM" if you've made a debit card withdrawal. (You know those irritating little slips of paper the machine spits at you? Keep them.)

2. Write down the date of the cheque or cash/debit withdrawal.

3. Write a description of the cheque (by whom it is to be cashed, for example, American Express or Auntie May), or where you used the debit card for a purchase, or simply write "Personal Cash" if you took money directly out of the bank by ATM or through a teller.

4. Record the amount of the cheque, debit purchase, or cash withdrawal in the "Payment/Debit" column.

5. Here is the tricky part (and as a product of the New Math generation, you may feel free to use a calculator): subtract the payment/debit amount from the balance on the line above and record this number—your new balance—in the "Balance" column.

TIP: If you ever realize that a cheque you wrote is going to bounce, call the person to whom you wrote the cheque and let them know right away—before your credit rating is affected.

Remember your pre-authorized payments

Perhaps you have pre-arranged a bill payment so that it will come out of your account automatically on a set day each month. Don't forget about these pre-authorized payments! They will mess everything up (and cost you more money in bounced cheques). There is usually a page in the back of your Cheque Register that has a chart to record the amount of these payments and the day each month they will be withdrawn from your account. At the beginning of each month, record these transactions in your Cheque Register so you don't forget them and end up bouncing a cheque or going into *overdraft*. (Here's another fun new word for you! An overdraft is an amount of money the bank will "lend" you to cover a cheque if you don't have enough money in your account. This prevents the embarrassment of bouncing a cheque but—and here's the hitch—the bank charges you a fee for this service. Do your best to avoid it.)

The Magic and Dangers of Compound Interest

What's the plan? To make a million? You can do that. Start by calling the bank and making an appointment with an investment counsellor to set up your personal investment plan. It doesn't matter if you have only $100 to start. What matters is starting early and being consistent.

If you have a full-time, or even part-time, job and your employer automatically deposits your paycheque, you can even arrange with the bank to have money withdrawn automatically from your account and put into a savings plan on the same day that your cheque is deposited by your employer. You decide how much you want the bank to withdraw. It's a start! The trick is to keep going. Ask your bank about conditions, and be very sure you know all the rules before you start the plan. This is why it's a really good idea to have a face-to-face meeting with the investment counsellor. Ask questions.

Compound Interest

"Simple interest" is "rent" paid for the use of money. But "compound interest" is interest that is paid not only on the principal (initial loan), but also on the interest it earns. Simply put, it is interest paid on interest.

For instance, if you invested $1000 in a bank with an interest rate of 10 percent compounded annually (once per year), then in the first year of your investment you would earn $100. If this were simple interest, you would continue to earn $100 per year for the period of your investment. However, if the interest is compounded, you earn interest on your interest. The amount of compound interest for the first interest period is the same as for simple interest. However, for further interest periods, the amount of compound interest increases compared to simple interest.

Here's how it works:

	Simple Interest	Compound Interest
Year 1	$1000 * 10% = $100	$1000 * 10% = $100
Year 2	$1000 * 10% = $100	$1100 * 10% = $110
Year 3	$1000 * 10% = $100	$1210 * 10% = $121
Total Interest	$300	$331

So, here's the magic part: with 15 percent interest for 25 years, $10,000 would grow to $330,000!

Remember, don't worry if you don't have $10,000 to save; compound interest has no minimum on which it will pay. If you have only $100 to deposit, deposit it. The sooner the better. Each year reaps even more rewards.

What is the downside?

If you are on the receiving end of compound interest, there is no downside … you simply watch your money grow magically! But if you are on the paying end, you are paying interest on interest! Compound interest can dig you into a debt hole so big it will take years for you to climb out. If you are living beyond your means and borrowing to fund that lifestyle (like our federal government does), soon you'll be so deep in debt you can't even pay off the interest, let alone the original debt. Thanks to compound interest, your debt snowballs each month—which is why you should pay off your credit cards, in full, every month. (See Credit Cards, page 351).

What Zero Percent Financing *Really* Means

You've seen the ads. You might even have been tempted. If you buy from them, they lend you the money for free. What have you got to lose?

What they don't tell you is that the cost of that "free financing" is built into the price of the item you want to buy. So, if you're interested in a $20,000 car, you could borrow money from a traditional lender and pay $5000 in interest, or you could buy it with "zero percent financing" for $25,000.

Same goes for those "No Money Down!!!" or "Don't pay a thing till ..." events. Don't be fooled by exclamation marks. They'll get your money, one way or the other.

Your Financial Health

You pay attention to your physical health, get your flu shot, see a doctor, because you want to be sure that you're doing everything you can to stay healthy. Well, you should be paying the same attention to your financial health, because you don't want any unpleasant surprises in that department, either!

First things first: get organized. Over the years you will accumulate a truckload of paperwork, some of which is important, others not so much. Sometimes the consequences of not being able to find a document can be quite serious. (Yes, worse than losing your "little black book"!)

Records and Documents You Need to Keep

When deciding what to toss and what to hang on to, it's best to err on the side of hanging on. Here are some of the bits of paper that you'll want to find someday.

- Copies of receipts for home improvement projects and major purchases—including warranties.
- Medical health records.
- Education records, diplomas and transcripts, awards received.
- Letters of recommendation.
- Birth certificate.
- Passport.

TIP: Make copies of your birth certificate, social insurance number card, and passport. Keep originals and copies separate—if possible, leave one at your parents' place, with a trusted friend, or in a bank safe-deposit box.

- Lease or mortgage papers.
- Bank statements.
- Bankbooks, cancelled cheques, and unused cheques.
- Credit card statements.
- Credit card information—you should have a list of all your credit card numbers, PIN numbers, and numbers to call in case of stolen or lost cards.
- Tax records.
- Investment records.
- Employment records.
- Club memberships
- Your Spending Plan.

You can shred or tear the day-to-day receipts for credit card or ATM transactions after your monthly statements arrive.

You will need to find a filing cabinet (check second-hand stores) or a file box (available at some dollar stores) for your important papers. If you're still not quite settled and moving around a lot, keep the box at your parents' home. Set up folders for each of the following category of documents or receipts:

- Folder for each bank account.
- Credit cards: one folder for statements and one for receipts.
- Home: separate folders for rent receipts or mortgage statements, hydro, cable, phone, and other monthly utilities.
- Car: folder for lease or bill of sale, folders for repairs, gas.
- Income tax and tax-deductible items: folder to keep previous years' tax forms, and a folder for any tax slips, T4s, and receipts for the present year.
- Employment records: folder for paycheque stubs and any other employment-related documents.
- Folders for warranties and receipts for major appliances/electronics, etc., and any instruction manuals.

One of the best indicators of your financial health (besides the fact that you're not at the food bank or seeking handouts from us) is your credit rating. Let's look at that next …

Credit Reports

Q: Do you have a good credit rating?

    a. Whaa?

    b. As far as I know, but I have never checked.

    c. No. About the only place I can borrow from these days is the library.

Darling, pick:

    d. None of the above are good answers.

What is a credit rating?

A credit rating sums up your reputation as a borrower by evaluating your debt in the past and how well you have managed to pay it off. Who decides? That's what credit bureaus are for. They are private companies that sort of "spy" on you and your money management—or lack thereof. They give you a rating from 1 to 9, with the best score being 1. In order to be a 1 you must have paid your debts on time or within 30 days of the due date. Anyone who wants to lend you money (creditors) can contact the credit bureau to find out how good you have been about paying back your debt.

It does sound a little Orwellian, doesn't it? But it's not all bad. Once you have a credit rating—and provided it's a good one—you can get a car loan, mortgage, all those grown-up things you've been dreaming about. Get behind on your payments and you'll end up with a trashed credit rating—and higher insurance rates, little chance of borrowing for big purchases, larger security deposits when you go to rent an apartment, and maybe even missed opportunities for jobs or graduate school. After all, who wants to take on someone who is irresponsible?

How do I get a credit rating?

- To be rated you have to have had credit for at least six months.
- The easiest way to establish a credit rating is by getting a credit card. (If you're a college or university student this might be a great time because lenders are more willing to take risks with you, knowing your parents will be there to bail you out.) But be careful. If you use the credit card and pay off the balance on time, you develop a good rating. If you abuse the credit card and are late on payments or, worse, make no payments at all, that's not so good.

- For now, just get one credit card, preferably one with a low or non-existent annual fee and low interest rates. More than that and you'll look too risky to creditors.
- Use your card regularly but don't charge more than 30 percent of the card's limit, or more than you can pay off in a month. One easy way to establish a good rating—if you can stick to it: for one full year, buy a tank of gas and then a few days later pay the balance online.
- Another quick way to establish a credit history is to piggyback on someone else's good credit—like good old Mom or Dad. You can either be added to their credit card as an "authorized" or joint user, or get someone to co-sign a loan for you.

How do I keep a good rating or improve my rating?

- Close inactive or unnecessary accounts. Too much available credit lowers your score.
- Schedule bill-paying once a month, and wherever possible, set up automatic payments for your bills so you don't have to stress over paying them on time.
- Don't charge more than you can pay off in a month.
- Stay below your credit limit on credit cards and pay off your credit cards in full each month.
- Contact the credit card company if you miss a payment, and never miss more than 2 payments.

If you run into financial trouble, don't stick your head in the sand and hope it goes away. It won't. If you can't pay the bill one month, contact your creditor (that's the company you owe) and fess up. No, you will not have thugs at your door with a baseball bat—but you might be contacted by a collection agency. First, though, try to make arrangements with the creditor to make up the missed payment. If you're upfront about it, most creditors will work with you to develop a payment plan before they resort to filing information with the credit bureau.

If you're overwhelmed with debt, try negotiating a lower interest rate with creditors, or contact a good credit-counselling agency. But dear, don't ever let it get that bad. Good credit is important, not just to help you get good rates when you're ready to buy a home or a car, but also to help you get a good job, a decent apartment, or reasonable rates on insurance. If you max out your credit cards or get behind in your payments, it can haunt you for years.

Debt Is a Four-Letter Word

Honey, do you know what they're calling you and your friends now? The Debt Generation. Yup—that's your claim to fame! They say your age group is characterized by high expectations, expensive tastes, and an "I want it all now" attitude. Your generation—according to the folks who study these things—tends to spend every cent (and more) earned and is not concerned because "everyone has debt." You believe you deserve to live life to the fullest in your youth—after all, there's plenty of time for saving later.

Not exactly something to be proud of.

Of course it's not all your fault. We, as parents, have pampered you, catered to your every need, and tried to shelter you from the real world for as long as we could. We only wanted the best for you! And it's not your fault, either, that temptation is always in your face—and borrowing is so darn easy. Besides, you've got a lot on your plate right now. And you're finally out in the real world making some real money (more or less), so why the heck can't you just enjoy it?

Enough excuses! You *can* enjoy the money you make—just not the money you *don't* make. That's the thing about being a grown-up: the buck stops here. There is no better time than now to start to make a dent in your debt, or to avoid it altogether. Here's why:

> **Been** there
> **Done** THAT
>
> Oh, I don't know. Clipping coupons—that's just not for me. I'm not the frugal type. None of my friends are. We talk about how bad it is that we're not saving our money, and then next thing you know, we're heading out for a night on the town.
>
> —SCOTT, 21

- You've just started to make money and so you are used to living on the cheap.
- You're flexible—no baggage (spouse or kids), and you're still probably willing to have a roommate or take public transport to cut costs.
- You don't have a mortgage or minivan payments.
- You can still travel cheap, stay in hostels, backpack.

If you take care not to accumulate debt now, or at least get out of any debt you have, you won't have to live the starving-student lifestyle when you're middle-aged. You will end up way ahead, financially, of your indulgent, overspending peers.

How to Avoid Debt

Take care of your "needs" first

Learn to distinguish between "needs" and "wants." "Needs" are the necessities of life. There are actually very few items in the "needs" list. Most things fall into the category of "wants." Unlike "needs," "wants" can be different for each person, and the price tag attached can differ too.

You *need* food and water and a safe place to sleep. Clothing is helpful—keeps you from being cold or indecent. Anything beyond that's a bonus. Really. You don't have to have a car or bus fare. You could walk. Drinkable tap water is a "need"; the fancy bottled stuff is a "want." Your TV might be black-and-white and get only three channels but it's still a "want." You don't even need that. Read a book at the library or watch TV at a friend's place instead. It's easy at your age to get caught up in image and status. Think about it: will you get enough enjoyment out of that new home theatre system you just bought to continue paying for it for the next 15 years when it has become obsolete? Take pleasure in the things you have; don't obsess over the things you don't have.

Ask yourself the following questions

Before you use credit to buy something, ask:

- Is this a "need" or a "want"?
- If it is a "need," do you really need it now, or can you wait?
- If you do need it now, what can you give up in order to afford it?
- If there is nothing you can give up, what will be the cost of using credit?
- Can you afford the monthly payments?
- When can you reasonably expect to pay the credit off?
- What will be the extra cost of borrowing on credit if it takes you that long to pay it off?
- Now, ask yourself one more time: is this really necessary, and is it worth the extra money it will actually cost in the end?

Maintain an accurate account of your finances: Balance your chequebook, keep accurate records of all your purchases, and stick to your Spending Plan.

Leave your debit card at home: Pay for everything with cash.

Avoid credit card debt like the plague: Don't charge to your credit card unless you can pay the entire balance monthly. Keep track of your credit card receipts and set aside an equivalent amount of money so you will have it on hand to pay off the balance on your statement the minute it arrives.

Warning Signs That You Are in Over Your Head

You might be in financial trouble if you are:
- Unable to put any money away in savings.
- Using savings to pay debt.
- At or over your credit limit on all your credit cards and accounts.
- Missing payments or due dates for your bills.

No amount of whining will get you out of debt. You need to take immediate action and follow these steps:

1. Set a goal for when you can realistically be debt-free. You can use an online debt calculator (like www.Bankrate.com) to determine how much you need to pay each month.
2. Put your credit cards on ice—literally. Put them in a plastic bag and put them in the freezer.
3. Do not charge anything new. You can't get out of the hole if you keep digging it deeper.
4. Determine where you can cut back so that savings can go toward debt. Look at your Spending Plan to see where cuts can be made. (See tips for cutting expenses on page 345.)

5. Pay off credit card debt first. Start with the higher-interest credit cards and work your way down until the lowest-rate card is paid off.

6. Once your credit card debt is gone, charge only what you can pay off each month.

7. Now look at your other loans. If your loan agreement does not include pre-payment penalties, consider making extra payments, even doubling your payments. Increasing a $203 minimum payment to $403 on a $20,000 loan will have you debt-free in 5 years instead of 10.

8. If you're still having trouble, or if you just can't seem to control your spending urges, consider contacting your local consumer credit counselling service.

Student Loans: Not All Debt Is "Evil"

So, you decided to invest in yourself and your future, you've been studying hard for the past few years, and graduation has finally arrived. You landed the job. You made yourself a Spending Plan. You're sticking with it. Time to make some serious money with those extra letters behind your name. Yes, life is good.

Then, *wham!* You get the letter in the mail: Canada Student Loans. Payback time!

Take a deep breath, then dig out the loan agreement that you signed so many years ago. Here's what you probably agreed to:

Full-time students

- You must begin to repay your loan 6 months after the day you completed or ended your full-time studies.
- Interest on your loan starts being calculated from this date as well.
- Rates and conditions for repayment are set at the time you begin repaying.

Part-time students

- Same terms as full-time students, only you have to also make interest payments on your loan while you are still in school.

You might have heard rumours of other students having their loans waived. Yes, this did happen at one time in the distant past. But this is the new millennium; don't count on it now. There are sometimes ways you can get relief on the interest, reduce your loan, and—on the rare occasion—have your loan "forgiven." To see if you qualify for deferment or partial cancellation, or to find out how to set up a repayment plan, visit your student assistance centre or www.canlearn.ca. For Ontario Student Assistance Plan (OSAP) loans, check out http://osap.gov.on.ca. Remember that missing or defaulting on payments can hurt that all-important credit rating.

TIP: Make sure you inform your student loan office if you move. If they don't know how to contact you and you miss a payment, you'll end up with bad credit.

When You're on the *Other* Side of Debt

Your pal's hit some hard times. He could really use a small loan, and you've been doing really well in your new job. Should you lend him a few bucks? It's a dilemma. You don't want to look like a tightwad. On the other hand, you've heard stories about people who've been stiffed by friends. Research shows that the majority of people surveyed have seen someone skip out on a friend, or a relationship end, because of unpaid debt. So what do you do?

First of all, if it's just a small amount, if you're not sure your bud's going to be able to pay you back, if it's a one-shot deal or you just don't want the hassle of hassling him, you can always offer the money as a gift. Once. Or you can just say sorry, you know of someone who lent a friend money and now the friendship's messed up and you really don't want that to ever happen to you two. If you have any other suggestions to help him out of his fix, soften the "no" with that.

If you do have the money and decide to lend a hand, be sure to keep a record. Don't make a big formal deal out of it. Just matter-of-factly grab a piece of paper and jot down the loan amount, the date of the loan, and a schedule for repayment. Sign it, and get him to sign too. That way you've got a record when payback time comes. And if payback doesn't come, you can send a few reminders your friend's way, but if he doesn't come through in the end, you'll just have to chalk it up to experience. Maybe a deadbeat friend wasn't much of a friend after all. Next time, "neither a borrower nor a lender be"—as Shakespeare put it.

The Opposite of Debt—Savings

What a concept—savings! I mean, what's more important—a plasma TV or a comfy nest-egg making money for you? (No need to answer that.) Believe it or not, you will get older, and you will want to retire some day. And the sooner you begin to save, the sooner you can do whatever the heck you want.

Registered Retirement Savings Plans

A Registered Retirement Savings Plan (RRSP) is a personal savings plan registered with the Canadian federal government that allows you to save for the future without being taxed on those savings. It's the Canadian government's way of helping you save money for your retirement.

I know, thinking about retirement is the farthest thing from your mind. After all, you're just starting out. You have lots of time to save. Well, honey, that's just it! You do have lots of time to save. Just think of the possibilities if you start socking it away now! It's all about compound interest. You do remember what that is, don't you? If not, turn back, right now, to page 363 and read.

Why You Should Start Your RRSP Today

Having money in an RRSP is not a guarantee that you will be able to retire comfortably. However, it is a guarantee that the investments will gather compound interest—without being taxed—as long as the funds are not withdrawn. This is called "tax-deferred growth." Notice I didn't say "tax-free." You do have to pay tax on the profits in your RRSP, but not until you withdraw the money. Ideally, you won't be removing your money until you are retired and in a much lower tax bracket, therefore paying far less tax on this income.

The second major benefit of contributing to an RRSP is that it gives you a tax credit. You can deduct the amount of money you put into your RRSP against your taxable income and end up either paying less tax, no tax, or even getting a refund. For example: If your taxable income is $30,000 and you invest $2000 in an RRSP, your taxable income is reduced by $2000 and becomes $28,000. At the lowest tax bracket, 26 percent, that is a savings of $520 (26 percent of $2000). Better in your pocket than the taxman's!

You can borrow from your RRSP to help pay for your first home (the Home Buyer's Plan), or for your education (Lifelong Learning Plan).

Convinced? Then get to it! It's easy. Any financial institution (bank, credit union, etc.) or investment house can open an RRSP account for you, as well as offer advice on investments within your RRSP. You can even set up an RRSP account online on the website of pretty much any of the major Canadian banks, as well as online investment brokerages. How much money do you need? That depends on the types of investments in your account and how they are being managed. You can have an institution manage your RRSP or you can manage your own, called a self-directed RRSP.

Managed RRSPs

- Your money is invested in a government-registered bank account in the form of GICs (guaranteed investment certificates) and/or stocks and mutual funds.
- The investment manager that manages your account makes all the necessary investment decisions on your behalf. (If you have trouble deciding what to have for dinner, this is definitely the route to go.)
- Fees and costs involved in managed RRSPs vary widely, depending on the types of investments and the way they are managed, so read the fine print! The least-expensive management fees start at approximately 1.5 percent of the value of your investment portfolio (the amount of money you have invested in RRSPs), including administration fees, commission, and transfer fees. The most expensive managed RRSPs charge around 2.5 percent of your investment portfolio, plus annual administration fees and transaction costs.

Self-directed RRSPs

If you're still having trouble balancing your chequebook, don't even consider a self-directed RRSP. At this stage in your life, you have too many other decisions to make, and your future financial security is not worth risking. Leave it to the professionals ... please!

When can I contribute?

You might only hear people talking about RRSPs in February, with the March 1 deadline fast approaching. This is when the banks and investment houses produce huge advertising campaigns. However, you can make contributions any time during the calendar year and up to 60 days (before March 1) of the following year, and still be eligible for an RRSP deduction for the current tax year.

How do I know how much I can contribute each year?

There is a limit to how much money you can actually put into your RRSP each year. This limit is based on your previous year's earned income. You can check with the Canada Customs and Revenue Department for the current maximum amounts (www.cra-arc.gc.ca/). The following is a summarized guideline:

- You can contribute to your RRSP until December 31 of the year you turn 69.
- You can contribute 18 percent of your earned income from the previous year, up to a maximum of the annual contribution limit for the taxation year.
- The exact amount you can contribute to your RRSP for the current year can be found on the Notice of Assessment you get from the Canada Revenue Agency after they process your previous year's tax return. Remember this is one of those pesky forms you must save!

What happens if I contribute too much?

Relax. You can contribute $2000 more than your contribution limit without penalty. Note that this is not an annual thing—it's the maximum you can over-contribute in your lifetime. If you exceed this limit, you are penalized heavily until your next assessment, when you will be able to contribute your usual amount, less the amount over $2000 that you contributed.

What if I want to, but I don't have any money to contribute?

- Check your budget. Can you tinker with it a bit, find a way to reduce other expenses? Think of it as paying yourself first—investing in your future. For ideas, go back to page 345.
- If you really can't contribute, or can't contribute the entire amount, don't worry—the government allows you a "Carry Forward." You use your unused contribution limit in later years when you have the money to invest.
- Remember, investing even a little now makes a huge difference later. For example, let's say you start investing $1000 per year for 40 years starting at age 25—and miraculously keep it up until you are 65. At 10 percent interest, compounded annually, you will have almost $445,000 in the bank—and you only invested $40,000! Now let's say you wait until you are 45 before you start, and invest $2000 per year for 20 years, when you turn 65. Assuming the same rate of interest, you

will have close to $115,000 in the bank. In both cases you invested $40,000, but by starting at age 25, you end up with almost $330,000 more. Aren't you glad you are still so young? Don't you just love that compound interest?

Preparing Your Income Tax Return

Remember how freaked out your dad and I used to get at the end of April—all those papers strewn across the kitchen table, the tapping away at a calculator, the riffling through filing cabinets? Guess what? It's your turn. No, you can't skip this part and marry an accountant. Just sit down and let me explain what this is all about.

You live in Canada; you have a job. By law, you must:

- File a tax return for each year's income by the deadline of April 30 of the following year.
- Pay the correct amount of tax each year on time.
- Give the CRA (Canada Revenue Agency) the information necessary to assess the tax return for the year.

Even if you don't owe money, there are still plenty of good reasons to file a tax return. You could be:

- Entitled to a GST credit.
- Eligible to carry forward your tuition education amounts.
- Eligible for a tax refund (even if you didn't pay any tax).

Let's face it, if you haven't had the urge to become an accountant before now, completing your own tax return is not likely to create a sudden desire to do so. After all, the most popular guide to preparing your income tax return is more than a thousand pages long. It's possible you have more exciting things to do than read that. However, it is a good idea to try to complete your own return at least once and then get a professional to do it. Compare the two returns. You might be surprised and discover you are a tax genius, or you will see how many errors you have made, or costly deductions and tax credits you have missed.

If you attend post-secondary school, you might find accounting students willing to help for a low fee or no fee, with the professors supervising. Some community centres also offer low-cost tax-filing services for students and seniors. There are tax software programs if you want to try it yourself. Or for $50 and up, you can hire a professional

More than You Really Wanted to Know

You Snooze, You Lose: There is a penalty for filing late which includes the taxes due, an initial penalty calculated as a percentage of the taxes due, and interest on the outstanding balance for as long as it remains unpaid. (This interest is calculated at a very high rate.) If you don't file a return at all, you are guilty of an offence, and if convicted, subject to a fine and possible imprisonment.

(like H&R Block). Don't make the mistake of paying extra for "instant cash back." You don't need to spend the extra for instant cash because it should only take two weeks after filing by Internet. Surely you can wait that long!

Other advantages of using a tax preparation agency:

- If you don't get the maximum refund that you're entitled to on your taxes, they may refund their fee.
- If they make an error on your tax return that costs you any interest or penalty, they may reimburse you for those costs.
- Some provide 12 months of tax support with every return they complete.
- They may offer online services where you can complete your taxes.
- Some offer discounted services for students … and even throw in a free pizza!

And finally, you could always ask (beg/bargain/pay) Mom or Dad to give you a hand. After all, they've been doing this happy job for a lot of years.

Tax Record-Keeping: What You'll Need to Hang on to

- T4 slips: Anyone you have been employed by in the calendar year must provide you with two copies of a T4 slip on or before the last day of February following the calendar year to which the slips apply. The T4 is a record of how much you earned.
- T5 slips: This is a record of your investment income. For example, you will get a T5 from your bank for any interest earned on your account in the calendar year.
- Your paystubs from each month. Make sure they add up to the same amount as on your T4.
- Receipts for deductible expenses, such as charitable donations.

TIP: Save all receipts related to your job, or your search for one—things like resumé services, trade magazine subscriptions, dues for professional association membership. You might be eligible for tax savings.

- If you are a student:
  —You must download your tuition credit form T2202a from http://www. cra-arc.gc.ca. Click on "Forms and Publications."
  —Keep rent receipts from your landlord.
  —Record moving expenses when you return home for the summer to work.
- Notice of Assessment: This is a notice issued by the CRA to a tax filer after the return has been processed. It tells the individual whether the CRA made any corrections to his or her return and what they were. It also lets the individual know:
  —Whether he or she owes more tax.
  —What his or her refund will be.
  —What his or her Registered Retirement Savings Plan deduction limit for the next tax year will be.

Once you have your papers together, it's time to begin. Visit your post office or the local Canada Revenue Agency office to obtain the necessary tax forms, or download and print them from the Internet.

Contact information for Canada Revenue Agency

The telephone numbers and address of your local tax services office can be found in the Government section of your telephone book, or at: www.cra.gc.ca. For help with taxation questions, click on "My Account."

Holding on to What You've Got: Smart Shopping Suggestions

Remember cruising the malls on a Saturday—you and your pals, whiling away the hours, whittling away at your wallets? Wasn't that fun! Shopping can still be fun, even though, as a fledgling adult, your wallet's nearly empty.

The marketing guys desperately want you to view shopping as entertainment, and they use every trick in the book—store layouts, slick ads, marketing research—to part you from your brass. Well, two can play at that game!

Here's what we'll call our game: How Little Can You Spend? In other words, how can you outwit the retailers? Who will end up with more of your cash—you, or the store? If saving money sounds like work, turn it into a game or hobby. Read the flyers, research the options, find out how to get the best deal, how to fix things instead of replacing them. Impress your friends with your new-found knowledge.

You don't have to turn into a cheapskate, go to work wearing a flour sack, or sleep on the floor. Simple things can make a big difference. Say you normally buy a $1 bottle of pop at the convenience store every day. Skip it. At the end of the year, you'll have an additional $365 in your pocket. Say you order a pizza every Friday night at $20 a shot. Don't. You've just saved yourself an extra $1040. Simple, no? And next time you find yourself tempted by a sassy pair of shoes, look at the price compared to your after-tax salary. *How* many hours do you have to work to pay for it? Do you still want it?

Here are some more frugal ideas:

- *Spread the word.* Let your friends know that you're trying to save your money, and then suggest alternatives for entertainment. They want to go shopping? Suggest a walk in the park. They want to dine out? Suggest a potluck. If you're lucky, they too will be happy to pocket the cash.
- *Learn to haggle.* Comparison shop, then ask if the retailer or service provider can match or beat the best price. See if they'll give you a break if you pay cash. If it's the end of a season, try to get a discount.
- *Keep a jar or bowl on top of the fridge.* Dump your spare change into it at the end of the day. Try not to think about it. Ever. Check it out at the end of the year. Surprise! Take it to the bank.
- *Lead yourself not into temptation.* Do you really want all those catalogues cluttering your mailbox and coffee table, tempting you to buy? Pitch them. Remove yourself from the mailing lists.
- *When you buy clothes, examine the label.* If it says "Dry Clean Only," think about how much you'll be spending to keep the outfit looking nice. Look for clothing that can simply be tossed in the wash. And if you do use a dry cleaner, go to its website. Not only might you discover a list of sales (e.g., 50 percent off dry-cleaning of winter coats in July), they often also post discount coupons.

- *Return things on time.* You're not saving anything when you use the library and then have to pay late fees every month. DVD rentals are really pricey if you add on a regular late fee. And video stores might say they've eliminated late fees, but if you read the fine print, you'll see the fees are still there.
- *Don't be lazy.* Raining? Skip the cab—pack an umbrella and walk. Or walk the three blocks to your own ATM and pocket the $1.50 you'd otherwise spend at the closer machine.
- *When money falls into your lap, bank it.* The birthday cash from Grandma, the unexpected tax refund, the minuscule pay raise—sock it away.
- *Scan the newspaper flyers.* It will help you learn about prices and avoid overpaying. If you see a good deal, but you get to the store and they've run out, ask their Customer Service Department for a raincheck, which lets you buy the item at the advertised sale price later, when they've restocked. You can also bring a flyer from one store to another store and ask if they will honour the competitor's advertised prices. Many stores do. If you don't get newspaper delivery, you can usually find the flyers displayed at the store's entrance, or check them out on the store's website.

TIP: Always put your receipts and product information in the same place so you know where to look if you have to return something or have it repaired.

- *Don't buy something just because you have a coupon.* Who cares if you save 75 cents, if it's something you would never buy otherwise?
- *Plan ahead.* If you are planning to stay in a hotel, then check out their website. There might be a discount coupon lurking there. Many websites offer coupons.
- *Limit "big ticket" expenditures.* Most people, when they're just starting out, move around a lot. If you spend your money on big things—like couches and fridges—you'll just have to lug them around with you.
- *Make the Internet work for you.* Comparison shop. Use eBay. Check out second-hand sources, like www.half.com, www.craigslist.org, etc. For bigger items, read the online reviews before you buy to make sure the product is as good as it sounds. If there's a product that you really like and buy often, Google the product's name and "+coupon."
- And if you're really inspired to live frugally, *check out the myriad of websites devoted to living on the cheap,* starting with: www.thefrugalshopper.com, www.simpleliving.net, www.frugaliving.com.

Beware the Following Sales Methods

Smart shoppers don't let themselves be snowed or bullied by these common techniques:

- Just because an item says "Sale," that doesn't mean it's a bargain. Know your prices, compare.
- Think carefully before you buy store membership reward cards or coupon books. Make sure you're not paying more than you'd save. Is this a store you'd otherwise shop in regularly?
- Stores often advertise lower prices based on manufacturer rebates—which many customers forget to send in. If you want the money back, stick it in the mail immediately. Keep your receipt and make sure you do get the refund.
- "Package deals" are no deal if you don't want the other items in the package.
- Loss-leaders are items that stores advertise at super-cheap prices to lure you into the store. Many times they will have very few of these items in stock. This is called the "Bait and Switch." Retailers hope you'll load up the cart with other items while you're there.
- Salespeople sometimes pressure buyers with deadlines ("Buy Now!") or limited quantities ("While Supplies Last!"). Don't be swayed by emotion or adrenaline or exclamation marks.
- Hidden costs: Read and listen carefully. There are often extra costs or disclaimers hidden in the fine print, or quickly scrolled on the TV commercial. Remember the fast-talking "*batteriesnotincluded*" guy who sold you toys between Saturday morning cartoons? He's still around, with more quick add-ons like "*shippingandhandlingextra.*"

TIP: Always ask about the store's return policy before you buy. Some have good return policies; others, not so good. They might provide only "store credit," which requires you to spend an equal amount on something else in the store. Look out for time limits for returns, return with receipt only, or no return on clearance items.

What to Buy When

You can usually count on certain items being reduced in price at specific times of the year. When you need to buy something retail, check here to see which month you're most likely to find it on sale.

January

- "White Sale" items, meaning things for your bed—sheets, pillowcases, etc.
- Exercise equipment and sports gear.
- Televisions.
- Computers.
- Winter wear: hats, boots, coats, scarves, and gloves.
- Air conditioners.
- Bikes and outdoor gear—old models making way for new.

February

- Furniture.
- Rugs.
- Curtains.
- Housewares, including china, glassware, and silverware.
- Stereo equipment.
- Jewellery.
- Chocolates.
- Mattresses.
- Fragrances, toiletries.
- Used cars.
- Resort and cruise wear.

March

- Gardening supplies.
- Luggage.
- Spring clothing.
- Frozen foods.
- Shoes.
- Laundry appliances.
- Winter sports equipment.
- Spring jackets and raincoats.

April

- Eggs.
- Anything Easter-related after Easter.
- Suits.
- Kosher food.
- Wallpaper and paint.
- Vacuum cleaners.

May

- More "White Sale" items, including blankets.
- Summer purses.
- Spring-cleaning supplies.
- Lingerie.
- Sportswear.
- Tires.
- Barbecue and picnic supplies.

June

- Summer clothing.
- TVs and portable music players.
- Refrigerators.
- Building supplies, renovation materials.
- Fabric.

July

- Air conditioners.
- Shoes.
- Bathing suits.
- Lingerie.
- Major appliances.
- Stereo equipment.
- Rugs and carpets.
- Summer sports equipment.
- Furniture.
- Used cars.
- Craft supplies.

August

- Furniture.
- More "White Sale" items, including linens and bedding.
- Camping equipment.
- Lamps.
- Pre-season fall fashions, including coats.
- Tires.
- Gardening tools, including lawn mowers.
- Barbecues.

- Air conditioners and fans.
- Back-to-school supplies.
- Bathing suits.
- Outdoor furniture.
- Local produce (fruits and veggies).
- New cars.

September

- Back-to-school supplies and clothing.
- Canned goods.
- Housewares, dishes, glassware.
- Bicycles and scooters.
- Car batteries and mufflers.
- Garden tools.
- Lamps.
- Carpets and rugs.
- Tools, painting supplies.

October

- Hosiery.
- Thanksgiving items.
- Outdoor sports and fishing equipment.
- Hallowe'en treats.
- Cars (toward end of month).

November

- Coats, fall and winter clothing.
- Blankets, comforters, quilts.
- Christmas items.
- Shoes, boots.
- Suits.
- Kitchen appliances.

December

- Toys.
- Party and gift items.
- Shoes.
- Coats.
- Used cars.
- The day after Christmas, Boxing Day, is loaded with bargains—look for jewellery, perfume, ties, wallets, and sweaters. It's also a good time to stock up on holiday wrap and cards at half-price or less.

TIP: If you are interested in buying something not on sale, ask the store clerk when it will likely be on sale.

Second-Hand Shopping

Honey, I take some responsibility here. When you were a baby I couldn't resist the Gap T-shirts, the handmade leather booties, and do you remember the Red River winter coat? That was just darling. But here's the thing: you can't afford to shop in malls any more—at least, not for everything. Let me introduce you to something called Second-Hand Shopping.

If the whole idea of buying "used" sends shivers down your spine (Eeww! I gotta go inside those smelly stores, touch the polyester pants, sit on the wobbly, cobwebby furniture next to the bag ladies …), then darling, it might be time to have another look. Second-hand is not what it used to be. It's cool, it's hip, it's where it's at … or at least, it would be, if more people just gave it a chance.

Buying used goods is cheaper, obviously, but there are other advantages. It's good for the environment—cuts down on manufacturing pollution and plundering of

Been there
Done THAT

Taylor brought some old clothes to donate to Goodwill and came back with more than he brought in. His friends compliment him all the time on the dandy corduroy jacket he found. Now they all shop there. They look very cool.

—JOANNE, TAYLOR'S MOM

resources; it does not add to the problem of Third World slave labour; and when you refuse to get sucked into the mass-marketing hype for trendy gotta-have-it whatevers, when you buy something with personality, you get a chance to express your unique personality.

Still, the overriding plus is price. It's amazing what deals you can find if you just take the time to shop outside the box. There are garage sales, classified ads, community billboards, estate sales, second-hand websites like eBay, community bulletin boards (check the board at your local grocery store), flea markets, thrift shops (which usually feature donated goods), and consignment stores (where people bring in their gently used items and share the profit with the storeowner). And then, of course, there's good old garbage pickup day. Remember that little night table by your bed back home? Guess where that came from! There's no shame in recycling; hold your head high and give dumpster-diving a try!

TIP: Don't buy anything that requires re-upholstering. It's expensive.

Of course, shopping second-hand is nothing like the mall. You won't find hip tunes, smiling salespeople, and racks and racks of your size in different colours. It is a little more work. It can require you to get up at dawn to hit the sales—and the deals—before the other bargain-hunters. But it can also turn into a fun and rewarding hobby if you follow some of the following rules:

- Shop often. You may not find what you want right away. Keep at it. Something's sure to turn up.
- Keep your mind open. Don't set out with a rigid idea of what you want. You won't find it—but you might find something else that will work just as well.
- Shop with cash. You'll have more bargaining power.
- Don't buy junk, just because it's cheap. Inspect the item carefully. Look for tears, breaks, and other things that you can't—or know you won't—fix. And steer clear of just plain ugly.
- Grab it if it's good. The nature of bargain-hunting requires you to make quick decisions, before someone else snaps it up.
- If you're shopping for furniture, make sure you can get it home. Bring a truck or a strong friend—or both.
- Never—ever—buy second-hand undies (but of course you already knew that).

What to buy used

- Clothing.
- Jewellery.
- Furniture.
- Computers.
- Housewares.
- Books.
- DVDs and CDs.

- Vehicles.
- Electronics.
- Appliances.
- Musical instruments.
- Software and video games.
- Sports equipment.

A Fool and His Money Are Soon Parted

We come into this world with lots of lessons to learn—but we also come with instincts. Use them, and remember these simple, sad truths:

1. Nothing in life is free.
2. If it sounds too good to be true, then it probably is.
3. The world is filled with people who want to take your money.

These shady folks are smart; you've got to be smarter. Familiarize yourself with these common rules and red flags so that you don't get sucked in.

- Don't release any personal information to anyone unless you are clear who it is, why they want it, and how the information will be used. Is the person asking for more information than he/she really needs?
- Don't ever let anyone pressure you into paying for something before you're ready. Watch for words like "final offer" and "urgent." Be wary of overly enthusiastic salespeople and offers that are too good to be true.
- Before you sign anything or pay money up front, thoroughly check out the business and the fine points of the deal.
- Read every detail before you sign anything. Make sure you understand it.
- Get a written contract or other documentation before you give out your credit card or other personal information.
- Don't do business with anyone until you've checked out their company's permanent address and phone number. If you don't know the company, contact the Better Business Bureau first. Steer clear of a company that only provides a post office box number, rather than a street address.

- Illegitimate companies often adopt names or logos that closely resemble respected companies.
- Never comply with a demand for payment to be picked up by courier or sent to a mail drop or post office box.
- A trial offer with "no obligation" to buy is one of those "too good to be true" deals. Usually there are strict requirements or conditions to the return, and you might find yourself locked into the purchase.

Suspect a scam if you see any of these warning signs:

- Phone calls, letters, or e-mails that ask for personal information for "identification" or "verification." This information can be used for unauthorized credit card charges or bank account debits.
- You are told that you have won a prize, but you have to pay something first.
- Work-at-home schemes that require you to purchase a kit or instructions.
- Unsolicited e-mails from well-known companies. They might be from criminals trying to get your credit card number or other personal information.
- Rigged ATMs. Choose another location if you notice anything unusual about the machine, or if you suspect someone is reading your PIN. There might be a hidden or cellphone camera recording you.
- Being asked to pay a processing fee for a loan.

Identity Theft

And you thought a house break-in felt like a personal invasion! Identity theft (the unauthorized use of your personal information) has long-term consequences, financial and otherwise. Basically it will really wreck your day, your month, your year. It's one of the fastest-growing crimes in Canada and the United States and it will be with us for a long time. The faster you recognize what's happening, the better off you'll be. Here are some obvious signs:

- Your bills and/or financial statements are not arriving on time.
- You are getting calls from collection agencies or creditors for accounts you don't have.
- An account has been opened in your name.
- Bank or credit card statements show withdrawals or transfers you didn't make.

- You get weird calls from credit cards companies, e.g., "Congratulations, you have been approved for ..."
- You get statements for credit cards you don't have.
- And our fave, you are denied credit because you are so over-extended. (Assuming that you are not.)

Okay, here's how to protect yourself (no guarantees):

- Check your bank and credit card statements *always.*
- Do not share personal information, and in Canada be careful who you give your social insurance number (SIN) to.
- Do not carry all your identification in your wallet.
- Care to do a little dumpster-diving? That's where the bad guys might find tons of your personal info because you have not ripped up or shredded your bank and credit card statements, receipts, and all sorts of other goodies.
- Shred old chequebooks and cut up old credit cards.

They got you anyway

Call your credit card company immediately, day or night. Depending on your area, call your bank, too. Next, call the cops. No, they won't send a squad car around with lights twirling and siren blaring, but they will file a police report, which means that you'll have started your own paper trail. Get a copy! They will also send the police report to your creditor. Hey, it's a start. Listen to their advice and follow through.

Resources

General financial information

www.yourmoney.cbc.ca

www.cfp-ca.org—Click "Public," then "Resources," then "Educating Youth." "Focus on Your Finances" is a free, downloadable, 32-page brochure aimed at 15- to 25-year-olds.

Stretching your dollar

www.freecycle.org
www.stretcher.com
www.half.com
www.craigslist.org
www.thefrugalshopper.com
www.simpleliving.net
www.frugaliving.com

Work-at-home job scams

http://www.workathomecareers.com/scams.shtml

Credit and credit cards

Financial Consumer Agency has a new tool, Credit Card Interactive. It helps you find cards that meet your needs and compare: www.fcac.gc.ca.

Calculate which credit card will cost you the least in interest and fees based on how you use your card at www.strategis.gc.ca. Go to "Site Map," then "C" for "Credit Card Costs Calculator."

Go here to check out your credit rating:
www.freecreditreportservice.com
www.consumerinfo.com
www.experian.com
www.freecreditreport.com
www.qspace.com

For a copy of your credit report contact:
Equifax Canada Inc.
Box 190 Jean-Talon Station
Montreal, Quebec, H1S 2Z2
1-800-465-7166

Trans Union Consumer Relations Department
P.O. Box 338-LCD1
Hamilton, Ontario, L8L 7W2
1-800-663-9980

Credit Counselling

In Ontario:
Credit Counselling Canada, Referral line: 1-800-267-2272
Ontario Association of Credit Counselling Services: 905-945-5644; 1-888-7IN DEBT
(1-888-746-3328)

Outside Ontario:
Alberta: 1-888-294-0077
Atlantic Canada: 1-800-539-2227
British Columbia: 604-527-8999
Manitoba: 204-989-1900
Newfoundland: 709-753-5812
Saskatchewan: 306-787-5387

   Also, in Toronto there are Credit Education Centres in 10 locations and a telephone counselling service: 416-228-DEBT (3328) or 1-800-267-2272.
You can also go online for a debt assessment: www.creditcanada.com.

Student Loans

www.canlearn.ca—this site has all the information you will need concerning getting a
   loan, repaying a loan, and calculating your loan payments, as well as a wealth of
   information on financial planning, budgeting, and keeping yourself debt-free.
For Ontario Student Assistance Plan (OSAP) loans, go to: http://osap.gov.on.ca.

Registered Retirement Savings Plans

Check out: http://www.investopedia.com/university/rrsp/rrsp10.asp

Income tax

For general information and forms:
http://www.cra-arc.gc.ca

For special student rates at H&R Block:
www.hrblock.ca/services/student_tax.asp

Identity theft

Go to www.rcmp.ca/scams/student_guide_e.htm for information on protecting your-self from identity fraud—one of the fastest-growing crimes in Canada.

14

Getting There

Leave sooner, drive slower, live longer.

—AUTHOR UNKNOWN

Honey, we know you miss your family now that you are on your own ... but we have a sneaking suspicion that what you miss just as much is the family car. Well, a car costs big bucks, so let's talk alternatives.

Taking Public Transit

Why not ride in a $300,000 vehicle that you have paid for out of your hard-earned paycheque? (Assuming you have paid taxes.) Depending where you live, public transit can get you there pretty efficiently, with buses, streetcars, or subways.

Some employers give fare subsidies as an incentive to employees to commute by transit. Universities often have separate deals with the transit companies and might offer free passes or student fares. Ask!

Find the quickest route to your destination by checking the transit company's website or phoning their information line. Printed bus and train maps are also typically available at libraries, bus depots, tourist information booths, and other civic locations. Get the route number. Buses display their route number and final stop in their front window. It's also helpful

TIP: If you are travelling to the United States and plan to use public transit while you're there, you can access the American Public Transportation Association for useful information, at www.apta.com/links/state_local/. Or call or fax: phone 202-496-4800 / fax 202-496-4321.

to find out how often the bus or streetcar arrives at your stop—the difference between an every-five-minutes bus and an every-half-hour bus can have a big impact on your day! Operators on the information phone line can also help you estimate how long your trip will take.

Never taken public transit before? Here are some suggestions:

- Arrive at least five minutes before the posted time.
- Make sure you're standing on the correct side of the street, at a regular stop or shelter.
- In the country or the burbs if you see your bus coming, it can't hurt to put out an arm to let the driver know you're waiting to be picked up.
- If you have any doubts about the route, *ask the driver* before boarding. Say "Good morning" when you get on and "Thanks" on your way out, especially if the driver has waited for you to catch up or shown any other special courtesy. If this is her regular route, you'll want a civil *nodding acquaintance* relationship. It pays to be nice.
- Unless you have a transit pass, tickets, or tokens, you'll need exact change.
- If you must get on a connecting bus, streetcar, or subway, take a *transfer* wherever you first board. It's good for a set time period (usually an hour) from when you get it. When you board your next vehicle, show or give the transfer to the driver. Remember that transfers can be used only at connecting points (e.g., getting off a northbound bus and onto an eastbound bus) and within the allotted time. So you can't get off the bus, walk six blocks, and get on another one, or get off the subway at a mall, go shopping and have lunch, and use your transfer to get home. If you have any doubts, ask a driver or other transit official.
- Move to the back of the vehicle whenever possible. Seats near the front are reserved for older or disabled passengers. Give up your seat to someone who needs it more than you do—your turn will come, one day.
- If you are going to be on the bus for a while, take a window seat rather than sitting on the aisle and making people squeeze past you to sit down at the window. And don't stand in front of the doors if you are not planning to exit any time soon.

Duh moment!

Hey, you are not in grade school any longer. Once you're off, don't cross the street until the bus has pulled away.

- Drivers usually announce major intersections or stops (in some places, this is now mandatory). If this is your first trip, tell the driver when you board which stop you are looking for, and sit near the front of the bus. Pull the black cord that runs above the window a block before your stop to let the driver know you want to get off. Disembark from the back door.
- In rural areas, if you are waiting for a bus in the dark on a regular basis, by all means be creative. A flashlight might be needed to get the driver's attention, and after a few nights he will start looking for you. (Do this in the city and you'll look like a dork.)

TIP: The Toronto Transit Commission offers a Request Stop program for women travelling on a bus between 9 p.m. and 5 a.m. If requested, the driver will let you off at a point that is not a regular stop, for passenger safety. This is great if your stop is farther from your home than feels safe to walk at night.

Bus Safety

If someone is being disruptive or putting the moves on you, move to another part of the bus. Tell the driver. In *most* cases the driver will be able to control other passengers. No one really wants to be tossed off a bus. Remember, though, before getting off the bus in a huff: you are safer on the bus than you are in an isolated spot.

Subway

If you are connecting with another form of transit (bus or streetcar), and you don't have a transit pass, don't forget to get a transfer when you enter the subway station, after you pay your fare. Usually these are provided by push-button machines that spit out the transfers (try to restrain yourself from pushing the button multiple times just for the fun of it!). Sometimes the bus or streetcar you need will come right into the subway station and you won't need the transfer, but unless you're really sure, better safe than sorry.

If you're travelling at night, be sure you know when the last subway train is leaving. Many cities have alternative all-night bus and streetcar service, and it's good to know about these so you have a Plan B if you find you've been partying a little later than you'd planned.

Be aware of safety on the subway platform. Stand with others, if possible, not by yourself. Some subway systems have special waiting areas on the platforms, with brighter lights, a closed-circuit camera, an intercom to connect you with the ticket collector, or other safety provisions. When riding the subway, avoid the end cars and empty subway cars. And as Petula Clark once sang, "Don't sleep in the subway, darling ..." Oh, guess you're way too young to remember that song ...

Bike to Work

Seven hundred people die in biking accidents in the United States every year. Hundreds of thousands get hurt. Know this: if you are on a bike and you have an altercation with a car, truck, or bus, you will lose, *no matter who is right.*

Don't let me discourage you. Biking uses the right kind of fuel—calories. And here's the bonus: it's cost-effective and easy on the environment.

Bike Fuel

Eat a decent breakfast fortified with calcium, vitamins A, D2, B12, and riboflavin, and carry a fresh bottle of water.

If you decide to ride your bike to work:

- Try to shift your work hours. Do what you can to avoid rush-hour traffic.
- Most people hop on a bike and take the same routes that buses and cars use, which are often the most congested. Look around for alternative routes, possibly with dedicated bike lanes. If allowed and safe, ride through parks.
- Care to win the "door prize"? I think not. Ride out, to the left. *Assume* the person in the parked car does not see you.
- Pull up directly behind a car at an intersection. The driver has a better chance of seeing you.

- Drive in the middle of the lane if you can keep up with the flow of traffic. If you can't, maybe you should think of an alternative route.
- It's hard to give up speed and momentum, but *stop* at the bottom of a hill before taking a fast right. A parked car might well door you big time when the driver gets out of the car.

TIP: Ride as if no one can see you.

To take the lane or not, that is the question ...

There are risks to both riding in the middle of the lane and riding to the extreme right. Your decision depends on the time of day (rush hour, light) and the conditions of the weather and road. It's your call, but think about this:

- Never take the lane on the downside of a hill. A car flying over the hill will simply take you out.
- Always take the lane when there is not enough room for a car to pass you safely.
- Take the lane in a traffic circle, otherwise a car will give you a *right-hook* as it exits.

Bike Check

- Check your front and rear tire pressure regularly, preferably with a pressure gauge.
- Check front and rear brakes by standing parallel to your bike. Depress the front brake and push your handlebars forward. The rear tire should lift off the ground. Now depress your rear brake while pushing forward. The rear tire should slide slowly forward. Check your cables for fraying. The chain and crank must be intact and in good working order.
- Tighten the quick-release skewers on your bike. They are located at the centre of your front or rear tires and/or on your seat post.
- Lift, then drop, your bike about 5 or 6 centimetres (2 or 3 inches) off the ground and listen for any rattling.
- Got your emergency road kit? It should contain a water bottle, a flat tire fix-it kit, an extra inner tube, rain gear, and, if you are on your own in the country, a cellphone.
- There must be a white light on the front of your bike and a red rear light or reflector on the back. A rear light is more visible than a reflector and usually costs less than $10.
- The bike must have a working bell or horn, a strip of white reflective tape on the front forks, and red reflective tape on the rear forks.

Cycling Gear

Wear the right stuff. A helmet is obvious, but think shoes, gloves, and clothes that allow some freedom of movement.

- A helmet will not prevent an accident—neither will a seat belt in a car—but both will reduce injury. A helmet can reduce head injuries by up to 85 percent, and helmets are mandatory in most areas for cyclists under 18. Assuming you have bought the helmet in a reputable store, and that it carries the recognized seals of approval, the next step is to wear it properly. Skip the high ponytails and up-dos. Have it fitted by the store staff, wear it down on your forehead, and strap it on.
- Cycling gloves can help protect your hands if you fall. And they look serious cool.
- In general, think about shoes and clothes that will work on your bike and allow freedom of movement.
- If your commute is less than 10 kilometres (5 or 6 miles), you might want to keep a fresh shirt at work. Bicycle panniers, available in different sizes, can hold your office clothes. Roll, rather than fold, your clothes before placing them in your pannier or garment bag to reduce wrinkling. Don't forget to remove your pannier when locking the bike up.
- Lucky you if there is a shower in your office. If not keep a facecloth, bar of soap, and deodorant in your desk drawer.
- Use pant-leg straps to protect your clothing from the chain.

Lock It Up

Most bicycle thieves carry tools for only one type of lock, so if your bike is a prized possession, use two different types of locks.

Make sure that a padlock does not dangle low enough to be smashed on the ground.

Lock both wheels to an immovable object. Or better yet, check whether your workplace has bike racks in an underground parking garage.

Finally, don't leave accessories like bags and lights with your bicycle.

Drive to Work

So, you've looked at all your transportation options and decided that the best way for you to roll is in your own car. I hope you've done the math.

Buying a Car

Start by asking yourself: "What kind of car do I need?"

- How many people do you need to transport?
- What kind of driving do you most often do? City? Country?
- How long is your commute? (Think gas mileage.)
- Will the car easily fit in your garage? Do you have a garage?
- How tall are you? If you are over 190 centimetres (or about six foot two), you just might not fit into a few cars—it's all about the *leg room*.
- Do you want a manual or automatic transmission?
- Do you really need four-wheel or all-wheel drive?
- Think safety features.
- Will you be carrying cargo?
- Will you be doing any towing?

How Much Can You Afford?

First of all, do these calculations at home, *before* you start looking around or visiting dealerships.

Get out your calculator. Your total monthly car payments should not exceed 20 percent of your monthly take-home pay. If you are taking out a loan, factor in the interest rate, the down payment, and the length of the loan. You will need a licence and insurance. Add on the cost of parking at home, and at school or at the office. If it's a new car, you can ask the dealer to estimate costs for the first two years. If it's an older car, depending on your mileage, you should factor in new tires, oil and filter changes, and, ohhh, a good $500 in basic repairs. Estimate the amount of gas that you think you will use, double it, and check the price at the pump. (Who said math would never come in handy?)

More than You Really Wanted to Know

Where does that *new car smell* come from? It's the odour from the glues used to assemble the car and, quite possibly, toxic chemicals from the vinyl and plastics. To be on the safe side, you might want to open the windows and park out of sunllight whenever possible. Just thought you should know.

Cost Cutters ✂

Do the Math, Month by Month

Car payments _____   Parking (at work) _____

Insurance _____   Occasional parking _____

Maintenance (min. oil and filter) $40   Gas _____

Parking (at home) _____

Lease or buy?

Buying a car makes sense if you have the down payment and the interest rates are low. Unlike leasing, you don't have to worry about a mileage penalty and you can sell the car if you get in a jam.

On the other hand, with leasing, you don't need a huge down payment, you can get a new car every few years, and there is no need to sell the car at the end of the lease—you just drive it back onto the lot. However, most leases have caps on mileage, so don't even think of taking that car to California. And when the lease is up, you are back into the monthly payment thing.

New or Used?

Forget the brand-new car, you can't afford it. And a new car will lose approximately 18 percent of its value in the first year. Instead, you might want to talk to your chosen dealership about cars that are coming off lease. Rental cars are not always treated well, but they are often sold off after only 20,000 kilometres (12,425 miles).

TIP: To remove decals or bumper stickers, cover the decal or bumper sticker with a cloth soaked in vinegar. Wait for a few minutes. The decals and bumper stickers should peel off.

When buying a used car from a lot, look into an extended warranty. And there's no need for power windows, power door locks, and heated seats. They drive up the cost of the car and, given that the car is second-hand, those are the things that will break first (and never get repaired, so you'll have just paid for something that doesn't work).

If you *must* buy a new car, then at least shop for a car at the end of the month, when dealerships are motivated to move the cars off the lot. Likewise, assuming that you are planning on keeping the car for a long time, buy last year's model just before the new cars arrive. That means shopping in September and October. And opt for safety features like anti-lock brakes and vehicle stability control. If you drive a lot in the snow, all-wheel drive is a good option, but if most of your driving is on well-cleared roads, then go for front-wheel drive—you'll get better fuel economy and save a bundle on repairs over the years.

Shopping Checklist

If you don't want to be at the mercy of the salesperson on the car lot or at the dealership, then know what you *need* as opposed to what you want. Comparison-shop. Use the Internet. There are tons of new options out there.

Here are some other tips to remember:

- Check your credit first. There's nothing like a trip to the bank for a reality check. Arrange all your financing in advance.
- Unless you plan to live in the car, check the cost of monthly insurance rates in advance. (Another reality check.)
- Read the warranty. I'll say it again: READ THE WARRANTY.
- Add-ons means that you are adding on to the dealer's/salesperson's paycheque. You need a radio and maybe air conditioning. Don't get carried away.
- Delivery date. *When?*
- Add up all the costs, everything, including pesky things like delivery costs and tire tax. (And remember—until you sign, you can still walk away.)

> ## *Been* there
> ## *Done* THAT
>
> I saw a sign outside a dealership that said, "Get a lease for $250. A month." I could afford that. Yeah, right. First of all, the down payment was half the cost of the car, and second, it wasn't $250 a month. It was $250 *twice* a month.
>
> —SHELLY, 24

The Dealership

The creepy salesman with the plaid jacket does exist, somewhere, but in well-run dealerships you'll likely find a cross-section of salespeople—including men and women, young and old, chirpy and quiet, laid-back and those creepy glad-handers that yell, "Hello there!" from across the sales floor.

You will be greeted as you walk in. This is the salesperson's way of claiming you. (Think of Fido marking his territory.) A good salesperson will leave you alone after that until you give the signal.

A poor salesperson will steer you toward the car he or she wants to move. Likewise, a salesperson who is evasive and confusing is someone to thank and run away from. And if he doesn't return your calls when you are preparing to buy, then he sure as hell won't when you need some questions answered. Remember, you are in the driver's seat here.

When you have picked out the car you want to buy, ask about your chosen car's availability. If you need a car by Tuesday, then you need to know if the delivery date is months away.

TIP: Oops, your brand-new used car just dripped oil on the driveway. Pour on a bag of kitty litter to soak it up. Wait until the litter has absorbed as much of the oil as possible, scoop up the litter, then go after the stain with hot water and laundry soap. Use a stiff brush. Chances are some of the stain will remain, but it's nothing a few hard winters won't fix.

Car Insurance

If you have a car, you need a driver's licence and car insurance. Obvious, perhaps, but it is surprising how many people forget this. Driving without a licence is against the law. You will get a whopping great ticket, or worse—and it can get much, much worse. If you have an accident, you will probably go to jail, lose your job, your girl/boyfriend, and look like a total loser to everyone you know.

How much car insurance you need and how much it will cost depends on your age, driving record, gender, the city you live in, and yes, even the model of your car. (Forget the racing stripe. It looks lame on a Honda Civic anyway.) Check around for rates.

Most important:

- Know what your insurance covers. Towing? Car rental while your car is being fixed? Roadside assistance?
- What is the deductible?
- Are there any additional charges?
- What about the warranty on repairs?

Deal only with a reputable insurance company. When in doubt, contact the Better Business Bureau.

The company you deal with has to be honest, and so do you. This is very important—*tell the insurance company everything they want to know.* If you have had three speeding tickets, tell them. And that $40 ticket you got three years ago for going just over the limit counts. If you don't tell them the whole truth and they find out—and sooner or later they will—they will have the right to withdraw your insurance at their discretion. Now, having been dubbed "unreliable," good luck finding a company to take you on. Most likely you will have to go into a pool of companies that will gang together to insure you. This is called "being in facility," and that's a very scary place, a sort of Purgatory for the almost uninsurable. The cost? Anywhere from $4000 to $6000 a year, for many years, usually between four and six. I repeat: *Tell the truth, the whole truth and nothing but the truth.*

> TIP: The Canadian Automobile Association (www.caa.ca) offers a lot of bang for your buck. Not only do they provide great roadside service, but they have a whole list of other membership perks, including hotel discounts. Don't leave home without it (or something like that).

Moving

If you are moving to a new province or territory you must get licence plates for the car in that province or territory. To get new plates, your vehicle will probably have to pass a vehicle safety inspection. The length of residence that requires a change of licence plates varies from province to province. Check with the local motor vehicle authority, which will be listed in the blue pages of the phone book. Drivers' licences might also need to be changed. And a test might be required. Don't procrastinate; you usually have only a brief period of time to make these changes.

> TIP: If you're heading to the United States for a long stay, check out the American Automobile Association (www.aaa.com).

Selling a Car

Pay the rent or move into your car? That's a toughie. Assuming that you have decided that the car has to go (good decision), step one is to price out its value. Start by going to the Canadian Black Book at www.canadianblackbook.com and click on "What Is My Car Worth?" Consult the Canadian Red Book, too, at www.canadianredbook. com.

When to sell? A soft-top will not sell as well in October as it will in May, and the value of sports utility vehicles goes up in winter.

Clean it up. You might want to have it detailed, but get a quote first. If you tackle it yourself, go the distance (Q-tips anyone?) and use a good air-freshener. A cheap paint job will actually lower the value, so if the car is a rust-bucket it might be better to go the trade-in route if you are planning to buy another car.

Good for you if you have kept an envelope in the glove compartment holding all your car maintenance receipts. A potential buyer will be impressed. (Black out any credit car numbers on the receipts before handing it over.)

Now you are ready to sell. It's a poker game.

Driving Safety

Don't you love it when some idiot challenges another driver because he *has the right of way*? So, what are you going to do about it?

Remember this: *No one* wins in a head-on collision.

Road rage? Take it inside. Go abuse a pillow or something.

Been there
Done THAT

My eighteen-year-old son tried to overtake another car. It wasn't the best decision, but he could have made it had the car [in front] not sped up and matched my son's speed. When another car came over the horizon my son could not pull in. It was a head-on. A man in the oncoming car died, and my son was in bad shape for a long time. My son went to jail on a charge of dangerous driving causing death. He didn't do well in prison. That other driver, the one who would not let my son pull back in, I often wonder about him.

—MOTHER

Here's the thing: most accidents happen in daylight, on a straight road, with good weather conditions. Accidents occur when a driver lets his or her guard down, is listening to or changing the radio station, lighting a cigarette, eating, talking, reaching for something, not paying attention, is distracted or sleepy. In bad weather, everyone drives more slowly, usually, and is focused.

Rural roads and secondary highways, with intersecting roads and cross traffic, are less safe. Stick to four-lane divided highways whenever possible. And if you see a car coming at you on a two-lane highway, keep your eyes on the edge of the road ahead of the car, maintain speed, and let the two right-side tires drive on the shoulder to avoid an impact.

> **More than You Really Wanted to Know**
>
> Aggressive drivers cause one third of all traffic crashes. But "multi-tasking" drivers (talking on the phone, playing with the radio, putting on makeup, eating, reading or even watching TV) are moving up the ladder.

If a drunk driver veers into your lane, honking or flashing your lights will only alarm him. Hit the brakes. Look where you are going, not at the car coming at you. You might have to slip two wheels off the road to avoid him. If you need to, hit the ditch.

Drowsy driving is just as fatal as drinking and driving

We all know now that alcohol slows reaction time, impairs judgment and the ability to process information, has an impact on behaviour, and decreases awareness and performance. But did you know that driving drowsy does the *exact same thing*? Granted, it's next to impossible to say how many accidents are caused by falling asleep or being drowsy at the wheel. However, single-car accidents in which the car just *falls off the road* or weaves into another lane, where there are no skidmarks present or evidence of any evasive measures, are often attributed to napping behind the wheel. Dying in one's sleep in bed at a ripe old age after a lovely dinner with great friends is a lofty goal, but the operative words here are *in bed*.

More safety advice

- At an intersection, even if you have the right of way, wait until the other car is stopped and you are sure he can see you before proceeding.

More than You Really Wanted to Know

You can get mugged, or worse, in a parking lot adjacent or attached to a bar, particularly on a Saturday night. If you hear shots, if something is going down, hit the dirt, roll under a car if you have to. (Preferably one that isn't moving.) Better yet, go to clubs with valet parking or take transit or a cab.

- At a stoplight, watch out for drivers running the yellow.
- Multi-tasking is overrated. Don't talk on the cellphone, smoke, or eat while driving.
- If you have to ask yourself if you're sober enough to drive, you probably are *not*. Call a cab.
- Check the back seat before getting into a parked car.
- If you lose your car in an underground parking lot, don't wander around. Call security and ask for help.

Winter Driving, or Invoking Your Inner Canadian (No Matter What Country You Are From)

When driving in the snow, do everything slowly. True, most drivers are more cautious in bad weather, but *don't* kid yourself: the first snowfall will result in a multitude of fender benders, or worse.

You need 100 percent visibility, *and* you need to clean the snow off the entire car, including the roof. Otherwise it will slide off the roof onto your windshield as you're slowing down, making you look like an idiot—a blind one. More seriously, it could fly off your roof onto someone else's windshield, causing an accident. Not nice.

On snow, your tires are just barely grabbing the road. Go slow and leave plenty of distance between you and other cars. Rapid movements lead to skids and then, too late, you are out of control. Feel the ground beneath your butt and press on the pedals as if there were eggs under your feet. Don't forget to stash a book in your winter safety kit. You will need it to kill time while you're waiting for the tow truck.

Tune up the car *before* the snow falls. To winterize a car, you will have to spend a minimum of $100. Check belts, hoses, water pumps, spark-plug wires, and distributor caps. Just find a good garage and say "Winter checkup, please." (You will find a good garage by word of mouth. Ask around.)

Switch to a thinner oil. You will also need to have the battery and spark plugs checked, gas line antifreeze checked, engine coolants replaced (to withstand lower temperatures), and a change of the windshield wiper fluid. Might as well have the air filter checked, cleaned, or replaced too. In a fuel-injected engine, a dirty air filter will need more fuel. Air filters cost about $20—you'll get your money back on gas savings.

Windshield wipers

You will need winter windshield wipers. Winter wipers are heavier than summer blades. They will wear out quickly if you use them in the summer. Try the ones with the rubber covering that reduce ice buildup. And while we are on the subject, you can go through a couple of litres of windshield washer fluid trying to keep your windshield clear on a messy day. Keep a few extra litres in the trunk. Watch out for the cheap stuff. It will freeze on your windshield. (I don't care what it says on the bottle!)

Note: Turn the wipers off *before* shutting off the engine. Otherwise, the blades might freeze on the windshield. In an effort to get the wipers unstuck, you might burn out the wiper motor when you turn the car back on.

Antifreeze

In most cases, you'll need a 50-50 mix of coolant to water. Do not go 100 percent coolant. The 50-50 mix has a lower freezing point and a higher boiling point than the straight stuff. (And you thought that your mother didn't know this stuff?) Why bother? The main function of antifreeze is to keep your cooling system from rusting. I think we can agree that rust in engines is not good. Coolant expands as it freezes, and there goes your engine block. If your engine block goes, so does that new plasma TV you've been saving up for.

Battery

If you need a new battery, get one now. *Note:* An engine is harder to start in winter because oil isn't as *fluid* as it is in the summer heat. Also, a battery loses power as the temperature drops. And since you are buying one anyway (think of the money you will save on the tow), get a big one. Just make sure it fits.

Cooling

Check the cooling system. You'd think it's a summer thing, but not necessarily. No or low coolant—no heat! At the very least, change your engine's coolant at the interval recommended by your manufacturer.

Gas

Keep the gas topped up in the winter. Gas is heat. If you get stuck but have gas you can idle the engine until the gas runs out, no harm to the engine. (Crack open the window a bit and make sure the tailpipe is clear of snow.)

Sand

Some well-meaning souls recommend loading the trunk with sandbags, apparently to give the car traction. This might work in a lightweight, rear-wheel-drive car. You could put a bag over the rear axle (usually toward the front of the trunk). But it's not a great idea to keep a bag of sand in the car itself. It can act as a projectile. Can you imagine the obituary? "Killed by a flying bag of sand." A small amount of sand, or kitty litter, however, can be helpful if scattered under tires stuck on ice.

Block heaters

These are standard in Saskatchewan and northern Minnesota. They cost less than a hundred bucks, plug into any old outlet, and almost guarantee that your car will start even on the coldest, frozen-nose-hair mornings.

Duh moment!

Got a nifty new block heater? Great. Just remember to unplug the car from the house before you drive away.

Snow tires

We have all heard the all-season tire pitch. It's a huge misconception that all-season radials *will do*. Will do *what*, exactly? All-season tires might be big, but size doesn't

TIP: Have scraper, will travel. Did you leave your certified, industrial-sized, overpriced, jazzy scraper at home? A plastic CD case or tape holder works like a charm.

count. They are made of a more flexible rubber compound, with small, tightly spaced treads, and are not designed for the snow.

Think of it this way: if you buy winter tires, your summer tires will last twice as long. To make the seasonal switch easier, buy four snow tires that are permanently mounted on steel rims. New steel rims start at about $50, but used ones go for half that amount. You will get the money back since it can cost about $70 a pop to mount and balance them on the old rims in the spring and fall.

If you absolutely can't afford four snow tires, two new snow tires (mounted on the wheels that are driven by the engine) are better than nothing. For all-wheel-drive cars, you really need four snow tires.

Note: Some tire shops offer to store off-season tires. Great, so long as the company doesn't do a midnight flit or file for bankruptcy. If you have the space, keep your tires in your basement or apartment locker.

> ### *Been* there *Done* THAT
>
> You gotta wonder at what goes through the brain of a guy changing a tire, with his rear end hanging out, on a major highway, in the dark. I mean, what's a tire worth? What's your life worth?
>
> —BEN, 32

Emergency Road Kit

In any season, there are a few very important things that you should have in your car:

- First-aid kit.
- Flares.
- Windshield scraper and brush.
- One or two space blankets (available in most hardware, camping, or travel stores).
- Pack of waterproof matches.
- Two fat candles.
- A few chocolate bars.
- Pair of winter boots, gloves, hat.

- Cellphone, but only if you promise not to talk and drive.
- Jumper cables (the heavy-duty ones cost about $70).
- And if you have money to burn, a 40-amp battery recharger runs about $850 (or $625 for a 20-amp recharger), and a 12-volt tire compressor goes for $70.

Been there Done THAT

It was my fault, the whole thing. I pulled out in front of a car. The other car hit me, spun out, and all I could see was the top of a baby seat. I remember getting out of my car and running toward the other car. I didn't look. I didn't see a pickup truck coming toward me.

—DAVE, 26

What to Do If You Are in an Accident

No matter how big or small a car accident is, it's a jolt to the system. You think you know how you will behave, but you really won't know until it happens. And buckets of blood splattered all over the place really does change everything.

If you are in a serious accident, all you should be concerned about are the lives of everyone around you, assuming you can actually move. Very cool if you have rubber gloves stashed in the glove compartment, but don't expect any understanding from anyone if you let someone bleed to death because you are afraid of AIDS.

After the Accident: Step by Step

Crash! It has a sound to it that you will never forget. Ask all the passengers if they are all right. Now look them in the eye and check them out for yourself. Seldom do people cry out after an accident. In most cases everyone goes silent.

Check out the occupants in the other vehicle. You can replace cars, not people.

- If you can move your car to the side of the road, do so. Flick on the car's hazard lights and put up flares or warning triangles. (The ones in your trunk, hopefully.) Stand away from the car and never, ever behind the car. If it's dark or there is no safe place to stand, get back in the car and buckle up.
- If anyone seems hurt or confused, call an ambulance/police immediately.
- Assuming that this is a fender-bender, write down the names, licence numbers, car registration, insurance company, and policy numbers from all the other drivers and vehicles involved. Also write down the model, make, and year of each car.

- Take down the names, phone numbers, and licence numbers of any drivers that might be witnesses.
- Draw a little diagram of what you think happened.
- *Important:* Do not get into a fight with the other driver about what happened. Just stay calm and remove yourself from the direct line of his/her wrath. Call the police if you feel threatened, or if the other driver will not show you his/her papers—which could indicate that he is driving without a valid licence or has no insurance.
- Write down the details of the accident, including the date, time, and location. (You will be amazed how much you will forget.)
- If the damage is more than $1000, call the police. They will tell you what to do next. In some cases they might come to the scene. In other instances they will direct you to a reporting centre or police station.

Accident kit (for your glove compartment)

- Cellphone.
- Pen and paper.
- Disposable camera.
- Mini phone book with emergency numbers (including your home number and the number of a taxi company). On the first page, write down the person that you want contacted in case of emergency.
- Have two copies of your *organ donation card*. Put one in this book in the glove compartment and keep the other one in your wallet.

Resources

For public transit in the United States

American Public Transportation Association, www.apta.com/links/state_local/. Phone 202-496-4800; fax 202-496-4321.

For car-related information

Canadian Automobile Association: www.caa.ca
American Automobile Association: www. aaa.com

Buying or selling a car?

Canadian Black Book: www.canadianblackbook.com

Canadian Red Book: www.canadianredbook.com

www.edmunds.com

www.autobytel.com

Lemon Aid by Phil Edmonston: www.lemonaidcars.com. This book is wonderful, and so is Phil.

If you want to avoid the hassle and cost of owning a car, check out www.carsharing.ca

Car Safety

Safe Road Home by Karen Goodman and Kirk Simon (Sterling, 2005). This book comes with a DVD: *Smashed: Toxic Tales of Teens and Alcohol.*

15

Etiquette

The great secret is not having bad manners or good manners …
but having the same manners for all human souls: in short,
behaving as if you were in heaven, where there are no third-class carriages,
and one soul is as good as another soul.

—GEORGE BERNARD SHAW

Why bother with etiquette? Consider this. A boy works his tail off in high school, gets brilliant marks, and nabs a spot at a top university. Same boy, now a young man, lands a fabulous entry-level job in the company of his choice. He rises through the ranks like a rocket. One fine day, Mr. Company President invites the young overachiever out to lunch with some clients. All goes well … until the young man rips off a chunk of bread, swipes his soup bowl clean, and pops the bread into his mouth. And so ends the career of the Boy Wonder—last seen pumping gas.

Okay, I exaggerate a little.

Fact is, manners count and etiquette is important. Let's define the two for the purposes of this book.

Manners are the basis of our society. *Please, thank you*, and *pardon me* might not seem like the glue that holds our world together, but think of the bedlam if doors swung in our faces, lineups turned into shoving matches, and guests (armed with eating utensils) charged the buffet table.

Etiquette, on the other hand, is manners choreographed. It's how we know, for example, that at the dinner table, the bread plate is the one *on the left* of our dinner plate! (Ever seen the chaos that ensues when one dunderhead grabs the wrong bread plate at a round table?)

All manners and etiquette are based on common sense. Or, in the words of Peggy Post, "Manners are a combination of common sense, generosity of spirit and some specific know-how." We'll assume you've got the sense and spirit part; let's work on the "specific know-how."

The Basics: Everyday Manners

Consider this: if everyone practised common courtesy (which is *not* really so *common*), would we have people robbing or shooting each other? How would that go?

"Excuse me, sir, may I have your wallet?"

"Thank you for asking, dear fellow, but I think not. Do have a nice day!"

It's not so hard, really. Here's all you need to know:

- Be nice.
- Be kind.
- Say *please*.
- Say *thank you*.
- Say *sorry*.
- Say *excuse me*.
- Give up your seat.
- Cover your mouth.
- Remember that friends are not personal therapists.
- Don't trap people on the telephone.
- Hold the door open.
- Close the bathroom door.
- Put the toilet seat down.
- The person closest to the elevator door exits first.
- Don't chew gum in public.
- Don't spit in public—ever!
- Bathe, every day, please.
- Don't neck in public.
- Don't blow your nose in a restaurant.
- Return what you borrow.
- Give people their personal space.
- Listen.
- Smile.
- Help.
- Suck it up.
- Clean up your pet's poop.
- No double-dipping.

- Return calls.
- Don't mistake gossip for conversation.
- Never yell at anyone, ever.
  The rest is gravy.

Duh|
moment!

How to Look like a Reject

- Use phrases from another language. (Pretentious and boring.)
- Drop names. (No one is impressed, really.)
- Whisper in someone's ear at dinner.
- Trash other people.
- Look over the shoulder of the person who is speaking to you.
- Interrupt.
- Contradict.
- Insult.
- Talk at length about an operation, your health, your colon, or the condition of your feet.
- Constantly play the devil's advocate.
- Argue for argument's sake.
- Tell a sexist or racist joke.
- Take stuff that isn't yours or fail to return stuff you have borrowed.
- Pigeonhole a professional in a social setting and ask for professional advice.
- Talk about your personal finances, in detail.

Meet and Greet

Walking into a roomful of strangers can be intimidating. The more you do it, though, the easier it gets. Whenever you can, practise talking to strangers. Yes, I really am telling you to talk to strangers. Forget all those old scary stories we told you. Strangers aren't always bad people. And besides, you're older now, and wiser—you can judge the situation.

Start small. Stop grunting at people. Say "Good morning" as you enter the elevator in your apartment building. Make eye contact and smile. It's not much, but it's a start. When the lady ahead of you in the grocery store complains about the price of tea, agree with her and talk for a minute. You'll get to know your neighbours, and you might even pick up some shopping tips. I'm not suggesting that you launch into a full-fledged conversation with innocent strangers. I am suggesting that you use your voice, eyes, and smile to break the ice. Try it for a few weeks. You'll see!

Going to an Event

You have now entered the realm of Big Boy / Big Girl stuff, and the kinds of conversations that you used to scoff at. (You think I didn't see your eyes rolling?)

Let's say you are going to a "Save the Borg" conference. Great. Presumably everyone at the conference has something in common—in this case, they're all Trekkies. Start talking at the coat check, to the next person in line. It doesn't matter what subject you pick—the weather, the cost of the conference, William Shatner's acting abilities. If you have talked to anyone for more than thirty seconds and he or she hasn't run screaming in the opposite direction, extend your hand and introduce yourself. By the end of the day you'll spot that certain someone in a roomful of strangers, and she'll seem like an old friend.

The Handshake

Never underestimate the impact of a handshake—it creates an instant, close-up, warm connection that is, nevertheless, acceptable for both business and socializing. And the younger you are, the more surprising and welcome your extended hand will be to the person you are hoping to make a good impression on.

The best handshake is brief and warm. Fluttery or dead-fish handshakes, jarring, arm-vibrating handshakes, bone-crushing, machine-gun, or boneless-hand handshakes will send a potential friend/client/boss racing for the door. Offer your hand upright and vertical, look the person in the eyes, and smile. Short of being introduced to Osama Bin Laden, *always* shake an extended hand, and say the person's name at the same time. Not only will this help you remember the name, but it will give that person an opportunity to offer the correct pronunciation: "Lovely to meet you, Bill, but it's Mick-eye not Mack-*kay*."

Handshakes are an equal-opportunity greeting—women, that means you should both offer and return them.

If the person you have been introduced to is handicapped, extend your hand anyway. He or she may reach out with their left hand or say something like, "I have arthritis, I am sorry I can't shake hands, but it's nice to meet you." There is no reason to get embarrassed.

How long, and how much pressure?

- The length of a handshake depends on the local culture. In the United States and Canada, one might shake about four and a half times and hold for a few more seconds. In South America, in particular, you may pump a hand a dozen times, then hold a while longer.
- In Europe and South America, expect to have your hand shaken several times a day. You might get hugged or kissed, too—lucky you. A woman might get kissed on both cheeks in western Europe. Then there is the three-cheek kiss. (Don't be rude, now.) That's in France.
- In Japan, generally, the lower the bow the more respect is being shown. It is crucial that you read up on the etiquette of any foreign country you are visiting, particularly Middle Eastern and Muslim countries.
- A firm handshake implies honesty and a strong character, but you don't want to see anyone wince. You might want to find someone to help you practise before a big interview.

How to kiss a lady's hand

You are in France, it's a social occasion (not a professional event), and you are out to impress. Fine. Gently take the extended hand in your right palm, raise the hand to mid-chest level, then bend over to meet the hand halfway

---

More than You Really Wanted to Know

Your handshake—what does it really mean?

1. *Palm down, or the "I am the Master of the House" shake.* People who extend their hand with the palm down force others to extend with the palm up. This is not good. It makes the palm-up guy feel like he is asking for money.
2. *Palm up, or the "sales shake."* This has an "at your service" feel. Not bad, but not great.
3. *Palm vertical, or the "let's play/work together" shake.* This is the cooperation shake. Perfect it.

and barely brush it with your lips. This is a high-risk manoeuvre so don't even try it if you're not confident that it will be welcome and look charming. But you never know— this tidbit might come in handy one day.

Business Cards

Business cards should never be over-sized. Large cards that scream *"Look at me, I wanna stand out!"* don't fit into wallets and end up in the trash.

Keep your cards handy so that you don't have to scramble through your wallet looking for one. When receiving a card, take it graciously and treat it with respect. In Japan, receive the card with both hands, bow, and place it carefully and respectfully in your wallet or purse.

If business cards are exchanged in a social rather than a professional context, it should be done as discreetly as possible, at the end of a conversation or, even better, the end of the evening. You don't want to deal them out at the dinner table like playing cards, or hold one up to show everybody the cool typeface you chose.

Introductions

Every time you are introduced to anyone, with the possible exception of a small child, stand up. Another possible exception is when your chum Floyd hollers across the room, "Hey Abe, it's me, Floyd." In this case a wave is acceptable. And since we are on the topic, *stand* when someone new enters the room for the first time. Keep standing until your guest is seated, the client is in the chair, and/or the Pope has given you leave to sit. Don't get too caught up in the male/female thing, think *respect.* Get up, smile, and extend your hand. If you meet someone in a restaurant and you are sitting, make that goofy pretend-to-stand gesture and hope to heck the person has the good sense to say, "Please, don't get up."

Once upon a time a married woman was introduced as Mrs. Andrew MacLeod. Try introducing a woman under seventy that way today and you might get flattened. We all live confusing lives, and many of the old introduction rules no longer apply. There are still some basics you'll need to know, though.

We'll start with the simple stuff. Your wife's name is Moonbeam Darling and your boss's name is Hank Plank. Traditionally, a person of lower social ranking is introduced *to* a person of higher social ranking. Following this rule, a man is introduced to a woman, a younger woman is introduced to an older woman, a junior employee is introduced to a senior employee, and so on. It might seem like a pointless distinction, but it does tend to start a conversation off in the right direction. So, we introduce Hank Plank to Moonbeam Darling, even if Hank is your boss.

"Moonbeam, I'd like you to meet my boss, Mr. Plank." If her last name is different from your own, or if your boss might not know that you are married, you can then move on to something like, *"Mr. Plank, I don't believe you've met my wife, Moonbeam Darling."* Simple, elegant, no fuss. Err on the side of formality—Mr. Plank always has the option to say, *"Please, call me Hank,"* and when he does he seems gracious and charming.

The point of introductions is to orientate everyone concerned. Let's say you are the host of a party. (The kind of party that does not involve shot glasses, reefers, nylon stockings, and oven mitts.) It's perfectly acceptable to say, *"Bunny, have you met Hank Plank? Hank, this is my editor, Bunny Bossyboots."* If you want to go further you might give the two something to talk about. *"Bunny, Hank was just saying that he has moved into that new complex down on Elm. Didn't you used to live there?"* If they start a conversation, you can excuse yourself and carry on with the hosting thing.

If the person is gay and you want to introduce his true love, try, *"This is Ryan Jones and his partner, Bob Smith."* Same for lesbians. If you are introducing business partners, just say so. *"This is Ryan Jones and his business partner, Bob Smith."* The same formula applies to unmarried but long-time–committed heterosexual couples.

Forget shepherding a new guest around the room and introducing him to everyone. Names will instantly be forgotten. Instead, introduce a newcomer to someone you trust will make him feel welcome.

Once you have been introduced to someone, repeat his/her name. *"Hi, Hank, nice to meet you."*

When "working the room" be aware of body language. If you see two people head to head and deep in conversation, that might not be the time to jump in with a boisterous, *"Hi, my name is Leo."* On the other hand, if you see a group of people talking, by all means stand near the group. With any luck, someone nearby will notice and step aside to include you in the circle.

Eye contact and a smile are helpful. When there is a break in the conversation, introduce yourself. The stranger will give his name, then introduce the others.

If you forget a name, no worry. We all do. *"I am so sorry, I'm having a moment here. Your name is...?"* Only a true bore would get offended. Unless it's your girlfriend's name you've forgotten. Then, you're on your own.

Beware of the guest who is all questions and no answers—there should be at least some give-and-take, no matter how much you might enjoy answering questions about yourself! And look out for the woman who wants to tell you every single detail of her last romance. All you're thinking is, "Lucky guy—*he* got away." Alas, you must listen as best you can, excuse yourself when you can, and realize that this, too, is part of the game.

You should never feel "stuck" in a party conversation. Etiquette allows such simple getaways as: "I believe I'll freshen my drink—it's been lovely to meet you"; "It's been delightful to meet you—I've just seen someone I must say hello to"; "I wonder if Bitsy needs help in the kitchen—I hope we'll have a chance to talk again another time." And you just go! It's okay!

Really, this isn't hard—it just takes practice. Now, if you are off to meet the Queen, well, that's another matter. Get yourself a big, thick etiquette book. And hurry.

More than You Really Wanted to Know

King Louis XIV's gardener was fed up with the upper-class louts trampling all over his lovely gardens. Said gardener got so ticked off that he put up "tickets" or "etiquettes" directing said rabble onto the correct paths. Alas, his efforts were to no avail. Louis stepped in (no pun intended) and issued an edict to his subjects to "Keep within the tickets" or "Keep within the etiquettes." We are happy to report that civility returned to the court—for a few more decades, anyway.

Conversation Killers

- "I work for the Revenue department."
- "I have a pain right about here ..."
- "You look different somehow ..."
- "You remind me of someone. Have you ever worked in a bank?"
- "You remind me of someone. What's the name of that actress, oh, just wait, it'll come to me ..."
- "I called you ten times. How come you don't return calls?"

- "I'm an accountant."
- "I love libraries."
- "No offence, but ..."
- "So you are a writer. Bet you wish your name was J.K. Rowling."
- "So you're a dentist. How much do you charge for a filling?"
- "I had the weirdest dream last night. I was standing on a rock ..."
- "I have to visit my parents in jail this weekend."
- "It's not that I am a racist or anything, but ..."
- "Not to play the devil's advocate or anything, but ..."

Duh moment!

Hats off in the house—always.

Clothing Basics

Guys, we're going to focus on you here, because we sense that you are more ... *challenged* in this area than your female counterparts?

For Guys

Here's what *Esquire* magazine recommends for every male's closet:

1. A white Oxford button-down shirt (to go with a suit jacket and tie, on its own for a more casual look with khakis or jeans, or under a sweater).

2. A lightweight V-neck sweater. The magazine suggests cashmere (which is pricey), but you should be able to find something similar on your reduced budget. It's best if it's not too heavy because that way you can wear it throughout the year—either with a suit or just jeans.

3. Nice jeans (as opposed to the torn-up, frayed-cuff pair you've worn since high school). If they're dark enough, you can get away with wearing them with your suit jacket as well as on the weekends.

4. White T-shirts for just about everything: sleeping, working out, or under your shirts or sweaters. Throw out the beer-logo shirts, *now*.

5. Black lace-up dress shoes can be worn to work and with nice jeans.

6. Navy suit. If you're only going to have one suit, stick with dark blue; it's the most versatile, since it can go with a shirt and tie or just jeans. Two- or three-button?

That seems to change with the fashions. I wouldn't sweat the details. Try on both and ask the store staff (or a trusted friend, preferably female) which suits you best.

7. Medium-width tie. It's the most versatile. Stick to something neutral so it goes with the most outfits.

TIP: Never, ever wear a holiday-themed tie. That cute tie Grandma gave you with the Santa on it goes straight to the back of the closet. I suppose it's okay to wear it on Christmas Day in her presence—but if you think you might even consider wearing it to the office Christmas Party (oops, I mean Holiday Party), then get rid of the thing immediately.

How to wear it

- Belts should match the colour of your shoes.
- Trousers are long enough if they have a light break in the front and cover your socks.
- Shirtsleeves should show more or less a centimetre (quarter-inch to half-inch) of cuff under a jacket.
- Socks should cover the shins when legs are crossed. Ah, that means that you are looking for "hose" in the man-store.
- Ties should land just above or at the belt.
- "French cuffs" mean that you need cufflinks. Do not wear cufflinks that blink.

Cracking the Old Code: What to Wear, Where

This is tough on everyone. Bottom line: the trick is to know just who is attending the affair you've been invited to. Will senior citizens be there, the crème de la crème, or is this a kids' benefit, in which case jeans are fine? Also relevant are the time of day, the planned activity, and the venue. You might be rubbing elbows with the super-wealthy, but if it's an afternoon sailing party you will feel very conspicuous (and possibly unwelcome) in stiletto heels or suit and tie.

There is nothing wrong with calling up the organizers and asking, "What's the dress code?" If it's an established event, then you might be able to Google it and look at past photos on various websites.

"Black tie"

If you see this on an invitation (aren't you the hobnobber!) then you are required to wear a tuxedo, if you're male. This consists of a French-cuffed tuxedo shirt with cufflinks, a bow tie, and a cummerbund. If all this is a little too stuffy for you, by all means break free—wear a *red* cummerbund if it's Christmas or Valentine's Day. Sorry, that's about as creative as you can get. The pants are black, shoes are black, socks are black. In summer you may substitute a white jacket for the black one.

Tuxedos populate upscale second-hand stores. Look for the length of the pants and the sleeves. Ideally, the suit should be bigger than you are. Now, take it off to a tailor and spend your money there. Another idea: buy one well-fitted black suit. Add the French-cuffed tuxedo shirt and all accessories and there you go.

Ladies, a long gown is appreciated in the evening, but variations on the theme are acceptable, so long as the overall effect is modest and elegant. Think little black dress—but not *too* little.

"Black tie optional"

When this is the dress code, you have a little more flexibility. Guys, if you have a tux, go for it (though be prepared to be the only penguin in the crowd). If not, a dark suit and white shirt with French cuffs may substitute. Ladies, again, a long dress is fine, but an elegant, dressy evening dress will suffice.

TIP: Should you buy your own tux? The rule of thumb is, if you are attending three or more formal events a year then the answer is yes. Renting a tux can cost between $80 to $200 or more, a night.

TIP: Got a great invitation but an empty pocketbook? Check out a second-hand store in an upscale neighbourhood. The swells don't want to be seen in the same dress twice and often turn in their nearly new duds for cash.

TIP: Got a hem emergency? Zip into a stationery store and buy double-sided tape to tape it up and make it through the night.

"Semi-formal"

Him: requires your basic suit and tie.
Her: a short dress, think cocktail length.

"Casual"

This one's a minefield. A casual summer afternoon at the boss's country estate means a blazer, cotton shirt, or golf shirt, light-coloured trousers, and loafers. You can leave your tie at home. Women, it's sundress time with— oh, go for it—a great hat and snazzy shoes.

On the other hand, if it's a casual deck party at the neighbours', then jeans, shorts, whatever, you're good to go. Don't get the boss's country estate mixed up with the weenie-roast next door.

"Come as you are"

The only time you would actually "come as you are" is if your house or apartment building were on fire. You might hear this ludicrous phrase from your neighbour who calls with an impromptu invitation to "pop by for a drink." Change into something respectable. No one needs to know that you wear bunny slippers and pyjamas bought at Disneyland.

Weddings

This can be tricky. What you wear depends on the time of the day. For men, it's easy: a suit is almost always the appropriate choice, but there are several exceptions.

- If the wedding takes place on a beach, crisp khaki trousers and a button-down shirt will do, especially if you are required to go barefoot.
- An early evening wedding calls for a business suit.
- Watch out for the night wedding; it might require black tie. If you don't want to be confused with the groomsmen, wear a set of suspenders instead of a vest or cummerbund.
- Ladies, I shouldn't have to say it, but don't outshine the bride. And even if the bride is wearing, oh caramel, don't wear white. Just … don't.

How to Tie a Windsor Knot

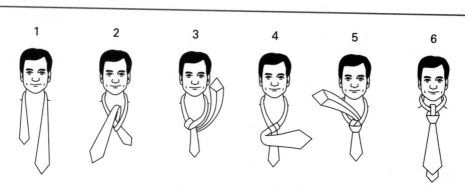

For wide shirt collars
1. Place the wide end of the tie to your right, hanging a foot below the narrow end.
2. Cross the wide end over the narrow end and pull through the loop.
3. Pull the wide end behind the narrow end and up to the right.
4. Cross the wide end in front of the narrow end.
5. Pull up through the loop.
6. Pull down through the knot in the front, tightening up to the collar.

How to Tie a Half-Windsor Knot

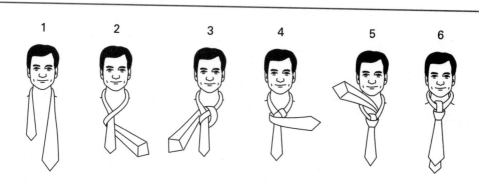

For standard shirt collars
1. Place the wide end of the tie to your right, hanging a foot below the narrow end.
2. Cross the wide end over, then underneath the narrow end.
3. Bring the wide end up and through the loop.
4. Cross the wide end in front of the narrow end.
5. Pull up through the loop.
6. Pull down through the knot in the front, tightening up to the collar.

How to Tie a Bow-tie

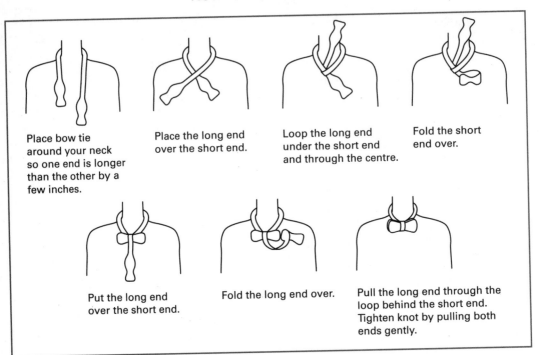

Place bow tie around your neck so one end is longer than the other by a few inches.

Place the long end over the short end.

Loop the long end under the short end and through the centre.

Fold the short end over.

Put the long end over the short end.

Fold the long end over.

Pull the long end through the loop behind the short end. Tighten knot by pulling both ends gently.

Cracking the New Code: What to Wear, Where

Didn't know there was one, did you? The *old* code is a cakewalk compared with the new code, which really isn't a code at all. Figuring out the subtext on an invitation is like deciphering the Rosetta Stone.

Here's an example. The invitation reads: *"Dress: Yes."* Sure, it's witty, but helpful? Should one assume that nudists were party regulars and the hosts have had a change of heart?

The new dress code is all smoke and mirrors designed by the cool kids in high school who are now all grown up. Use your head and keep your ear to the ground.

"Black-tie denim"

Graydon Carter (Canadian-born editor of *Vanity Fair* magazine) might not have invented the upper-body lower-body split, but he made it mainstream. It goes like this: big-bucks jacket on top (anything from velvet to tweed) and big-bucks jeans on the bottom. Men and women—same thing.

"Cocktail"

At last, a word Grandma will understand. This still means a great short dress for a woman and whatever it is he wears to work (e.g., a suit or jacket and great jeans). And if you work at home, please, no robe and slippers.

"Join us on the red carpet"

Ladies, do not go over the top here. No sweeping gowns, please. Leave that look to the starlet who is wearing a freebie or a loaner dress from a designer. A little black dress or glitzy pantsuit will do. Men are usually in black tie, but check with your host. It might well be "Black-tie denim."

"The opening"

If it's a *now* event, a *who's who* event, then this is the time to *wow*. Ladies, go to your hair stylist and get your makeup done. Exception: an opening for an art show in a private gallery is played way down. A multi-million-dollar reopening of a publicly funded art gallery is a whole other ball of wax. Make the call to anyone who has been there, will be there, or runs the damn thing.

TIP: You can see the snaps from previous years' events in old papers and magazines or online. However, bear in mind that the photographer was taking pictures of the organizers and the Mr. and Mrs. Big Bucks. There are plenty of others who are having a jolly good time and not dressed in birds-of-paradise costumes.

"The private party"

Wear something comfortable *that fits*. And ladies, think twice about wearing a stiletto heel in a private home. They can cause damage to your host's floors, and if the floors are made of reclaimed wood you might lose your heel in a knot. Either way, you won't have a good time.

"Business attire"

Office clothes, which means that if you are working as a mechanic you have to go home and change.

Clothes for all seasons

Your jeans look appropriate all year round—that's one of the reasons you love them so! But the sundress looks wrong in December, the tweed jacket looks silly in July, the long red velvet dress is out of place almost any time except Christmas, and the heavy wool navy-blue suit looks painfully uncomfortable at a barbecue. Face it, not all of your clothes will work all of the time—some things have to be put away and rediscovered when the temperature starts heading in the opposite direction. It's okay to buy a few seasonal clothing items, and use your common sense about what works when. White shoes might even look right after Labour Day if the temperature stays high!

Last word: try hard not to look as though you are trying too hard.

So there you have it—how to look like a grown-up. To summarize, sloppy doesn't work any more, and neither does wearing pants around your crotch or showing ten centimetres (four inches) of flesh below the navel.

It comes down to this: dress yourself with respect. You do not need a $3000 suit. What you need are clean clothes that suit you, the weather, your budget, and the occasion. And remember: your best accessories (sorry if this sounds corny) are always a firm handshake, a sincere smile, and good manners.

The Basics of Polite Dining

Meet Susie. She is seven years old and an "A" student, thanks to a multitude of tutors and an expensive private school. She takes ballet and violin lessons, rides a horse, and acts in all the school plays. Her proud parents just know that she will be a huge success and one day hobnob with the swells.

This morning little Susie had an egg on a muffin and a glass of milk. Lunch was a slice of pizza and pop, while dinner, consumed in the back of the minivan, was a hamburger. What's wrong with this picture?

TIP: About lipstick. One does want to look yummy across a candlelit table, but applying a whack of red lipstick to the lips, only to have it end up on the glass rims and napkins, will not endear you to your host. Go light on the lipstick, and dab, don't rub, your mouth with the napkin.

Nutrition aside, Susie has not touched an eating utensil all day. In fact, thanks to chicken nuggets, fish sticks, and PB&J, Susie rarely touches eating implements at all. Not surprisingly, Susie holds her knife like a barbarian and believes the best place to rest a fork is in her brother's thigh.

If you recognize this little girl then take note: Susie can be helped.

> **Duh !**
> **moment .**
>
> If you are choking, do not leave the room. You need help. A host would far rather see a dinner upset than find a guest in the bathroom dead with a hunk of prime rib in her throat.

How to Do the Sit-Down Dinner (As Seen on TV Circa 1970)

Maybe you too were raised in a minivan, but you're not doomed to eat from your lap forever. There is another way. Honey, meet the dinner table.

When the host says, "Dinner is served," it means *dinner is served.* Really. Now is not the time to run off to the bathroom, or to finish off that very important level of your video game. Now is the time to walk to the table, wait until your seniors have been seated (hold the back of Grandma's chair), and then *sit down.* Wait until everyone is seated, grace is said, and/or the host says, "Oh please begin."

Sitting at a table requires that your feet be on the floor, not tucked under your butt or twisted around the chair legs. Elbows off the table. (You must have heard that one before.) Your back is straight and against the back of the chair. No one wants to see you with one arm circling the plate and your other hand stabbing at the food.

Grace (the prayer, not your great-aunt) should be respected, regardless of your own religious beliefs or lack thereof. Some families hold hands around the table and bow their heads, while others simply bow their heads. Just do it. If you are asked to say grace you are allowed to decline politely, or you could try, *"For what we are about to receive, may we be truly thankful."* Grace is becoming less common these days, but still, do not eat anything until everyone is seated and the host has given you the nod, or said, "Please, go ahead." When in doubt, wait for the hostess to begin.

Your napkin should be placed on your lap as soon as you sit down. It does not belong clipped to a tie or tucked into a shirt or collar, unless you are eating lobster. If you excuse yourself mid-meal, place the napkin *on your chair,* not on the table. When you are finished the meal and everyone is rising, leave your napkin on the tablecloth beside your plate. Do not use your napkin to clean your face. And never, *never* use a napkin to blow your nose. *Ever.*

Duh |
moment!

Q. What's wrong with this picture? You arrive fashionably late for a dinner party carrying a dozen long-stemmed roses.

A. Your timing is all wrong. First of all, there is no such thing as "fashionably late" for a dinner party, only "rudely late," because serving dinner is all about timing. Beyond that, your choice of gift is not well suited to a late arrival. Just what a host wants to do—arrange flowers while dealing with coats, food, wine, and everything else. By all means, bring a hostess gift (a candle, a well-chosen memento—add a small card) and a bottle of wine. Flowers? Not so good. If you insist, they should at least be arranged in their own container or delivered by the florist before the guests arrive.

Eating is the *whole* point of a meal, so by all means chew, but with your mouth closed. And to state more of the obvious: do not salt, pepper, or season your meal until you have tasted it. Remove the spoon from the teacup after stirring. Cutting up your food all at once is something children do; cut and eat as you go. When squeezing a lemon, cup your hand around the lemon in an attempt to prevent the juice from going into your date's eye.

TIP: Don't pig out on appetizers, and don't ever take more than two at a time.

Appetizers

It's common to serve appetizers with pre-dinner cocktails. If you are standing and holding a glass, you are required to master the *glass and plate in one hand* trick. Hosts are aware of the potential problem and will often place handy tables around the room. Often appetizers are served when sitting, and occasionally the appetizer plate will accommodate the wineglass as long as a well-placed thumb holds the foot in place. (I am personally opposed to the glass-on-a-rope solution, but to each his own.)

If the hors d'oeuvres come with toothpicks, stab said appetizer with the pick, pop it in your mouth, and dispose of the toothpick by placing it on the side of your plate or on a designated dead-toothpick plate. Never, ever, put it back on the appetizer plate. That's just gross.

A word about bread

If you are obliged to cut or rip off a piece of bread from a baguette, refrain from holding the entire loaf with your bare hand—hopefully there is a napkin laid across it. Take one slice or piece, not a hunk, and break it gently into bite-sized pieces, one at a time. Do *not* split the bread or roll in half and slather on the butter.

TIP: Those empty foil wrappers your butter comes in? Fold them up and tuck them under the butter plate.

Instead, butter each small piece as you go. If you are sitting at the table, use the communal butter knife to transfer the butter from the butter dish to your bread plate (on the left). If you have a personal butter knife, placed across your bread plate or above your dinner plate, use it. It might seem complicated or contrived, but the purpose is simply to keep your germs to yourself.

Flat breads (Indian and Middle Eastern breads fit into this category) are usually big, round, and yummy. Tear off a large piece, put it on your plate, and then break it into bite-sized pieces.

First Course: Soup

The soup spoon is the big, round, shovel-like spoon to your far right. Scoop the soup away from you. When the bowl is nearly empty, tip it very slightly toward the middle of the table. The point here is that if the bowl slips, the soup spills onto the table and not into your lap. (Granted, both options are horrible.) When finished, you may leave the spoon in the bowl *if it's shallow.*

Hold the soup spoon as you would a pencil and lift it parallel to your mouth. The days of playing "zoom, zoom, open wide" are over, dear. Tip the spoon into your mouth (no need to clap your teeth over it) and sip.

A word about slurping. Don't give me that "in some countries slurping is a compliment" bit. (And by the way, same thing with burping.) Noise is rude. And don't clink your spoon against your teeth, either. Consume quietly.

Utensils

Here is some very good basic advice about our friends the knife and fork, from Lillian Eichler's *The Book of Etiquette, Volume II*, published in 1923:

> In using the fork and knife, one can display a pleasing grace, or just the opposite—awkward clumsiness. It depends on how well one knows and follows the rules. The

first rule to remember is that a knife is never used for any other purpose than cutting food. It is unforgivable to use a knife to convey food to the mouth—unforgivable and vulgar.

The knife and fork should never be held in the same hand and when not being used, one or both should be placed entirely on the plate, their tips touching at the center and the handles resting on the edge.

Well, that's all fine, but what if there's ... more than one fork in front of you? What to do?

This is totally simple. No matter how complicated the table setting is, just remember: start with the utensil that is farthest from the plate. Say it to yourself: *outside in.*

Impress Future Out-laws

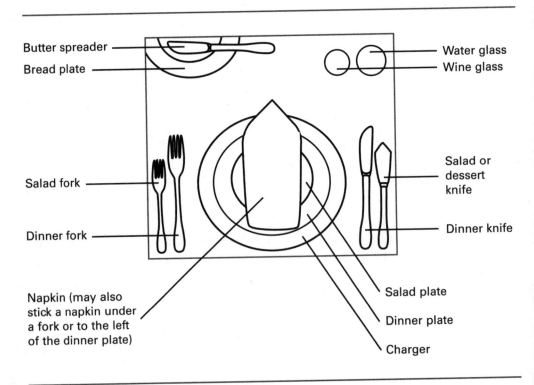

Butter spreader
Bread plate
Water glass
Wine glass
Salad fork
Salad or dessert knife
Dinner fork
Dinner knife
Napkin (may also stick a napkin under a fork or to the left of the dinner plate)
Salad plate
Dinner plate
Charger

The salad fork is like a dinner fork, but smaller. Where it's placed depends on what part of the meal the salad will appear in. If the salad is first, the fork is on the outside. If the salad is served mid-meal or after the main course to cleanse the palate (how very Norwegian), then it will be on the other side of the bigger dinner fork. Got it?

To the right of your dinner plate you will find the knives and spoons. The large spoon is for soup and the largest knife is the dinner knife. A flat knife that looks as though it would not cut soft cheese is your fish knife. The blades of the knives face the plate.

And one more thing. In a restaurant, if someone at the table drops a utensil on the floor, have the server pick it up and remove it to the kitchen. Leave a utensil on the floor, unless it poses a risk. At a private home, pick it up and place it to one side. On no account should a utensil be retrieved from the floor and used without being washed. Yuck.

Glasses

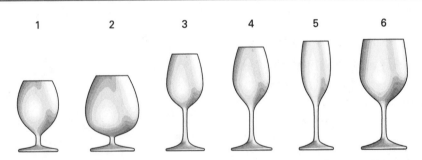

1. Water: Holding this full body glass by its short stem helps preserve the drink's chill.
2. Brandy: Roll between both hands, then cup it in one hand to bring out the bouquet of the brandy.
3. White wine: Hold this smaller glass with a wider bowl by the stem to pre serve the wine's chill.
4. Burgundy reds and Pinot Noirs: Taller than the white wine glass, with a wide bowl.
5. Champagne: A narrow glass that reduces the wine's surface area.
6. Red wine: The larger of the wine glasses, hold this glass where the bowl meets the stem.

Duh moment!

That big plate under the dinner plate is called a "charger." It is decorative. Do not eat off of it. In a restaurant it will be removed before dessert.

The water glass, usually the largest, is placed directly above the dinner knife. Wine glasses are to the right of the water glass and the champagne glass sits behind the wine glasses.

Which glass is which? In the good old days the big glasses were for red wine and the smaller glasses were for white wine. Champagne glasses were fluted or had a shallow bowl. Now it's all a little trickier. There are glasses for different types of wine—Riesling, Chardonnay, etc.... Give me peace! Let the host pour the wine; you just relax and drink.

Tricky Foods and How to Eat Them

Mastered all that? Now you're ready for the high-wire act—no net!

Spaghetti

Does one twirl or drill?

Let's consult the bigwigs on this one. If Miss Manners had her way (that's Judith Martin to her husband), one would use only a fork. Said instrument is planted firmly on the plate, twirled, then lifted to the mouth. Problems occur when the spaghetti first arrives and one cannot simply find the bottom of the plate. Mrs. Peggy Post allows the cutting of pasta, using spoon and fork as the preferred utensils. Yikes, Peg!

The Drill

My preference is for *the Twirl*: Lift a few strands of pasta onto your fork and place the tines against the round part of the spoon. Twirl. Eat. Practise this in the privacy of your own home. And dear, mix sauce into the pasta gently. No need to look as though you are mixing up a batch of cement.

The Twirl

Steamed clams

Served hot or cold, clams should be open when on your plate and ready to eat. Discard any unopened shells onto a spare plate. Do not eat unopened clams or anything that smells or looks odd. (*Before* cooking, the clams must be closed.)

TIP: Avoid spaghetti, French onion soup, and lobster on first dates and dinner with the boss.

Oysters

You are presented with a raw oyster. Yummy. Take your fork and make sure that the oyster is not attached to the shell. Drop in a dollop of sauce or squirt a bit of lemon if you so desire. Hold the oyster in the palm of your hand, bring it to your lips. Tip it into your mouth and swallow whole (not the shell, of course!). Raw oysters should be eaten only in reputable restaurants or homes where the cooks know what they are doing. In fact, there are enough food safety concerns surrounding oysters that you might want to avoid this choice altogether. (See page 165 in the chapter Making It Edible). Just use your head.

Fish

If you are ordering *whole* fish at a restaurant, ask that it be filleted in the kitchen. (That means that the bones are removed.) If you forget and an entire fish is served to you, smile and send it back to the kitchen with a request that it be filleted. Just trust me on this one.

About the fish fork and the fish knife—these two implements have seen their day but occasionally they make a reappearance. The fish fork has a bar between the tines and creepy little barbs on each side. The fish knife is flat, like a mini cake knife, and designed to push the fish flesh away from the bone.

Lobster

There's really no pretty way to eat lobster. Wear protective clothing and enjoy. You will need a nutcracker and small forks or picks. Hopefully the back of the lobster has been cracked in the kitchen. Snip the tips of claws and let the liquid drain out (preferably onto your plate rather than your lap). Twist the claws off at the knuckles. Crack the knuckles open and remove the meat. Crack the claw in half and remove the meat. Pull off the legs. Twist the tail from the joint where it meets the body. Use a pick or small fork to push the tail meat out. Dip the lobster in melted butter. You might want to mix a little pressed garlic into the butter, but be careful not to overwhelm the flavour.

You can eat the green liver, or *tomalley*, straight from the lobster, or mix it with lemon juice or butter and spread it on crackers. Just ignore the guffaws from the yahoos beside you. They don't know what they're missing.

French onion soup

You'll need a spoon and a knife. Dip your spoon into the hot cheese and bread. A quick twist of the wrist while holding the spoon and, with a little snip from your knife, a neat little package of cheese, bread, and broth may now be delivered to your mouth.

TIP: If you have a cold, stay home or leave the table. Blowing your nose in public will turn your fellow diners' stomachs at the best of times. To the Japanese, however, this is a real no-no.

Eating Japanese

Sushi is delectable raw fish or vegetables served on top of, or rolled up with, a fat, finger-sized roll of rice. The green stuff that comes with it is called wasabi (think of it as Japanese horseradish). A bowl will be placed in front of you—pour a small amount of soy sauce (not more than you need) into the bowl, take a small portion of the wasabi, and, gently now, mix it into the soy sauce. Now you can take your sushi and *dip*, not *dunk*, it into the sauce. Sometimes the chef will add the wasabi between the rice and the fish, so

TIP: Should you bring your hosts a small gift, do not expect them to open it in front of you. It is not the Japanese way. And be sure to wrap it nicely. Send a thank-you note for the dinner the next day.

no wasabi in the soy sauce in that case. To add a caveat: mixing wasabi and soy sauce is often considered "Western-style." In Japan, this exercise is frowned upon.

Sashimi is raw fish without the rice. It is usually served on shredded radish.

The opaque, orangey stuff is ginger and designed to clear the palate between bites of different fish.

High-end Japanese restaurants usually have *tatami* rooms—private rooms surround by paper doors, with low tables. In many cases there is a hole, or pit, under the table allowing feet to dangle. If not, then men usually sit cross-legged and women normally drop their knees to one side. Best of luck with your circulation. Remove your shoes at the door of the room. (Please tell me that you have remembered to wear nice socks.)

If you are out to impress your Japanese host, say *"Itadakimasu"* before the meal, which means "I gratefully receive." After the meal, say *"Gochiso-sama,"* which expresses gratitude and means, literally, "It was a feast."

There are definite rules when it comes to using chopsticks. Don't use them to point at people, move your plate, or wave in the air. If eating from a communal plate, flip them around and use the blunt end to pick up food and move the food to your plate. Never pick up food and put it on another person's plate.

Eat up. It is impolite to leave food on your plate. The rule is: if you can see it—eat it!

Sake, usually served hot, is rice wine. Easy here—the cheap stuff will give you one hell of a hangover. Pour out the sake for your neighbours. They, in turn, will fill your cup. Toasts are simple. Wait until everyone has a drink and then shout the Japanese version of "Cheers!"—*"Kampai!"*

More than You Really Wanted to Know

It's bad luck to leave your chopsticks in a bowl of rice. If you do, ghosts may join you for dinner.

Using chopsticks: Note: Japanese chopsticks are smaller, with thin tips, while Chinese chopsticks are longer and thicker, with square ends.

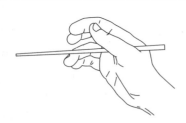

One chopstick rests between the base of the thumb and the palm. Use the ring finger to hold the lower part of the stick. Squeeze the stick down with the thumb while pushing it up from the ring finger.

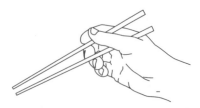

Use your thumb, and index and middle fingers to hold the chopsticks like a pen. The tips of the sticks should line up.

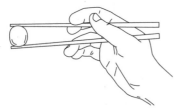

Move the top stick up and down toward the bottom stick to pick up food.

After much practise, your chopsticks will function like a pair of pincers.

Putting on the Ritz

When you make reservations at a high-end restaurant, they might ask for your credit card number. Be warned, they mean business. Welcome to the big time. Making a reservation is a perk. In return for being *on time* there is no waiting and you will be shown to a nice table. If your plans change, you should call as soon as possible and cancel. Anything else is simply rude.

Inquire about the dress code when making the reservation. And if someone in your party is in a wheelchair or wearing a cast, ask also about washroom accessibility. Some idiotic restaurants will say that they are *wheelchair accessible*, meaning you can get in the front door but, oops, the bathroom is up or down a set of stairs.

If you have a reservation, even though the restaurant might be crowded it is perfectly acceptable to make your way to the head of the line and say, "My name is Joe Blow and I have a reservation for six."

Men check their coats; women may choose whether or not to keep theirs with them. Some restaurants do not want to be responsible for checking an expensive coat.

It's not necessary to tip the maître d', but if you frequent the restaurant and plan to make this your home away from home, go for it. The maître d' or "host" will show you to your seat. If the table is against the wall, the woman traditionally faces the crowd—all the better to see the world come and go. (While the man, of course, has eyes only for her.)

The Menu

"Table d'hote" or *"Prix fixe"* means the entire meal is pre-planned, with limited choices and a set price. This often happens at holidays, in golf clubs and private clubs, for special events, or in small restaurants with a specialized menu.

"A la carte" means that you choose from the menu and pay the price listed for each separate item, unless specified. (Some meals will come with a soup or salad included.)

If the server reels off the specials and does not give the price, don't hesitate to ask.

If you are at the restaurant as someone's guest, you should be sensitive to your host's financial limitations and the high cost of fine dining. Wait to see if your host is beginning with an appetizer before you commit to the expensive, though no doubt delicious, *Brie en croute.* For your entrée, plan to order from the middle of the menu, where the items are usually moderately priced. If you are the host, you can signal your willingness to offer your guest the top-price items by ordering one yourself or recommending one: "Do you like lobster? I hope you'll try it, I understand it's excellent here."

Hailing the server like a flag-waver at a car race is a bit much, while whistling, hissing, or snapping your fingers is way over the top. It should take no more than eye contact, a raised eyebrow, and a smile in a high-end restaurant, or a half-raised hand in a family restaurant, to hail the server. Yelling, "Hey, over here!" will get you terrible service and send your guests running for cover. And bear in mind that the only people who can get away with calling servers "sweetheart" are seriously old men clutching oxygen tanks.

Menus are posted outside the restaurant, usually in a glass case. But let's say you missed that, or you are in foreign parts. And let's say you sit down at the table, open the menu, and have a heart attack. A plate of pasta is $62.50? (Okay, so it has some lobster tossed in, big deal.) If you can't afford it, simply close the menu, tell the waiter that you have reconsidered, and leave. No big deal, and no reason to get embarrassed. What? Like you're going to meet this guy at the laundromat?

The Wine List

The wine steward (or "sommelier") is the person who knows wine. If you avail yourself of his or her services, tip 20 percent of the wine bill. But wait a sec, it's fine to say, "Thank you, but we can manage." Really! A bottle of wine can set you back the rent. Don't be the big shot—know what you are buying and how much it costs. A really sensitive wine steward will recommend a bottle of wine, then point it out on the wine list. He's actually trying to show you the price.

Dining Details

Most restaurants will set the table with one set of cutlery. Did some of your cutlery disappear after your appetizer? In a family restaurant, it's probably wise to remove the cutlery from the plate that is about to be whisked off your table—you might never see another knife again! In a high-end restaurant, an observant server will bring you fresh cutlery, and if not, feel free to ask that it be brought. (How much are you paying for this meal again?)

Occasionally vegetables and potatoes are served in side dishes placed around your plate. Your best approach is to spoon the veggies onto your plate, but it's no *faux pas* to eat them directly out of the dish. (Just to make this perfectly clear—I am talking about single servings. On this side of the Atlantic, never, ever, eat out of a communal vegetable dish. Use the large spoon provided and put the vegetables on your plate.)

The Cheque, Please

When you're ready, signal the server with the universal symbol for "Cheque, please"— imaginary pen scribbling on imaginary notepad.

It's boring to watch people fight over the cheque. Equally annoying is the cheque-dodger or the one who constantly forgets his wallet. If you know you are planning to pick up the tab, it's not a bad idea to say so before food is ordered: "This will be my treat, tonight—no, really!" How frustrating for the empty-pocketed student to order a glass of water and the house salad, only to find out later he/she could have had the *filet mignon* (or at least the pasta special!).

If someone else offers to pick up the tab, you can protest *genially* and reach for your wallet, but if your would-be host insists, then back down quickly, with gracious thanks. If the bill has arrived and you're not sure if you are expected to pay or not, try, "Well, what does my contribution come to?" which should cue the other person to say either, "Put your wallet away—I thought you knew this was my treat!" or "Looks like about $120—no, you had most of the wine, make it $150." How sad!

If no one is treating, and the meals were roughly equivalent, best to divide the bill equally among the diners. If this would be terribly unfair to any of your party (after all, the vegetarian pasta special with a glass of mineral water is a far cry from the veal with several glasses of red wine followed by chocolate cake), then you can either ask for separate cheques *before* you order, or work the totals out quickly and discreetly, remembering tax and tip, and err on the side of generosity, just in case you overlooked something in your haste.

Check the bill for errors—briefly, please—tip accordingly (mental math, no calculators), and place your cash or card on the tray or in the envelope provided. If there is no tray you are likely in a more casual establishment and might be expected to pay the cashier at the front.

How to Open a Bottle of Champagne

Obviously, this is an issue for at-home entertaining, not restaurant dining, but if you are going to splash out on a bottle of champagne, you want to serve it properly, not waste a drop, and make the best possible impression on your guest or guests. Think Humphrey Bogart holding a glass of 1926 vintage Veuve Clicquot while gazing into Ingrid Bergman's eyes in *Casablanca*: *"Here's looking at you, kid."*

Here's the right way to do it:

1. Chill the champagne to 7 degrees C (45 degrees F) for three hours in the refrigerator or thirty minutes in an ice bucket.

2. Remove the foil and wrap a towel around the bottle. Yes, it looks snazzy, but it's really to help to keep the cork from flying away and to catch any escaping bubbly.

3. Hold the neck of the bottle while securing the top of the cork with your thumb. Twist off the metal cage that circles the cork. Keep your thumb on the cork. Hold the bottle at a 45-degree angle.

4. Turn the *bottle*, not the cork. Go slowly. No shaking the bottle, please, you don't want to waste the champagne by making it into a fountain.

5. Release the cork gently—don't "pop" it—and pour the champagne down the side of the glass (like pouring beer). Use champagne flutes rather than the wide, shallow glasses—keeps the bubbles bubbling longer!

6. Done. Toast! Drink!

TIP: Carry small bills or appropriate change so you always have something handy for quick tips (doorman, valet, etc....)

Tipping

As long as people who serve the public are paid less because of the expectation that they will make up for the lack of income with tips, then tipping will be an expected and necessary part of our culture.

Restaurants and Bars

Stiff the server at your peril. However, with the exception of a pre-set service charge on your bill, you are in control of how much you tip.

- Lunch servers generally expect a 10 percent tip, while dinner is usually 15 percent. Give 20 percent for exceptional service. If a service charge has already been added, you may leave an extra 5 to 10 percent for great service. The tip is calculated on the bill before tax.
- Maître d's can be given anywhere from $2 to $5 for a special table.
- Busboys do not expect a tip. Coat checks are $1 per item.
- At buffets where a server brings you drinks, tip a dollar or two.
- Leave bartenders serving drinks at the table $2 to $3, or 20 percent if he or she is running a tab.

Hotels, Resorts, Motels

- The doorman: $2. (Keep in his good books. Over the course of your stay he might give you restaurant tips and flag down the cab that gets you to the airport in time.)
- The bellman who helps with luggage: $2 to $5. (More if he takes your bags up to your room and does a security check, shows you how the TV and radio work, and so on. Give him $5 to $10, plus $1 a bag.)

- A parking attendant: $2 (free valet parking doesn't mean you get out of tipping).
- The concierge: $5 to $10 (if you ask for show tickets or sightseeing advice).
- Leave the maid $1 per day, or more if you need extra towels and shampoos. (Call the desk first and ask if a 15 percent service charge is added to the bill.)
- If you call down for extras like an iron or more pillows, tip the housekeeper $1 to $2.
- Pool-side attendants may be tipped $1 for bringing you dry towels.

Airports

- Porters usually receive $1 per bag, minimum $3 for the job. (They often know where reserve taxis are.) In some cases there is a set rate that is noted on their cart.

TIP: Don't tip airline attendants for bringing you a drink or your meal up in the air.

Taxi Drivers

- Tip taxi drivers 15 percent of the fare and an extra 50 cents for each bag.
- Limo drivers get 15 percent of the total bill.

Cruises

- As a rule, the tips are given out on your final night. Expect to fork out from $20 to $30 per day per couple in tips.
- Check out the "cruise preparation kit." It comes with envelopes for you to put your money in just before you depart.

Miscellaneous

Darn near everyone expects a tip for what, in the real world, is just good manners. Still, you gotta do what you gotta do …

- *Emergency roadside service:* $5 to $10. Has he put his life in jeopardy to help you? Give him $50.
- *Hairdresser:* 15% of total.
- *Assistant* (the person who washed your hair): $2 to $5.

- *Personal trainer:* $50 once you have reached your goal. Some clubs discourage tipping. If your trainer is employed by the club, as opposed to a freelancer, give him or her a small gift instead.
- *Car wash attendant:* $2. More if you are a regular.
- *Valet parking:* $2 to $5.
- *Kid who checks your oil at a gas station:* $2.
- *Furniture delivery guys:* $5 a person. More if they have to remove doors to get the sofa into the house.
- *Kid who helps you with your groceries:* $2, unless the store discourages tipping.
- *Courier:* The larger companies typically do not accept tips. If this person delivers to you regularly, give a small gift at Christmas.

What if you are stone-broke and simply do not have the money to tip that helpful roadside service guy or maid at the hotel? Send an e-mail or note to the person's employer. If the employer pays attention, it might end up being more valuable to your helper in the long run than a cash handout.

Dear Sir or Madam,

Last night I was stranded on Highway 44. Mr. Hero, your employee, came to my rescue. The service was excellent, fast, and helpful in a very stressful situation.

Sincerely,
Gordon Ran-out-of-gas Smith

Party Time

Once, a party was a bunch of friends and a two-four. Now that you've entered the adult world, social events take a little more planning ... okay, they take a lot more planning. Here are a few tips Mother never told you (sorry!).

1. Invite more women than men. Sexist, a wee bit, but women tend to circulate more.
2. Mix it up. The seminary graduate and the fine arts grad might have more in common than you think. Mix up ages, too. But think twice about having your little sister and her "hot" best friends join in. For one thing, underage drinking is a

TIP: If smokers at your party have stunk up the place, next day place a wide bowl of white vinegar in the corner of each room and leave it for twenty-four hours.

totally bad idea (and don't kid yourself—they will drink). For another, in a fog, your own, older friends might misjudge the ages of invited guests. Bad, bad idea.

3. Are you past the age of massive party gate-crashing? Invite lots of people for an all-out bash. Half won't show.

4. Keep the food plentiful and bite-sized. You'll need tons of food on hand, plus a few frozen pizzas in the freezer just in case. If it's a big party, set up lots of bottled water, pop, and juice around the room. Lots of food in your guests' stomachs and lots of non-alcoholic beverages will minimize the damage from stupid-drinking.

5. Be clear about what your guests can expect. If you invite people for 7 p.m., for example, they will expect dinner.

8. Have something for everyone to eat—think vegetarian, kosher, food allergies. If you are concerned about peanuts, just don't serve them.

9. How much wine to buy? The conservatives will say one-half bottle of wine per invited guest or three bottles of beer per person. I'd double that, but you'll figure out what works best for your crowd by trial and error. It's fine to ask people to BYOB (Bring Your Own Bottle). A word about serving hard liquor—*one tequila, two tequila, three tequila, floor.* You are responsible for what you serve. Watch your guests, and be prepared to deal with guests who drink too much (get them a cab, pinch their keys). Stay sober yourself!

Preparing the Premises

Make sure any candles you light are protected and not likely to tip over. Check that the smoke detector is working. Provide smokers with a Smokers' Corner, preferably outside, with a big, safe ashtray.

Unless you want your chums to inspect your medicine cabinet (they will anyway), leave mouthwash, disposable cups, and headache pills on the counter. Clean the bathroom well, including the

TIP: True, most coats end up piled on the bed. But if your boss arrives wearing a cashmere coat, hanging it is a good idea—preferably not on a wire hanger. (The only items that belong on wire hangers are dry-cleaned shirts.)

tub. (Closing the shower curtain won't really help.) Empty the dishwasher, the wastebaskets, and set out containers in obvious places for garbage and for recycling bottles and cans.

If you are having this party in a house (as opposed to an apartment), walk around outside and make sure there are no obvious pitfalls—like an empty swimming pool or unlit staircase.

TIP: Want a polite way to say "bring food"? Try "bring a dish to share."

Invite the neighbours in an attempt to prevent them from ratting you out to the cops. Another option is to tell them when the party is expected to wrap and—here's the clincher—give them your phone number. Better that they call you at 3 a.m. and yell at you than the aforementioned police. If the party really does get out of hand, noise-wise, hand-deliver a small present (flowers, chocolates, whatever) with an apology to your neighbours the next day.

Get the hell out of my house, I'm tired!

The party is over. You're tired. Your guests are not! To state the obvious—stop serving drinks when you want the party to end. And at the risk of sounding like Grandma, you might want to put on a pot of coffee half an hour before you want your guests to get the heck out. (The smell alone might be enough of a "get out" signal.) You could try, "Well, thanks for sticking around to clean up!" and hand the lingerers a garbage bag—

worst-case scenario, you get some help. But if you have really had enough, stand up and say, "It was great having you over. Thanks for coming." Remain standing, then slowly walk toward the door. Or offer to call a cab.

Big Events

At this point in your life, there are two, possibly three other types of social events (beyond parties) that you will be attending: weddings, funerals, and the occasional baptism or christening. (As you grow older, add bar mitzvahs and bat mitzvahs to the list, but that's getting ahead of ourselves.)

The Wedding

You have just been invited to a wedding. Great! Before you say yes, though, consider the cost. Will you have to travel to the wedding? Will you be staying in a hotel? Will you need a new suit or dress? Can you afford an appropriate gift?

Note: Occasionally, if you are a rather casual friend or acquaintance of the couple, you might be invited to attend a wedding ceremony (especially if it's in a church) but not the reception, so read the invitation carefully. This is within acceptable etiquette and springs from the old-fashioned notion that the ceremony itself is more important than the big old party that follows.

Whatever your answer, try to respond to the invitation within forty-eight hours or you're bound to forget. This is very important, and a cause of great wedding-planning stress, because accurate numbers are needed for the caterer, for organizing the seating at the reception, and lots of other details. If you cannot attend, a gift is not required (but you can send one anyway). You might also want to go the extra mile and send an e-mail or telegram to be read out at the wedding. (Telegrams are way classier. Send it to the reception care of the Best Man.)

If it's a "Yes":

- Dress according to the wishes of the bride and groom. (If the groom says "jeans," I'd double-check with the bride or suitable representative.)
- Never, ever show up with an uninvited guest, and do not call up and ask to bring a friend. Likewise, do not assume that children are welcome unless they are explicitly invited.
- Turn up on time.

- You will probably be ushered to a seat for the ceremony. There's a general assignment of "friends of the groom" to one side and "friends of the bride" to the other, but it is perfectly fine to say to the usher, especially if you are attending solo, "Oh, I see some friends are already seated—would it be all right if I joined them?" Usually it's a relief to the usher to know where to put you.
- Smile to the people sitting on either side of you. If appropriate, whisper your name and relation to the bride or groom.
- Unless the marriage service requires you to disrobe and pledge your allegiance to some offshore demigod, just go with the flow—that is, stand and sit when you are expected to. (Do not take Communion unless this is your habit.)
- Do not get drunk at the reception.
- Tell the bride that she looks beautiful, no matter what!

TIP: What not to say: anything whatsoever about the past sexual experience or past girl/boyfriends of the bride or groom.

If you are invited to a wedding from a culture you are not really acquainted with, remember: weddings in every culture are a celebration. Call and ask about appropriate dress, any customs you should be prepared for, potential faux pas, and acceptable colours for your attire. Turn up on time and bring your smile. Happy, respectful, and sober is all you really have to be.

The Gift

Send the gift through the delivery service at the store, mail it, courier it, have it dropped off by carrier pigeon, but *do not* bring it to the wedding. A gift table is usually set up at the wedding reception, but this is how gifts get lost, stolen, or damaged. Cards get misplaced, and the bride and groom might never know it was you who gave them the one-of-a-kind cheese tray.

Note: If you send a gift and, after a suitable amount of time, you have not received any kind of acknowledgment, call and check (tactfully) that the gift did in fact arrive. Keep the receipt when you buy the gift and request that a gift receipt be enclosed with the present.

Just for fun: If you are attending a Jewish wedding, and you would like to give a cash gift, note that eighteen is a lucky number (along with multiples thereof). Eighteen stand for the letter *"chai"* which in Hebrew which means "life." So, if you're giving money, give $18, $36, $54, and so on.

Baptism or Christening

This one's a no-brainer. Unless you have been asked to be a godparent (in which case, speak to the minister or priest about your role in the service and what is expected of you down the road), then all you have to do is turn up on time with a baby present. (Better yet, deliver the present a few days before the big event.) If you're not used to attending church, the dress code is "subdued and respectful." The good news for women is that hats are never wrong in church, and can be worn throughout the service (so long as they are not too big and ostentatious).

Most christenings take place during an otherwise routine church service, so be aware that you will have to participate in the whole thing. (You might want to inquire as to the kind of service you are in for and how long it is likely to be.) Make sure you have a $5 bill in your pocket for the collection plate. If it's a private ceremony, then it will last a mere fifteen minutes or so at a preset time. Expect to be fed well at a celebration after the ceremony.

The traditional gifts are silver spoons or rattles or some other keepsake, but any baby-related gift is fine. Books and teddy bears are fine, too.

Funerals

Sadly (no pun intended), many funerals have turned into parties. That may be fine in the case of a memorial, which usually takes place weeks or even months after a death, but a full-out wingding immediately after a death can be very hard on the people very close to the departed. A little decorum, m'dear.

In most cases, news of a "passing" or death is conveyed quickly and efficiently by telephone. When you hear the news, and assuming that you are not totally distraught, it is perfectly acceptable (and often very welcome) to offer to pass the word along, especially if you're in touch with people that the family might not be aware of or have a way of contacting. It is also acceptable to call people who might not have known the deceased personally but are chums of the family. (Many will not attend the funeral but would like to know, and have the opportunity to send a condolence card.) When you first learn about a death, ask if the funeral will be private and, if not, whether there will be an announcement in the newspaper giving the details. Be sure to ask the name of the paper. Do *not* say, "Thanks for calling but we have tickets to the game on Thursday. (The deceased) wouldn't want us to miss that."

Don't wait to be invited—unless there is some indication that the funeral is private (in which case details will not be announced publicly) you should assume that you are welcome to attend. There is no RSVP involved, either. You do not have to call and say you can't come, and in fact unless you are a close relative this is not news the family particularly wants to hear. If you can't be there, just send a card. (See below for tips on writing a condolence letter.)

The newspaper announcement will have all the relevant information, including the times of the "viewing" or "visitation" (a time to "pay your respects"—see below). If the announcement says, "In lieu of flowers" it means don't send flowers. Instead, you may send a contribution to a charity, usually named by the family. The address may or may not be in the actual announcement but, in most cases, you will find envelopes of the organization at the funeral home. Pick one up, and send in a cheque. The charity will inform the family of your donation. If you would like to be absolutely sure that the family knows that you have sent a cheque, mention it in your condolence note (but not the dollar value, which would be crass).

Be careful about sending balloons and such. This might be appropriate at a memorial that is designed to be a *celebration of life* but it's rarely acceptable at a funeral.

The condolence note

When writing a condolence note, be aware that this is one of those things that you are allowed to do awkwardly, because it is more important to *do it* than to *do it well*. Use an attractive note card, or even a store-bought sympathy card, as long as you promise to write something personal and not leave it to Hallmark to express your thoughts. Address it either to the person closest to the deceased or, in some cases, the person *you know well* who is affected by the death. Say something as simple as, "My thoughts are with you at this difficult time," or go a little further and offer a brief memory of the deceased and how much he or she will be missed.

Dear Aunt Ellen,

I was so very sorry to hear of Uncle Frank's death, and wish I could have been with you and the rest of the family at the funeral. I'll cherish my memories of fishing trips with Uncle Frank, and I'll always remember his wonderful sense of humour and cheerful laugh.

Know that my thoughts are with you, and of course with my cousins, at this difficult time.

Your niece,

Charlotte

Most important part? Do this as soon as you think of it, or you won't do it at all and you'll feel bad when you realize the family has been saying, "Did she hear that Frank died? We never heard a word …"

Appropriate Clothing

Black clothing is no longer expected of those who attend a funeral, but *dark, subdued, respectful, tasteful* should be your watchwords.

Ladies

Wear a dress or a suit, please, although a skirt or dress pants with a tasteful blouse will work as well. Cleavage, front and back, should not make an appearance, even if the deceased worked at Hooters. Nix leather or backless anything. And just because that little black cocktail dress is the *only* black thing you have does not mean it's suitable funeral attire. To continue the *don't* list, don't wear flip-flops, running shoes, or over-the-top jewellery.

Been there
Done THAT

Rob was the quarterback of the school football team and incredibly popular. He was killed in a car accident, and his parents and family just fell apart. The funeral was terribly sad. His dad just sat and sobbed. Instead of expecting his parents to celebrate his life, we, as his teammates and friends, organized our own memorial at a favourite pub a few weeks after the funeral. We, of course, told the family about it. The funny thing was, Rob's dad showed up. He loved hearing all the stories we told. I will never forget that night, and I'll never forget Rob.

—AILENE, 22

Gentlemen

Given your age, you might or might not have a dark suit, but I hope you have a plain white shirt, a jacket, a tie, and some shoes that are not running shoes. Dress as well as you can, and remember that you are there to say goodbye. It's how you *behave* that counts, not the colour of your shoes.

The Christian Funeral

A Christian funeral might or might not include a *viewing* at the funeral home, with an open casket. (You do not have to go up to the coffin and have a look-see if you do not want to.) If this is called a "visitation" the casket might be present but closed. Usually this will happen at set times announced in the newspaper notice, and you are welcome to come by, sign a book, look at the photographs that are often scattered about, speak to any family members present, and leave. This can take five to thirty minutes but seldom longer. This is called a "condolence call" or "paying one's respects." You might consider doing this if you want to reach out to the family but are unable to attend the funeral.

TIP: Think you won't need Kleenex in your pocket or purse? Think again. You have no idea what might get the tears started. Be prepared!

The funeral service itself might be at a church or in a chapel at the funeral home. It can take an hour or so, seldom longer. Remember that the type of service has likely been chosen and planned by the deceased's grieving relatives. It might not be your idea of what would be appropriate for the deceased, but that's an opinion you should keep to yourself. You might find, in fact, that the funeral the family has chosen gives you a different perspective on someone you thought you knew. If you can't honestly say, "It was a lovely service, and just right for (the deceased)," simply express your condolences to the family, or say nothing at all.

If there is a casket, there will most likely be pallbearers. If you are asked to be a pallbearer (a great honour), your job will be to escort the coffin into the church or chapel (a "processional") and out again (a "recessional"). Most coffins are placed on a stand with wheels, therefore you do not have to actually carry them. In the rare circumstance where the coffin must be hoisted up, the funeral home staff will do the lifting. There will be plenty of people around to guide you through this. Don't worry about making a mistake. In some cases the casket remains in place and is only removed after the guests have left.

Arrive a little early. Wait at the back of the church or chapel if people are being escorted to their seats. Fellas, if you arrive with a woman, she will take the escort's arm and you will follow behind. (Got that, ladies?) Don't change seats unless you want to give one up to someone who is older or disabled. If you are not escorted to a seat, be aware the first few rows are generally reserved for family, who will likely enter last. If the venue is full, stand at the back of the room unless told to go elsewhere. (Many funeral homes have a private room set aside with an audiovisual feed for very large funerals.)

Unless the deceased is a family member, you are not required or expected to go to the cemetery. If you do go, expect mud. A funeral home employee will place a sign on your car. (It is a *clean* car, right?) Turn on your headlights and join in the funeral procession, driving slowly and following the directions of police officers along the route. Once at the site, park and gather around the plot. The pastor, priest, or minister will say a prayer. The coffin may or may not be lowered into the ground. Flowers are usually laid on the coffin.

If the body is cremated, the service remains the same. The family may or may not go to the crematorium. If so, a short service might be held there.

The reception may take place in the funeral home, church hall, or at a private home. Be sure to connect with at least one family member while you're there, so they don't have to say, later, "I saw Cousin Joe, did anyone actually talk to him?" Say nothing but nice things about the deceased and keep that "funny" story about how he stuck you with a bill or slept with your girlfriend to yourself. It won't be funny on that day. "I'm so sorry," covers a great deal of ground. Do not say, "Call me if there is anything I can do" unless you mean it. In fact, there is a lot of work that happens after a funeral in terms of sorting out belongings and taking care of legal and financial affairs. That is very hard on everyone. If you can be of assistance, great!

Unless you are a close and very helpful family member, you should not be the last to leave the reception. Don't stay too long—no matter how much you might be

> **Been** there **Done** THAT
>
> I can't tell you how many guys turn up in the parking lot with ties in their hand saying, "Can you tie this for me?"
>
> —FUNERAL DIRECTOR

enjoying seeing old friends and relatives, this is not a party. Offer to give an elderly aunt a lift home, if you can, but otherwise make a gracious exit. If the reception is at the funeral home or church hall, there might be a semi-secret get-together for the nearest and dearest to follow, but no matter what rumours you hear, wait for someone to say, "You will come back to Aunt Ellen's with us, won't you?" Otherwise, get lost.

A memorial service usually takes places some weeks or months after the death, when people have had time to get their heads around it and plan something more celebratory. It can take many forms—a "celebration of the life of," a great party, or a more sober affair to honour and reflect on the life and contributions of the deceased. Likely you will get an invitation in the mail. While there is seldom an RSVP on the invitation, it would not be out of line this time to call if you cannot come. If there is an RSVP on the invitation, reply within forty-eight hours.

The memorial service might be in a church, complete with prayers, hymns, and eulogies, or it might be in a rented hall and include musical entertainment and champagne. The invitation should offer some hints. Dress accordingly—but the earlier cautions about cleavage and bling still apply.

The Jewish Funeral

Jewish funerals are held soon after the death (usually within twenty-four hours, as embalming the body is forbidden by Jewish law). Since the grief of the mourners is very fresh, no matter what a party guy he was, don't expect one of those "celebration of life" roaring wakes with kegs of beer. The rituals depend on whether the deceased was Orthodox, Conservative, or Reform.

Rarely does a funeral take place in a synagogue. It will likely take place in a chapel or funeral home. Dress conservatively, or in black. Orthodox and Conservative Jews do not include flowers in the chapel, although the Reform traditions might. (Confused? Make a call to the funeral home and ask.)

At the entrance to the chapel there will be a box of *yarmulkes* or *kippot*—head coverings for men and boys. All males are required to wear a kipa (singular of *kippot*). Reach in and take one. Stick it on your head and off you go. You may or may not return it at the end of the service.

Women are not required to cover their heads, although there are usually lacy head coverings offered near the *kipa* box. The exception are the synagogues that are egalitarian and ask that both males and females cover their heads as a gesture of respect.

In the Orthodox tradition, men and women sit separately. Just go with the flow. The coffin will not be open. It will be a plain pine box without any adornments.

The service will include readings by the rabbi, a eulogy by a family member or friend, and often a cantor chanting a psalm.

The family leaves the chapel first.

At the cemetery, the first prayer, called the Kaddish, is recited. Males then either throw a handful of earth onto the coffin or, in the more Orthodox and Conservative tradition, peel off their jackets and pick up shovels. Remain until the coffin is covered or the grave is filled.

"*Shiva,*" the Hebrew word for "seven," takes place over the next seven days. Family usually visits during the first three days, while friends and neighbours come later in the week. Make this *condolence call* at a convenient time, afternoon or evening. Do not visit on the Sabbath, which is Friday sunset until Saturday sunset. In an Orthodox home, the bell will be covered. Knock and enter. The door will be unlocked. Speak quietly, say something nice, and leave with words like, "May God comfort you." A shiva visit might last between fifteen and thirty minutes—do what feels right. A short service happens in the morning and evening. Stand.

The Buddhist Funeral

A Buddhist funeral resembles a Christian one. The funeral usually takes place in a funeral home, with prayers and a eulogy, within a week of the death. The casket will be open and everyone is expected to view the body. Stand beside the casket, bow slightly, and move on.

Everyone is welcome to attend the cremation or burial, but guests do not participate. After the service, guests are often invited back to the house. Do not visit the home of the deceased before the funeral.

The Islamic Funeral

This takes place two or three days after the death and is generally conducted in a funeral home. Family, friends, and neighbours may make condolence calls before the funeral.

The coffin is always closed. The short and simple service is conducted by an imam. Muslims are never cremated, and guests are welcome to come to the gravesite.

Mourning following the funeral lasts forty days, and condolence calls are welcome during this period. By all means, send flowers to the home.

The Hindu Funeral

A Hindu funeral takes place at the crematorium. The body is kept at home for twenty-four hours or less before the cremation. Friends and neighbours may visit the family and the deceased at the house during that period. Flowers are welcome. The body is taken from the home directly to the place of cremation. All are welcome to sit and hear the service, which is conducted by a family member or priest. The body will be in full view. Stay or go for the actual cremation, it's up to you.

In most cases there will be a reception at a family home after the cremation. If you make a condolence call later in the week, it is customary to bring fruit.

The Non-Religious Funeral

In some cases, a friend or family member might play the role of a subdued MC and introduce various people to deliver short eulogies or speeches. If you are asked to speak, a brief, sweet story about the deceased that elicits smiles or laughter is appropriate. Anything that qualifies as a "joke" is inappropriate. The deceased might have been able to eat five pies without using his hands and wash it all down with a barrel of beer, but likely his parents don't need to be reminded at this moment. Remember to talk about the deceased and *not about yourself.* What not to say: *"Bill was a great influence on my life. I was down and out when he picked me up from the gutter. He helped me see the light. Without him I would not be president ... "* Yadda, yadda, yadda.

If ever there is a time when you can stumble or fumble while speaking in public, this is it. Don't worry about your presentation. A favourite poem (preferably one that does not begin, "There once was a girl from Kilkenny ...") may be read instead of a short speech.

The common theme of all funerals is *respect.* Offer that, and no matter what, your presence will be welcome.

And no, there are no collections at any funerals. You don't need to bring money.

Electronic Etiquette

I know, you can't imagine giving up your text-message or your e-mail. No one is asking you to. It's just that the Internet can be such a rude and sloppy place. If you insist on making the virtual world your primary realm of communication, please, do your part to keep it civilized, okay? And that goes for your phone behaviour as well!

E-mail Etiquette (Or "Netiquette")

I can't begin to tell you about text-message etiquette: it's almost a contradiction in terms. But with e-mail, it's simple: whatever etiquette rules apply in real life, apply them also here.

- Live is ast and the medium is the mes but the there are oder peple tying to red this so plase check your spel and gramher.
- Keep it short. Get to the point.
- Always put something recognizable in the Subject Box, even if it's just your name and a hint of what's inside.
- Jokes are great—just don't send them on. Same goes with anything that says, "If you pass this on to two people good luck will arrive by midnight."
- At some point you will forward an e-mail that is not meant for the receiver. Mistakes happen. Apologize profusely. Flowers are an option. If you should be on the receiving end, forgive and forget.
- Never, ever, forward an e-mail without permission from the original sender. If you do have permission, do not change the message.
- Don't ever send anything written in anger (also known as a *flame*). You will regret it. The joy of snail mail is that, by the time an angry letter is written, and by the time you have tracked down an envelope and stamp and located one of the dwindling number of mailboxes, most of us will have thought better of the whole

> ## Duh moment!
>
> A few students used anti-Semitic and racist comments in an e-mail. Guess what? Their teachers read it, their friends read it, and their friends' parents read it—and the entire e-mail ended up on the front page of two national newspapers. Good. They deserved to have their butts kicked, or worse. That aside, how would you feel if your e-mail was splashed all over the World Wide Web? Well then, don't write it.

thing and ripped it up. If you should be so unlucky as to receive a flame, ignore it. It drives flamers crazy.

- TYPING IN CAPITAL LETTERS MEANS THAT YOU ARE SHOUTING. That's not nice. Stop it.
- Answer an e-mail with a reference to the sender's remarks. That sounds complicated, so here's an example. Do not write:
"Fine"
"Sure"
"OK"
"NO"
Put the words in context: "Timmy, you asked me to marry you, and the answer is no."
- Who has the last word? In real life we say goodbye. I don't know why we don't do that with e-mails. Consider the feelings of the receiver. A sharp cut-off might make a recipient feel as though he has been dumped. Close off your last e-mail with, "It's been great talking to you. I'm sure we'll be in touch at Christmas."
- E-mail cards only work for people under 30 (and only for under-30s with high-speed Internet). Not to generalize here, but your grandfather would appreciate a snail-mail birthday card.
- By all means, learn "emoticons." Emoticons are facial expressions made by a certain series of keystrokes, like the smiley face :) . For a complete list that you might want to print and post above your computer, go to www.computer-user.com/resources/dictionary/emoticons.html. *Exception:* if Grandma is new to this e-mail thing, then forget it. She has enough to contend with.
- You don't need to start an e-mail with "Dear Potty Dottie," or end with "Sincerely yours, Dozy." However, beginning with the recipient's name and ending with your name is always a good idea.
- Pity those of us with dial-up. Don't send attachments bigger than 50K without permission.

Netiquette at Work

What's the difference between sitting on the bottom rung of the corporate ladder and being midway up the climb? (This is not a joke, by the way.) Often, it's the tone of your e-mails. To succeed in business, a certain "formality" is required. (I know, you hate that word.) Goofy quotes, smiley faces, and jokes are *out* if the plan is to get to the top.

Read on.

- Start a business e-mail formally, using Mr. or Ms., and be prepared to switch to a more informal form of address once you have received a reply. Outside of North America, a formal address to an equal or a superior is always expected.
- Think short and sweet. Start with your subject line: make it clear and compelling.
- If you want people to respond, end the e-mail with a question. You will soon find out if your e-mails are being read.
- We can't see you, or your body language! You might think people will understand that you're just being sarcastic, but you don't know what kind of mood they'll be in when they read it. What may be interpreted as funny one day may be misinterpreted the next.
- Take a step back. Consider setting a five-minute buffer between when you write your e-mail and when you hit Send. Go get yourself a cup of coffee. Come back. Re-read.
- Always respond to an e-mail. If you can't keep up, get help.
- Use spell-check and the thesaurus.

> **Duh moment!**
>
> Never, ever answer e-mails at night after you have had a glass of wine. Never!

Cellphones

Let's cut to the chase here. Cellphones have lost their cachet. We know you have one. Five-year-olds carry them in their Blue's Clues backpacks, for Pete's sake! So let's make this short and snappy. Repeat after me.

- I will keep my phone on vibrate *always.*
- I will not holler into a cellphone in public even though my grandfather is on the other end and keeps yelling, "Speak louder!"
- I will not subject fellow elevator captives to my cellphone conversations.
- I will not set the ringer to annoying compositions, goofy songs, or sappy renditions of James Blunt.
- I recognize that wearing more than two wireless devices on my belt makes me look like Buddy Holly in Grade 8. Likewise, wearing an earpiece and talking to the air

makes me look like the Borg, or an escapee from a place one visits only on Sundays between 2 and 5 p.m.

- I will not dial while driving. Wait, I will not talk on a hand-held phone at all while driving.
- I will not sit down at a table in a restaurant and dump my phone beside the condiments. If the deal is that important, my trusty assistant will contact me by telepathy.
- P.S. What to do if you have lost your cellphone? Go to the Finances chapter, page 357.

Land Lines

You should assume that the person you are calling has Caller ID, and if you've dialed a wrong number, apologize. *Really* apologize if you woke some poor guy up on a Saturday morning at six. (Who do you call at six in the morning, anyway?)

Don't call people without children before 9 a.m., or people with children after 10 p.m. Don't make business calls on the weekend unless it's really urgent.

Here's the big question: how many messages do you leave on an answering machine before giving up? The minimum is one, the maximum is three. Perhaps you are calling someone to ask him or her out on a date. Call twice. It's perfectly fine to assume that he or she did not get the message the first time. Two calls are enough. Only call a third time if you have been leaving messages with someone under ten years of age or that brain-freeze stage between thirteen and eighteen. (A pox on anyone who leaves messages that run to the end of the tape.) Keep your message clear and concise, and leave your phone number—always.

Headphones—Use Your Head

Speaking as an old-fart here, there's nothing more annoying than sitting next to someone who's lost in their own little iTunes world. Unless of course they are forcing me to listen to their tunes too, thanks to a volume control dialed way up high. Then it's more than annoying—it's stupid and it's rude.

If you insist on tuning out the world with headphones, then please use your head. Keep the volume low enough that your neighbour doesn't have to hear a constant *shuka-shuka-shuka*. Not sure? Test it on a friend. And if you're listening while shopping, be polite to the salespeople and remove the buds when it's time to make a purchase.

So, there you go, everything you need to know to leave a good impression in this big wide world. It's not rocket science, just common sense. You'll notice that etiquette and good manners have more to do with considerate behaviour and excellent social skills than choosing the right fork at the dinner table. The person with great interpersonal skills, empathy, communication, and an ability to see the point of view of others will always, always win the day.

Resources

Miss Manners' Guide to Excruciatingly Correct Behavior and *Miss Manners' Guide for the Turn-of-the-Millennium*, both by Judith Martin.

Emily Post's Etiquette, a 2004 update of the original classic by Peggy Post, great-grandaughter-in-law of the great Emily. Peggy Post has published a good many other titles on the subject of etiquette, such as *Emily Post's the Etiquette Advantage in Business: Personal Skills for Professional Success* and *Excuse Me, But I Was Next ...: How to Handle the Top 100 Manners Dilemmas.*

16

Travel

If you reject the food, ignore the customs, fear the religion
and avoid the people, you might better stay home.

—JAMES MICHENER

We want you to travel, see the world, experience new sights and sounds, *yadda, yadda, yadda* … but pardon us if we worry! It's part of a parent's job description. And there's lots to worry about. The world has become a scarier place. There's political strife and terrorism, of course. Then there are parasites, snakes, spiders, and food poisoning. And just think of all the diseases you could run into: typhoid, hepatitis A, yellow fever, malaria, cholera, rabies, influenza, and traveller's diarrhea, to name a few.

Your desire to see, taste, and experience a new country is laudable, but spending time in a Mexican prison will not bring you any closer to experiencing "the real Mexico." Obey the laws. Read the damn signs. Leave Greek antiquities on the ground. Wear what you are told to wear. Don't pet strange animals. And follow the rules of the road, even if every person driving a car in China or France seems to have his/her own personal code of road behaviour.

If you are determined to explore a bit, read on. What you'll get here are hundreds of tips, plus websites from the United States, Canada, and Britain, with a few Aussie sites tossed in for fun. Most of the sites listed have dozens of links that will send you all over the place. We are not recommending any one site over any other. These are just to get you started.

Out of Town but in Your Budget

Hate to put a damper on things, but you'll need to think about how much this fun in the sun is gonna cost.

1. Figure out how much you can afford to spend.
2. Make a list of costs: travel expenses, food, accommodations, daily activities, entertainment, souvenirs. Now double it!
3. Don't get upset if Number 1 and Number 2 are miles apart. Prioritize and eliminate!
4. Look for travel packages. Be creative.
5. Travel expenses in your destination country can eat up a big chunk of change. In Europe, look into the price of a rail pass. In North America, it is often better to rent a car. Remember to add in the cost of gas, taxes, and insurance.
6. Make sure that you set aside some emergency funds.

Find a Ticket!

What's the best, most reliable, or cheapest way to buy a ticket that will get you on your way? Here are some suggestions.

Travel agents: Most travel agents receive commissions from the vendors (airlines, hotels, tour agencies). They pay—you do not. A travel agent has access to deals that often are not available elsewhere. They can take the headache out of searching for the cheap ticket or the right vacation, and they often include travel insurance in their packages.

Internet: Thanks to the Internet, travel prices have gone down. At sites like Expedia, Orbitz, and Travelocity you can find great deals on airfares, hotels, and package deals. And you can do it all at three in the morning! But it takes time to compare all the different rates.

Guidebooks and newspaper reviews: The Saturday travel section always has something to offer. And travel guidebooks are your new best friend. Hit the library and read them for free.

Booking directly: If you have the flexibility and can leave on a dime, tour and cruise companies often offer half-price (or lower) rates. Get on their e-mail lists.

Cost Cutters

Cheap airline tickets are available if you are willing to fly standby. This you know. What you might not know: you can get on your favourite carrier's e-mail list and they will tell you when the sales are on. Also, check out www.cheaptickets.com, www.lowestfare.com, and www.priceline.com.

Before-You-Go Checklist

- Pay off your credit cards. At the very least, make sure that you have enough credit available on them for emergencies. And read the fine print concerning the card's policies. Some provide insurance.
- Call your credit card company and tell them where and when you will be travelling. If you have never set foot out of the country and suddenly start charging hotel bills in Paris, they might stop payment until they know for certain that you are the one on the move.
- Hire or bribe a friend to keep your walkway clear of snow and pick up the mail and newspapers. Ask also that he or she walk around the outside of your house to check for a break-in. Cancel the paper if you are away for any length of time, say, over two weeks, or offer it to your trustworthy neighbour for free.

- Call your bank and make sure that your debit card will work at your travel destination. (See "Handling Money While You're Away," page 493.)
- Check that your home or renters' insurance is up-to-date.
- Pay bills ahead of time to prevent cancellation of a service.
- Check home security, including smoke detectors.
- Make a reservation at a doggy hotel for Fido.
- Put your plants in the bathtub with some water, assuming there is a little light in there. Otherwise, sweet-talk a friend into watering them.
- Give a neighbour the phone number of a family member in case of an emergency (e.g., break-in, fire, flooded basement, etc.).
- Give someone a copy of your itinerary.
- Buy travel insurance.

TIP: Do not leave a message on your answering machine stating that you will be away. Or if you do, make sure you leave your home unlocked so thieves won't damage the door upon entry. (Kidding, kidding …)

Documents, Please?

Make sure you have the documents you'll need for your trip. In addition to your passport and required travel documents (visas), do you have or need:

- A driver's licence? Is it up-to-date?
- Travel insurance forms?
- A rail or bus pass?
- A hostelling membership card?
- A record of recent vaccinations, depending of course on the country you are travelling to.

And consider getting these cards and passes:
- In the United States, you can get an International Student Identity Card (ISIC). It provides discounts on food, accommodations, and reduced entrance fees at some tourist sites, as well as a 24-hour emergency helpline and insurance benefits. You must be a full-time secondary or post-secondary school student and 12 years of age or over.

TIP: Before you hit the big 2-6, get yourself a Eurail pass. After that, you are no longer eligible for the youth discount.

- The International Youth Travel Card (IYTC) offers some of the same benefits as the ISIC. You must be 25 years old or under and not a full-time student. The cards cost around $22 U.S. You can buy them at a student travel agency, or visit the International Student Travel Confederation (ISTC) website (www.istc.org) for more information.

- The International Student Exchange Card (ISE) is great if you are between 12 and 26. There are discounts to be had and some medical benefits, access to a 24-hour emergency helpline, and student airfares. The card costs $25 U.S. Call 1-800-255-8000 for more info, or visit www.isecard.com.

- If you're planning to travel in Europe, consider a rail pass, www.raileurope.co.uk. If bus (coach) is your plan, go to www.busabout.com.

Be Worldly, Sure, but Be Safe

You are out of the country at last. It's all daiquiris and white beaches. Yeah, well ...

- *Protect your stuff.* Don't flaunt it. Leave Grandma's heirloom necklace at home.
- *Stay sober.* You might be on vacation, but the bad guys are hard at work, particularly in nightclubs and fun spots. And don't leave your drink unattended. Do you think that's just a girl rule? Think again.
- *Keep your mouth shut.* Okay, you have just met the nicest girl/guy. Really, she/he is *fab*, the bee's knees, and you have always been a great judge of character, even when you've packed away three martinis. But what the heck, honey? Do not tell

TIP: Write down all the information you will need upon arrival at your destination on one piece of paper and keep it with you. This includes the names, addresses, and phone numbers (cell number, too) of any hotels you'll be in or people you will be staying with. Here's the big tip—copy the name of the hotel and its address in the original language (e.g., French, Italian, Greek). True, most taxi drivers will recognize the name of your hotel despite it being mangled beyond recognition by your terrible accent, but this will not always be true.

her/him your room number! If you must make a lunch date with Ms./Mr. Paragon of Goodness, pick a public place and take an enlightened look at this specimen of perfection in the light of day.

- *Travel insurance.* Read the policy—such a novel idea! Buy it, and carry the claim numbers and a copy of the policy with you.
- *Keep cash in different places*—an inside pocket, breast pocket, your sock. That way, hopefully, if you get mugged, you won't have to give it all away.
- *No drugs*—none. Ever. You are a complete idiot if you do. Period.
- *Don't hitchhike*—unless you are running away from a bunch of people with guns.

Passports

You don't plan to travel outside of North America, so you think that you don't need a passport? Wrong. You do. Get one now. Who knows, you might get a call from Regis and Kelly and win a vacation!

Canadians and Americans can pick up passport forms at the post office, passport office, or any court of law.

Travel Documents Necessary to Enter the United States

As of January 31, 2008, if you travel to the United States by land or water, a U.S. law will require you to present:

- a government-issued photo ID, such as a driver's licence;

and

- a birth certificate or a citizenship card;

or

- a valid passport;

or

- a NEXUS or a Free and Secure Trade (FAST) card;

or

- for those 18 and under, a birth certificate.

NEXUS is a system allowing faster border crossings for pre-approved frequent travellers; FAST is a similar system for importers, carriers, and registered drivers.

Canadian citizens flying to or through the United States must present a valid Canadian passport.

To find out more about a NEXUS card and to keep up-to-date, go to the Canada Border Services Agency website at www.cbsa.gc.ca. This site will provide you with information on cross-border shopping and ever-changing passport rules.

Passport Maintenance

Be sure to photocopy the page of your passport with your photo, passport number, and other identifying information. Also photocopy any visas, travel insurance policies, plane tickets, or traveller's cheque serial numbers. Carry one set of copies in a safe place, apart from the originals, and leave another set at home. You might also want to carry an expired passport or an official copy of your birth certificate in a separate place (i.e., not with your current passport). (See the note about "dummy wallets" below.)

Fancy leather passport wallets are very nice, but carry yours in a small plastic sandwich bag. It might look a tad goofy, but your passport has to last five years, and the plastic will keep it clean and dry. Your passport includes a page listing names of people who can be reached in case of a medical emergency. Keep another copy of this list in a separate place. Also, list in your passport any allergies or medical conditions.

Lost Passports

If you lose your passport while you are travelling, immediately notify the local police and the nearest embassy or consulate of your home government. You will need all information recorded on your lost passport, ID, and proof of citizenship. (That's why you carry your ID in two different places, and why you photocopied the first two pages of your passport.)

Been there
Done THAT

I decided to take my fourteen-year-old brother with us for a quick trip down to New York. I had no idea that I needed a notarized letter from our parents to take a minor out of the country. We found a lawyer near the airport and managed to catch our plane. But that wasn't the really awful part. The Customs people found my little brother's fake ID card. So much for that trip. What a mess.

—BRYAN, 24

In an emergency, ask for temporary travelling papers that will permit you to re-enter your home country. Get a copy of the police report. This will help you get a new passport once you are home.

The passport is a public document that belongs to your home government. If you must surrender it to a foreign government official, and you don't get it back in a reasonable amount of time, inform the nearest embassy or consulate.

If your passport turns up after you have reported it missing, send it back to the originating office. It will be destroyed.

Travel Insurance

How much risk are you willing to take? To put it another way, how much risk is your *family* ready to take? Because if you have just broken your neck in South America bungee jumping, guess who'll have to foot the bill? You'll end up scared and damaged, and your family could end up with major financial problems.

Tip: Try calling your insurer's hotline (usually an 800 number) before you go, just to make sure that it is working.

Travel insurance covers four basic areas: medical/health problems, property loss, trip cancellation/interruption, and emergency evacuation. (There is a fifth type—see "High-Risk Travel Insurance," page 497.)

Buy the travel cancellation/interruption insurance direct from the carrier. It can be a little more expensive but there is less hassle if you need to claim it.

Be sure to get insurance that pays for repatriation to your home country (not necessarily the country where you bought the insurance) and—here's the kicker—pays medical costs up front. Here's why.

Let's say Sam is teaching English in Japan for a year. He takes a header on a soccer field. The head was fine but he breaks his leg. Darn. Here's what might happen:

a. His insurance will cover a First Class ticket home if the doctor in Japan agrees that his leg cannot bend. If the leg can bend, then too bad, he's stuck in Economy. The insurance company will pay for a regular return ticket back to Japan once the leg is fixed.

Or …

b. The insurance will pay for his operation, and all his extra needs, in Japan.

Sounds like a fair deal, doesn't it?

Actually, no. Most policies pay all expenses upon receipt. That means that Sam and his family have to pay up in advance and wait for the insurance company to send a cheque. In other words, they could be on the hook for many, many thousands of dollars.

Luckily, Sam has a policy that pays *up front*. That means that the doctor and the hospital bill the insurance company directly.

U.S. Medicare does not cover foreign travel. Canadian Medicare's coverage is limited too. If you are Canadian and zipping into the United States for a little cross-border shopping and you come head-to-head with a runaway beer truck, you are not covered by Canadian Medicare.

Travel insurance is always your responsibility. Many schools, colleges, and universities have no requirements regarding student health insurance during overseas travel.

Even the best study-abroad programs often lack travel safety standards. In fact, there are no mandatory transportation and travel safety standards for study-abroad programs. More disheartening is the fact that health insurance is not always a mandatory requirement. This isn't meant to discourage you from participating in such a program, but take responsibility for yourself. Investigate thoroughly.

Some homeowners' insurance policies cover theft during travel plus loss of travel documents (passport, plane ticket, rail pass, etc.) up to $500 U.S. Find out if yours does.

The International Student Identity Card (ISIC) provides basic insurance benefits to U.S. cardholders. Go to their website and read the fine print: www.istc.org. Cardholders have access to a toll-free, 24-hour helpline for medical, legal, and financial emergencies overseas.

Been there
Done THAT

Our hotel room was looted while we were in the dining room. They took a laptop, iPod, my son's PSP, and our digital camera. I thought, "Well, at least we have insurance." It turns out that under our policy electronics were covered only up to $500. The laptop alone was $3800.

—LINDA, 36

American Express (1-800-528-4800) grants most cardholders automatic collision and theft car rental insurance and ground travel accident coverage of $100,000 U.S. on flight purchases made with the card.

Honey, are you travelling to a scary place? (Be still my heart.) Then you'll find more on high-risk travel insurance at the end of this chapter.

It's in the Bag

So, now that the serious stuff is behind us, let's deal with the fun part—beginning with packing your bags.

Backpack or the bag-on-wheels ("wheelie"): which to pick? Well, where are you going? If you plan to loll around on a beach, then opt for the wheelie. You have a better chance of keeping your clothes in wearable condition if you drag around a suitcase on wheels. (Yeah, you'll look like Granny. Get over it.)

If you are heading off the beaten path, choose a backpack with an attached daypack and a zipper that goes around the entire pack. (Try dragging a wheelie down a mud road in Africa. Not pretty.)

There are bags that are on wheels with a backpack hidden in a zippered compartment. They are not designed for serious backpackers but are great if you are in a pickle and need to make fast tracks. Eddie Bauer sells a bag that might work, although it's on the small side.

Spend real bucks on the backpack, but don't opt for a showy please-rob-me-I'm-an-American-Fat-Cat bag. The best bags have thick shoulder straps, a belt, and a zippered compartment that hides the back harness, thereby turning the backpack into a regular soft suitcase.

TIP: Want to see the world on someone else's dime? Find a job that includes travel, before you have a family or a mortgage to tie you down. Or if you've ever wanted to explore another part of the world, do an Internet job search of that area.

TIP: Try the backpack on in the store. Load it up with something heavy. (Is there a book department? Does the salesperson have any ideas?) Go for a walk up and down the aisles. Is it comfy?

If you plan to hold on to your money you'll need a money belt. I know they look dopey, but think how dopey you'll look standing in the local cop shop, railing to the heavens after you have been pickpocketed. Leather money belts are heavy and get sticky, while plastic gets gooey in the heat. Choose a heavy cotton money belt, and don't keep all of your money in it. Beach boys and girls might want to buy a waterproof pouch that can be worn swimming. Yep, they exist.

A padlock and chain are handy to bring, particularly if you are staying in a hostel and want to lock stuff up. They're also useful if you rent a bike. Don't even try putting the lock and chain in your carry-on luggage; the airport security guys will not be amused. If you tend to lose little things like keys, you might want to make it a combination lock instead.

Tip: Money belts that are hidden between stomach and shorts need only hold your passport and cash. Make sure they are washable cotton, they get smelly fast.

To cut down on clothes, colour-coordinate everything. Male or female, black and white is the easiest combination. Two pairs of black pants and two white shirts/blouses, two white T-shirts, black sweater, black jacket, three pairs of black socks, black shoes or white sneakers. If you are heading for the beach: five T-shirts, shorts, flip-flops, two bathing suits, one hoodie.

Add a warm jacket or wool sweater, a rain jacket (Gore-Tex® is both waterproof and breathable), sturdy shoes or hiking boots, and thick socks, and you're ready to hike the fjords.

The fabric of your clothes is more important than the style. You want them to be wrinkle-resistant and fast-drying. And think long and hard before dragging all your work-out clothes around with you. Will you actually use them?

At the risk of repeating myself, your clothes should not scream, "Look at me, I'm a rich idiot from North America!" And respect the local traditions, especially if you plan to visit religious or cultural sites. Dress modestly. Do some research—try asking the

Tip: If you feel someone following you, put your hand on the belt before turning around and looking the guy in the eye. Some pickpockets will try cutting the belt from behind.

Canadian embassy or consulate in the city you are visiting for advice. Long sleeves and head coverings might be necessary for women (so carry a sweater and a light scarf, it's not a big deal). Short skirts and short-shorts are not considered appropriate in more conservative countries, so don't wear them—or your skimpy bikini—unless you know you'll be staying in the tourist enclave. And that goes for males, as well. Leave the T-shirts with vulgar slogans at home. And, oddly, your hairy legs do not send ladies' hearts aquiver. Imagine! Wear long pants.

TIP: Going to meet the Queen, are we? Lay out dressy clothes separately: shoes, socks, suit, hanky, and all. Otherwise you'll forget a crucial part of the outfit—like the shoes.

Before you start cramming stuff into your bags, lay out only what you absolutely need. Then take half of it away. Next, lay out the longest items on the bed and place shirts, tops, and whatever on top. Wrap the long items around the shorter stuff and place it in the bag. Tuck underwear and socks into shoes. Some people swear by placing tissue in between layers of clothes. Zippered freezer bags are good for creams, shampoo, and anything that might leak.

Do not throw all your medications into a single container to save space. They must be in their original containers and properly labelled—it's an airport security thing. And you might need to have the prescription renewed. (Take the container, and hopefully the prescription too, into a drugstore. The pharmacist might take pity on you and give you enough pills to last the trip—no guarantees.) Carry the prescriptions with you on the flight (although you might want to keep a second stash, also properly labelled, in your luggage.)

Note: Depending on the current air travel restrictions you might not be able to take a bottle of liquid medication. Talk to your doctor about a pill form of the same medication.

Wear a medical alert tag if you have a serious medical problem. Drug stores carry tags for common conditions. Better yet, contact the MedicAlert International Foundation (1-800-825-3785; www.medicalert.org) and ask about their twenty-four-hour hotline access to your records. Hey, four million members can't be wrong.

Pack a spare foldable, squishable bag that can instantly and miraculously hold all the presents and new clothes you buy. It's tempting to buy a really cheap bag, but eventually this baby will have to stand up to the airport baggage handling guy named Bubba who has anger-management issues.

TIP: A matchbox can hold needles, pins, and the pack of coloured thread lifted from the hotel bathroom.

Sleeping Arrangements

Some hostels require that you provide your own sleeping bag or "sleep sack," which is a folded sheet that is sewn down one side and along the bottom. (Make your own and bring it with you. It can double as a laundry bag.)

At any point in your travels, might you sleep on the ground? If the answer is yes, opt for a cotton-lined, not down-filled, sleeping bag. Down gets totally awful when wet and will not keep you warm.

As for bedbugs, alas, you will come across them sooner or later. Pack large plastic garbage bags and duct tape. Duct tape the bags to the suspicious mattress. It works—for the most part.

Duh moment!

Condoms. Boys and girls, bring them with you. True, you can buy them in just about any country, but who knows what you'll be getting? The quality varies wildly. Stick with what you know.

Extras to Pack (Just Because You Never Know)

- Outdoor equipment, like a plastic water bottle, compass, waterproof matches, pocketknife, sunscreen, and hat.
- Needle and thread, and duct or electrical tape for patching jobs.
- Packet of laundry detergent.
- Alarm clock.

Been there *Done* THAT

I travel with my hockey team. I think I have stayed in every cheap, disgusting hotel in the Midwest. Here's what I've learned. If you want to check for bedbugs, rip off the top blankets suddenly, then turn on the lights. If you see one, then there are zillions. Bedbugs don't party alone. And check the seams in the mattress. That's where they hang out.

—ROBERT, 18

Duh
moment **!**

Learn a Language in 60 Seconds

First of all, if you believe *that*, do not leave home. You'll get hurt!
But you can buy a phrase book and learn the basics. Carry the book everywhere.
Try out the basic phrases on taxi drivers, servers in restaurants, and anyone who works at the hotel.

TIP: Bring disinfecting wipes or tissues—lots. Case in point: the washrooms at Dhaka International airport in Bangladesh come fully equipped with a mug and running water. That's it. Disinfecting wipes work really well on food stains, too. Betcha didn't know that.

- Safety pins.
- A few rubber bands.
- Cheap dollar store flashlight.
- Small calculator.

Converters and adapters

A North American appliance will be fried by the electrical outlets in Europe and Asia. Buy an adapter (which changes the shape of the plug) and a converter (which changes the voltage). Both are available for about $20. Don't make the mistake of using only an adapter (unless appliance instructions explicitly state otherwise). For more on all things adaptable, check out www.kropla.com/electric.htm.

Tips for Modern-Day Air Travel

Before you leave:

- *Packing.* Know before you go what the current restrictions are for carry-on and don't even think of arguing about it. (This is where a travel agent comes in really handy. Check your carrier website close to the time of your departure for specifics.)

Do you really want to toss your new iPod in the trash? You might have to choose between keeping your flight or your favourite electronic gadget.

- *Clean out your bags before flying.* What's tucked in the dozens of zippered pockets that you have forgotten about? Has your best friend borrowed your bag to go camping? Oh look, a Swiss Army knife tucked into the bag's lining! "Lucy, you have some 'splainin' to do!"

- *Prepare for the grand search before you leave home.* Headed for the metal detector? While it might be impossible to remove that steel plate in your head, you can wear sensible shoes. (No steel-toed boots or stilettos held together by pins. Wear slip-ons.) Don't wear an underwire bra. Pack your carry-on bag so that it is easy for the screener to rummage around. And depending on the airport, you might also bump into armed military personnel, bomb-detection equipment, sniffing dogs, and photo ID checks at the gate prior to boarding.

- *Get your ticket or boarding pass before you arrive.* It is usually possible to change your seat at the gate or at a passenger service area inside the secure area of the airport.

- *Make sure all allowable electronic stuff is charged up and works.* And if you really want to be careful, stay away from the shooting range for a few days before you board a plane. Depending on the airport (Belfast, for example), gunpowder residue on your hands might keep you grounded. Who knew?

- *Arrive early.* The recommended time for international flights is two hours, but arrive earlier if you have to line up at the ticket counter.

- *Water.* Gulp down a bottle of water before you get on the plane. On the plane, drink more. (Depending on the current regulations, bring at least one bottle and/or take what's offered on the plane.) The walks back and forth to the bathroom are good for you. Some reports suggest that deep-vein thrombosis, which increases the risk of blood clots, occurs in as many as one in ten long-haul travellers. And note, only travel amateurs drink excessive alcohol on long flights.

- *Ticket, boarding pass, and ID.* Keep them within reach the entire time you are in the airport and on the plane. That means you don't leave them in the seat pocket on the plane.

- *Be nice to airport personnel*—even if you want to rattle their teeth. (No, especially if you want to rattle their teeth.) They have new-found power and they know how to use it. If you get totally pissed off at a security guy who seems to be enjoying his power just a wee bit too much, then get the guy's badge or ID number and take it to the airport authority.

- *Dress for success*. It's a fact: travellers who are appropriately dressed will pass through security and passport checks faster. Wait, there's more. Airlines do not want their First Class section cluttered up by a smelly, unkempt bore. To increase your chances of getting bumped into Business or First Class, comb your hair, be polite, and stand up straight. (You might also tell them that you are on your honeymoon, have been travelling for twenty-four hours, your dog has just died and you are on the way to its funeral.)

And I know you know this, but I'll say it anyway:

- Don't ever make jokes to or with airport security people about anything.
- Don't babysit anyone else's stuff in the airport. And don't offer to babysit their kid, either, while they run off to the loo. Normal parents do not leave their children with strangers.
- Don't carry anything but your own bags across a border.
- Don't hook up with anyone just before you cross a border. If you meet someone, say goodbye, cross the border, and hook up again on the other side. If they have anything they shouldn't in their luggage, you don't want to be rounded up as an accomplice.
- Don't leave your bags anywhere, and don't, for heaven's sake, walk around with a bag that can be opened by someone passing buy. (Nix the zipperless carry-alls.)
- Don't ever lend your passport to a friend who looks like you. Think that that's too obvious for words? I wish it were!

Been there
Done THAT

We were both seventeen years old, blond, same body shape, same nose—we could have been brothers! Besides, he was my best friend. My passport was four years old. In other words, the picture in my passport was taken when I was thirteen. Brad wanted to go to Mexico for five days, so I just lent it to him. His parents found out, my parents found out. Man, it was like the earth exploded or something. I mean, it was a joke, just for fun! No harm done. He didn't get caught—not by the authorities, anyway. I think he's allowed out now, but then he just turned twenty-five.

—ART, 25

And here are some quick tips from the been-there-done-that old folks:

- Taxi, sir? Forget the lineup at the airport exit. Zip up to the Arrivals and snag a taxi that has just dropped someone off.
- If you need your luggage fast, check it in as "fragile." It is usually put on top and the first to arrive. (This has been known to backfire.)
- If you are going to a major hotel, holler down the line of waiting wannabe taxi passengers, "Anyone going to the Fairmont?" It takes a little chutzpah but you'll save a bundle.
- In Second and Third World countries, where taxi fares depend on how rich you look, agree on the fare before you get into the taxi. And think twice about allowing your bag to be locked in the trunk. You might get out and the taxi could take off—with your bag.

Lost Luggage

The bad news is that according to the U.S. Transportation Department the odds are about one in two hundred that your bag will be lost or misdirected. Do the math: that means that one passenger on every flight will stand forlornly at the luggage carousel crying, "Why me?" *Because it was your turn in the lost-luggage lottery, that's why.*

Label your bags. That doesn't mean scribbling your name on a scrap of paper that dangles off an elastic band. Slap on, *glue* on, your contact information. No, you don't need to announce your name and home address to the world. Use your business address if you must. Just make sure your bag has at least a hope in hell of eventually arriving in the same city as you—via New Delhi, perhaps. Put your name and address in the bag as well.

The tie-a-yellow-ribbon thing is a bit old, but do tie something onto your luggage to identify it if it's the basic black variety. Plastic garbage bags can help protect your new luggage. They look a little odd as they come around the luggage carousel at the airport, but heck, you'll be able to spot them right away.

If you can limit yourself to a carry-on only, and you can either bring it with you onto the plane or gate-check it before boarding (that means dropping a small bag into a baggage cart just before boarding and picking it up as you deplane), then lucky you. It's the preferred way to travel because:

- You don't have to ask for help from anyone or run around looking for a luggage cart.

- You don't have to worry about your bags ending up in another city or country.
- Theft is less likely.
- Re-booking a missed connection is easier. (No worrying about your luggage making its own travel plans.)
- No need to hang around the luggage carousel for twenty minutes.
- Some cabs charge extra for luggage and large bags that must go in the trunk.

What About Your Camera?

Pickpockets love digital cameras, and who can blame them? Keep an eye on yours.

If you're using old-fashioned film or a video camera, airport security X-rays can fog film (despite disclaimers to the contrary). Buy a lead-lined pouch at a camera store, or ask security to hand-inspect it. Pack your film in your carry-on luggage, since higher-intensity X-rays are used on checked luggage.

And while we are on the topic of pictures, *do not*:

> ### *Been* there *Done* THAT
>
> I was snapping a picture of my uncle in Belfast and a military truck drove into the background. My film was confiscated, but I kept my camera.
>
> —SARA, 21

- Take photos in shrines or religious buildings.
- Take snapshots of local rituals, especially cremations (think India). How would you like it if some nutty tourist burst into your granny's funeral and started snapping away? Not nice.
- Take photos of people because they look quaint. Senior ladies on junks in Hong Kong will send their large grandsons after you. Ask, and expect to give them a few coins for the privilege of taking their picture.

Never take pictures of military vehicles or facilities (including naval vessels) or even oil refineries in any country. Best thing that can happen is that you lose your film; the worst is that you are accused of espionage.

TIP: Have Gun, Will Not Travel: What not to take on board a plane? Well, forget your cross-bow, darn it. In Canada, find out at www.catsa-acsta.gc.ca. Go to "Travellers" and then click on "Permitted and Prohibited Items."

TIP: If you're travelling from west to east, stay out of the sun until the day after you get there. If you're flying from east to west, go for a brisk walk as soon as you arrive.

Jet Lag

Everyone has a favourite jet lag cure. Mine is going to bed earlier than usual for a few days before I leave, and thereby adjusting my body to a new sleep pattern. I nix all caffeine two to three days in advance of leaving and drink lots of water before and during the flight. I change my wristwatch to the local destination time the minute I get on the plane and once I have arrived (preferably at night) I go straight to bed after swallowing two glasses of wine.

People might tell you to try over-the-counter sleeping pills. Be sure to try any over-the-counter drugs *before* you leave in case you suffer a reaction. (Popping a few sleeping pills onboard the plane might result in you speaking in pig Latin to all sorts of armed individuals upon arrival—best to know in advance.)

Been there
Done THAT

I always bring a full-size $5 pillow with me on the plane. I couldn't possibly sleep on those Chiclet-sized pillows the flight attendants hand out, and I don't suppose they are cleaned very often. The airplane blankets are not too bad. I drink a bottle of water, sip a glass of wine, plug in my earplugs, cover my eyes with an eye-mask, and go to sleep. At the end of the flight I leave the pillow behind in the seat.

—RASHADE, 24

Girl Travel

It's a sad fact: women, no matter what their age, are more vulnerable on the road. Best advice—travel with someone. Next, wear appropriate clothing—long sleeves for starters, shoes instead of sandals (all the better to make a run for it), and modest knee-length skirt or baggy pants to ward off leering eyes.

Been there
Done THAT

I wear a gold band on my right hand. I'll switch it to the left hand (wedding finger) if I feel uncomfortable. It's amazing, but there are many men out there who really will not put the moves on a women if they think she's "taken." Weird but true.

—MANDY, 23

More tips for female travellers:

- Try to book your flight, or arrival, so that you land in the daytime. No need to muddle around a foreign city at night.
- Pay a few extra bucks and stay in the safe part of town.
- Keep sunglasses handy if you want to avoid eye contact.
- If you take an overnight train, opt for the top bunk. It's the out-of-sight, out-of-mind strategy.
- Pick up a cab from a hotel taxi line rather than flagging one down on the street.
- Wait for the next hotel elevator if you don't like the look of the company onboard.
- If you feel uncomfortable going into a hotel parking garage, ask that your car be brought up to the door, or have a hotel employee escort you to the car. Don't be shy—ask!
- Can't say this too often—trust your instincts.

Call Home! We Love You ... Really ... Sort Of ...

I'm sure you'll be having the time of your life, travelling the world in search of adventure, but spare a thought for your poor, worried family and check in once in a while, please?

Telephone

If you're counting on using your cellphone, you should be aware that almost all areas of Europe use Global System for Mobiles (GSM). For your cellphone to function in Europe, it must be GSM-compatible and have a SIM (Subscriber Identity Module) card, which gives you a local phone number and connects you to the local network. SIM cards can be purchased from any European carrier. Companies such as Cellular Abroad (www.cellularabroad.com) also rent cellphones. In other countries, most of Africa for example, you can buy a cheap phone, plus airtime, for peanuts. They work.

A calling card is probably your cheapest option for telephoning home, although they are not acceptable everywhere (in some eastern European countries, for example). Calling card calls are billed collect or to your account. Contact your phone service provider. While you have them on the phone, ask about getting a PIN for your account. That will allow you to bill your account from any phone.

Direct international calls from pay phones anywhere are usually easy without a calling card, but watch the price. Pre-paid phone cards, and sometimes major credit cards, can be used for direct international calls, but these still tend to be expensive. Just use the phone to check in, say you're fine, make sure no one has died at home, and hang up.

Do not use your hotel room phone to make calls unless it's absolutely necessary or you have worked out a deal with the front desk. The charges are ridiculous. And if you do ring up charges there is no harm with haggling at the front desk to have those charges reduced. Ask for the manager.

Snail Mail

Easy for you to send a postcard home, but how do we get in touch with you this way? American Express's international travel offices offer a complimentary Client Letter Service for cardholders. They will hold mail for up to thirty days and forward it upon request. Some offices even grant these privileges to non-cardholders. Call them in advance of leaving.

E-mail

Internet cafés are springing up in cities around the world. Try them—it's a great way to avoid phone charges. While it is possible to make a long-distance connection with your home server, this option is slow and expensive, and usually frustrating. The easiest way is to use a Web-based server (Yahoo, Hotmail, gmail, etc.).

If you're bringing your laptop with you, go to www.roadnews.com and www.kropla.com for the latest news. Just remember: laptops are fragile, and in hot countries they get ... well, hot. Use yours for short periods and prop it up so that air can circulate underneath.

Mom and Pop can send money via Western Union. Agree on a password before you leave home. Go to westernunion.com for locations and details.

Accommodation

On the first night of your arrival in a new and unfamiliar overseas country, make absolutely sure that you are booked into a decent hotel. (Two- or three-star minimum.) You will have no idea how long your plane will be delayed, and you will likely arrive tired, disorientated, headachy, and jet-lagged. Find a cab (ask how much the ride is going to cost you in advance), go to the hotel, take a shower, sleep, and the next day, refreshed, you can find some digs that better suit your budget.

Hotels

Privacy is the number-one benefit of a hotel stay. There is also less hassle, and it might be cheaper for larger groups. If the suite costs $250 and there are five of you splitting the cost, then you're better off there than booking five beds at $60 each in a hostel. Careful, though—some hotels will charge per person, and you'll need to factor in those pesky taxes.

Privately owned hotels usually offer better value and a greater degree of personality than their big-name chain counterparts. In some locales, a cheap "hotel" more closely resembles a hostel.

More than You Really Wanted to Know

Tipping: In most European countries a pre-set service charge is already on your bill. In countries where it is not expected, or where very little is expected, don't over-tip. You might make it difficult for other travellers and for the locals to carry on their business. In Japan, tipping is considered rude, and in North America, beware the irate server if you don't tip! There's a neat tipping table at www.tramex.com/tips/tipping.htm. It doesn't cover all countries, but it will give you a good idea of expectations.

Everything on the hotel bill is negotiable, so ask about the extra charges. Some hotels will charge a buck and a half for a local call. Long distance charges are nuts. Parking is extra. There might be charges to carry your luggage to your room—even if you carry your own bags! Just say no. Specifically, say, "Are there any extra charges that will appear on my bill?"

In North America you can usually whittle the bill down by showing your CAA or AAA card (Canadian or American Automobile Association). Go to the hotel website and see if there are any coupons for reduced rate. Also, try the relevant tourist association. They often have coupons or give special rates.

The services

The concierge (*con-see-air-ge*) provides a complimentary hotel service. He or she is in the main lobby, sitting behind a little desk, waiting to offer you advice, directions, and services. This person will help you buy those hockey tickets. Tip him or her very well.

A *coolhunter*—a hip local who has the inside scoop—might be provided by a very high-end hotel, but you will pay dearly for his or her services: think

Duh moment!

Inquiring Minds Want to Know

You don't really think that a rapist/robber/general bad guy is going to knock on your hotel door and say, "Open up so I can rape and pillage"? No, the bad guy on the other side of the door is going to talk, and possibly dress, appropriately. Think about it. Did you really order extra pillows? Do you really think the hotel is sending you up a free fruit basket just because you are nice? Don't open the door unless you know who is on the other side. Unsure? Call down to the front desk and inquire.

$600 to $1000 a day. This person becomes your personal tour guide and gets you into the best places in town … presumably. If you have the bucks, call the hotel at least three weeks ahead to secure this service.

Packing checklist for a hotel stay

- Toothbrush and paste.
- Deodorant.
- Razors.
- Hairbrush and comb.
- Cream.
- Makeup bag.
- Prescription medicine.
- Headache or over-the-counter drugs.
- Small bottle of laundry soap.
- Zippered baggies.
- Contact lenses and solution, plus glasses. (Carry the prescription.)

If you are doing any hard travel, hiking or pilgrimages to parts unknown, opt for daily-use contact lenses. They are a little more expensive, but an eye infection in Africa is an experience you don't want.

Hostels

Primarily for students and youth, hostels provide no-frills, inexpensive lodging. They are also a great place to meet like-minded travellers. Many offer kitchen access, laundry, lockers, and common rooms. Some hostels are clean and safe, but the range in quality is huge. Talk to travellers you meet and get recommendations. Just as in a hotel, when checking in ask about any hidden or extra charges.

Packing checklist for a hostel stay

Besides the usual stuff that you might take into a hotel, bring:

- Towels.
- Soap.
- Talcum powder to keep your feet dry if you are doing any hiking.

B&Bs or Guesthouses

B&B: bed and breakfast—that means that breakfast is included. Rates are generally cheaper than hotels and the rooms are usually homier. You might have to share a washroom with other guests. When you book, ask if there is an ensuite available. Parking is almost always free. Dinner is not usually offered, which can be a problem if the B&B is in a charming village that does not have a restaurant. Ask. The new breed of B&Bs is often run by owners off-site, so, for better or worse, you might not find yourself chatting with Ma and Pa Kettle in the parlour every evening. Okay, so maybe you like that sort of thing …

College Dorms

Universities and colleges in major tourist destinations often rent out beds at below-hostel rates during the summer. McGill University in Montreal, Quebec, for example, has a full-service hotel, not dorm, atop a residence (it's called New Residence Hall on Avenue du Parc).

Prices are great and usually the location, close to downtown, is even better.

These rooms are usually reserved for visiting professors or parents of students but are often available to all in the summer. During the university year, and in a pinch, just say that you are a prospective student visiting to check out the school. Don't even try this during the first week of September or at graduation.

Most universities rent out actual dorm rooms during the summer. Double-check the location. Even if the university is in town, the dorms might be on the outskirts. And they sometimes require reservations. Call ahead.

Camping

Schlepping camp equipment around is impossible unless you are in a car. However, if you don't have a vehicle you might still be able go the camping route. Some campgrounds rent tents, and sometimes there are cabins onsite. You will probably need reservations. Check out the surrounding area and look for a security guard. Oh, is there electricity and running water? They come in handy.

Private Homes

Travellers are occasionally offered rooms by locals. Think carefully. The price might be right, but there is absolutely no way of knowing if these rooms are safe or, more to the point, if you will be safe in these rooms. A tourist office or an agency in the town will have a list of private homes that rent rooms.

"The Rellies"

Staying with your long-lost auntie and uncle is cheap, financially anyway, but there are still costs involved. You have to be nice—really nice—even after a long day hiking the hills and dales of Scotland. They'll probably want to show you their favourite sights, which might not have been on your own agenda. And you'll have to fit in with their lifestyle, not vice-versa. If you are now a practising vegan, mention it in advance, let your hosts know that you will be looking after your own food needs. And no midnight raids on the fridge. Nor can you come staggering back from the pub after last call, unless the family is staggering along with you!

Do not leave any lingering long-distance phone charges. Use a calling card or reverse the charges to your home number. Auntie-dearest might fork out $75 for a roast beef dinner but she'll likely resent the $5 phone charge. Weird but true.

Arrive with a decent hostess gift—a bottle of wine for a week-long stay does not cut it. Nor does giving a hostess gift get you out of buying a meal for the family during your visit. If you really are down and out, take the small fries out for dinner at MacDonald's and give the old folks a night off. Babysit or offer to shop for and cook a meal, if that's within your range of talents.

Ask specifically about house rules and respect them. Beyond that, take in your surroundings. Not everyone has lots of water—most people pay for it, and some are actually on a well. Keep your shower short. If you are in the country and the family have a septic tank, a commodity your city-self knows nothing about, ask! The family may use the *"If it's yellow let it mellow, if it's brown flush it down"* rule. Use the recycling bin, and for heaven's sake clean up after yourself! Ask about the family's typical week—if four people have to get out of the house by eight in the morning it might be best if you just sleep in. Don't pinch their bathroom supplies without asking. (I am referring to shampoo and toothpaste, not toilet paper.) If you have sightseeing plans, tell your hosts. They might want to come along or help you plan your bus route. The key here is to be the guest you would want to have in your home. How would you feel if your cousin ten times removed stopped by your house for a week and left the bathroom towels on the floor, drank your beer without replacing it, and borrowed your car and did not pay the parking ticket? Remember the old adage: "Fish and visitors stink after three days." And now that you know the family's likes and dislikes, leave your bedroom tidy and an appropriate gift on the bedside table. Don't forget to send a thank-you note when you get home.

Stay Well

Unless you plan to spend at least part of your holiday yelling through a bathroom door, listen up. Most travellers will spend hours comparing hotel prices but totally ignore prevalent health risks in their chosen destination. For example, malaria and dengue fever are the big worries in Africa and southeast Asia. In the Caribbean and South America, it's infections from worms and other parasites. Respiratory illness is a possibility in south-central Asia. Need I go on?

Been there
Done THAT

It was my first morning in Nassau after a fabulous night spent chowing down on something yummy called conch (a dee-lish seafoody thing). I woke up, pulled on my new bikini, grabbed a towel, and raced to get a good sunning spot on the beach. I lay down, and that was it. Game over. The sky spun horribly. I leaned over and puked into the sand. The rest of that lovely trip was spent in a dark hotel room with a bucket beside me. I had to take a wheelchair from the hotel room to the taxi, then another wheelchair got me through the airport—with me still throwing up the whole time. I have no idea what the Bahamas look like. Do know one thing: won't eat conch again.

—CLAIRE, 22

In 2004, 50 million travellers visited the developing world, and about 8 percent became sick enough to require medical help. One-third of those who became infected fell ill a month or more after their return, and one in ten became sick six months after the trip. North American doctors often fail to recognize some of these exotic diseases, or diagnose them too late.

If you do get sick, it is vital that you tell your doctor where you have been and what you did while you were there. Keep in mind that you can get malaria on an airplane. If you suspect that you have contracted a tropical disease, contact the biggest hospital in your area and ask for the department that deals with tropical diseases. If you are in a small town and in the United States, contact the Centers for Disease Control in Atlanta.

And do some research yourself. You know how to work a computer, you know your symptoms—get to work.

Vaccinations you will need

Ask your doctor what is recommended for the area you are travelling to. Vaccinations should include hepatitis A, and if you are planning to be sexually active get hepatitis B, or a combination of the two. Vaccines are also available for typhoid, yellow fever, and polio. Make sure you are up-to-date on your routine shots—tetanus and diphtheria every ten years and flu shot annually. The "Travelers' Health" page on the Centers for Disease Control website (www.cdc.gov) is a good resource.

Commonsense tips

- Do not pet stray animals. Rabies still exists, and there is a worldwide shortage of rabies anti-serum. Not a pleasant way to die. Stay away also from birds, bird markets included.
- Stay off motorcycles and scooters. They are the most common cause of death and injury while on holiday. Next in line are accidents involving water (drowning, speed boats, etc.).
- Get the recommended vaccinations way before you leave.
- Use sunscreen—lots! Fill your cupped hand. That's how much sunscreen you need per application. (For more on this, see "Taking Care of Skin" in the chapter When Good Bodies Go Bad.)
- Use bug spray with DEET. Bring a pump spray instead of aerosol can. (It's less likely to be taken from you at the airport.)

TIP: The tasty sauce on the falafel might have been the cause of your stomach problems, but, just as likely, it might have been the way the food was handled. Do your best Dr. Niles Crane impression (remember, Frasier's brother?) and use antibacterial wipes on your hands, on restaurant tables, and in bathroom facilities. Really.

- First-aid kit—got one?
- Wash your hands and carry a ton of disinfectant wipes with you.
- Clip your fingernails short. (This makes it easier to keep your hands clean.)
- Don't go barefoot. Dog and cat hookworm can be picked up by walking around in bare feet.
- Do not eat food from street vendors.

Traveller's first-aid kit

- Bandages.
- A pain reliever.
- Antibiotic cream.
- A Swiss Army knife (not in your carry-on luggage).
- Tweezers.
- Decongestant.
- Motion-sickness remedy.
- Diarrhea or upset-stomach medication (e.g., Pepto Bismol or Imodium).
- An antihistamine.
- Sunscreen.
- Insect repellent.
- Burn ointment.
- Package of oral rehydration solution (ORS) (very helpful should you end up with traveller's diarrhea).
- Optional: Aspirin, puffers, prescriptions in the drugstore bottle.

And Just in Case You Don't Stay Well

Carry up-to-date, legible prescriptions or a statement from your doctor with trade names, manufacturers, chemical names, and dosages. Better yet, before you leave, put together a written copy of your medical history with your name, address, and home phone number, as well as a relative's number, your blood type, immunizations, your doctor's name, address, and office and emergency phone numbers, a list of any ongoing health problems, such as heart disease or diabetes, a list of medications you are currently taking and pharmacy name and phone number, allergies, and prescription for glasses or contact lenses. That way you'll have the info available should you be too shaken up or ill to provide it yourself.

If you do get sick while away, find a hospital where English is spoken or doctors trained in North America are available.

Keep all medication in its original containers and in your carry-on luggage. (You might not be able to carry liquid prescriptions. Check.) If these are critically important meds (i.e., you'll die without them), ask your pharmacist to make you two original containers and put one in your carry-on and the other in your luggage, in case one is lost.

Traveller's Diarrhea, or "Riding the Porcelain Bus"

According to the World Health Organization (WHO), "traveller's diarrhea" affects 20 to 50 percent of all globetrotters. (Now you will *stop* making jokes about Depends.)

If you have three or more loose bowel movements in a twenty-four-hour period, you have it. Diarrhea might just be a nuisance, but it *can* be serious if it's accompanied by any or some of the following symptoms: nausea, bloating, fever and chills/sweats, blood in stools, dehydration (feeling thirsty, peeing less often, dry skin, exhaustion, wooziness or faintness), vomiting, abdominal cramps.

Traveller's diarrhea is seldom fatal, but pregnant women, infants, children, the elderly, and those with compromised immune systems need to be especially cautious.

Where did it come from? Food or drinks contaminated with bacteria, viruses, and/or parasites (such as protozoa) are the usual culprits, with bacteria accounting for the majority of infections. It can also be picked up from unhygienic public toilets.

Don't want it? Then before you go, ask your doctor's office about the signs and symptoms of bacterial, viral, and parasitic traveller's diarrhea. Ask the doc about prevention and treatment (anti-diarrheal and antimicrobial drugs). Depending on your destination, many doctors, travel medicine programs, and clinics will offer a prescription for antibiotics to take with you. Also, talk to the doc about carrying a supply of Cipro or Floxin if you are heading to a country where the hospitals are scarier than the disease. And have a look at this website: www.travellersdiarrhea.com.

Prevention will not guarantee that you will escape it, no matter how careful you are. Still, it helps to always wash your hands before meals with an antiseptic or antibacterial gel or pre-packaged wipes. (Duh! Don't tell me you didn't know that.) And even in a first-class hotel or big-bucks resort, there is no guarantee that the water is clean. Don't drink tap water unless it has been boiled really, really well. Hot tea, coffee, and other drinks made with boiled water—as well as bottled or canned pop, beer, and wine—are your best bet. Some locals re-bottle pop and water, so check the cap and the bottom of the bottle for a small hole that has been resealed. Make sure the top *cracks* open. Wipe the outside of the bottle or can with all those disinfectant wipes you have stashed in your pocket. (*Note to self:* Stash disinfectant wipes in pocket. Also excellent for clothing stains. Did we mention that already?)

More tips to keep you off the can:

- Nix ice cubes in drinks and foods. This means no ices or popsicles either.
- Skip foods that were rinsed under tap water, such as raw fruits and veggies (e.g., salads). Peel fruit yourself.
- Hot food should be served piping hot and cold food served cold.
- Don't eat anything raw or poorly cooked. Some fish and shellfish might not be safe to eat even when fully cooked because they can contain poisonous biotoxins. (Not to be a buzz-kill or anything, but many experienced travellers just don't eat shellfish when travelling.)
- Generally avoid unpasteurized milk and other dairy products. (Except in Quebec and France, where the unpasteurized cheese is delicious and safe. They know what they are doing!) Likewise, avoid raw anything unless you are in Japan. (They know what they are doing, too.)
- Steer clear of food and drinks from street vendors.
- No singing in the shower—in other words, keep your mouth closed while showering or swimming. (Your neighbours will thank you, too.)
- Use bottled water to wash your face (especially around your eyes) and brush your teeth.
- Do not swim in stagnant pools of water, and swim only where the locals swim.

> ### *Been* there *Done* THAT
>
> I always say, let the diarrhea run its course (assuming that it's a mild case). Hate to say it, but let the bacteria *out!* Drink plenty of boiled water and hunker down for a day or two.
>
> —LINDA, A MOM

So What If You Get It Anyway?

Dehydration is the main concern. Drink lots of non-alcoholic fluids. Caffeine can exacerbate diarrhea. Bottled or canned water and other soft drinks are usually best. If you are worried about what is in the local bottled water, switch to carbonated water—it's harder to fake.

If you do become dehydrated, drink a special oral rehydration solution (ORS) to restore your water and electrolyte (salts, such as sodium and potassium) balance. Hopefully you've thought ahead and brought along pre-prepared packages of ORS powder. They are available at some drugstores. (Talk to your doctor about ORS.)

In the meantime, don't eat if you're not hungry. If you are, eat non-greasy, low-fibre foods. Think baby food—bananas, plain rice, unbuttered toast, boiled potatoes, salted soda crackers.

Handling Money While You're Away

TIP: Bring enough local currency to last for the first 24 to 72 hours.

You arrive at a small airport and discover that the currency exchange booth is closed. Worse, your credit card is refused for reasons unknown and your debit card doesn't work. Now is the time to pull out cash. A few U.S. dollars have been known to work wonders, but local currency is a definite plus, too.

When you need to exchange money, go only to banks that have, at the most, a 5 percent margin between the buy and sell prices. Post offices generally offer good rates, too. It's tempting to convert large sums at once, since you lose money with every transaction, but pickpockets are watching. You should never carry around a wad of cash. Convert only what you need.

With the use of debit cards, traveller's cheques are being used less often, but if you do carry them, make sure that they are in small denominations. (List the numbers of the cheques and keep the list in a separate place. They can be replaced if lost, which is why they're so useful to have.) You will need your passport as proof of ID to cash them.

Technically, debit cards can be used just about anywhere, but you'll have to do some planning. Not all bank machines are created equal outside of North America, nor are

Been there
Done THAT

I travel all over the place—Africa, South America—but I was mugged in London, England. I handed over my wallet. The guy pulled out the "cash," tossed the wallet on the ground, and took off. I wonder if he ever spent that Canadian Tire money?

—ERIC, TRAVELLER

TIP: Most thieves are opportunists. To foil them, put your wallet under your clothes rather than in your back pocket. And when you are travelling in countries where stick-ups are common (now there's a phrase you don't hear too often any more), carry a dummy wallet. Keep your old driver's licence in it, along with out-of-date credit cards, some photos, and a decent amount of cash. Hand it over to the bad guy or gal, cash and all. You're only out the cash—a small price to pay. Better yet, toss the wallet on the ground and scram. Hopefully you'll get a head start as he bends down to pick it up. And a word of warning: use old ID, not false ID. The guys at the border have problems with people who carry two different sets of ID.

they necessarily accessible around the clock. In Vietnam and rural China an ATM is a rare bird indeed.

If there's an international logo on the back of your card, such as Cirrus or Plus, it will usually work. Company websites, such as www.mastercard.com/atm and www.visa.ca, can help you track down a nearby ATM. Bank machines in foreign parts typically accept a four-digit PIN—not a five- or six-digit PIN. *Talk to your bank before you leave.* Finally, if you forget your PIN while overseas you are out of luck: it is impossible to create a new one over the telephone.

(Last word on bank machines: why do they have Braille on drive-through machines? Just asking!)

Been there
Done THAT

I put my bank card into the machine and was about to punch in my number when I just stopped and looked at the machine for a moment. Something didn't feel right. I punched "Cancel" and my card returned but it was hard to pull out. I put my hands on either side of the frame of the bank machine and pulled. The entire (fake) front came off in my hands. I called the police. Apparently, this is how the bad guys get PIN numbers. There is a recording device in the fake front. The police said that my account would likely have been cleaned out by morning.

—JOAN, 40

What Your Embassy Can Do for You—or Not

Let's say you're sick, broke, or you did something really stupid and got caught. Doubtless you have seen the movies where the misunderstood, hapless tourist makes a run for the embassy gates. "Go, Billy, go!" The gates open (gunfire in the background) and the poor soul falls into the arms of a fellow American/Canadian/Brit, and is saved. Cue music.

Uh, no.

Do something dumb in a foreign land and you will pay the consequences. You are obligated to obey the laws of the land. Twenty years in a Turkish slammer will teach you a thing or two.

Learn the laws of the visiting country in advance. For instance, there is a ban on bringing chewing gum into Singapore. (Apparently, it's also against the law to pee in an elevator in Singapore. The thought had never crossed our minds, but still, it's a good thing to know.)

A consulate or embassy might provide you with a list of local lawyers who speak English, but they will not get one for you. Nor will they provide legal advice. If you need a lawyer, you might want to try calling a local transnational business and asking for their recommendation.

Duh ! moment !

There are about 6000 Americans arrested in more than 90 countries and 1500 are languishing in foreign jails, according to the U.S. State Department. Now *that's* gotta be fun. In Singapore, if they catch you dealing drugs they will teach you a lesson—they'll hang you. Won't do that again, will you? And let's not talk about the accommodations in Mexico, Korea, Thailand, Argentina, Turkey—all bad. Most of the poor sods in foreign jails are there on drug-related charges.

Here's how it happens. You are on holiday. And look, everyone is smoking a little weed. Heck, you can buy it on every street corner. Besides, you have it on good authority that the local authorities look the other way. After all, you are a tourist, dropping your hard-earned bucks into the local economy. They don't want to cause you trouble.

Right ...

Don't touch the stuff. Never. Don't go near it. If offered, put on your best "Who, me?" grin and get the hell away from anyone who is selling. *Now!*

+

More than You Really Wanted to Know

Criminal Records

It is illegal to visit any country with a criminal record. This includes crossing into the United States. Don't even think of trying to sneak in! If you are caught, you may be arrested, detained, and/or deported, and your car might be seized. You will need to apply for a waiver. Go to www.pardonservicescanada.com. Expect to pay for the service. You should also talk to your lawyer. Or call 1-8-NOW-PARDON.

A consulate or embassy can provide you with an emergency loan, replace a lost or damaged passport, transfer funds, but all for a fee—there is no free lunch here. The consulate or embassy can also contact relatives or friends in an emergency and your next of kin in case you die. (Not that you will care much at that point.) But they will not post bail, pay fines, get you out of prison, or investigate a crime. Nor will they make travel arrangements unless the situation is dire (flood, war—the big stuff). They will not store your bags, get you a work visa, help you find accommodations or a job, perform a marriage ceremony, compensate you for a delayed flight, pay your bills, or accept mail.

However, if you become an expatriate and take up residence overseas, by all means let them know that you are in the neighbourhood and you may get invited to expat parties. Or not.

There is an Emergency Consular Service for Canadians that operates twenty-four hours a day. If you leave a recorded message, make sure you tell them where you are and leave a number where you can be reached. There is also a number you may call collect: 613-996-8885.

Where Canada does not have direct representation in a country, arrangements are usually made with another country's embassy or consulate. Canada has such an arrangement with Australia, for example. Go to www.voyage.gc.ca and check "Country Travel Reports" for specific information.

Give-Your-Parents-Heart-Attack Travel

I know. You are more likely to get killed within five kilometres of your own home. And I get all that call-of-the-wild thing. *Still* … if you are even thinking of travelling off the beaten path, do your homework. Start monitoring the news. (And if the channel you are watching includes parenting tips from Britney Spears, you are watching the wrong news show.)

- Be sure to double-check entrance requirements at the nearest embassy or consulate for up-to-date information before departure. U.S. citizens can consult www.pueblo.gsa.gov/cic_text/travel/foreign/foreignentryreqs.html.
- Again, especially useful for travel to the developing world is the World Health Organization: www.who.int.
- To begin to understand the impact of AIDS in Africa (a good idea if that's where you're headed), start with www.stephenlewisfoundation.org. Also, www.unaids.org.
- Check out the website of the British Foreign and Commonwealth Office (FCO) and keep current on terrorist threats: www.fco.gov.uk. *Big note here:* if you visit a country that the FCO advises against, your insurance might be rendered invalid. Check!

For U.S. citizens …

Prior to your departure, you should register with the nearest U.S. embassy or consulate through the State Department's travel registration website (https://travelregistration.state.gov/ibrs/ui/). Registration will make your presence and whereabouts known in case it is necessary to contact you in an emergency. In accordance with the Privacy Act, information on your welfare and whereabouts may not be released without your express authorization. Remember to leave a detailed itinerary and the number or copies of your passport or other citizenship documents with a friend or relative in the United States.

TIP: Favourite book for off-the-grid travel: Robert Young Pelton's *The World's Most Dangerous Places* (HarperCollins). To view the online version, go to www.comebackalive.com. (I could not have said it better myself.)

High-Risk Travel Insurance

Yes, it is possible to get travel insurance for countries not on the Must-Visit-Before-You-Die list. Tell the prospective insurance company the *truth*, for heaven's sake. If you are going to search for The Lord's Resistance Army in Uganda (why?), tell the company that. In turn, they might tell you to take a long walk off a short pier (i.e., no insurance for you, buddy), but better to know that in advance. Some companies will provide kidnapping insurance (if that makes you feel better). See the Resources section under "Travel Insurance."

What to Bring Home

Gifts for your parents are a must, of course! A last stop at the duty-free ought to do it. But collecting and carrying gifts for everyone back home and souvenirs for yourself might leave you broke and cause luggage problems. (You have packed that extra, foldable bag, right?) Really, the best keepsakes are goofy things you can glue into a travel diary (beer labels, cigar bands, postcards, outrageous restaurant bills, etc.).

If you pick up a cheap piece of art at a local market, keep the bill or you might be suspected of trying to abscond with an artifact. And we know that you know better than that. Souvenirs must be legal. Check out www.canadianheritage.gc.ca/travel. The government takes this very seriously.

Gap Year Ideas

So you're thinking of taking a gap year and spending it travelling. How nice! But it's not enough simply to decide to take a break between high school and university or between university and a real job. Gap years take tons of planning and research. If you don't plan in advance, then you will likely end up on the sofa, and before you know it the year will be over and you'll be no further ahead.

Begin by thinking outside of the box. How about volunteering as a castle-cleaner in France? Or maybe you can help protect the endangered loggerhead turtles in Greece? What about studying abroad? There are hundreds of work-as-you-go programs. Many big cities are eager to employ foreigners, especially for work that requires interaction with tourists.

Teaching English as a Second Language (ESL) is extremely popular. In most cases, companies hire in North America and provide support in the host country. This support varies, so it's critical that you talk to someone who has worked for the company of your choice in the country of your choice. There are loads of places where you can get training in ESL or TEFL (Teaching English as a Foreign Language) or TESOL (Teachers of English to Speakers of Other Languages). You will need an undergraduate degree, to begin with, and the course can take anywhere from a few months, if it's intensive, to a full school year. Make sure that the diploma you are after is worth the paper it's printed on. Call your local school board or college and start there. Or hit the web (see Resources section, "Teaching English as a Second Language").

If you already have a degree or two, you might want to apply directly to a university and teach seminars or classes in China or Africa. In return for teaching seminars on specific topics (depending on your major or interest), you might score room and board. Chances are you won't get paid for this, but you will have an intimate glimpse into a world you would otherwise not see.

No doubt, a year overseas sounds exciting—but is it right for you? Here are some questions to ask yourself:

- Have you had any experience of international travel? (The trip to EuroDisney in France does not qualify.)
- Do you have a strong political, economic, and geographic knowledge of the country you are interested in?
- How are your personal coping and adapting skills? They should be excellent. For example, do you fly off the handle easily? Look at how you have behaved in high-stress situations. How did you react?
- Is the country right for you? Start by finding out about that country's belief systems, modes of behaviour, and attitudes. (In some countries, the attitude toward women might be a relevant concern.) Become active in cross-cultural groups, and take a language class. Your sense of humour and curiosity will keep you going.
- Are you quick to judge people or apply the standards of your home country as a measure of what's right? In order to work in a foreign country you must understand the people and their culture. Start by thinking about your own culture. Even in Western cultures, there are huge differences that are not apparent at first, or even tenth, glance.

Just for Canadians

You will need a work permit or special visa for work or study. The requirements differ depending on the length of your stay. If you're considering a stint abroad, start your

> ### Been there
> ### Done THAT
>
> I gave a two-hour talk on manners and etiquette in North America in a very small university in a remote Chinese city. I worked incredibly hard preparing this lesson. After it was over, the only question I got was, "Is your hair really that colour?" I am blond, and yes, it's really my colour. It was totally fun.
>
> —SUSAN, 22

search at www.letsgo.com, Let's Go's brand-new searchable database of tips and opportunities for alternatives to tourism, organized by country, continent, and program type. You can also go to www.youth.gc.ca or call 1-800-465-7735.

Katimavik is a national youth volunteer service for Canadians between seventeen and twenty-one. Over a seven-month stretch you'll go to three different regions of Canada. It's tough to get in, but those who do say it's worth the effort. Check out www.katimavik.org, or call toll-free: 1-888-525-1503. See Resources section under "Volunteering."

Working holidays: In most cases work is not provided. You have to go get it. You will need a valid passport, usually a return ticket, and sufficient funds for the trip. Contact each embassy for specific details and be aware that websites change; you may have to let your fingers do the walking. See Resources section, "Working Abroad."

Recruiting agencies: There are zillions of recruiting agencies around the world. Most tend to specialize—engineering, education, or home help, for example. You have to begin somewhere. See Resources section under "Working Abroad."

Dear, we want you to go, really. But we want you back too, and with all your body parts in the right places. Take care!

Resources

General

Pick up a copy of *YouthLink*, a Government of Canada publication, in the reference area of your public library and look under "Travel." You might also want to go to www.canada.gc.ca for more general information.

Go to www.youth.gc.ca, click on Travel, or call 1-800-465-7735

Foreign Affairs Canada: www.canada123go.ca

A useful resource: www.transitionsabroad.com

Check out www.canuckabroad.com for helpful ideas and suggestions.

Institute for Global Communications: lots of stuff here. Great feminist links. www.igc.org

The Gap Year Book (Lonely Planet): www.lonelyplanet.com

The Big Guide to Living and Working Overseas by Jean-Marc Hachey (Intercultural Systems) includes a CD-ROM with a searchable index and over 3000 hotlinks. Formally called *The Canadian Guide to Living and Working Overseas*, it's been updated and expanded and contains more than you'll ever want to know, for both Canadians and Americans. All of its information is easily accessible online at www.workingoverseas.com—most of it for free (the free web edition contains 70 percent of the print edition). But if you are serious, get the book.

Booking airline tickets

expedia.com

orbitz.com

travelocity.com

www.cheaptickets.com

www.lowestfare.com

www.priceline.com

Student/youth travel cards

International Student Travel Confederation (ISTC) website: www.istc.org

International Student Exchange Card (ISE): 1-800-255-8000; www.isecard.com

Rail and bus passes:

www.raileurope.co.uk

www.busabout.com

Passport applications

Canada: Canadian Passport Office, Department of Foreign Affairs and International Trade, Ottawa, ON   K1A OG3: 613-994-3500 or 1-800-567-6868; www.dfait-maeci.gc.ca. Available online, at post offices, passport offices, and Canadian missions.

United States: 1-900-225-5674 ($0.35 per min.); www.travel.state.gov/passport/ passport_1738.html. Apply in person at any federal or state courthouse, authorized post office, or passport agency (in most major cities). See "US Government, State Department" in the telephone book for addresses. Processing takes six weeks.

Travel insurance

Canada: www.bluecross.ca/travelinsurance.html

United States: www.bluecross.com

Private insurance providers:

STA offers a range of plans that can supplement your basic coverage: www.statravel.com

Travel Assistance International: 1-800-821-2828; www.travelassistance.com

Access America: 1-800-284-8300; www.accessamerica.com

Berkely Group: 1-800-797-4514; www.berkely.com

Globalcare Travel Insurance: 1-800-821-2488; www.globalcare-cocco.com

Travel Guard: 1-800-826-4919; www.travelguard.com

High-risk travel: Lloyds of London, www.lloydsoflondon.co.uk; Asset Security Managers Ltd, U.K., www.asm-uk.com; The Chubb Corporation, U.S., www.chubb.com/business/ep/kr; American International Group, www.aig.com

What's banned, what's allowed on flights

Canadian Air Transport Security Authority: toll-free 1-888-294-2202; www. catsa-acsta.gc.ca; U.S. Transportation Security Administration (www.tsa.gov); Britain's Department for Transport (www.dft.gov.uk)

Tipping advice

www.tramex.com/tips/tipping.htm

Medical information

MedicAlert International Foundation: 1-800-825-3785; www.medicalert.org

Centers for Disease Control and Prevention, 1600 Clifton Road, N.E., Atlanta, GA 30333, USA: 404-639-3311; Public Inquiries: 404-639-3534 / 1-800-311-3435; www.cdc.gov or www.cdc.gov/travel

www.travellersdiarrhea.com

World Health Organization International Travel and Health website: www.who.int/ith/en/

Travel Health Online: www.tripprep.com/scripts/main/default.asp

HealthLINK: Medical College of Wisconsin International Travelers Clinic website: http://healthlink.mcw.edu/travel-links.html

Banking

www.mastercard.com/atm; www.visa.ca

westernunion.com

Aid to travellers

Canada: www.voyage.gc.ca; "Country Travel Reports"

United States: Overseas Security Advisory Council, www.ds-osac.org; Bureau of Diplomatic Security, www.ds.state.gov; U.S. Department of State Travel Warnings and Consular Information Sheets, www.travel.state.gov/travel_warning.html; U.S. Department of State, 202-647-4000.

United Kingdom: www.fco.gov.uk.travel

Australia: www.dfat.gov.au/consular/advice/advices_mnu.html

News updates for travellers

www.roadnews.com

BBC: www.news.bbc.co.uk/hi/english/world

The New York Times: www.nytimes.com

Associated Press: www.newsday.com/news/nationalworld/wire

AfricaNet: www.africanet.com

Middle East: www.menic.utexas.edu/medic/menic.html

Help for high-risk travellers

United States: www.pueblo.gsa.gov/cic_text/travel/foreign/foreignentryreqs.html; U.S. citizens should register with the nearest U.S. embassy or consulate through the State Department's travel registration website (https://travelregistration.state.gov/ibrs/ui/

For travel to the developing world, World Health Organization: www.who.int

For travel to Africa: www.stephenlewisfoundation.org; www.unaids.org

British Foreign and Commonwealth Office (FCO): www.fco.gov.uk

The World's Most Dangerous Places, by Robert Young Pelton (Harper Collins). Online version at www.comebackalive.com.

What can you bring home?

Canada: www.canadianheritage.gc.ca/travel

Alternatives to tourism

www.letsgo.com

Society for Educational Visits and Exchanges in Canada (SEVEC): a group youth exchange for children between 11 and 18, www.sevec.ca

Roadtrip Nation: the brainchild of three Pepperdine grads who drove across the country in an RV. The result is a documentary series on PBS. Roadtrip Nation now operates three RVs for summer trips; students can apply for a free spot. RTN also provides Roadtrip grants for students who hit the road on their own and agree to film interviews: www.roadtripnation.com

A Japanese cultural and exchange program: www.jetprogramme.org

CESA Languages: learn Russian in Russia, Japanese in Japan, and so on— www.cesalanguages.com

The Goethe-Institut / Inter Nationes: teaching German language and culture worldwide—www.goethe.de/deindex.htm

Center for Study Abroad: this is a worldwide program, U.S.-based, that's fully accredited—www.centerforstudyabroad.com

AFS (American Field Service): this organization got its name in World War I. There are more than 10,000 students and adults involved in their cross-cultural program every year. The programs are in 50 countries. See www.afs.org.

Working abroad

General

Vacation Work Publications: great books, and very reasonable prices. They will send you a catalogue of all sorts of ideas. www.vacationwork.co.uk

Students Working Abroad Program: www.swap.ca

Working Holiday, for Canadians between 18 and 30:

in Australia: www.immi.gov.au

in Japan: www.embassyjapancanada.org

in Germany: www.germanembassyottawa.org

in Korea: call the Embassy of the Republic of Korea in Ottawa, 613-244-5034

in New Zealand: www.nzhcottawa.org

in Sweden: call the Embassy of Sweden in Ottawa, 613-241-8553

in the United Kingdom: call the British High Commission in Ottawa, 613-237-2008

Overseas Jobs: it's an all-in-one job opportunities site, www.overseasjobs.com

A site to alert gappers to scams and country-specific hazards: www.gapaid.org

www.escapeartist.com

www.jobsjobs.com

Teaching English as a Second Language (ESL)

In Washington, D.C.: www.lado.com

In Europe: www.TEFL.net/tcd or www.tesall.com

In England: www.cambridgeesol.org

International House operates in 40 countries: www.ihworld.com

A great Internet meeting place for ESL & EFL teachers and students: www.eslcafe.com

An ESL teacher's board. This one is jam-packed too: www.eslteachersboard.com

World Learning Inc.: maybe you speak English, but teaching it is another thing. Teacher training, along with a raft of cultural programs for professionals and youth—www.worldlearning.org

Recruiting agencies

In America: www.ajb.dni.us

In Europe: www.europa.eu.int/eures

In Australia: www.jobsearch.gov.au

In New Zealand: www.job-bank.winz.govt.nz

In Canada: www.jobset.ca

In the U.K.: www.jobcentreplus.gov.uk

Volunteering

Katimavik program: 1-888-525-1503; www.katimavik.org

www.canadian-charities.com/charityentry.html

www.volunteer.ca

www.givingandvolunteering.ca

www.charityvillage.ca

The GAP Activity Projects, U.K.: sends close to 1400 young people each year to volunteer overseas in over 30 countries. Volunteers work overseas for 4 to 11 months. You must be 18 at the start of their GAP placement and must attend a GAP interview in the U.K. And it's an educational charity. www.gap.org.uk

For Americans: The Federation of American Woman's Clubs Overseas (FAWCO) is an international network of 76 clubs in 34 countries with a stated mission to "improve conditions for Americans living, working and retiring overseas." Go to www.fawco.org, and click on Links.

17

And AnotherThing ...

Adulthood is a journey—not a destination.

I know you're not going to read this, but humour me. Before you head out the door, give this chapter a quick scan, because if adulthood really is a "journey," then you are going to need a road map—a way to keep from getting banged up by the speed bumps, distracted by the detours, or lost along the way.

Detours and Speed Bumps

Fear

> *Only when we are no longer afraid do we begin to live.*
> —DOROTHY THOMPSON

Don't let fear paralyze you. Whether it's fear of embarrassing yourself, fear of failure, or fear of wasting time and money, fear is something to be analyzed. Pinpoint your fear. Write it down. Try to understand it. Then put it behind you.

Failure

> *I have not failed. I've just found 10,000 ways that won't work.*
> —THOMAS A. EDISON

Failure is a good thing. Make mistakes. It helps you find out what you don't want to do. As long as you don't actually die, kill someone, or cause irreparable harm, the most important lessons you will ever learn will not be from your successes but from the flops you survive along the way.

Not Everyone Is Going to Like You

Life didn't promise to be wonderful.
—TEDDY PENDERGRASS

Big life lesson here. Sometimes you will not get the job because the interviewer just didn't *like* you. Or a lover will dump you because he/she really *isn't* that into you. Life is messy; it can hurt. You won't be able to choose what happens to you, but you will be able to choose how you respond. So maybe this dream didn't come true, but if you have enough of them, one day, one dream will.

Negative Thoughts

The universe is change; our life is what our thoughts make it.
—MARCUS AURELIUS

I don't buy into that "positive thinking can cure cancer" idea, but thinking on the bright side can definitely make the ride through life (and/or chemo) easier and better. Got a negative thought? Smack yourself upside the head—and switch it with a positive.

Bad Times

We do survive every moment, after all, except the last one.
—JOHN UPDIKE

Bad times don't last. Turn it into your personal bumper sticker. Ride out the bad times; get help if you need to, talk with someone if you can, but hang in there—for this too shall pass.

Anger

He who angers you conquers you.
—ELIZABETH KENNY

We usually hold on to anger because it makes us feel as though we have the moral high ground. We become the hero of our own story. Feels great, doesn't it? But if you cultivate anger, harbour it, and let it fester, it will make you bitter. Use anger to create change. Be angry about world poverty and do something about that, instead.

Anger's Nastier Cousin: Rage

Anger is a killing thing: it kills the man who angers, for each rage leaves him less than he had been before—it takes something from him.
—LOUIS L'AMOUR

The minute you "go postal," you have lost all. No matter what moral high ground you once *thought* you stood on, no matter how right you might have been, if you let your rage go, it's over, you lose. Don't even *think* you can pretend it didn't happen. And don't give *poor me* excuses. Apologize.

Rudeness

A true gentleman is one who is never intentionally rude.
—OSCAR WILDE

A wise person once said, "Treat everyone with politeness, even those who are rude to you—not because they are nice, but because *you* are." How you behave is who you are. Slam a door in a stranger's face and the world has just had a look into your soul.

Signposts and Rules of the Road

So those were the speed bumps—things that will slow you down or run you off the road. Here are the helpful habits that can make your journey a little smoother.

Laugh

You grow up the day you have your first real laugh—at yourself.
—ETHEL BARRYMORE

Children laugh four hundred times a day, while adults laugh only fifteen times. Laughing lowers blood pressure, relieves tension, boosts immune function, kills pain, rests the brain, increases creativity, and reduces insomnia, depression, constipation, and fatigue. So who do you think is smarter?

Say "Thank You"

During my second year of nursing school our professor gave us a quiz. I breezed through the questions until I read the last one: "What is the first name of the woman who cleans the school?" Surely this was a joke. I had seen the cleaning woman several times, but how would I know her name? I handed in my paper, leaving the last question blank. Before the class ended, one student asked if the last question would count toward our grade. "Absolutely," the professor said. "In your careers, you will meet many people. All are significant. They deserve your attention and care, even if all you do is smile and say hello." I've never forgotten that lesson. I also learned her name was Dorothy.

—JOANN C. JONES

'Nuff said.

Make the Right Decisions

Good judgment comes from experience, and often experience comes from bad judgment.

—RITA MAE BROWN

How do we know what *right* is? What seems right today might be wrong in five years. When it comes to making the tough decisions, ask yourself: How will I feel about this decision a year from now? How will I feel five years from now? How will my decision affect the people I care about? Sometimes you will have to reassess your decisions. That doesn't make you a quitter. Just go back to the beginning and think again.

Forgive and Remember

The stupid neither forgive nor forget; the naïve forgive and forget; the wise forgive but do not forget.

—THOMAS SZASZ

Someone done you wrong? Find the lesson in this experience, and move on.

Take Care of Your Body

> *A man too busy to take care of his health is*
> *like a mechanic too busy to take care of his tools.*
> —SPANISH PROVERB

Experts now say that by the year 2150, people will live for 150 years—and be healthy (assuming they've taken good care of themselves). Are you treating your body as well as you treat your friends? Are you building health, or building disease? Your body is your vehicle on this journey. Fuel it well.

Believe

> *Believe in your luck.*
> —JANINA WODECKI, WISE GRANDMOTHER

If you work hard, you will become lucky. Funny how that works. You also need to believe in yourself—and in something deeper, too. Look for what touches your spirit—whether you find it in a place of worship, a sunset, on a nature walk, on a yoga mat, or on the golf course. Find something that gives you strength.

Write It Down

> *Fill your paper with the breathings of your heart.*
> —WILLIAM WORDSWORTH

Wealthy Greek shipping magnate Aristotle Onassis used to keep little notebooks in his back pocket. He would record the name of everyone he met. Do the same. Take notes on life—names, dreams, fears, or worries. Vent, purge, brainstorm, babble. Burn or flush the angry stuff. Keep the rest to read later, reminding you how far you've come, and where you still plan to go.

"Do unto Others as You Would Have Them Do unto You"

How can anyone improve on the Golden Rule? It's so universal that it is recorded in at least eight world religions.

Judaism: What is hateful to you, do not do to your fellow man. This is the entire Law; all the rest is commentary. (*Talmud Shabbat* 31a)

Christianity: All things whatsoever ye would that men should do to you, do ye even so to them: for this is the law and the prophets. (*Matthew* 7:12)

Islam: No one of you is a believer until he desires for his brother that which he desires for himself. (*Sunnah*)

Confucianism: Surely it is the maxim of loving-kindness: Do not unto others that you would not have them do unto you. (*Analects* 15:23)

Buddhism: Hurt not others in ways that you yourself would find hurtful. (*Udana-Varga* 5, 18)

Zoroastrianism: That nature alone is good which refrains from doing unto another whatsoever is not good for itself. (*Dadisten-i-dinik*, 94-5)

Brahmanism: This is the sum of duty: do naught onto others which would cause you pain if done to you. (*Mahabharata* 5,1517)

And a personal favourite:

Taoism: Regard your neighbour's gain as your own gain, and your neighbour's loss as your own loss. (*T'ai Shang Kan Ying P'ien*)

Marry Well

> *I was married by a judge. I should have asked for a jury.*
> —GROUCHO MARX

A bad marriage can screw up kids, ruin careers, cause financial hardship, and generally make a mess of your life. Sex wanes, and looks fade—so marry someone you really *like*. You need equality in your marriage—a teammate—as in your life. Think of marriage as a bird: if one wing isn't strong, no matter what, the bird will not fly.

Volunteer

> *You cannot do all the good the world needs,*
> *but the world needs all the good you can do.*
>
> —ANONYMOUS

You will meet people, you will make a difference, and in your own small way you might actually change the world. But an important aspect of volunteer work is finding the ways in which it can be personally rewarding—not in terms of money, but in the sense of expanding your horizons, learning more about your world and the people in it, and coming to understand that the more you give, the more you have.

Give

> *We make a living by what we get, we make a life by what we give.*
>
> —SIR WINSTON CHURCHILL

Just because you can't give a lot, that doesn't mean you shouldn't give anything. Give what you can. It's not the size of your gift that counts, it's the size of your heart.

Get Involved

> *In the end we do not remember the voices of our enemies,*
> *but the silence of our friends.*
>
> —MARTIN LUTHER KING, JR.

Have you heard this lately? *"I don't want to get involved."* Watch the people who say it. They're the ones life passes by.

There will be occasions when you will need to stand up for your beliefs, speak out for the underdog, or reach out to a hurting friend. Those times might feel very challenging. But when we walk through life as passive bystanders, we allow injustices to go uncorrected, bullies to terrorize their victims, and hardships to be suffered unnecessarily. Be the person who looks at life straight on, not the one who looks away. As Mahatma Gandhi said, "We must become the change we want to see."

Read

We read to know that we are not alone.
—C.S. LEWIS

Read novels and non-fiction; read for knowledge and for pleasure and for escape. Reading enriches our minds and takes us out of ourselves, so that we can see the world from a broader, less self-centred perspective.

Dream

Dreams are free, so free your dreams.
—ASTRID ALAUDA

It all starts with quiet. Go for a walk. Find some space in this busy world. Try canoeing the northern lakes, hiking Alberta, or planning a tour of Europe's museums. Free your dreams—and then *chase* them.

Work Hard

Bite off more than you can chew, then chew it.
—ELLA WILLIAMS

Success takes work, and not all the work you do will be fun. But each hard slogging brings you closer to where you want to be. Give your jobs your all—big or small.

Final Words

If at first you don't succeed, do it like your mother told you.
—AUTHOR UNKNOWN

Be good. Be kind. Have fun. Work hard. Play well. Make friends. Learn new things. Drive safely. Wear sunscreen. Go to the dentist. Bad times don't last and things will get better.

Okay, enough! Go! You have the tools, you can do this! With any luck, your journey through adulthood will be a long and happy one. Enjoy the trip. (Oh … and don't forget to call!)

Acknowledgments

The authors would like to thank: Dr. Alphonse DeLucia, cardio-thoracic surgeon; Dr. Mark Shuren, oral and maxillofacial surgeon; Alison Berecz, RN; Susan Fyshe, MHSc, RD, Nutritionist; Brett Caldwell, CA; Anne Zarzour, reader, cheerleader; Micheline's Lunch Ladies; Shelley Grieve, researcher and teacher; Detective Kim Philby, York Regional Police; Peter Bellm, Halton Honda, Burlington, Ontario; Laurel Dubrawski, reader; Elizabeth Grandbois, reader; David MacLeod, reader; Downtown Brown (you know who you are); Barbara Berson, editor; Katie Hearn, production editor; Eleanor Gasparik, cold reader; and Zack Dubrawski—*you're* good to go but welcome to stay (a *little*) longer. Special thanks to all those who shared their road stories from the journey to adulthood; and most especially, our thanks to Catherine Marjoribanks for her tremendous support, advice, and professionalism above and beyond the call of duty.

Index